M000096731

STATES WITHOUT NATIONS

NEW DIRECTIONS IN CRITICAL THEORY

NEW DIRECTIONS IN CRITICAL THEORY

Amy Allen, General Editor

New Directions in Critical Theory presents outstanding classic and contemporary texts in the tradition of critical social theory, broadly construed. The series aims to renew and advance the program of critical social theory, with a particular focus on theorizing contemporary struggles around gender, race, sexuality, class, and globalization and their complex interconnections.

Narrating Evil: A Postmetaphysical Theory of Reflective Judgment,
MARÍA PÍA LARA

The Politics of Our Selves: Power, Autonomy, and Gender in Contemporary Critical Theory,
AMY ALLEN

Democracy and the Political Unconscious,
NOËLLE MCAFEE

The Force of the Example: Explorations in the Paradigm of Judgment,
ALESSANDRO FERRARA

Horrorism: Naming Contemporary Violence,
ADRIANA CAVARERO

Scales of Justice: Reimagining Political Space in a Globalizing World,
NANCY FRASER

Pathologies of Reason: On the Legacy of Critical Theory,
AXEL HONNETH

JACQUELINE STEVENS

STATES WITHOUT NATIONS
Citizenship for Mortals

COLUMBIA UNIVERSITY PRESS   NEW YORK

COLUMBIA UNIVERSITY PRESS

Publishers Since 1893

New York   Chichester, West Sussex

Copyright © 2010 Columbia University Press

Library of Congress Cataloging-in-Publication Data

Stevens, Jacqueline, 1962–

States without nations : citizenship for mortals / Jacqueline Stevens.

p. cm. — (New directions in critical theory)

Includes bibliographical references and index.

ISBN 978-0-231-14876-4 (cloth : alk. paper)—ISBN 978-0-231-52021-8 (e-book)

1. Liberty.   2. Citizenship.   3. Inheritance and succession.   4. Marriage.
5. Eminent domain.   I. Title.   II. Series.

JC585.S74 2009

323.6—dc22   2009012178

Columbia University Press books are printed on permanent and durable acid-free paper.

This book is printed on paper with recycled content.

Printed in the United States of America

c   10 9 8 7 6 5 4 3 2

References to Internet Web sites (URLs) were accurate at the time of writing. Neither the author nor Columbia University Press is responsible for URLs that may have expired or changed since the manuscript was prepared.

DESIGN BY **MARTIN N. HINZE**

For Sarah and Rue

To fight aloud, is very brave—
But gallanter, I know
Who charge within the bosom
The Cavalry of Woe—

Who win, and nations do not see—
Who fall—and none observe—
Whose dying eyes, no Country
Regards with patriot love—

We trust, in plumed procession
For such, the Angels go—
Rank after Rank, with even feet—
And Uniforms of Snow.

EMILY DICKINSON
(C. 1859)

Contents

Preface

Despite the Mexican-Spanish zone that reaches from Los Angeles to San Antonio and leaps over to Saint Augustine, despite the profound influence of the American Indian on our early development, the pioneering in the Mississippi valley and the northwest by French and French-Canadians, the ten percent contribution to the population made by Negro and mulatto, and all the weight of 39 million "Foreign white stock" in the country, there are still some who repeat the shibboleth and call us an Anglo-Saxon nation.

FREDERICK DETWEILER,
"THE ANGLO-SAXON MYTH IN THE UNITED STATES" (1938)

The chances of factual truth surviving the onslaught of power are very slim indeed; it is always in danger of being maneuvered out of the world not only for a time but, potentially, forever. Facts and events are infinitely more fragile things than axioms, discoveries, theories.

HANNAH ARENDT, "TRUTH AND POLITICS" (1967)

In "Truth and Politics," Hannah Arendt meditates on the backlash against her account of Adolf Eichmann's 1961 war crime trial in Israel.[1] Her five lengthy articles on Eichmann's management of Jewish removal from Germany, first published in the *New Yorker*, detail specific Jewish elites' support—if not initiation—of one Nazi plan to shift the Jewish population from Europe to Palestine. Eichmann wrote of being instructed by his boss Reinhardt Heydrich,

Hitler's chief of staff for Jewish expulsion and genocide, to read "Theodore Herzl's *Der Judenstaat*, the famous Zionist classic, which converted Eichmann promptly and forever to Zionism."[2] In 1905, Herzl called for the international Jewish nation to pull together and establish a state in Palestine. Profits from selling Jewish property in western Europe would subsidize the settlement of the poor Jews from eastern Europe.[3] Arendt offered damning evidence that in the 1930s the Jewish Agency of Palestine, modeled along the lines of Herzl's plan, was taking advantage of Germany's anti-Semitism and coordinating Jewish expropriation and resettlement with a passion that may even have exceeded that of the bureaucrat in the docket.

Arendt noted Eichmann's description of the "emissaries from Palestine, who would approach the Gestapo and the SS . . . to enlist help for the illegal immigration of Jews into British-ruled Palestine."[4] Arendt says that they were "not interested in rescue operations" but wanted to select "suitable material." Paraphrasing another study of these actions, Arendt wrote, "they were probably among the first Jews to talk openly about mutual interests and certainly the first to be given permission 'to pick young Jewish pioneers' from among the Jews in the concentration camps."[5] For Arendt to describe these actions and others, such as Jewish financiers working with Eichmann's bureaucracy to pay for Jewish passage to Palestine, was taken by some as a wanton attack on justice,[6] as if the world could not condemn a war criminal if the commitments of a nationalist organization that experienced slaughter, the Zionists, were discussed in the same breath as the goals of an imperialist nationalist organization that perpetrated that slaughter.

Arendt's "Truth and Politics" (1967) engages critics of her Eichmann narrative by explaining the challenge of speaking the truth in the face of politics rather than by refuting specific charges. However, Arendt is doing something more specific than resisting the pressures of a vague political agenda. She is telling the truth in the presence of nations. Stories that would question a nation's honor and founding myths evoke especially venomous renunciation and reprisals. This is worth examining. Arendt's work in this area had a long history. Twenty years earlier, Arendt showed the same honesty and clear thinking, but under conditions that were even more fraught with political danger. In 1944, when the Jewish community, including Arendt, a recent refugee, was horrified by the millions of Jews being killed in Europe, she disparaged the Zionists attempting to establish an exclusively Jewish nation-state:

The social-revolutionary Jewish national movement, which started half a century ago with ideals so lofty that it overlooked the particular realities of the Near East and the general wickedness of the world, has ended—as do most such movements—with the unequivocal support not only of national but of chauvinist claims—not against the foes of the Jewish people but against its possible friends and present neighbors.[7]

Arendt believed the exclusively Jewish nation-state being contemplated would be seen as parasitic on an imperial power and despised by its neighbors,[8] and she challenged American Zionists to back a proposal endorsed by many other intellectuals and states: a federated state of Arabs and Jews.[9]

Arendt's rebuke to an organization with the noble mission of representing a people being massacred was courageous, but why this was so is also perplexing. As much as Arendt bravely endured attacks for lending support to anti-Semitism, her audience resisted facts they should have been desperate to learn. Indeed, this was Arendt's point when she disparaged the shift among "Jewish left-wing intellectuals who a relatively short time ago still looked down upon Zionism as an ideology for the feebleminded."[10] In 1944, the war was still on, the Einsatzgruppen were still destroying the Jews of Europe, and it would be four more years before the United Nations would establish Israel. Political dramas affecting the region were still unfolding, and Arendt had reason to believe that if she warned the American Jews that the European émigré leadership urging a purely Jewish state was tainted by bigotry and Nazi affiliations[11]—on which Arendt also had commented during this period—the American Jews would demur from continuing on that path.[12] In the event, Arendt was right on the facts and astute on her predictions about the consequences of Zionists pursuing this course.

So why were her claims in 1944 treated with disbelief or dismissed as opinion? Once the Jewish community was made aware of the truth—that the Zionist leadership was chauvinist and had been openly collaborating with Nazis—one might expect that American Jews would find the Jewish Agency collaborators despicable and would reject their ideas and leadership for a Jewish state. (Chaim Weizmann was the president of the Jewish Agency of Palestine and Israel's first president.) Instead, the American Jewish intelligentsia ignored not only its own earlier aversion to Zionism but also its hatred of Nazi policies of expulsion and with the Jewish intelligentsia became a collaborator with the collaborators. This is not behavior unique to those who supported the establishment of Israel but, as Arendt pointed out, the modus operandi for all national movements. This especially dramatic example of people giving their full support to causes, ideologies, and people they would, absent their national attachments, otherwise despise suggests that truth's contest with nationalism goes deeper than the everyday challenge truth faces in politics, to irrational psychic attachments that supersede logical, instrumental ones.

It is tempting to see the nation as the means through which people express their traditions, communities, and histories and to imagine that it poses problems only in circumstances of nationalism, but the most apparently pacific nation does not exist without the possibility of virulent nationalism. In the early 1990s, the main concern among scholars of the nation-state was its demise and replacement by a global corporate network that would be based in the United States and penetrate and absorb markets worldwide, creating a single hegemonic capitalist empire.[13] This expectation changed after the 2001 attacks on the World Trade Center and the Pentagon, though these events were only history's most recent reminders of the nation's ever-present possibilities of systemic violence. The rapidity and ease with which President Bush shifted from encouraging an open border with Mexico to locking up long-term residents in detention facilities by the tens of thousands[14] is similar in kind if not degree to the experience people in the former Yugoslavia described, when their neighbors became their attackers. If the nation were not an enduring form conducive to the rapid instigation of irrational, systemic violence, then these shifts could not occur so easily and seem, after the fact, so predictable.

The United States used to be perceived as a government committed to advancing an uncompromising human-rights agenda. Such an image was attacked by the Right as naïve, by the Left as hypocritical, and by the far Left as diabolically imposing the West's particular values in the name of universal ones. That criticism has become passé. And the White House under the Bush and Obama administrations is not the only government institution to use the cover of national security to abrogate rights recognized by U.S. and international law. In 2007, the Democratic-controlled U.S. Senate twice rejected the most draconian immigration bill considered by Congress since the early twentieth century—because it was too permissive. Both versions of the bill that the Democratic leadership worked furiously to pass would have established English as the national language, deported legal residents who were convicted of drunk driving, established a national database of all aliens applying for employment, built a seven-hundred-mile fence along the U.S.-Mexican border, established a program for aliens to live and work in the country without being eligible for citizenship, and required undocumented aliens applying for legal resident status to pay thousands of dollars in fees and leave the country.[15] The liberal immigration-law centers in the country all opposed the bill.[16] And yet all eleven Democrats who voted against S. 1348 and the five who voted against S. 1639 did so because they, like the Republicans who opposed these measures by strong majorities, thought the bills were too easy on aliens.

Senator Claire McCaskill (D-MO) explained her nay vote: "when someone breaks the law, they should be brought in front of our criminal justice system and be accountable to the courts."[17] The two Democratic senators from Montana issued a joint press release: "Baucus and Tester said that the bill aimed at reducing the number of illegal immigrants entering the country makes it too easy for an illegal immigrant to get a work visa, does not go far enough in strengthening the country's borders, and does not have tough enough enforcement measures."[18] Of course, there is another way to prevent people living here illegally, and that is to allow anyone residing here to do so without sanction. The bill's author, defending these measures as the best that he could do for immigrants, was Senator Edward Kennedy, whose civil rights credentials were otherwise in excellent standing. Yet, in exchange for burnishing his bipartisan reputation, he was willing to reject the advice of liberal organizations he otherwise supported and urge the passage of a measure that would have criminalized the presence of longtime residents in this country.

Ironically, buried in S. 1639 was language to establish a Commission on the Wartime Treatment of Jewish Refugees. The bill would have charged the commission with reviewing "the United States Government's refusal to allow Jewish and other refugees fleeing persecution or genocide in Europe entry to the United States."[19] It also required a "review of Federal refugee law and policy relating to those fleeing persecution or genocide, including recommendations for making it easier in the future for victims of persecution or genocide to obtain refuge in the United States."[20] Thus, toward the end of a bill that would have codified a labor underclass based on birthright, Congress also was being asked to recall its aversion to the consequences of these political partitions and exclusions based on nationality. Admittedly, guest-worker programs are not death camps. The goal of this book is to demonstrate their connection, to reflect on why so-called liberals make exceptions from their larger principled worldviews to endorse policies whose outcomes they would be expected to reject, and to explore alternative policies for states without nations.

STATES WITHOUT NATIONS

INTRODUCTION

When mud huts or straw shelters, incapable of resisting the inclemency of the weather, sufficed for the living, tumuli were raised for the dead, and stone was used for sepulchres before it was used for houses. It is the strong-builded houses of the dead that have withstood the ages, not the houses of the living; not the temporary lodgings but the permanent habitations.

MIGUEL DE UNAMUNO, *TRAGIC SENSE OF LIFE* (1954)

It is not the consciousness of death but the flight from death that distinguishes men from animals.

NORMAN BROWN, *LIFE AGAINST DEATH* (1959)

Humans, from the Latin *humus*, are creatures of the earth, "the *earthy* one, the *earth*-born."[1] Other creatures come and go, and therefore also are earthy, so to speak, but only humans are mortals, beings conscious of their own mortality. Mortality has enormous implications for politics. Most obviously, governments use the fear of death to manipulate obedience. If the threat of one's destruction is the most extreme example of coercion, and if governments have a monopoly on the legitimate use of coercion, then governments have the preeminent means of guaranteeing obedience, or so the story goes.[2] Death is not a perfect incentive system. Honor and justice may be more important than self-preservation. Socrates advocated death over obedience to an unjust democratic sovereign: "A man who is good for anything ought not to calculate the chance of living or dying; he ought only to consider whether in doing anything he is doing right or wrong."[3] Telling the Athenian jury that he would not compromise his principles even if it meant a death sentence, Socrates said he did not know what became of the dead and therefore, in ignorance, he had nothing to fear.[4]

Also aware of death's ambiguity, the seventeenth-century theorist of the social contract Thomas Hobbes arrived at the opposite inference. In a recently ended civil war, Christian soldiers had shown themselves willing to risk death to support their view of God. This willingness to die for a religious cause made Hobbes uneasy, and he told his readers it was more rational to fear certain violent death from breaking their covenants with the state than to fear an uncertain eternal hell from breaking their covenants with God: "Because there is no natural knowledge of man's estate after death, much less of the reward that is then to be given to breach of faith, but only a belief grounded upon other men's saying that they know it supernaturally or that they know those that knew them that knew others that knew it supernaturally, breach of faith [with the sovereign] cannot be called a precept of reason or nature."[5] In other words, Christians should know that life is good and it would be irrational to risk life now for a future that might be less felicitous.

In addition to these commonly debated questions about how the fear of death and other bodily harms incites compliance with state prohibitions, mortal citizens have two other characteristics with political implications that extend far beyond questions of authority. First, mortals are conscious of being born from another mortal's body. Second, half are conscious that anatomy denies them the ability to similarly give birth. Envying the ability to reproduce children from their own bodies,[6] men compensate by presiding over entire reproductive units, political societies they create by law.[7] A political society's kinship rules for creating families to repopulate as larger hereditary groups derive from men's desire to control by law intergenerational attachments available at birth only to mothers, meaning those who give birth. This is because the intergenerational world is fantasized by men, first as young boys, as the biological prerogative of mothers, and not because of maternity's essential preeminence in securing intergenerationality, which may be produced in an infinite variety of contexts and communities (chapter 5 explores these ideas in detail). Intergenerational groups with hereditary rules for membership are mortality's neurotic and even psychotic symptoms. Nationality, ethnicity, caste, clan, and, in the last several hundred years, race are the conveyances for mortal narratives, the way men assure themselves through law the feeling of security they feel is denied by anatomy. The hereditary group that uses the legal convention of fatherhood to put men into certain relations with children—with whom they may lack a genetic relation—is an invention designed by creatures preoccupied with fantasies about the significance of bearing children and who seek to overcome their finite lifespans.[8]

Many of the ideas in these chapters build on my earlier book, *Reproducing the State*, which shows that certain intergenerational groups often considered natural, for example, the family, the nation, ethnicities, and races, are actually produced by laws, kinship laws in particular.[9] *Reproducing the State* contrasts the law's use of birth for membership in hereditary kinship groups with religious groups recruiting through death narratives. *Reproducing the State* also analyzes the muddled legal status of religious groups under the U.S. Constitution. On the one hand, the state singles out religious devotion for special protection by admonishing the government to ignore religion, an injunction not equally available to other membership groups, thus favoring religion. But, on the other hand, the state's preeminence over religious groups is performed by its prerogative to outline the scope for religious devotion in the first place.[10]

Reproducing the State engages primarily with the theories and histories of these affinities. It devotes little space to the daily political consequences of kinship laws today and virtually none to exploring alternatives. *States Without Nations: Citizenship for Mortals* begins where *Reproducing the State* ends, documenting the specific harms that kinship rules cause and explaining the benefits of changing them. Some points are reiterated to avoid confusion, but a reader who wants a historical and theoretical explication of how political membership rules lead to affinities we call national, ethnic, racial, and familial and who wants to understand how these differ from religious ties should consult that earlier work.

Current Social Science Research

Hereditary groups entail insiders and outsiders. As native or foreigner, citizen or alien, us or them, the mortal subject has been a longstanding protagonist in wars among states and other political societies, as well as in civil wars. These conflicts have invited scholarly study. Recent investigations by social scientists challenge the view that intra- and interstate wars are caused by ethnic or religious conflicts.[11] James Fearon's and David Laitin's article, the most frequently cited among the many multivariate regression studies by political scientists studying civil wars, claims conflicts that may appear to be based on hereditary or religious attachments are due to insurgencies engendered by weak states.[12] Their findings are based on research that has been challenged if not discredited by other scholars, who point out problems with the methodology,[13] datasets,[14] and the variable used to operationalize ethnic conflict.[15]

In a very different region of the academy, political theorists using historical and philosophical texts to reflect on systemic mass deaths propose that violence organized by official or semiofficial functionaries is a symptom of nationalism unique to modernity. The consensus position is that the modern state has created something Giorgio Agamben calls "bare life," a disrespect for humanity that he says began with the population policies of Nazis and subsequent governments using what Michel Foucault called "biopower," meaning the use of power to produce a specific human body and its behaviors, often in the guise of what is naturally or scientifically desirable.[16] Agamben writes: "The fact is that the National Socialist Reich marks the point at which the integration of medicine and politics, which is one of the essential characteristics of modern biopolitics, began to assume its final form. . . . The physician and the sovereign seem to exchange roles."[17] However, the use of eugenics and policies to privilege the reproduction of citizens over aliens had assumed this form thousands of years before Hitler's ascendance. Plato's *Republic* describes using marriage law as a form of breeding and advocates eugenics,[18] a practice widespread in antiquity.[19] States accommodated and even encouraged infanticide if offspring were deformed or were born to anyone other than married citizens.[20] Plutarch writes: "Lycurgus [a seventh century B.C. Spartan king] was of a persuasion that children were not so much the property of their parents as of the whole commonwealth, and, therefore, would not have his citizens begot by the first-comers, but by the best men that could be found."[21] Not only did the sovereign claim the right to supervise his subjects' breeding, as did the Nazis, but Lycurgus advocated state-controlled infanticide, appointing committees to whom fathers could bring their offspring for inspection.[22] Meanwhile, Athenians deemed the offspring of foreigners and unmarried couples unfit for citizenship.[23] In other words, the physician and the sovereign had intermingled duties.[24] Moreover, Agamben's narrative ignores the genocides of Asia. China and Japan were never colonized but have been responsible for slaughters that follow logics of ethnicity.[25] Some of the largest episodes of group slaughter in the twentieth century had nothing to do with the history of the modern European biopolitics that Agamben believes responsible for the Nazi's genocide.

The Mortal Citizen

The phenomena Agamben describes are symptoms of longstanding diseases afflicting the mortal subject or, in democratic regimes, the mortal citizen. Rather than dismiss the longstanding centrality of kinship or religion to systemic violence (as do the social scientists) or claim a special status for twentieth-century European biopower, this book explores the deadly consequences of the institutions through which humans seek to transform their condition from one of finitude to one of infinitude. The intent of destroying death by overcoming its premise with war and myths of eternity, as well as laws assigning men reproductive privileges, occurs primarily through the family, nation, and religion, all of which promise immortality.

Paradoxically, the groups whose allure is the control of circumstances of life and death are the ones that have led to mass slaughter. That is, governments create the kinship rules for the families into which we are born, giving us our nationality, race, and other hereditary identities. Religions also stake out control over birth and death through baptism rites, the promise of an afterlife, and the claim to be able to risk their members' mortal bodies in religious wars. Only hereditary or religious groups expect this self-sacrifice and demand the systemic destruction of nonmembers; other types of groups, including those that cultivate fierce loyalties and compete, do not. In short, institutions emanating from collective fantasies of living forever—in memory or spirit—are the ones that incite us to kill and die. Since the fear of death to which these institutions respond exists for all mortals and not a time-bound epoch, the methods most useful for their study come from philosophies of the soul.

From Plato through Freud, a variety of reactions to the narratives denying mortality have appeared, the most politically astute being G. W. F. Hegel's observations, discussed in chapter 1, that the need for recognition as belonging to a particular hereditary group may be such an acute psychological—not biological—drive that one might risk one's own death and kill others. Hegel also shows that the family is not the pregiven building block of the nation but its consequence, because before anyone can start a family, the nation-state must dictate what a family looks like. One wife or four? States claim the monopoly on the prerogative to define the family because only legal kinship rules playing on fantasies about birth and death ensure national attachments that might lead large populations to risk their lives and to kill others.

States do not cultivate these attachments for instrumental purposes. There is no conscious or even evolutionary imperative selecting for birth narratives as the most successful way to inculcate the loyalty instrumental to conquering other nations.[26] Instead, it is the irrational fantasies underlying the desire to control birth and death that give us the kind of states that enable war. Hegel pointed out that human beings see themselves as capable of conquering their fears of not being recognized, of effectively being dead, only by establishing institutions that replace their feelings of impotence, fragility, and banality with a consciousness of feeling powerful, immortal, and distinctive.[27] Family law is created by the state or any other form of political society, including tribes or medieval kings. The legal family provides the political script used to appease fears of death, as does the nation whose membership is legally determined by birth. Nations and other hereditary or religious communities are the only groups that can stage wars because only they—not, for example, interest groups, sports clubs, and especially corporations—can promise remembrance. To enhance the conditions of memory, people will sacrifice themselves and kill others.

Hitler elicited commitment on this basis, stating, "We are the last who will be making history in Germany."[28] When Hitler learned that a German general had surrendered in Stalingrad in 1943 instead of fighting to the death, Hitler told his colleagues:

How easy he has made it for himself! . . . The man should shoot himself as generals used to fall upon their swords when they saw their cause was lost. That's to be taken for granted. . . . What does "life" mean? Life is the nation; the individual must die. What remains alive beyond the individual is the nation. . . . So many people have to die, and then one man like that comes along and at the last minute defiles the heroism of so many others. He could free himself from all misery and enter into eternity, into national immortality, and he prefers to go to Moscow.[29]

But what does this mean, this narrative of a desire to "enter into eternity," and why is it so intimately tied to nations and religions?

By the standards of liberals or secular humanists, such claims seem fantastic, but they are only the more obvious examples of the normal function of the nation and religion. Hegel, the German nation's most insightful and ultimately misguided theorist, explained that political societies implementing these rules and norms were a symptom of humanity's specific desire for recognition guaranteed through groups with institutionalized memory, especially the nation-state, just as he endorsed religion's promise of eternity as a comforting palliative for mortal anxieties. Norman Brown writes: "Hegel was able to develop a philosophy of history only by making a fresh start and identifying man with death. And he develops the paradox that history is what man does with death, along lines almost identical with Freud's. . . . There are no social groups without a religion of their own immortality, and history-making is always the quest for group-immortality."[30] History gives comfort to mortals, the possibility that intergenerational memories may compensate for biology's single lifespan. And the nation-state, able, for instance, to cut through large swaths of mountains to erect miles of war monuments, build archives, fill museums, and determine the kinship rules distinguishing the lineage of its society, is history's most reliable repository and guarantee of an audience.

The Mortal Citizen as Pathological

Unlike Hegel, who embraced the institutions wrought through mortal fantasies, Freud did not celebrate the irrational and deadly means for obtaining affirmation. Hegel exalted war as a moral imperative whereas Freud stipulated its necessity.[31] Freud pointed out that the apparently beneficent, communal, and supportive institutions of nation, religion, and family—the culmination of civilization—insidiously and complexly cause the very death and suffering against which they appear to protect us. Hobbes, Freud writes, misunderstood the raison d'être of political societies, which was not to alleviate violent death through a sovereign who would protect against violent death but to ensure it:

> When we start considering this possibility we come upon a contention which is so astonishing that we must dwell upon it. This contention holds that what we call our civilization is largely responsible for our

misery, and that we should be much happier if we gave it up and returned to primitive conditions. I call this contention astonishing because, in whatever way we may define the concept of civilization, it is a
certain fact that all the things with which we seek to protect ourselves
against the threats that emanate from the sources of suffering are part
of that very civilization.[32]

Describing the suffering brought about by wars and families, which both arise
from laws civilization imposes to establish nation-states and kinship groups,[33]
Freud writes that these rules are not evidence of a higher consciousness
among humans but of a death drive: "We cannot see why the regulations made
by ourselves should not . . . be a protection and benefit for every one of us. And
yet when we consider how unsuccessful we have been in precisely this field of
prevention of suffering, a suspicion dawns on us that here, too, a piece of un-
conquerable nature may lie behind—this time a piece of our own psychical
constitution."[34] Freud contemplated the violent history of the world, including
his own experience of World War I,[35] anti-Semitism,[36] and later, the threat of
the atomic bomb.[37] Based on his clinical practice and his reading of history
and current events, Freud derived the hypothesis that the family, nation, and
religion were such destructive institutions that they only could have developed in a species cultivating its own death.[38]

Freud knew such a thesis would face resistance. Especially challenging for
readers then and today was Freud's insistence that the family was not primarily a site of safety, intimacy, and respect but, at its best, fraught with repression
and guilt and, at its worst, violence. We have commandments against killing
and commandments that require parental respect, Freud suggested, not because humans are averse to such acts but because absent such rules, the family's incipient chaos and murder would be realized.[39] Freud's family drama
features a son who desires to kill his father in order to establish sexual access
to his mother. As a result, the son feels guilty about this desire and fearful of
his father, whom the son believes shares his rivalrous fantasies (and, being
bigger, is in a better position to make them happen).[40] Of course, sons rarely
kill their fathers, but such a psychic drama is not pleasant to endure, repressed
or otherwise, and, Freud held, it expressed itself in other forms of organization as well, such as when men banded together to overthrow a tribal or monarchical father figure.[41]

Discussing the parallels between the fantasies of individual sons and the
myths of entire cultures, Freud asked rhetorically: "If the development of civilization has such a far-reaching similarity to the development of the individual

and if it employs the same methods, may we not be justified in reaching the diagnosis that, under the influence of cultural urges, some civilizations, or some epochs of civilizations—possibly the whole of mankind—have become neurotic?"[42] While much in Freud's ahistorical and extremely partial account of the family, nation, and religion is extremely dubious, Freud's diagnosis inspires conscious reflection on the family, nation, and religion, especially their pathologies.

National and Ethnic Violence

From 1900 to 1987, 203 million people were killed in war or genocide.[43] Of these deaths, 170 million were noncombatants.[44] Hundreds of millions more have died from war-related disruptions of food supplies and disease. Public-health officials are now studying state violence as a health problem.[45] From an epidemiological perspective, having an ethnicity, nationality, race, or religion is a risk factor for violent death as much as childhood obesity is a predictor for diabetes.

Death in the Family

In every country in the world, wives and children are most at risk of physical abuse and death within their families.[46] The most likely perpetrator in an infant or childhood homicide is not a stranger or a step-parent but a genetic parent.[47]

Religious Violence

A letter to the editor quotes a Gallup poll stating that 61 percent of Americans believe that religion can solve most of today's problems and asks, "what sort of problems do they have in mind? Certainly not the kind mentioned [in the article] where we are told that 10,000 human beings are dying each month in Darfur, Sudan," as a result of religiously inflected ethnic cleansing.[48] The Roman Catholic Church, promising purity and righteousness, has been responsible for warfare since its inception.[49] Lately, the Catholic Church has been revealed as the world's largest organized protection racket for pederasts. In the documentary *Deliver Us from Evil*, a man whose daughter was raped by their priest breaks down in tears because his diocese and many others supported the perpetrators of the violence and not the children abused.[50] To date, the Catholic Church has paid close to $2 billion to settle the lawsuits.[51]

Poverty

Borders associated with fixed national territorial communities are responsible for nonemergency boundaries of compassion. In other words, the nation-state comprises the limits for empathy, regardless of the location where the most suffering occurs. As long as problems lie outside one's intergenerational group—for example, of family, ethnicity, nation, race—or one's religion, then they may be ignored, and equitable, pragmatic solutions can be dismissed as utopian. As a result, one billion people do not have safe drinking water,[52] 2.4 billion do not have basic sanitation,[53] two billion people do not have electricity,[54] almost a billion people are undernourished,[55] and 15 percent of disease results from childhood and maternal nutritional or weight deficiencies.[56]

STUDYING POLITICS FOR MORTALS

The information above is not new to this epoch but documents persistent crises that each year seem more incongruous in light of the technical and legal accomplishments across all civilizations. The same culture that gave us Plato's lofty ideals about justice produced the murder of Socrates and the slaughter of occupied colonies during long stretches of siege and warfare. The hand-to-hand, face-to-face assassinations and raids that killed about 800,000 Rwandans in 1994[57] occurred during the same short period it took for Intel to solve its "floating chip error." Intel spent millions of dollars on a new design that would save a few seconds here and there for the small portion of the planet owning a computer; not a single plan was implemented to save millions of what social scientists call "disability-adjusted life years," that is, the early deaths resulting from wars. Faced with the bold facts of suicide missions on behalf of nations or religions, even the guru of rational-choice theory, Jon Elster, has conceded that the economic model of behavior is wanting: "Sometimes the parable of the scorpion and the frog seems to have more explanatory power than might be claimed by any model,"[58] suggesting that psychological processes eluding rational-choice theory are motivating group violence.

Referring to the failure of scholarly studies to shape immigration debates, Bonnie Honig writes: "Rational arguments about the costs and benefits of foreigners fail to settle (though they may inform) the politics of immigration because the issue has as much to do with identity as with interests."[59] The point holds as well for other identities experienced as hereditary or religious, such that they are normalized and mobilized to cause great harm,[60] leading to the ultimate form of devastation, war. In his pathbreaking work *The Great Illusion* (1913), the Nobel Prize winner Norman Angell made the point that wars were not simply evil but a bad risk, even those begun for instrumental reasons:

> A victorious nation, it is said, could dominate territory, and occupy it for her own merchants, shutting out those of rivals. Well, fortunately, here we can talk on the solid basis of experience. History furnishes numberless instances where the thing has been attempted. And in every instance, without any single exception known to the historian, they have all failed. Spain tried it with half the world for an experimenting ground, and the more she applied this principle of exclusivity the poorer she got.[61]

Angell's work to start a peace movement suggested his own faith in civilization's learning curve—that having these lessons pointed out would be sufficient to wean world leaders from repeating past errors.

Freud's "Future of an Illusion" (1927), perhaps an homage to Angell, also grasped war's irrationality and attempted to explain the persistence of illusions such as those Angell had identified: "We call a belief an illusion when a wish-fulfillment is a prominent factor in its motivation, and in doing so we disregard its relations to reality, just as illusion itself sets no store by verification."[62] Wars, because they are fought in the name of the family, nation, or religion, promise so much, especially immortality, that their persistence is not surprising. People support their leaders, tyrants and democrats alike, who organize slaughter in the name of these associations not because of greed, values, or even power, as leading social scientists have asserted (see notes 11–13 in this chapter), but because citizens fear death and these groups sustain the illusion of immortality. If Angell were right and people fought for money, then they would be moved by his analysis, but if war is not based on poor economic calculations but a psychotic denial of death, then further work is needed.

In short, social scientists researching the conditions that give rise to war and civil war, as well as researchers assessing less confrontational strategies to advance a hereditary or religious group's interest in zero-sum environments, have been studying a question that does not speak to the underlying causes of the conflicts that interest them. To paraphrase, they have been asking, "Why and when do some states, nations, ethnicities, and religions go to war and others do not?" Research here addresses the question, "Why do some groups settle conflicts through mass slaughter, and others do not?" And it poses a series of thought experiments designed to respond to the question, "What are the changes necessary for this to end?"

The first question is addressed by drawing on psychoanalytic theory and legal history to highlight how hereditary and religious groups extend narratives forged in childhood fantasies about birth and death. These are groups that kill and solicit suicide. Groups not using criteria of birth or death for membership—the vast majority of organizations, from cities to philanthropies—settle their conflicts to ensure worldly benefits and not immortality.

The second question, how to thwart these actions, is explored through imagining the dismantling of the laws and rules that implement these fantasies. Because there is much fear associated with losing these hereditary and religious contexts as presently organized, this book considers these anxieties directly and pragmatically and explores the principled political theoretical underpinnings of these laws.

PROPOSALS FOR CHANGE: FOUR THOUGHT EXPERIMENTS

Abolishing Birthright Citizenship

To eradicate hereditary population differences that fuel violent conflict, states would need to stop producing the laws that create nations, from the Latin *nasci*, meaning birth. Chapter 1 describes current and historical rules for birthright citizenship producing national attachments and reviews tensions in so-called liberal theories defending these practices. Chapter 2 contemplates alternative rules for membership based on criteria of active and not passive citizenship and discusses potential objections.

Abolishing Inheritance

One reason to worry about migration from the open borders, chapter 2 proposes, is the great disparity in wealth between rich and poor countries. But if wealth left at death were to be collected by a global agency and disbursed to provide for basic needs worldwide, not given to the nearest relatives, then this might reduce the incentives for economic migration. Chapter 3 provides a detailed analysis of statistics on the concentration of wealth, reviews the laws controlling estates in the United States and abroad, and discusses the three dominant defenses of inheritance laws: individual choice, capitalist accumulation, and family sentiment. Chapter 4 explores a proposal to abolish inheritance laws and distribute the wealth in these estates through a provisions agency funding clean water, health, education, and other basic needs.

Abolishing Marriage

Chapter 5 draws on anthropological research on kinship, pointing out that marriage rules do not reflect existing genetically discrete groups but concretize an experience of hereditary attachments underlying systemic, mass violence. And marriage creates fathers, by putting men into relation with children from another generation. The marriage rules for the United States and elsewhere are described and the religious and secular defenses of these rules reviewed. Chapter 6 portrays an alternative model of intergenerational care, one based only on the needs of biological dependence and not on anxieties about mortality and men's inability to give birth.

Abolishing Land Rights

The proposal to prohibit private ownership of land is a bit different from the first three. Land ownership does not follow obviously from kinship conventions. Also, unlike the first three proposals, the prohibition against purely private ownership of land already is in effect to some degree through "eminent domain," the government's prerogative to seize land for its own use, claimed by all nation-states. The problem with private land rights is that they make it legal for individuals from one generation to make decisions with potentially permanent adverse consequences for future generations. Such rights are disrespectful of the limits of mortality.

Chapter 7 reviews facts and laws concerning land ownership. The chapter's history of laws governing land use develops the claim that land rights exist by the grace of one's government. Defenses of private land rights put forward by political and economic theorists are evaluated before examining the benefits that might accrue were individuals denied even provisional title to land they use, instead awarding lifetime leases.

Religion and the Nation-State

Chapter 8 analyzes three possible relations of religious groups to the nation-state. Although some religious groups and especially individuals exist in a state of pure antagonism to all nations, religious groups' use of mass, systemic violence to force the conversion or subjugation of other religious or hereditary groups rarely occurs separate from nation building or racializing projects.[63] Religious groups independent of any sovereign power have opposed ethnic oppression, but religious groups that favor these practices and forced religious conversion tend to do so in conjunction with, or as, a state. Thus laws eradicating the hereditary basis of state violence might also ameliorate the tendency of religious groups to perpetrate large-scale violence.

Methods for an Open Society

I have included as an appendix a chapter explaining my method for using empirical data to refute existing theories and advance alternatives. The appendix explains how the method I use is consistent with critical theory that draws on Immanuel Kant's work on reflective judgment. I am especially engaged with how Kant's ideas animate Karl Popper's and Arendt's epistemologies, whereby examples are developed for falsifying or generalizing scientific and political theories. I also compare the view of change for which I argue here with the teleological vision advanced by Jürgen Habermas. Readers who are concerned about epistemology may want to read the appendix first.

The proposals above differ from those advocating world government.[64] Rather than stipulating the rapacious individual of neoclassical economics, who needs to be restrained by force—a new world order to replace the current anarchic international order—the thought experiments here contemplate breaking the legal templates producing violent conflicts and the major causes of widespread poverty. Absent the underlying incentives that make us partial to those we regard as our ancestors and progeny, a global sovereign authority designed to manage the excesses of nationalism is unnecessary. Rather than a world government, which could at best episodically repress but not eliminate ethnic fighting, government institutions in current sovereign boundaries might be used to change what appears as human nature—ethnic loyalties, nationalism, militarism.

THE NEW ABOLITIONISM

In light of the ubiquity of nation-states and the laws supporting them, these proposals may sound far-fetched. But this has been the case for numerous other causes that at one point appeared natural and necessary but that eventually became unthinkable. The origins and demise of slavery are good precedents for imagining a trajectory for the demise of laws sustaining nationalism and war. Slavery once was as widespread as birthright citizenship, inheritance, and marriage are today and was endured by monarchies and democracies alike. For about 4,600 years, war was the activity whereby soldiers kidnapped alien populations and brought them home as slaves[65] or used their forced labor to colonize new lands.[66] Once slavery became separated from the project of nationalism and war and became a private affair in European colonies, legal slavery quickly drew to an end[67] and is practiced today only in secret.[68] The public today would not tolerate slavery as a result of war but does not bristle at systemic death. If the Bush administration had acknowledged that despite their best intentions over twelve thousand Iraqi civilians had been enslaved by U.S. soldiers during the first months of the invasion, the outcry would be overwhelming. But the same number of Iraqi civilians killed outright by the U.S. military[69] provokes little reaction. Is it possible for societies to become as collectively repulsed by systemic death and other harms of the nation-state as by the legal ownership of aliens? If ideologies sustaining slavery could be overcome, then perhaps this contains lessons for abolishing the nation-state, the legal entity responsible for war's practices of slavery as well as killing.

The Roots of Slavery in War and Nations

An examination of slavery for the purpose of discovering a path to overthrowing the nation may seem ill advised. Because one popular practice is held in disrepute hardly legitimates or enables radical change of other longstanding institutions. Otherwise, one might call for ending voting rights. Slavery, practiced today in pockets of Africa, Haiti, and the Dominican Republic and sweatshops in North America, has no principled defenders, while the global system of nation-states, like voting rights, is so widely accepted that its moorings come in for little discussion and less condemnation. Moreover, slavery and nationality seem to have many substantive differences. The psychological and physical differences between the master and the slave contrast with those between the colonizer and the colonized or between citizens in wealthy countries and those in poor ones. Yet, although the institutions of slavery and that of a world of nations provide numerous differences, some important similarities exist as well.

Understanding the parallel and overlapping aspects of slavery and nation-states may promote both an awareness of the need to change our current form of governance and provide a model for achieving this. There is, of course, an extensive historiography of slavery, and the following schematic description is offered with apologies for the many omissions of detail; the examples are selected for illustrative purposes and not meant to be exhaustive. The reason for this specific comparison is that slavery is not just a convenient example of a pervasive, oppressive system that was abolished. Slavery is the penultimate expression of national violence, the alternative, still widely accepted in theory and practice, being the enemy's death.

An additional reason that analogizing slavery with the constraints of the nation-state system may seem odd is that many, especially in the United States, have focused on studying the institution as a largely economic and not political endeavor. But slavery, though it provided forced labor that may have increased a conquering nation's productivity, was not instituted for this purpose. Just as cheap prison labor is a side effect of criminal law and does not lead us to infer our penal system exists so states can produce cheap license plates, the economic benefits of slave labor were happy consequences for those nations that proved victorious in war. Slaves either were sold by governments to raise revenues or given to reward loyalty and valor among a king's conquering soldiers and nobility.[70] In its first guise, one that was in effect for thousands of years before U.S. plantation slavery, it was a way of fixing another nation's compliance. The origin of the Arabic word for slave is *asīr*, originally meaning "captive."[71] And the root of the English "slave" is from the Byzantine Greek *sklabos*, meaning Slav, a reference to the people conquered and enslaved during the period of the Holy Roman Empire.[72] Similarly, referring to their foes, the Latin word for slave was *aegyptius*, or Egyptian. In Hebrew, the word for slave was *ebed*, meaning righteous punishment of one's enemies sanctioned by the Lord, especially Canaanites.[73] Enslavement or its threat were how rulers attempted to subdue their foes.

In this vein, Hammurabi's code for the Babylonian empire of the late second millennium B.C. outlines a reciprocal system of enemy capture that was the basis for regulating slave ownership: "If a chieftain or a man (common soldier) be caught in the misfortune of the king (captured in battle), and if his fields and garden be given to another and he take possession, if he return and reaches his place, his field and garden shall be returned to him."[74] Such a capture was seen as a communal harm and not individual bad luck, such that if a merchant bought a slave and returned him to his homeland, the merchant would be paid "by the temple of [the freed slave's] community."[75] If that temple had no funds, the king himself would pay, not the slave's family: "His field, garden, and house shall not be given for the purchase of his freedom."[76] Knowing that his soldiers risked capture and enslavement in war, Hammurabi reduced the adverse consequences of this, increasing the willingness of his subjects to fight, by publicly proclaiming that if anyone returns a Babylonian slave he will be paid for this, a guarantee backed by the king himself.[77] Hammurabi issued a further law obviating intragroup slave ownership, by depriving property rights to those attempting this: "If while in a foreign country, the buyer shall buy a male or female slave belonging to another of his own country; if when he return home the owner of the male or female slave recognize it: if the male or female slave be a native of the country, he shall give them back without any money."[78] Slavery was what one endured in war, and Hammurabi, to ensure cohesion, wanted to make sure his subjects understood that in exchange for fighting on his behalf he would do what he could to guarantee their freedom.

In the Mediterranean up through the fifth century B.C. there was largely indifference as to whether slaves were from neighboring nations that spoke the same language or from other regions. After the wars between the Persians and the Greeks, there was some feeling among the linguistic Greeks that they should unite against a common foe, not one another. Plato's *Republic* voices such a sentiment, expressing a preference that Greeks will be "lovers of Greeks," and if they have internal quarrels, they will not punish other Greek nations with a "view to their enslavement or their destruction."[79] During this period, the Persians largely captured Greek and then Roman populations, and the Greeks and then Romans captured Persians, as well as each other. Although in times of pique or desperation Greeks of one nation would resort to enslaving Greeks they had colonized, they never enslaved those from their own nations. One authority on the history of slavery observes that the "survival of true slavery required some form of social or psychological discrimination," which is evidence, David Brion Davis claimed, of "ethnocentrism and of slavery's ultimate dependence on real or simulated ethnic barriers."[80] Until the mid-sixteenth century, slavery was of a piece with sovereignty and warfare. The slaves of antiquity were those unfortunate soldiers and often civilians of "other" nations whose lives of servitude were the price of life itself.[81]

Such national antagonisms were also the basis of another system of exploitative labor, feudalism, which has, like slavery, often been misinterpreted as a strictly economic system. Serfs were of different ethnic backgrounds from their lords, the people who had been victorious in war and laid claim to prisoners of war and their descendants,[82] so in many places the status of serf and slave were indistinguishable: "French legal scholars translated the words *servitus* and *servus* from the Justinian Code as *servage* and *serf*," Davis explains, and "regarded the French serf as legally subject to the almost absolute authority of his owner, and as alienable by sale, exchange, or gift."[83] Similar laws applied in England as well.[84]

Social contract theorists as late as the seventeenth century also discussed slavery as an artifact of war, as they debated whether consent to slavery given on the battlefield could legitimately obligate one thereafter. Tellingly, it is warfare that provides the contexts for choosing between accepting subjection as a subject or a slave. War over who will be sovereign raises the same problems of obligation for the potential slave as for the potential national subject. Both must accept a government's sovereignty under threat of death.[85]

True, at points rulers were eager to convert their slaves into currency, and in preparation for war "kings and their generals summoned the slave-traders to them in their camps to offer for sale in advance the large number of prisoners they felt sure they would capture,"[86] but these prisoners were obtained as part of a larger struggle for political domination, really for colonization of other territories, not to obtain money for its own sake. Although there was always a side trade in humans kidnapped by what were essentially gangs who would sell slaves to wealthy subjects or citizens, as well as to kings, this practice emerged from slavery's roots in state warfare. When the legitimacy of acquiring slaves from warfare came undone by agreements among Christian nations to stop taking slaves, even in just wars, slavery began its demise. In the relatively short period of a few hundred years—after slavery became detached from war and came into its own right as a racialized economic institution dedicated to supplying forced labor—its accepted, legal existence came to an end.

Rules for birthright citizenship are of a piece with those that produced slavery. Slavery, like birthright citizenship, also was an institution that was around for most of recorded history and whose initial adversaries were met with claims that its abolition was misguided if not impossible.

The Nation's Violence: Death, Slavery, Aliens

Having laid out the historical specificity of slavery's spot on the timeline of war and the nation, the inquiry can become more finely grained, as we turn to war's less dramatic but also frequently deadly near-relations in the nation-state system.

The reason slavery is thought evil is that it puts a person from one kinship or religious group in potentially permanent control of another, and the reason this is thought intolerable is that it violates the condition of natural freedom that liberals associate with the essence of what it means to be a human being. A condition of servitude based on the arbitrary accident of birth is thought unfair and unjust, as opposed to imprisonment and even forced labor based on poor choices such as stealing. Even if none of us is completely free, because of biological conditions of, say, needing to eat and have shelter, not to mention the constraints of our social and political conditions, the slave's room for advancing desires is unconscionable because her degrees of freedom seem so close to zero. Moreover, for most slaves in most places, this was not a temporary position but one's condition for life, depriving even the hope of exercising will later.

The institutional constraints of nationhood impose burdens similar to those of slavery or apartheid.[87] Though it is not a single household or property to which one is confined, the nation's borders are regulated through the use of force in order to circumvent free movement. The national of one state is no more free to leave her homeland at will than a slave could exit the household. Whether it is internal patrols that keep people in or those of other countries to exclude foreigners, the device of birthright citizenship means that from the perspective of a potential emigrant, the effect is the same: most must reside in the state into which they are born. Indeed, the phrases "homeland," as in "homeland security," or "domestic," in "domestic policy," themselves convey a parallel between the family home and the national one, neither of which one chooses nor is all that easy to leave behind.[88]

The direct physical coercion of slavery, although it may find echoes in colonial administrations, is not a feature of the nation-state system per se. But just as the basis of slavery has been ethnic or other intergenerationally based group differences, it appears that the mutual antagonisms informing economic policies and the indifference to the suffering of others in social policies share the same taxonomies. Just as intergenerational group differences—for example, ethnicities and races—invite exploitation through overt violence, they also provide templates for the more mundane trade policies that seek to protect home markets at the expense of foreigners and to privilege the improvement of the economic well-being of one's own nation's relative prosperity, even when indices of suffering and principles of fairness would suggest attention to alleviating hardships elsewhere.[89]

On average, variations of wealth among countries are higher than variations within them.[90] Millions of deaths from disease, famine, and microbes in water occur because governments allocate resources based on borders, not needs. While this is unfair, the real brutalization of humanity from living in this condition goes far deeper. In every region of the world, the nation-state alone is responsible for people who drown, suffocate, die from dehydration, or are killed by bandits if they attempt to circumvent border patrols and enter a country without government papers authorizing their presence; families, lovers, and friends who are not willing to take these risks and have their relations severed when governments refuse them visas; hundreds of millions of immigrants spending decades in a country without documentation and who are denied services readily available to citizens and who endure anxieties about deportation;[91] and people whose chances of economic advancement are thwarted by confinement to national labor markets. These horrors are global, but because the United States is at the forefront of preaching the virtues of the free movement of capital, its policies preventing the free movement of people invite special scrutiny.

"The sun-bleached bones are kept in a cardboard box in a locked cabinet—a skull, a thighbone, several ribs and vertebrae, pieces of a pelvis," the AP article begins. "To Lori Baker's trained eye, the remains found in a lonely corner of south Texas near the Rio Grande tell of a boy, about 13. Some of his clothing was homemade, and he carried a dark cloth knapsack bearing the name of a Mexican university."[92] Baker was a forensic scientist working in 2001 on a project to identify the more than 1,300 dead bodies that had turned up along the U.S.-Mexican border, people from all over South America whose last days were lived in fear of capture, then of death, whose nightmares came true for just one reason: laws excluding them in the name of national difference. From 1995 to 2005, more than three thousand people died crossing the U.S.-Mexican border—in other words, about the number killed on September 11, 2001.[93] Internationally the statistics are more dire. In 2006 alone, for instance, three thousand Africans are thought to have drowned trying to make the 11,400 mile boat journey to the Canaries.[94] If these were escaping slaves, the dreams, fears, and manner of death would be more similar than many care to realize.

Early death is only the most obvious of many harms the nation-state causes. The nation-state also injures hundreds of millions of legal and illegal refugees and aliens facing daily obstacles that range from the silly to the depressing to the terrifying, and there are hundreds of millions living this way. Perhaps the most miserable are displaced persons and those in refugee camps, thirty-seven million people living without a home, a job, a future.[95] The camps often attract violence and rape by soldiers; each one offers its unique challenges. In Ivory Coast, Liberians displaced by their civil war could substitute their fear of immediate death for anxieties about having their children kidnapped from the camps to be given guns and made into soldiers.[96] Permanent refugee camps, with populations segregated from their host countries, would not exist if nation-states allowed free movement.

And then there are the tens of millions outside the camps, who live in countries without the state's permission. Yuliana Huicochea moved to the United

States when she was four years old; ten years later, after her school bus was stopped returning from a high school field trip to Canada, she faced deportation: "'I'm scared,' said Ms. Huicochea, then a sophomore at Phoenix College, who declined to say what country she immigrated from. 'I don't know any other place. My whole family is here. This is where my education is, my dreams, my goals. I don't know what I would do anywhere else.'"[97] Over twelve million people in the United States live in fear of similar discoveries, disruptions, and dislocations,[98] simply because of nationality.[99] Many work for three dollars an hour in sweatshops and service-industry jobs.[100] About 800,000 are farm workers, earning low seasonal wages that may be withheld on various pretexts; the worker has no legal recourse, an incommensurability in power not lost on employers.[101] A survey in Holland of employers using undocumented workers gave as the main reason their low cost,[102] which is also why "80 percent of the coffee in the Dominican Republic is picked by Haitians" and why maids in Hong Kong are Indonesian, among whom nine out of ten are underpaid and "with many receiving half the legal minimum wage."[103]

On an even more mundane level, there are the hardships caused not for any actual violations of the law but for mere confusions—albeit the sort of misunderstandings that thrive in a climate of foreignness and borders. Consider Iraqi-born Saad Kavarizadeh, who was fourteen when government security forces deported her family to Iran, forcing her into the world's largest refugee population of 2.4 million.[104] Kavarizadeh says security forces told her that her ancestors were Iranian, although she did not previously know this. Now she lives in an Iraqi refugee camp: "'In Iran they call us Iraqis, but they kicked us out of there,' said Mrs. Kavarizadeh, whose children where educated in Farsi in the poor Ahwaz neighborhood where they live. 'If we go back to Iraq, they will call us Iranians. I am miserable in this big country, but I don't know what I would do in Iraq. They confiscated everything, including our future.'"[105] The Nuremberg laws in Germany did something similar, taking people, Jews, who considered themselves citizens and using ancestry to deport them.[106]

The United States episodically has removed long-term residents and even citizens. This occurred most dramatically in the 1920s and 1930s, when approximately one million U.S. residents of Mexican ancestry, of whom 400,000 were legal residents or citizens, were deported.[107] This began again in the late twentieth and early twenty-first centuries, as immigration sweeps, especially by police, prisons, and jails, are resulting in the deportation or detention of U.S. citizens by the Immigration and Customs Enforcement Agency for months and even years.[108] Robert, a U.S. citizen, told me that he was certain that if his last name were "Johnson" and not Hispanic he would have been sent home after he served his sentence in the Los Angeles County jail, instead of being herded with a group of brown-skinned or Hispanic-surnamed inmates into a room where they were screened for alienage. After his interview, Robert was put on a bus and taken to a remote detention center. His wife, also a U.S. citizen, was furious at the government and at Robert for failing to return home to support his family. Feeling pressure from his family to be home instead of waiting to appeal a decision against him, Robert signed papers stating he was a Mexican citizen and then reentered the United States from Tijuana. Later, when police took Robert's driver's license after a barroom brawl, they sent him to another detention center, and Robert again signed papers agreeing to be removed to Tijuana. Apprehended on this second reentry, Robert explained his situation to a border-patrol agent, who charged Robert with illegal reentry and falsely impersonating a U.S. citizen. Threatened with both charges, Robert, assigned a criminal public defender who did not understand citizenship laws, pled guilty and served three years in a San Diego prison. At this point, he had figured out the law sufficiently to explain his citizenship status to an immigration judge. She released him on bail so that he could locate the documents necessary to confirm his U.S. citizenship.[109]

The reason that the individuals depicted above are so lost and their avenues of appeal so futile is that there are no individual-level solutions to their problems. An individual cannot choose to live in a world without nation-states and the strange and harmful laws sustaining them, especially those that draw on psychic attachments to myths of heredity and religion.

The Nation as Inevitable? Lessons from Slavery

Over the course of millennia, even in societies that have given us our foundational beliefs in justice, few launched serious political or even intellectual campaigns against slavery. Plato and Aristotle praised the institution. A historian writes, "One would have thought that the problem of slavery should have been mentioned in all these designs for a perfect social system, but it is not explicitly questioned in any of them; indeed it is accepted throughout."[110] For well over one thousand years after the slave revolts led by Spartacus in Rome,[111] there were virtually no public debates about slavery, which was closely interwoven into the fabric of the Western and Eastern Roman empires.[112] Enshrined in law from Persia through northern Europe, the existence of slavery incited no more wonder during this period than women's subordination to their husbands or dynasties maintained by birth and marriage and not a popular vote. Even Thomas More, the most populist of the sixteenth-century humanists striving to overcome the immiserations of serfdom, did not question slavery but endorsed it,[113] as did, of course, the U.S. government as late as 1861.

The rare early modern humanist critic of slavery would condemn only particular aspects of the institution but, seeing slavery as part of the law of nations, did not propose slavery's abolition, which was seen as tantamount to suggesting abolishing war.[114] It is true that slavery still exists, as do antislavery organizations, but because the ethical consensus on slavery is so clear, there is little thought given to its basis and earlier legitimacy. The complete rejection of the institution has meant that there is little in the popular imagination that makes the connection between the barbarities of slavery and those of warfare or notes slavery's vestiges in the nation-state.

Even after acknowledging that nations and families have been sites of cruelty, suffering, and violence, some might maintain that nation-states and the families they constitute need only to be reformed, perhaps seriously, but not to be eliminated entirely. This is the path taken by most mainstream political theorists today, discussed in chapters 1 and 2. But if it is liberal to believe that individuals should be rewarded on the basis of their own skills and work ethic and not that of their forebears, then liberals cannot defend citizenship or wealth's distribution based on birthright or marriage, for instance, arguments that will be explored in later chapters.

Slavery's serious opponents not only pursued changing the opinions and behaviors of slave traders and slave owners but sought slavery's abolition in law. Those who cared about slaves insisted that the state stop enforcing property rights granting them ownership of people. Slavery's cessation did not require the state to do anything other than abolish its own legal sanction of the practice. When legal slavery ended, public opinion, which so long accepted slavery as necessary, turned its back on the institution entirely.

A vast majority of people endorse the nation, family, and religion as they are at present. But, as we see with slavery's legal abolition and many other changes of state policy, when the law shifts, the character of normality and common sense swiftly follows. For instance, in 1954 a majority of the public supported the notion of "separate but equal" underlying the segregation of public schools, a view that reversed itself after the Supreme Court's ruling in *Brown v. Board of Education* (1954). In 1973, when states had laws against abortion, one-third of the public said women should be able to have abortions. Today, two-thirds of the U.S. public supports abortion rights.[115] In 2000, about

INTRODUCTION

23

half of those in Vermont opposed civil unions, but shortly after the state legislature allowed same-sex civil unions, only 21 percent opposed them.[116] In 2003, the Massachusetts Supreme Court ruled bans on same-sex marriage unconstitutional, leading to a shift from 60 percent opposing same-sex marriages to 64 percent supporting them.[117] In Maine, several years after same-sex civil unions were legalized, opposition groups failed to muster the necessary signatures to place a measure on the ballot to end the practice.[118] Although Californians passed a constitutional amendment banning same-sex marriage, opposition to this measure had increased from 39 percent against Proposition 22—a 2000 referendum prohibiting state recognition of same-sex marriage—to 48 percent for Proposition 8.[119]

TRAJECTORIES OF CHANGE

Public-health experts are gaining significant media attention for their documentation and critiques of war's harms, and this is one group that might successfully prompt public questioning of national and religious violence, as they have in the cases of domestic violence and gang violence. The statistics on women's visits to emergency rooms as a result of partner abuse were widely cited in legal studies insisting on new policing and arrest practices for domestic violence. In the 1980s and 1990s, public-health scholars reframed criminal and family violence so that they were not legal and private problems, respectively, but perceived as common medical problems deserving the attention of all facets of government.[120]

Today, public-health experts are bringing the same concerns and methods to bear on their studies of intergroup violence. For instance, in the World Health Organization's *World Report on Violence and Health*, the authors, including James Mercy, who wrote an early article on gun violence as a public-health problem, are now focusing on civil wars.[121] Two articles in the British medical journal *Lancet* review the war mortalities in the Democratic Republic of Congo and Iraq as public-health concerns, and in 2002, the *British Medical Journal* devoted an issue to exploring the public-health implications of war.[122] The authors of the *Lancet* articles do not prescribe medication but rather an increase in peacekeeping troops[123] and a call for the U.S. government to document civilian deaths,[124] respectively. Both articles condemn the violent methods used to settle group conflicts; the authors of the Congo study write: "Maintenance of the status quo is unacceptable: the east remains in conflict and hundreds of thousands of civilians continue to die unnecessarily as a result."[125]

However, just as the palliatives of earlier times—peace treaties or restrictions on the use of certain weapons—were not strong enough for the disease being fought, the same remedies called for by today's public-health experts will also fail if not joined with those of other movements responding to problems of birthright and citizenship laws in other domains. Attempting to stop mass group violence by asking sovereign states not to use cluster bombs is like requiring criminals not to use Chevrolets in high-speed chases. Enforcement would be difficult, and the effect of such a prohibition is irrelevant; other cars are equally fast. Among the millions who were maimed and killed in Rwanda, not a single person was harmed by a cluster bomb. Meanwhile, harms to body and spirit from the distinctions of kinship and birthright citizenship afflict populations in ways that are less visible but no less harmful than immediate violence. Losing a child to a landmine or to starvation from being in a stigmatized racial group is equally devastating.

New techniques and specific prohibitions are not sufficient to quell the mass violence induced through hereditary and religious attachments, while Kantian incitements to cosmopolitanism, such as those offered by Martha Nussbaum and Jürgen Habermas, do not provide the grounded critique necessary to realize their values. To maintain that populations shaped by the laws and ties of the territorial nation-state, including its birthright membership rules, might be persuaded by Nussbaum's well-intentioned lessons of a "thick universalism,"[126] or to maintain that reason is going to triumph over nationalism just because that's how reason works in the world, as Habermas insists,[127] is to fail to critically engage the present. A focus on the details of present laws and their instantiation of templates predisposing publics to psychotic, violent outbursts requires a finely grained reading of the variations and generalities of attachment that our political institutions produce, not just the good and bad principles these may reflect. Critical theory finds its energy in discerning through apparent distortions of and constraints on freedom and thinking a range of possibilities for their supersession. In the first book of the New Directions in Critical Theory series, Amy Allen, the series editor, writes that critical theory "offers an empirically grounded critical diagnosis of the central crisis tendencies and social pathologies of the present" and "charts paths for future transformation."[128] Drawing on German philosophy beginning with Kant and developed by Hegel, critical theory develops concepts of the psyche and dialectics between thought and practices, especially the many ways that law constitutes attachments that so-called liberal theory understands as natural. Such conceptual tools necessary for what Allen describes as critical theory's mission of grasping the "depth of power's influence on the subject" without denying possibilities of autonomy[129] is missing from the analyses of John Locke, Jeremy Bentham, John Stuart Mill, Isaiah Berlin, John Rawls, and Michael Walzer.[130]

The purpose of theorizing states without nations (and, relatedly, without inheritance, marriage, and private ownership of land) on behalf of citizenship for mortals is to provide perspective on the psychic and legal contingencies underlying mass, systemic violence and economic inequality and to initiate a dialogue about alternatives. The quietism in mainstream politics and scholarship on kinship rules and religion as fairly obvious, longstanding, and pervasive sources of death and suffering suggests formidable psychological obstacles. Implementation of these proposals seems, at best, a challenge. But current institutions of birthright seem neither defensible nor sustainable. No one in the twelfth century foresaw capitalism, much less a majority of the world's governments as even nominal democracies. Naysayers in the sphere of social change, those who extrapolate the future from the present, are the ones whom history has repeatedly defeated. Because our time on earth is so incredibly brief and the fear of death so intense, families, nations, and religions have filled an acute psychic need—ironically at the expense of life itself. Here are some thought experiments for institutions designed not out of anxieties about mortality but, as Hannah Arendt put it so clearly, to honor this time between past and future, out of love for the world and not to escape it.[131]

CHAPTER ONE

THE PERSISTENCE AND HARMS OF BIRTHRIGHT CITIZENSHIP IN SO-CALLED LIBERAL THEORY AND COUNTRIES

Even the super powers cannot ignore the reality of worldwide protests. The ongoing state of nature between bellicose states that have already forfeited their sovereignty has at least begun to appear obsolescent.

JÜRGEN HABERMAS, 1990

The conflict between Russia and the former Soviet republic of Georgia moved toward full-scale war on Saturday, as Russia sent warships to land ground troops in the disputed territory of Abkhazia and broadened its bombing campaign to the Georgian capital's airport.

NEW YORK TIMES, AUGUST 10, 2008

We shall not turn over any Kurdish man to Turkey, not even a Kurd-ish cat.

JALAL TALABANI, IRAQ'S PRESIDENT AND ETHNIC KURD, 2007

CITIZENSHIP RULES

Laws and Practices in So-called Liberal Societies

Those who believe so-called liberal societies embody the end of ideology,[1] the end of history,[2] and the end of legally mandated birthright-status relations[3] must find the rules for citizenship in contemporary societies a bit confounding. Rules for political membership in the most enlightened countries of the European Union vary little from preliterate communities and the premodern states of antiquity. From Afghanistan to Zimbabwe, about 97 percent of us will have our prerogatives and burdens of citizenship determined by birth.[4] In Afghanistan, the Republic of Congo, Honduras, Monaco, Senegal, and Zimbabwe, not to mention the United States, England, and Japan, indeed, in *every single country in the world*, citizenship is determined primarily by birth, either to one's legal parents or from being born in a particular country.[5]

Not only does the birthright-citizenship criterion violate liberal norms at the level of the individual, but it is also at odds with classical liberal arguments for the "invisible hand" and free markets, including the free movement of labor. Restricting the supply of labor based on alienage is an artificial interference with economic laws of supply and demand that, the theory holds, will result in decreased productivity relative to a labor market that lacked such inhibitions. U.S. Secretary of Homeland Security Michael Chertoff admitted as much in 2007, when he explained that the measures he was implementing to expel undocumented residents would be bad for business: "There will be some unhappy consequences for the economy out of doing this."[6] A lobbyist for a business consortium opposing the Department of Homeland Security measures said, "It's going to be awful; the harvest is going to be awful. People will feel it when they go grocery shopping, when they read in the newspaper that we're importing our meat from China."[7] While it may seem counterintuitive to enact a policy that decreases the productivity of one's own economy, birthright citizenship requires this.

In short, the rules for determining citizenship are not based on calculations that might advantage one's own group but that sort the teams' composition in the first place, so to speak. No one can say whether a practice is going to benefit "my" group until the rules for determining these groups have been established. The birthright criterion for citizenship is flawed, at least based on theories of classical economics and genuine liberal political theory, because it excludes potentially productive citizens. In 2004, 43 percent of lawful resident admissions to the United States were granted to immediate relatives, including spouses, children under twenty-one, and parents.[8] There are no restrictions on the number of new residents in this category.[9] Another 23 percent of legal resident admissions were given to nonimmediate relatives under "family-sponsored preference admissions."[10] In sum, 67 percent of newcomers to the United States were admitted because of kinship ties, and 16 percent were given legal residency because of their skills or wealth.[11] (Foreigners may apply for a legal resident card if they are "willing to invest at least $1 million in businesses located in the United States,"[12] but only 129 of the 155,300 legal resident cards issued in 2004 went to people in this category.)[13] The United States waives the requirement of legal residency altogether if one has "performed active military duty during World War I, World War II, Korea, Vietnam, Persian Gulf, [or] on or after September 11, 2001"[14] and provides an express lane for veterans interested in obtaining legal residency, but only a few thousand have become U.S. citizens via this route. This means that while the Department of Homeland Security is threatening fines and criminal sanctions against private employers whose workers lack documentation, the military will be cheerfully recruiting nonresident aliens. An immigrant can be hired by one branch of government security to kill Iraqis but will be imprisoned by another branch of government security for picking a tomato. These numbers seem to be increasing and will go up further if Congress passes pending legislation that would allow citizenship to undocumented immigrants who were in the United States since they were fifteen and have served just two years in the military. Offering citizenship to encourage aliens to join the army resembles the dynamic between war and slavery in antiquity, when regimes would use slaves captured in one place for colonizing adventures elsewhere.[15]

If countries really did behave like sports teams or businesses and wanted to recruit the most talented individuals, then state governments would both encourage the immigration of those who brought the most economic benefits and seek to expatriate the poor and unskilled, a drag on the national average. A country with membership rules adhering to the axioms of rational-choice theory and concerned with prosperity would prefer members who are skilled, wealthy, and fluent in its dominant language, for instance. Everyone would be expected to meet the minimum standards for any valued attributes, not just aspiring immigrants who now must memorize information about the country's history and political institutions that natives ignore. Just as sports teams do not allow uncoordinated children of sports stars to join their teams, those not up to a country's standards would have to leave, regardless of their place of birth or ancestry. The analysis here is not arguing for meritocratic standards of citizenship but highlighting the irrationality of arguments claiming that it is immigration and not birthright citizenship that lowers a country's standard of living.

Birthright citizenship does not even guarantee a citizenry knowledgeable on its own political institutions. Most citizens, including students at top universities in the United States, are not minimally versed in the basic principles and institutions of this country. Columnist Rosa Brooks writes in the *Los Angeles Times* that a survey from 2006 "found that although 52% of Americans could name two or more of the characters from 'The Simpsons,' only 28% could identify two of the freedoms protected under the 1st Amendment. Another recent poll found that 77% of Americans could name at least two of the Seven Dwarfs from 'Snow White,' but only 24% could name two or more Supreme Court justices."[16] Brooks makes the case that those who fail should be deported, a tongue-in-cheek rebuke of the knowledge we require of immigrants taking the new citizenship test.[17]

The gatekeeping policies of the United States resemble those of the six countries randomly selected for analysis, many very poor, mentioned above. This is curious. The absence of variation in citizenship criteria is another indication of their independence from market mechanisms. Were countries using immigration policies in order to increase their revenues, then one would expect to see variation among their policies. Rich countries might be expected to do much more to exclude potential newcomers than would poor countries, as it would be more likely that a random newcomer would be poorer than the average current resident. Reciprocally, the opposite would be the case in poor countries. However, as we see from the chapter's sample,[18] wealthy and poor countries have similar rules for citizenship. The Republic of Congo, with an average GDP of $900 per person, and Monaco, with average GDP of $27,000 per person (2002 estimates), both restrict citizenship largely to those whose parents are citizens.[19] An ad hoc example also illustrates this point: among the several hundred EU citizens who applied for Turkish citizenship between 1995 and 2003, none of them had their applications approved.[20] During the same period, tens of thousands of Turkish immigrants were accorded EU citizenship, the plurality in Germany.[21] To be clear, the point of these examples is to emphasize the inconsistency of these norms from the expectation on the Right and Left alike that government policies are largely influenced by crude market principles and the pressures of large corporations. While capitalism is not on its way out, it has met a fierce ideological and political foe in the guise of nationalism. Likewise, those who may not care about defending capitalism have ideological investments in equality and freedom that are also incompatible with birthright citizenship. Embraced by most on the left and right alike, the inclusions and exclusions relying on birthright citizenship call for further explanation.

So-called Liberal Political Theories of Citizenship

In the 1970s and 1980s, some feminists began exploring inconsistencies in so-called liberal thought indicative of the theorists' sexism. The purpose was partly to suggest that the work of social contract thinkers was inherently masculinist and not liberal and partly to provoke rethinking relations between men and women that would be consistent with the liberal norms suggested for men's relations among one another, although many feminists for various reasons rejected the liberal project altogether.[22] Carole Pateman's *Sexual Contract* points out that John Locke contemplated an enduring sphere of private, familial, sexed inequality as the basis for imagining a public realm that would put men on equal political footing.[23] Susan Okin finds a very similar aporia in the work of John Rawls. His *Theory of Justice* sets aside the family from inquiry into norms of justice.[24] Pateman, Okin, and many others show the blind spots of Enlightenment authors.

To account for the different standards Locke applied to the familial and political spheres, Pateman draws on psychoanalytic theory. Pateman suggests that the parallels between Freud's story of the band of brothers overthrowing the father in order to be masters of their respective households[25] and Locke's incitement for English men to shake off the monarchy and dominate their families is evidence of history's and Locke's misogyny. Okin does not delve into deeper psychological motives but seems to attribute Rawls's exclusion of family roles from the "original position" to old-fashioned sexism. Their inquiries initiated numerous other studies across many fields into the seemingly anachronistic resilience of the illiberal family and other hereditary groups, including the nation and empire, in work by a number of theorists who called themselves liberal. The postcolonial critiques of liberal theorists, discussed below, do not overtly connect the theorists' views on kinship rules with the authors' racism and imperialism, but the attachments of Locke,

Jeremy Bentham, and John Stuart Mill, among many others, to family, nation, and racialized imperial power are rooted in their anxieties about mortality that did not give way to their otherwise individual-level, rational analyses. Sexism, the institutionalization of men's legal dominance of intergenerationality they cannot obtain in nature, is also an artifact of these anxieties, and will be discussed in chapters 4 and 5. There are a handful of theorists whose work expresses consciousness of these attachments and rejects them.[26] This is liberal theory; those theories that do not extend their deontological analyses to all people and all activities may call themselves liberal and may even provide the intellectual historical origins for the term,[27] but if the concept is to have meaning, then self-declarations are not sufficient evidence.

In light of their opposition to feudal uses of heredity for resource allocation, as well as the incompatibility of birthright with market principles, one might expect those claiming liberal credentials to call for open borders. But prominent twentieth- and twenty-first-century so-called liberal democratic theorists have tended to endorse rather than repudiate birth criteria for citizenship.[28] For instance, Isaiah Berlin defends the views of Johann Gottfried Herder, a late eighteenth-century philosopher and poet who believed people were born with national spirits (Volksgeist and Nationalgeist) particular to their ancestors.[29] A staunch defender of "the individual" against totalitarian and fascist ideologies of the twentieth century,[30] Berlin argues nonetheless that nationalism's premises of common blood and culture are benign and fill a "profound natural need,"[31] an assumption subsequent liberals have embellished to adduce an enclosed hereditary community's self-determination as an individual right. For example, the 1948 United Nations Declaration of Human Rights includes the "right to a nationality."

Rather than mount a critique of nationalism, so-called liberal theory works within ancestral paradigms of membership, a concession to "inevitability" not made in the case of other prevailing practices in earlier times. An article by the political philosophers Avishi Margalit and Joseph Raz makes this approach explicit, explaining that their method elevates common practices and intuitions to moral principles: "We assume that things are roughly as they are, especially that our world is a world of states and of a variety of ethnic, national, tribal, and other groups. We do not question the justification for this state of affairs. Rather, we ask whether, given that this is how things are and for as long as they remain the same, a moral case can be made in support of national self-determination."[32] The answer is "yes." Margalit and Raz infer the characteristics of the groups providing a principled basis for the relevant units of self-determination, what they call *encompassing groups*, "membership of which is important to one's self-identity."[33] Margalit and Raz observe that these communities do not depend on achievement but that one "belongs because of who one is,"[34] meaning the experience of being born into a particular identity and not of having earned it.[35]

In a related project—establishing rules for distributive justice—the political theorist Michael Walzer[36] also endorses birthright citizenship: "The distinctiveness of cultures and groups depends upon closure and, without it, membership cannot be conceived as a stable feature of human life."[37] The birthright-citizenship rule for closure holds even though Walzer also insists that society's benefits be allocated on the basis of the skills appropriate to earn them and criticizes aristocracies and other birthright legal privileges. Closure for a specific political society should be based on birth, Walzer insists, because any other criterion risks endangering families. *Jus soli*, membership by birth in the territory, is also allowed, so as not to disadvantage those whose parents were born elsewhere.

Walzer's assertions depend as much on the value he finds in such hereditary communities as on their inevitability: "If states ever became large neighborhoods, it is likely that neighborhoods will become little states. Their members will organize to defend the local politics against strangers.... To tear down the walls of the state [is not to create] a world without walls, but rather to create a thousand petty fortresses."[38] Local police would take over those functions now held by federal border guards. Instead of Americans keeping out Mexicans, San Diegoans would keep out all non–San Diegoans. The hypothesis assumes a universal propensity for nationalism and xenophobia.

Mustering support for using birth and kinship rules, Walzer quotes from a late nineteenth-century political scientist, Henry Sidgwick, who also favored policies of ethnic and national discrimination: "National and patriotic sentiments ... appear to be at present indispensable to social wellbeing,"[39] a belief shared by another so-called liberal, John Rawls. Rawls specifically defines "liberal peoples" as those whose membership is determined in the first instance by heredity, not shared liberal values. Rawls quotes for this point John Stuart Mill, an author whose liberalism also was constrained by racism and imperialism (or whose racism and imperialism was revealed through his liberalism, depending on the critic).[40] Mill asserts that to exist as a political community, people need to have the "common sympathies" found in "race and descent."[41] Only political societies formed on this basis, Rawls infers from Mill, share the requisite "community of recollections; collective pride and humiliation, pleasure and regret, connected with the same incidents in the past."[42] Rawls provides no account of how heredity per se provides a "community of recollections" but appears to be relying on Freud's unscientific belief that "memory traces" exist in our genes,[43] failing to acknowledge other possible instances of collective pride and memory. Rawls was intimately familiar, for instance, with how the Harvard University community of students and alumni passed on rituals, memories, and had a sense of collective pride in belonging to a closed community where membership is only contingently and not predominantly determined by descent or race.[44]

So far, the proposition is that Berlin, Raz and Margalit, Walzer, and Rawls have adduced from the correlation of birth with citizenship a causal as well as necessary relation. They assert a feeling of belonging, family, and values as the justifications for birthright citizenship. If a community of birth accomplishes such solidarity, then although other routes for establishing community are feasible, the route via birthright still might deserve special respect because birth consistently is a sufficient condition for such feelings. In other words, alternative membership rules might or might not work, but birth always works. This position is taken by Jules Coleman and Sarah Harding, who reason that *as a consequence of birth*, "to be an American ultimately is to accept liberal, political ideals."[45] The evidence for this is scant. What about the birthright Americans in the twenty-one states who voted to include a ban on same-sex marriage in their state constitutions? Would Coleman and Harding endorse calling in Homeland Security to deport those who voted for such measures, as they lack the toleration consistent with alleged American values? Should these states secede?

Paradoxically, one writer who epitomizes the very intolerance Coleman and Harding define as un-American is Henry Sidgwick, the scholar from whom Walzer quotes with approval. Not only is the statement that embracing toleration is an American value contradicted by the authors' failure to tolerate nonbirthright immigrants as citizens, but it also calls attention to the normalization of such exclusions as consistent with a deceptive nominal liberalism that makes the weak argument seem so powerful. The acceptance of this reasoning is symptomatic of the syllogism: the United States=liberal, the United States=birthright citizenship, ergo, liberalism=birthright citizenship. Sidgwick's invocation by Walzer only makes sense in this context, because there seem no other grounds for citing Sidgwick's work as evidence for even putatively liberal claims for hereditary citizenship. Sidgwick is no Plato, or even Herder, but a racist, sexist nineteenth-century scholar whose chauvinist essays might be called anachronistic even for his own time. Along with insisting on the inevitability of nationalism, Sidgwick also thought it unlikely that "civilized" peoples would abjure imperialism, as empire gave colonizers satisfaction "inseparable from patriotic sentiment";[46] undesirable that married women be granted the suffrage;[47] and "expedient" to exclude people from voting "on the ground of race alone . . . if the general intellectual or moral inferiority of the race excluded is sufficiently clear."[48] Using the nativist Sidgwick to cull arguments limiting immigration is like quoting approvingly from a sixteenth-century tract allowing for witch drowning as long as the heretics sink.

It is worth noting that Walzer and Rawls explicitly embrace the tradition of social contract thought, meaning that they hearken back to projects of Hobbes, Locke, Rousseau, and Kant dedicated to discerning the mechanisms by which an individual's consent to a society provides its legitimacy. In fact, an article predating Rawls's own statement of his views on immigration concludes that Rawls's "veil of ignorance" in the "original position" would lead one to "insist that the right to migrate be included in the basic liberties for the same reasons that one would insist that the right to religious freedom be included: it might prove essential to one's plan of life."[49] Rousseau, associated more with the counter-Enlightenment than the Enlightenment, was the lone social contract theorist who claimed birth a reasonable basis for determining political membership. The others looked to individual choice or conquest. Locke writes that tacit consent to a government simply based on residence entails obedience to its laws but "makes not a man a member of that society," even if residence is acquired through birth in the territory or to subject parents. "Nothing can make any Man so," Locke continues, "but his actually entering into it by positive engagement, and express promise and compact."[50] This norm, however preferred it is by Locke, has never been enforced in any country.

Subsequent so-called liberal theorists have largely abandoned Locke's endeavor to use explicit consent as the basis of legitimate government. Most so-called liberal democratic theorists simply accept prevailing practices of birthright, seeing these as a truly authentic condition for citizenship. They understand that birthright citizenship is the basis of the nation and justify the former by celebrating the latter. Some propose alternatives that are even more illiberal than our present laws. In a book avowedly invigorating liberal and not hereditary norms for citizenship, Peter Schuck and Rogers Smith "urge that the festering problem of illegal immigration should be combated, and the national commitment to liberal consensualism vindicated" by denying citizenship to those whose parents are in the United States illegally:[51]

If mutual consent is the irreducible condition of membership in the American polity, it is difficult to defend a practice that extends birthright citizenship to the native-born children of illegal aliens. The parents of such children are, by definition, individuals whose presence within the jurisdiction of the United States is prohibited by law. . . . If the society has refused to consent to their membership, it can hardly be said to have consented to that of their children.[52]

Schuck and Smith want to increase legal immigration but feel they have pinpointed a poignant contradiction—birthright citizenship for children of illegal aliens—that they want to ameliorate. However, they do not propose ending birthright citizenship for those whose parents are legally in the country, and they do not explain how what they characterize as good legal and ethical decisions (to have legal status in a country) made by one's parents is a liberal decision rule for determining children's citizenship. Moreover, the authors provide no evidence other than the nativism of those responding to opinion pollsters to support their characterization of illegal immigration as a "festering problem." They suggest that a social contract needs to take into account the preferences of those within it, but they do not defend this claim against counterexamples of, say, free movement within federated countries, including the United States, whereby those born in a destination state cannot refuse admission to interested newcomers and short-term residency requirements initiate membership on an equal political footing with those born there.

The apparent consensualism Schuck and Smith seek is not at the level of the individual, which would entail free movement, but is a "mutual consensualism" requiring each generation's majority to decide on population movements. Thus the hallmark of this approach is norms of democratic rule, allowing the majority to invoke birthright privileges of citizenship parents (to override the Fourteenth Amendment's requirement of birthright citizenship) and not individual consent. Yes, social contract theory poses some paradoxes—what happens if an individual wants to consent and the sovereign is not amenable?—but this requires grappling with these hard questions. Redefining the challenge of individual liberty for modern so-called liberal states by eliminating birthright citizenship for one class defined by ancestry (children of undocumented residents) and not another (children of legal residents) is a somewhat curious exercise. Once one acknowledges birthright citizenship is an illiberal criterion, then it seems odd to continue to use it for anyone, including the children of citizens.

A similar criticism holds for a very different proposal advanced by Ayelet Shachar and Ran Hirschl, who advocate taxing birthright by assessing levies on the populations of wealthier countries.[53] Their reasons for pursuing this proposal and not a truly liberal one of allowing free movement is precisely the problem: they want to maintain the prerogative of nation-states to exclude based on birthright. They admire the attachments they find created by intergenerational communities and dismiss as unrealistic and undesirable their being superseded by free movement.[54] Considering only the economic inequalities of birthright citizenship, Shachar and Hirschl fail to calculate the full extent of its damages.

THE BENEFITS AND HARMS OF BIRTHRIGHT CITIZENSHIP

There are three categories of reasons for suggesting that birthright citizenship should be abolished: pragmatism, rationality, and justice. The sections below review some of the assumptions and assertions in the immigration literature, suggesting that once immigration and citizenship are empirically better understood, then fears of change may be assuaged, at least those based on pragmatic worries and not on unconscious aspirations for controlling reproduction and achieving immortality—birthright citizenship's actual function and the reason it has been so pervasive. A world without birthright citizenship and nations might do something far worse than threaten one's job. It might tip confused fears about a meaningless, finite life into melancholic certainty. A pragmatic cost-benefit analysis that adds up the brutal consequences of such national attachments provides ample utilitarian reasons for reconsidering criteria of birthright citizenship and motivates attention to the psychological reasons for its persistence.

Pragmatic Analyses

This section on birthright citizenship's costs and benefits assumes that birthright citizenship achieves the practical benefits its supporters claim. It assumes that birthright citizenship protects "my" job and that I do not care about anyone else, maintains "my" homogeneous culture and tradition, and ensures that taxes paid by native inhabitants are not spent on undeserving newcomers. The further stipulation is that the views of those in countries with the lowest rates of emigration should be weighed more heavily than those held by those in countries with relatively higher levels of emigration, as the former could be assumed to suffer more from open borders than the latter. For instance, the pragmatic concerns of U.S.-American residents, where fewer than 1 percent emigrated last year, would be weighed more heavily than those from Mexico, from which about 3.7 percent emigrated in 2005.[55] This last point means that, as a matter of calculating preferences, a utilitarian would assign more significance to the desires of a population born in a particular territory over those moving there at some subsequent point. For the purposes of this analysis, particularist benefits from birthright-citizenship rules in wealthy countries will be weighed very heavily, and the preferences of natives in countries with stipulated government burdens from immigration and low emigration rates valued more than those in countries with higher emigration rates.

This is a pragmatic assessment, which means that these views may be more heavily weighted, but these are still preferences and not "rights" that would trump all other claims, even if rights could be construed as absolute.[56] (Rights and justice arguments are assessed below.) This section establishes a framework for evaluating stipulated benefits of exclusion against its costs, for which evidence will be provided: (1) systemic, mass violence; (2) insecurity from the threat of war; (3) long-term tyrannies; (4) trafficking and superexploitation; (5) inefficiencies in labor markets; and (6) global as well as ethnic apartheid.

MASS, SYSTEMIC VIOLENCE

War casualties worldwide remain enormous.[57] Since World War II, when between fifty and seventy million people were killed, over twenty-three million people have been killed in major wars.[58] More recently, between 2003 and 2007, 377,000 people, largely civilians, have suffered brutal, violent deaths during militarized conflicts—the equivalent to the fatalities from 125 World Trade Center attacks,[59] but this receives little public discussion. There is a war on terrorism but not a war on the far more deadly fighting of war itself. Hundreds of millions also have died off the battlefields because of wars during this period. And nationality also sets the stage for sovereigns to kill internal enemies as well. Hitler said, "If I don't mind sending the pick of the German people without regret over the spilling of precious German blood, then I naturally have also the right to eliminate millions of an inferior race that multiplies like vermin."[60] Such a statement raises questions about why people go along with this, serving as soldiers or mass executioners. How can political leaders call on these national attachments toward the end of killing?

Yael Tamir, who had Isaiah Berlin as a teacher and is a so-called liberal who endorses this mass psychology of violence on behalf of (so-called) liberal states, explains how nations incite nationalist militarism: "The importance of endowing the state with a national task that creates a link between the present generation, its ancestors, and future generations [necessary for men to fight] cannot be overstated; it helps individuals conquer the fear of death by promising them an opportunity to enter the sphere of the eternal."[61] Tamir quotes literary sources ranging from Shakespeare to Milan Kundera affirming that mortality's nemesis is the nation, but she fails to explain why the nation and not, say, writing a play or a novel would be sufficient to alleviate the anxiety, as these too promise the "opportunity to enter the sphere of the eternal," to wit the performance of Shakespeare's plays worldwide five hundred years after he wrote them.

The nation is not unique in allowing an opportunity at immortality but for guaranteeing this. Such a promise cannot be made if it depends on people having the genius to write great literature. Belonging to a nation places one in an apparently certain and natural relation to the past and future. Losing the birth criterion would weaken the potential of governments to expect loyalty by shows of violence: if people experienced themselves as bound to states only by individual consent and not birth, the history of local townships and other political communities in which membership is by residence and not birth suggests these citizens would be unlikely to fight, a result one might expect a so-called liberal theorist such as Tamir to endorse and not repudiate.[62] The commitments evoked by birthright, including the "Birthright Israel" project to elicit support for Israel (the country Tamir says exemplifies the object of her concerns) from Jews worldwide,[63] are precisely the ones that Tamir is calling on to support militarism and are at odds with genuinely liberal projects, despite Tamir's claims otherwise.

For liberal theorists claiming to embrace Kantian paradigms precluding instrumentalizing individuals in service of a larger cause, nothing is more irrational or undesirable than war. In "Perpetual Peace," Kant describes war deaths and injuries as the unhappy outcomes of an international system where, lacking a single sovereign, governments are predisposed to violent conflicts. This echoes earlier social contract views of what happens under conditions of competing sovereigns, for instance, Locke's statement that: "force, or a declared design of force, upon the person of another, where there is no common superior on earth to appeal to for relief, *is the state of war*."[64] Absent a world government, wars are necessary.

Tamir acknowledges that war's inevitability in social contract thought has invited criticism and rebuts pacifists by justifying nationalism and war: "Nationalism should be seen not as a pathology infecting modern liberal states but as an answer to their legitimate needs of self-defense. [Without nationalism,] the atomism, neurosis, and alienation [afflicting] liberal states . . . may leave them defenseless."[65] If governments do not invoke metaphors of immortality to inspire citizen self-sacrifice, then some very good states will fail, Tamir suggests. She fails to realize the reciprocal inference: if governments, liberal or tyrannical, do not have metaphors of immortality to goad citizen risk, then no one will be attacking in the first place. Tamir acknowledges that her main motive to write in favor of militarism is to defend Israel's armed defense of Jewish sovereignty,[66] a case that highlights this point. Palestinians voted to elect a government and are equally willing to advance their national interests through armed struggle.

One possible defense of Tamir's position might be that other neighboring states that are not democracies, the so-called evil regimes of Syria or Iran, could force or trick their citizens into fighting and thus put legitimate governments in a weakened position. However, Tamir is not making the point that liberal democracies only fight defensively. Tamir seems to realize that especially in the case about which she is writing, nationalism may well drive democratic publics to war, but she does not reflect on the importance of this. In other words, although her explicit argument is that liberal democracies need armies, the underlying premise and facts suggest that this need for armies is because of nationalism and not liberalism. Israel could have been founded as a federation of Muslims and Jews, but instead its leaders chose to establish a specifically Jewish state in which membership is obtained by ancestry. Armies are not formed to defend liberalism but, rather, political sovereignty, especially the control of kinship and membership rules that establish the particularity of the nation. The state, either elected or a dictatorship, uses law to inculcate these commitments throughout the population, so that the contrivance of the sacred nation seems normal and necessary.[67]

In other words, the nation and other hereditary commitments, as well as religion, are the exclusive formations leading to systemic slaughter and not a generic flaw in something like human nature. To expand on a similar point made in the introduction, if sheer devilry alone induced people to organize and prey on pacifists, then we would expect to see much higher levels of organized violence than currently exists. For instance, Enron, run by people convicted for stealing and lying in a manner that severely hurt hundreds of thousands of their workers and shareholders, was never moved to war. The political theorist and apologist for the Nazi regime Carl Schmitt explains:

> Under no circumstances can anyone demand that any member of an economically determined society, whose order in the economic domain is based upon rational procedures, sacrifice his life in the interest of rational operations. To justify such a demand on the basis of economic expediency would contradict the individualistic principles of a liberal economic order.... To demand seriously of human beings that they kill others and be prepared to die themselves so that trade and industry may flourish for the survivors or that the purchasing power of grandchildren may grow is sinister and crazy.[68]

Schmitt dedicated the famous essay "The Concept of the Political," from which the above quotation comes, to a friend who had died in battle after World War I, unbeknownst to his friend, had come to a close.[69] Schmitt is commemorating his friend's death as exemplary of the violence "the political" requires, especially when it is instrumentally pointless. Schmitt does not acknowledge that this, too, is crazy. To the contrary, he defends the logic of killing as key to what he calls "the political" but is more specifically "the national" and "the religious."

In their article on citizenship, Michael Kearl and Anoel Rinaldi also provide part of the explanation for why the nation or religions, and not other groups, can inspire this sacrifice by observing that the nation-state "provides the individual with not only with *spatial transcendence* (such as the pride when seeing the American flag on Mars), but *temporal transcendence* as well."[70] They quote a student of Durkheim, Robert Hertz, who himself died in World War I, writing, "Indeed, society imparts its own character of permanence to the individuals who compose it: because it feels itself immortal and wants to be so, it cannot normally believe that its members, above all those in whom it incarnates itself and with whom it identifies itself, should be fated to die."[71] Kearl and Rinaldi conclude, "The state, like religion, confers immortality on each of its elect."[72] It is this immortality that makes the state's expectation of the most extreme form of self-sacrifice—risking death and killing others—possible. Purely economic organizations do not allow such insanity. Even Shell Oil, defending itself against a lawsuit charging it with complicity in a government's murderous human-rights abuses in Nigeria, is not itself torturing people; it is giving funds to a nation-state that is doing so, in exchange for that government's protection of its oil exports. Shell is funding a government run by one ethnic group that is using violence to quell challenges to its authority by other ethnic groups and democratic organizers.[73] Many nonstate groups with ethnic, racial, or religious commitments also have behaved in this way, for example, tribes or insurgent groups united by religion, ethnicity, or race inciting civil wars or genocide in African countries such as Rwanda, Somalia, Ethiopia, and Sudan—in other words, those groups that also confer immortality on their members.

Apparent counterexamples of communist insurrections and revolutions (and their bloody repression, say in South America) or even the anticolonial war against the British in 1776—where institutions of governance seemed at stake, not hereditary attachments—also fit this pattern. In many cases, ethnic loyalties underlie party differences (discussed below), and all civil wars are fights over controlling the destiny of a nation (from the Latin *nasci*, meaning "birth") or initiating a new one, not over controlling or inaugurating a non-intergenerational group or organization whose worldly stakes are not worth the loss of life.[74] Counterexamples are cities with autonomous police departments, which, despite their independent monopolies on the use of force and even when corrupt, do not organize to fight other cities. This suggests that perhaps shorn of the intergenerational and sacred accoutrements enabling the myths of immortality, states, too, would be nonviolent.

INSECURITY AND PROXIMATE HARMS FROM WAR

In addition to the actual deaths war inflicts, living in war's proximity and potential is itself harmful. If one thinks only of the devastation from the early twenty-first century's largest conflicts in Iraq, Afghanistan, Israel-Palestine, Lebanon, Sudan, Chad, Somalia, the Democratic Republic of the Congo, and harms affecting states adjacent to them as well—filled with refugee camps and displaced people—it is clear that war directly traumatizes tens of millions of people. Each refugee is enmeshed in a web of others, meaning hundreds of millions of friends, lovers, and relatives who must worry and mourn. Wars also have devastating health consequences,[75] including significantly heightened rates of tuberculosis, malaria, AIDS, and other infectious diseases.[76] Between 1994 and 2003, about thirteen million people died as a result of war, compared with 669,000 total deaths from natural disasters.[77] A study measuring disability-adjusted life years (DALY) based on the war-related contraction of twenty-three diseases found that sixteen million DALY were lost due to international and civil war *in 1999 alone*.[78]

Wars also impose enormous opportunity costs, as funds go to militaries instead of health, sanitation, and educational capabilities. In 2004, governments worldwide spent about $1,035 billion on their armies.[79] If these funds were spent on health care for the 2.3 billion people living in low-income countries, per capita expenditures would increase 1,858 percent, from $24 to $446 annually.[80] Although military expenditures, especially on personnel, may appear to be a part of the social-welfare state and not an alternative, as William Connolly suggests,[81] the flourishing of programs enacted to defend a nation's sovereignty through force—and not the less overtly violent regulatory regimes Michel Foucault envisions during the period after the king has been beheaded—requires some attention. Indeed, the nation-state's ability throughout history to establish itself as sacred and not simply a welfare consortium is one of juridical power's continuities and not an epistemic break on which Foucault strategically, I believe, insists. On what other basis could his writings almost entirely marginalize the most important traumas of the twentieth century, namely World War I and World War II? It is possible that some forms of state control could be exercised by regulatory regimes but not war. War requires the old-fashioned death of combatants and civilians organized by a state on behalf of agendas that are virtually unchanged since antiquity: the coercive power over an intergenerational—that is, immortal—people and territory. To the extent that the state exists primarily as a means of organizing for interstate violence, it requires expenditures on a military. In other words, the old-fashioned lens locating power in legal institutions still provides the best tool for understanding why the state is investing in the military.

If, absent the imperatives of psychic investments in immortality promised by nations and religions, these funds were freed for other purposes, their disbursement would be far more than sufficient to offset the costs associated with immigration's alleged harms and could be used to address the underlying structural problems for which immigration is often a red herring. For instance, the anti-immigration group Federation for American Immigration Reform estimates that illegal and legal immigration combined cost the United States $66 billion in 2002. For the sake of argument, even if this figure were $100 billion, were the United States to eliminate military spending, this would still leave a balance of over $370 billion *annually*.[82] Even assuming a 90 percent reduction and not elimination of military spending, a generous amount analogous to corporate funding for their own private security, these funds would be more than sufficient for the basic crime-prevention needs of the federal government and leave a tremendous surplus for high-quality social services.[83]

The threat of war inherent in a system of nation-states with closed borders has other economic costs as well. In their study of U.S. savings rates, economists Bruce Russett and Joel Slemrod observe that "to the degree that Americans, or people of other nations, have reduced their savings because of expectations of war, national savings pools available to support investment are smaller than otherwise."[84] This research was done in the shadow of nuclear threats. The study suggests that people living in a potential war zone, which is the case for large parts of Africa, are not going to pursue the strategies of capital accumulation necessary for developing the means of production leading to higher standards of living.[85] Another version of nationalism's war costs was the "war on terror" launched by the Bush administration and sustained by President Obama, despite promises to the contrary by candidate Obama. Only nationalism would allow a sovereign to turn a major criminal event that might cost at most tens of millions of dollars—for the FBI to find and arrest the responsible foreigners—into a military invasion whose total cost will be in the trillions.[86]

BIRTHRIGHT CITIZENSHIP SUSTAINS TYRANNICAL GOVERNMENTS

Describing the plight of Jews under the Nazi regime, Hannah Arendt writes: "It is always relatively easy to get out of a country illegally, whereas it is nearly impossible to enter the place of refuge without permission and to dodge the immigration authorities."[87] In addition to the harms of war and budgetary inefficiencies, birthright citizenship also thwarts if not prevents the emigration of people threatened by genocide and other forms of tyranny, eliminating an effective, nonviolent means of passive resistance. Dictators and their enemies are extremely sensitive to the possibility of emigration. Knowing that repression without border controls would lead to mass exodus, dictatorships with the resources to prevent emigration devote them to this task. "It is nearly impossible to secure compliance with drastic state demands if people are able to vote with their feet," the political scientist Ari Zolberg observes.[88] The regime of the former Soviet Union exemplifies this. The demise of the USSR was not caused by glasnost but by the collapse of the Berlin Wall. The USSR's oppression of its population, not to mention that of dictatorships from Hitler's Germany to Hussein's Iraq, also benefited from the restriction of movement to other countries. In 1989, if West Germany had applied the same policy to East Germans that a unified Germany now applies to potential immigrants from

Libya (generally refused), the Communist Party might still be running East Berlin.

Understanding the effect of immigration policies on the longevity of other regimes, the U.S. government encourages emigration from Cuba to the United States and refuses to allow entrance to Haitians.[89] The United States makes it especially easy for Cubans to come to the United States because it is very interested in Cuban regime change but supports the Haitian government, though not because of any fellow feeling for Cubans as opposed to Haitians.[90] Reciprocally, when the U.S. government is anxious about migration, it changes the regime directly, as did the Clinton administration in Haiti. Fearing a massive exodus and refugee crisis from the civil war, U.S. troops were sent to install a new and supposedly more stable government led by Jean-Bertrand Aristide.[91]

Illegitimate regimes benefit from the restrictive immigration policies of their neighbors. In most countries run by tyrants, emigration is not curtailed by the regimes themselves, which often lack the resources to police wide swaths of their borders. Rather, neighboring countries fearing the incursion of political and economic refugees take care of this. Iraqis under Saddam Hussein were kept in place by the border guards of Turkey, Iran, and Syria. North Koreans are forced to labor for the regime of Kim Il-Sung as much by the North Korean border patrol as by the vigilant Chinese, who regularly repatriate refugees back to North Korea.[92] Many countries are formally committed to accepting as political refugees those fleeing from direct state persecution, but in practice their commitments are hollow. For instance, despite well-documented evidence of sectarian violence in Iraq, the United States has continued to turn down Iraqi requests for asylum, imposing a five-hundred-per-year quota.[93]

The notion that governments are responsive to population flows is a simple extension of the logic behind economic sanctions. Limiting financial resources from a global economy is a strategy to weaken an existing repressive government and provide it with incentives to change. Extending such an approach to the subjects of an oppressive government by allowing them to leave and depriving governments of their resources strikes a similar blow. It is difficult to tax and recruit for the police, necessary for an unpopular regime's survival, without the warm bodies to contribute revenues and to serve. Allowing free movement saves populations from such hardships without the logistical and violent costs of intervening superpowers or a world government.

The major source of underground slave labor—most of it sexual or child labor, and much of it both—is war refugees. This black market has been estimated to bring in profits outstripping those of drug smuggling.[94] Sociologist Vincenzo Ruggiero found that in 1997 there were about two hundred million people enslaved worldwide.[95] Much of this slave trade occurs among African families in war zones, selling daughters as young as ten into marriage to occupying soldiers, believing that obtaining a husband is a path to honor foreclosed if the same soldier were to rape her, a likelihood in these camps.[96] A study of sex slaves from traffickers in Hungary found that the "primary reason for emigrating was war, notably from Kosovo, Afghanistan, Sierra Leone, and Liberia."[97] And women from other countries and settling elsewhere in Europe reported similar experiences, for instance, the Algerians who were trafficked due to their fears of Islamicist attacks.[98]

The problem is not North-South or First World–Third World inequalities but the national border itself, as when employment agencies conspire to import "guest labor," knowing that the confiscation of passports upon arrival in regions far from home or in government embassies will lead to indentured servitude and worse. A reporter describes Filipino women escaping from a house in Kurdistan where they been locked for a month and "made to work for free after their passports, cellphones, and plane tickets were taken away."[99] In 2002, Kurdistan began importing labor from Ethiopia, Indonesia, the Philippines, Bangladesh, and Somalia, with the workers frequently tricked into thinking they were being taken to other countries and not to Iraq: "'At the airport [in Dubai] they grab our luggage and push it through the X-ray machine, then they start shouting at us, 'Go, go, your contract [is] in Kurdistan.' We are confused. We don't know what to do.'"[100]

Human trafficking is distinguished from smuggling based on the autonomy of the individual migrants. The woman about to be killed in a raid on a refugee camp by drugged soldiers, who ends up friendless, broke, and without a passport, locked in an apartment in a country where she does not understand the language differs from those with more degrees of freedom in their choices to plan a move and to have the same police protection and rule of law available to other residents. Trafficking is facilitated not only by wars but by birthright citizenship itself.

The condition of being undocumented is the mechanism that allows employers to become virtual slaveholders; their ability is predicated on the legal and related psychic condition of the alien as a foreigner that affects all countries, including advanced industrial societies.[101] According to a UNICEF study of Africa, countries may be a "destination and also a source country for trafficking. Nigeria is a case in point, as it is a country of origin for women and children trafficked to twelve countries, but at the same time a country of destination for women and children arriving from ten countries, many of them the same as the countries of origin for Nigeria's arriving trafficked immigrants."[102] More than 90 percent of the trafficking in Africa stays in the same region, though the people are moved outside of their country of origin.[103]

Trafficking people among countries imposes costs of time and resources. Nonetheless, traffickers receive substantial benefits from moving women and children outside their native countries. Birthright-citizenship rules help in subordinating people living outside their countries of origin. Local police ignore the rule of law and take bribes for trafficking because foreigners are not their problem, a belief conditioned by knowledge that the officer is not a problem for the country from where these strange women and children come. If no one were illegal, then this would increase police investigations into violence and sexual abuse and thus increase the costs of the trafficking business, establishing higher points for profitability, which might deter at least some of the present culprits.

Nation-states no longer use slavery as a direct instrument of war, but the nation-state facilitates an illegal slavery through birthright citizenship. If episodic violence persists in a world without birthright citizenship, the worst consequences for refugees would be the burdens of social dislocation and alienation. These are undesirable, but the safety nets of truly universal access to health care, housing, and education would still make it possible to live with dignity and hope, not to mention security in the feeling that one has legal rights wherever one lives. Without birthright citizenship, families would not be confined to these camps but could freely settle with expenses covered by a provisions agency (and without marriage there would be no bride-wealth, a further incentive for impoverished refugees to sell their daughters).

INEFFICIENCIES FROM INEQUITIES

Since 1984, the *Wall Street Journal* editorial board has issued an annual call to add an amendment stating "There shall be open borders."[104] Opposing legislation eventually passed in 1986, the so-called amnesty law, for being too repressive, the *Wall Street Journal* board penned the only position truly in keeping with liberal values. (The sentiments speak directly to the 2007 debates on the immigration reform measures as well, also attacked from the right as "amnesty" and yet deeply reactionary.)[105] In 1984, the *Wall Street Journal* editorial board wrote:

> The nativist patriots scream for "control of the borders." It is nonsense to believe that this unenforceable legislation will provide any such thing. Does anyone want to "control the borders" at the moral expense of a 2,000-mile Berlin Wall with minefields, dogs and machine-gun towers? ... The instinct is seconded by the "zero-sum" mentality that has been intellectually faddish this past decade. More people, the worry runs, will lead to overcrowding; will use up all our "resources," and will cause unemployment. Trembling no-growthers cry that we'll never "feed," "house" or "clothe" all the immigrants—though the immigrants want to feed, house and clothe themselves. In fact, people are the great resource, and so long as we keep our economy free, more people means more growth, the more the merrier.[106]

The editorial board is not only pointing out the growth benefits of free movement but for the most part making a liberal political argument against the oppression of heavy-handed government.

The many scholarly studies of immigration undertaken since this appeared support the *Wall Street Journal*'s position. The first detailed study of the tax burdens undocumented immigrants impose on state budgets, undertaken by the state government of Texas, found that while undocumented immigrants used $1.16 billion annually in services and benefits such as education and health care, they contributed $1.58 billion in taxes and user fees.[107] Undocumented immigrants increased the state's productivity by $1.72 billion annually.[108] To understand the impact of an unexpected, large influx of unskilled immigrants on the labor market, economist David Card examined Miami's economy after the Mariel Cuban boatlift in 1980. His study found that although the labor supply increased by 7 percent, there was "no evidence that the Mariel influx adversely affected the unemployment rate of either whites or blacks."[109] Other research on newly opened labor markets, as well as prospective models, also support the conclusion that free movement leads to increased incomes in the countries of origin and in destination countries.[110] One widely cited scholar, George Borjas, has undertaken studies showing varying levels of overall negative and even neutral impacts from immigration,[111] but his colleagues have refuted these on the grounds that his models do not include enough variables to accurately replicate labor-market dynamics.[112]

In a study that has been reproduced,[113] economists Bob Hamilton and John Whalley estimate that open borders would dramatically increase worldwide income. They write of their model: "In most cases the gain exceeds worldwide GNP generated in the presence of the controls suggesting that immigration controls are one of the (and perhaps the) most important policy issues facing the global economy."[114] In their model, eliminating these controls increases incomes substantially in poor countries and helps rich countries as well.

Finally, according to the economist Gillian Hadfield, a "social welfare function defined over original residents presumes rather than demonstrates that original people are the people among whom resources should be distributed.... If economists are to participate in the normative debate over immigration ... it seems there can be no starting point other than a global social welfare function."[115] Hadfield then shows that just as the lack of an exit option for citizens enhances the power of dictatorships, the inability of labor to compete in a global market artificially enhances the bargaining power of capitalists, increasing economic inequality and absolute immiseration: "those exploited by highly unequal distribution and therefore suffering the consequences of low productivity have nowhere to go and thus the loss of an imperfect 'resource' is not threatened."[116] Hadfield extrapolates from the emigration restrictions behind artificially low wages in Communist regimes to immigration restrictions today: "it is interesting to ask what the domestic political, ultimately economic consequences for some poorer countries might be if mass emigration were facilitated by reduced immigration restrictions in the developed countries."[117] He reasons that functioning labor markets would translate the diminished supply of workers into higher wages for them.

The economist Bruce Scott writes: "The immigration barriers in rich countries ... foreclose opportunities in the global village to billions of poor people.... In effect, the strict dictates of sovereignty allow wealthy nations to continue to set the rules in their own favor while allowing badly governed poor nations to continue to abuse their own citizens and retard economic development."[118] Scott's larger argument is that neoclassical economists are overlooking major factors leading to uneven development by focusing only on market forces for goods and neglecting labor barriers. Josiah Heyman explains that "compared to normally exploited, resourceless proletarians (day-laborers, farmworkers, domestics, etc.) undocumented immigrants work faster and harder for the same pay (and less frequently for lower pay), and struggle to avoid or limit workplace authority less often. Given this scenario, it is easy to attribute to the U.S. government the role of direct labor control."[119]

By maintaining a two-tiered system of labor—one wage for Mexicans and another for Americans—corporations reap the benefits of superexploitation, a situation for which legal status alone is responsible.[120]

ETHNIC AND RACIAL APARTHEID

Finally, when nation-states produce birthright citizens, they issue a stamp of a permanent, unalterable, and yet entirely political difference: ethnicity.[121] An ethnic group is any population that identifies with a past, present, or aspirational nation-state. Ethnicity is not based on generic cultural attributes but on affiliations experienced as hereditary. Nation-states also produce the imprimatur of race, when kinship rules used for membership trace an observed or imagined physical characteristic associated with a political territory of origin.[122] Racialization is a legal process that occurs within each country, the details for which may vary; each country provides racial categories their foundational legal space: the political territory for a racial designation is either a single nation-state or their aggregation into a region or continent. These are the groups that result not only in war but also in other deleterious habits of daily life, such as informal slavery, prejudice, segregation, and the reinforcing conditions of abjection accompanying the above.

The ultimate expression of such differences occurs under legal apartheid, when a society takes the mark of a hereditary racial or religious difference and assigns rights on this basis. Familiar examples include South Africa before 1992, the Nuremberg laws of 1935, and before that Jim Crow in the United States. In these cases, states developed hereditary criteria for supposedly pure or mixed kinship groups and used these to determine citizenship and legal rights. Israel continues to fit this criterion, as Avram Bornstein shows in his analysis of the restrictions the Israeli government places on its non-Jewish residents, in contrast to the full rights of citizenship available, if requested, by nonresident Jews worldwide. Bornstein echoes Josiah Heyman's analysis that unlike what a Marxist would predict, the "economic forms of violence are largely opportunities emerging from racial forms of violence."[123] In other words, non-Jewish Israeli settlers occupying government-subsidized housing are benefiting economically from the stolen resources of Arab landowners and not from capital from immiserated laborers.

Interestingly, Bornstein's analysis of the economic exploitation of the Arabs invokes Heyman's work on the U.S.-Mexican border. Although many in the United States consider their country liberal, unlike Israel, both—all countries—determine membership primarily by birth. Moreover, the policies

THE PERSISTENCE AND HARMS OF BIRTHRIGHT CITIZENSHIP

50

and technologies of the U.S. border gave the Israelis their blueprint. The electric fences, ditches, surveillance cameras, and intense patrolling in Israel first appeared in southern California.[124] President Jimmy Carter's book denouncing Israel as apartheid[125] obscures the larger problem. Paradoxically, Carter's administration was responsible for initiating heavy policing along the U.S.-Mexican border and supporting sanctions against employers hiring undocumented immigrants. In a 1976 speech, President Carter warned, "unauthorized immigrants had breached [the] Nation's immigration laws [and] displaced many American citizens from jobs."[126] Unable to pass legislation resisted by agribusiness, Carter appointed a blue-ribbon commission that echoed his proposals and "served as the basis for subsequent debate and legislation regarding observing immigration control."[127] Joseph Nevins writes: "The increase in federal resources dedicated to boundary enforcement commenced in the latter half of the administration of President Jimmy Carter.... There was a significant upgrading of equipment, for example, ranging from increased construction of fences to the deployment of helicopters and improved ground sensors," technologies that were not used in the West Bank until two decades later.[128]

The U.S. government's handling of equal-citizenship claims in the midst of ethnic and racial classifications provides some insights into the ways in which synchronic norms of equality (what one sees when looking at a snapshot of U.S. laws in a given moment) may be trumped by diachronic legal narratives of hereditary and religious differences (the cumulative story of our laws, populations, and institutions). Precisely because of the laws and myths outlining the United States as a place where people expect equal respect regardless of ancestry and religion, the image of the other United States—warmongering, racist, bigoted against non-WASPs—eclipsing this profile provides a canvas for considering these tensions. In a later work, *Dying to Live: A Story of U.S. Immigration in an Age of Global Apartheid*, Nevins describes how the U.S. government used force not only to appropriate territory in the aftermath of the Mexican-American War but also to displace the majority Mexican Californians who were residing there—as well as the precolonial natives.[129] Meanwhile, a number of state and federal laws then created, within the United States, an apartheid-like system of segregation for people of Mexican ancestry, "regardless of whether or not they were U.S. citizens."[130]

The legal and informal racial and ethnic discrimination against U.S. citizens of Mexican ancestry is an excellent natural experiment revealing how the materialization of legal boundaries within one contiguous landmass in

North America provides a template that may overwhelm other laws on the books. The sovereign difference between the United States of Mexico (Estados Unidos Mexicanos) and the United States of America as facts on the ground and also as kinship laws embodying a population's sense of their own and others' ancestry may at moments overwhelm the legal equality of birthright citizenship enshrined in the U.S. Constitution.

Section One of the Fourteenth Amendment states:

> All persons born or naturalized in the United States, and subject to the jurisdiction thereof, are citizens of the United States and of the State wherein they reside. No State shall make or enforce any law which shall abridge the privileges or immunities of citizens of the United States; nor shall any State deprive any person of life, liberty, or property, without due process of law; nor deny to any person within its jurisdiction the equal protection of the laws.

Beginning in 1868, everyone born in the United States was a citizen, and all male citizens had to be treated equally by the state, but this was at odds with other juridical imperatives. Both the condition of equality and the condition of exclusion and hierarchy held out promise for appeals to natural law, but the former did not have the same fantasies at their disposal. The appeals to nationality and family have not only immortality but also a certain quality of material inevitability. The borders mapping Mexico and the United States and the kinship laws that create a narrative of familial-based national or ethnic origins, on the one hand, and the words creating equality among all those who are citizens by birth in the United States, on the other, are similarly fictive, invented by politicians and used for a particular purpose. The former have been given a material immortality denied the principle of birthright equality. The Fourteenth Amendment is a law, but its imbrication in government and a world system that denies free movement on the basis of birth renders the aspiration to equality an aspiration and not a legal institution. The law for equality has a few lines and for their performance some judges. The laws of hereditary difference have been lived for millennia through nations and families.

Before turning to the egregious violations of the Fourteenth Amendment in law and practice, its failure to be effectively implemented should not be confused with its being ignored altogether. The history of the United States, as for all countries, is one of a struggle between the voices on behalf of rationality and equality, on the one hand, and those urging the imposition of rigid distinctions based on ancestry and religion, on the other. For instance, despite the racist motives underlying the 1882 Chinese Exclusion Act and subsequent restrictions on immigration from that country and others with majority non-white populations, the Fourteenth Amendment's definition of equal citizenship based on territorial birth was never compromised. Instead, it has been used by the federal courts to bludgeon immigration agents and legislators for their indecency and inhumanity toward U.S. citizens and often alien residents.

For instance, an 1879 decision condemning San Francisco supervisors for passing a law requiring haircuts within one inch of the scalp for arriving male prisoners, on the "pretense" of health reasons, said the measure was an additional punishment and constituted "wanton cruelty" toward Chinese inmates because of the political and cultural significance of their queues (long, braided ponytails).[131] In China, not having one during this period was grounds for being charged with treason.[132] Overturning the law, the judges wrote:

> In our country hostile and discriminating legislation by a state against persons of any class, sect, creed or nation, in whatever form it may be expressed, is forbidden by the fourteenth amendment of the constitution.... And the equality of protection thus assured to every one whilst within the United States, from whatever country he may have come, or of whatever race or color he may be, implies not only that the courts of the country shall be open to him on the same terms as to all others for the security of his person or property, the prevention or redress of wrongs and the enforcement of contracts; but that no charges or burdens shall be laid upon him which are not equally borne by others, and that in the administration of criminal justice he shall suffer for his offenses no greater or different punishment.[133]

The opinion, written during the same period of mobilization to exclude Chinese immigrants from the United States altogether, states: "It is not creditable to the humanity and civilization of our people, much less to their Christianity, that an ordinance of this character was possible."[134]

In many cases, the federal courts were intent on ensuring that regardless of the legislation restricting incoming foreigners, all those born in the United States would be considered on an equal footing. The fact of one's parents' alienage and one's race should be disregarded. In a decision granting habeas relief and harshly condemning the immigration enforcement agency for its poor treatment of a U.S. citizen of Chinese ancestry, held for weeks under the

Chinese Exclusion laws as the authorities disregarded evidence of his citizenship, the court comes down strong on the rights of citizenship, even if this may undermine border-control policies: "It is better that many Chinese immigrants should be improperly admitted than that one natural born citizen of the United States should be permanently excluded from his country."[135] The 1920 Supreme Court justices are relying on a plain reading of the U.S. Constitution, but the immigration officials also have a legal template underlying their racist and xenophobic intuitions as well. It is not surprising that within a country different discourses and social movements arrive at radically different understandings of how law should handle population taxonomies when we remember that these voices compete for attention within the same individual. From Thomas Jefferson the slave owner to President Truman, who bombed the civilians of Nagasaki and Hiroshima while using federal authority to racially integrate public schools, the laws and norms of equality and difference may function on many levels and in contradiction.

A synchronic reading of law would suggest that these three systems—the territorial, the familial, and the citizen who is juridical—could operate without ethnic, national, or racial discrimination. The sovereign countries of the United States of Mexico and America, respectively, on this reading, might control their borders, enforce kinship rules, and also guarantee equality under law to all citizens without passing, say, laws directed against humiliating some populations by unnecessary hair-cutting rules. However, once the importance of narrative and diachronic or historical time to law is understood, then it becomes clear that citizenship law at any given point in any single country is always on the verge of being undone by that country's home in the laws of nations and families. Thus, while it is tempting to say that it is theoretically possible for nationality and family to coexist with a principle of territorial birthright bestowing citizenship on an equal footing for all, this is precisely what is theoretically impossible. The problem is that so-called liberal theory has not understood these tensions between domestic and international forms of exclusion and inclusion and indeed has validated the aspiration of closed ancestral nations and kinship rules, on the one hand, and equal citizenship regardless of heredity, on the other.

Today, in part as a result of the illegal deportation of hundreds of thousands of Mexican American citizens and legal residents in the 1930s,[136] as well as a continuation of racist and nationalist paradigms embedded in political societies that are nation-states (meaning political societies throughout history), U.S. citizens are being treated in many of the same ways denounced by the courts at the turn of the twentieth century. Those who are born outside the country as well as those born inside the United States are being detained. Although they may not legally be deprived of their citizenship absent a process of expatriation, they are being illegally deprived of their rights of citizenship.[137] These violations include everything from false imprisonment at the border to coercing a guilty plea from a U.S. citizen accused of falsely claiming to hold U.S. citizenship. In the former case, an immigration agent refused to believe that the U.S.-born, Stanford doctor's passport was genuine. He handcuffed Chima Obi for six hours and told her husband, "These people will do anything to get in here."[138] The government eventually paid Obi $50,000 to settle her lawsuit. However, most of the U.S. citizens and legal residents the government illegally detains do not have the resources to file habeas petitions much less sue for damages for far more serious offenses, including imposing alien classifications on U.S. citizens in jails and prisons to pocket per diem reimbursements from the federal government;[139] holding U.S. citizens and legal residents in detention centers in order to coerce agreement-to-removal orders, even when the detainees are legally eligible to remain in the country either because they are U.S. citizens or legal residents;[140] holding U.S. citizens who claim to be born in the U.S. in detention centers without reasonable suspicion, much less proof, that these people are lying;[141] and failing to insure that those deported to Mexico are Mexican nationals.[142]

In sum, granting the empirically unfounded claim that immigration poses economic hardships on those in countries with net increases in its population, these costs pale compared to the price of war deaths, military spending, child and sex trafficking, slavery, refugee-camp life, insecurity, superexploitation, and apartheid for which birthright citizenship is largely responsible. Those defending birthright citizenship would be hard pressed to do so on principles of pragmatism if they accounted fully for its costs.

Birthright Citizenship Is Irrational

In addition to birthright citizenship being impractical, it is also illogical, unfair, and inherently unstable. Birthright citizenship rules symbolize a struggle to fix identity through kinship rules that are themselves fluid but treated as genetic and immutable. The creation and reliance on kinship rules to determine membership is a symptom of an unmet desire for certainty and immortality in the face of life's actual conditions of chaos and death.

THE TRIUMPH OF THE PASSIVE CITIZEN

For citizenship to live up to the promise of self-rule, equality, and autonomy that liberalism as an ideology promises, states must redefine citizenship so that it merges two qualities: the criteria for one's status as a member with the criteria for participation. So-called liberal democracies today—ostensibly committed to freedom, equality, and birthright—use standards for *passive citizenship* (who counts as a member) that are at odds with those for *active citizenship* (the prerogatives of citizens to shape law).[143] Ancestry is not a rational basis for awarding the privileges of active citizenship. Insofar as liberals have decided that nepotism is bad for running a business, how can they justify using this system for selecting citizens who will run a country? Even pseudo-intelligence tests, ones that did no better than randomly select for those who were ostensibly qualified, would be more in keeping with liberal norms than those of birthright, as the exclusions would be based on at least a pretense of preferring individual merit over birth. Or what about using the criterion of money—so that a state would reward those who are especially skillful while at the same time attracting capital? If the neoconservative pundit George Will can decry limits on campaign contributions as illiberal because liberals believe money is a fair proxy for voice,[144] then it would seem to follow that money also should be the right proxy for being able to choose a country. Whoever has a certain amount of wealth could join and vote. Or what about only awarding citizenship to people who are not just smart but who demonstrate special competences in the art of governance, say, those who have an especially strong grasp of laws and the constitution?[145]

Active citizenship or self-governance requires certain competencies. Not only the age of reason, as John Locke suggests, but local knowledge, good judgment, and a dedication to a state's well-being all would seem to be reasonable prerequisites for self-governance. Yet these criteria do not generally determine a country's citizens. Passive citizenship has no overlap with these capacities. Passive citizenship—being born to one or two citizen parents or within a particular country's borders—requires no skills at all.

So why do countries persist in using birthright citizenship for political membership? There seem to be two answers to the question of why nepotism makes sense when it comes to running a country and not a company. The first seems obvious: one's political society or polity is an extension of one's family. It seems no more unreasonable for citizenship and state benefits to be a birthright than it is to limit one's family this way. No one criticizes a parent for nepotism when she pays only for her own child's college tuition and not for that of her neighbor's more talented child.

The thinking here is confused in three respects. First, it assumes government benefits are confined to citizens. However, historically and recently governments have awarded aid to individuals who are not citizens. T. H. Marshall pointed out that the Poor Laws in England granted welfare provisions for women and children as a way to mark their political disenfranchisement and not as recognition of their citizenship:

> The Poor Law treated the claims of the poor, not as an integral part of the rights of the citizen, but as an alternative to them—as claims which could be met only if the claimants ceased to be citizens in any true sense of the word. For paupers forfeited in practice the civil right of personal liberty, by internment in the poorhouse, and they forfeited by law any political rights they might possess [until 1918].[146]

Marshall's description of the exchange of citizenship for food and shelter is a situation analogous to the social benefits granted to resident aliens in Europe, especially as governments may tend to a population's welfare while excluding it from prerogatives of governance.

Since 1996, the U.S. federal government has been passing legislation and regulations attempting to tie state benefits to citizenship, but Europe and some U.S. states take a different approach. Curiously, Marshall's observation has been not simply overlooked but reversed by Anthony Giddens and those who rely on it to parse Marshall, for example, Yasmin Soysal's misplaced criticism of Marshall in her book on the European welfare state:

> The order in which rights are extended to guestworkers challenges Marshall's theory of the formation of citizenship. According to Marshall's model, based on his reading of the British case, rights are extended to social entities that had previously been excluded from the polity, thus gradually transforming them into citizens. Marshall argues that citizenship rights evolve sequentially: civil, then political, then social.[147]

But, as quoted above, Marshall shows that social benefits can be, and indeed were, conferred in complete independence from the granting of political rights. Far from being a consequence of political rights, social benefits may be the condition for denying political rights, if they figure the recipient as lacking independence.[148] The very familial, paternalist image of the state invoked to defend state nepotism is precisely the image at odds with responsible, active citizenship. As Mary Dietz observes, a maternalist state provides no guarantees of participatory democracy, either: "An enlightened nepotism, a welfare-state, a single-party bureaucracy and a democratic republic may all respect mothers, protect children's lives and show compassion for the vulnerable."[149]

Second, restricting citizenship because it impinges on funds collected for "our" people misstates tax practice and theory. Taxation for most people is triggered by residence, including undocumented immigrants.[150] The U.S. tax code states: "The Code does not contain special rules regarding the treatment of illegal aliens. . . . For Federal tax purposes, non-citizens are treated as either resident or non-resident aliens."[151] To follow the principle of "no taxation without representation" thus would require citizenship for all aliens. Reciprocally, the right punishment for tax evaders would be exile.

The intuition that citizens pay and benefit from taxes is also historically ungrounded. States for millennia have aimed to extract taxes from anyone other than political decision makers. The people running the state have used their power to force others to pay for it. Governments have used a range of tactics pursuant to this strategy: raiding other states to steal some combination of booty, land, and people; sending out their own fleets to collect direct payments from captains of ships with foreign flags, and then duties known as "ship money" in England, to pay the navy for fighting pirates;[152] charging significant fees to citizens and foreigners in exchange for the government protection of contracts, the goal of various Stamp Acts in England and the colonial United States; and when all else fails, hiring "tax farmers"—impossible to distinguish from any other henchman in an extortion racket. Democratic Athens, medieval European kings, and Ottoman sultans preferred to extract their funds from foreign sources, turning to internal revenues as a last resort.[153] Kings would use war to capture slaves and then raise revenues by selling them to slave traders.[154] And heads of state would enhance their war machines by obliging protection rackets, giving treasure to countries with the strongest armies. Xenophon writes that Sparta's funds for its victory against Athens came from "money bought by the Persian alliance."[155] Although contemporary states may refund particular sales taxes to visitors (those who will not substantially benefit from the hospitals built from that money, for example), no state excludes noncitizens as a class from taxation— thus the millions of resident aliens and others worldwide who pay taxes abroad, with no political representation. If there were a true reciprocity between taxation and active citizenship, then birthright citizens might abjure voting in exchange for not being taxed, a trade-off no government ever has allowed.

Indeed, under U.S. law, those who expatriate themselves have the burden of proving they are doing so without a tax purpose. In 2004, Congress entirely separated citizenship from taxation, making it "possible for an individual to be treated as a citizen for tax purposes during a period when she is not a U.S. citizen under nationality law."[156]

The main principle governments seem to follow for revenue-raising strategy is finding the path of least resistance.[157] The shift away from external revenue raising through war seems a move of expediency over principle, especially after the toppling of monarchies led to a new tipping point. The ire of citizens who did not want to fight posed higher political costs than gains in war booty might redeem. Although even nominal democracies can for long stretches of time ignore their citizens' preferences, citizens seem more comfortable raising money by taxing themselves and not going to war. In any case, taxation without representation has been a longstanding practice for dictatorships and democracies alike. This is not an indictment of current immigrant claims for representation on the basis of their taxation but an observation as to why the question of taxation might be left aside from discussions of citizenship.

Justice

Finally, it is hard to imagine any single principle that so fails basic intuitions about justice than that which would confine one's life to an arbitrarily small circumference based on the nation-state within which one's place of birth happens to be located. There have been numerous persuasive moral arguments against birthright citizenship—from John Locke to Joseph Carens—all making the point that a requirement of individual freedom is the ability to make contracts and not birth the basis of obligations, including citizenship.[158]

Their objections to birthright citizenship and nationalism—that it is unfair and is inconsistent with values of active citizenship—do not resonate with the so-called liberal authors criticized earlier. Berlin, Walzer, and Rawls see the birthright nation as an inevitable expression of human nature. Their belief in the necessity of a birth narrative to undergird the belonging of statehood is a symptom of a fear of death, which they try to ameliorate by establishing laws for intergenerational continuity. Theorists asserting the imperatives of nationalism and the need for birthright citizenship do not review the available evidence among those who study these intuitions. If they did, then perhaps they would rethink the usefulness of assuming that nations and birthright citizenship are inevitable.

THE SPECIFICITY OF ETHNOCENTRISM

Groups Not Inherently Violent

The legal codification of nationality by birth might not be useful, rational, or just, but a large number of scholars under the influence of evolutionary psychology defend nationality and other so-called primordial affinities as expressions of human nature. Referring to the ubiquity of these divisions, they invoke evolutionary theory to suggest these behaviors are naturally selected for and part of human condition, just as the universality of male dominance and slavery led previous generations to believe legal patriarchy inevitable and slavery's abolition unnatural. Earlier generations of researchers and philosophers could produce reams of evidence proving the inevitability of these relations of domination, just as social scientists today can produce studies documenting the inevitability of violent conflicts between what they call "in" and "out" groups. When studying inner-city gangs, soccer hooligans, or even school-lunch seating patterns in racially diverse schools, they find that people culturally and socially segregate, enact their own unique rituals, adopt special symbols, and fight on the basis of these, which social scientists take as evidence that intergroup aggression of the sort witnessed in wars is innate.[159]

There are two difficulties with this inference from findings from controlled experiments on arbitrarily assigned "in" and "out" groups to theories of war. First, nonhereditary or nonreligious groups episodically kill at most in the dozens, not thousands or millions, a scale of destruction that distinguishes this violence from other forms of conflict.[160] Second, experiments have shown that random, synchronic assignments of group membership are insufficient to generate in-group loyalties and out-group animosities—or any attachments at all. In one famous experiment, 112 Dutch fifteen-year-olds were randomly divided into green and blue groups. The study concluded: "group classification per se appears to be insufficient to produce discriminatory evaluations."[161] Still, this article is frequently incorrectly cited to support the unproven hypothesis that the classifications were meaningful.[162] Before going through the results, the first point is that the few reported differences are statistically significant but very small. The largest difference in group ratings of their own qualities and those of the other group on a one-to-seven scale was 4.9 (in-group) and 4.58 (out-group), a far cry from the polarizing effects supposedly leading to war claimed for this research.[163] The study found that when a positive shared fate—the members received a radio—was arrived at by chance, then each group rated its members slightly more favorably than those in the other group. However, when the "experimenter delegated the responsibility for awarding the prize to one of the groups in the group treatment, 10 of these 16 subjects unexpectedly voted for the other group."[164] In sum, the differences were very small and inexplicably inconsistent. This research does not support the hypothesis that generic group membership motivates strong attitudes or actions based on in-group and out-group status. History as well as controlled studies indicate that when individuals are in competitive situations that do not enlist affinities to intergenerational or religious groups, then they may either ignore their labels, or they may be marginally more inclined to help their own members and hinder others, but not by means of systemic, mass violence. Political societies using ancestry for membership are not only behaving in a way that makes little sense as a matter of substantive or procedural justice but they are using divisions that needlessly predispose populations to great harms.

Evolutionary Contingencies: Nationalism and Natural Selection

The casual evolutionary assumptions informing the work above have more systemic proponents: natural and social scientists who adduce from ethnocentrism's survival evidence that the quality is useful. The evolutionary biologist E. O. Wilson has suggested that the nuclear family is nested in a modern-day equivalent of a clan, "bands of brothers" who establish rules regulating sexual access among themselves to ensure stability for competing against "neighboring groups."[165] The evolutionary result is tension with other groups and, inexorably, war:

> Any group of people that perceives itself as a distinct group, and which is so perceived by the outside world, may be called a tribe. The group might be a race, as ordinarily defined, but it need not be; it can just as well be a religious sect, a political group, or an occupational group. The essential characteristic of a tribe is that it should follow a double standard of morality—one kind of behavior for in-group relations, another for out-group.[166]

Wilson points to the Sinhalese and Tamil ethnic conflict in Ceylon as exemplary of this dynamic, explaining that when there is awareness of group difference, "xenophobia becomes a political virtue," and the result is violence. "History is replete with the escalation of this processes to the point that the society breaks down or goes to war. No nation has been completely immune."[167]

Similarly invested in claiming an instinctual basis for such fighting, sociobiologist Konrad Lorenz in his book on aggression writes that the "militant enthusiasm" of group membership is "dangerously akin to the triumph ceremony of geese and to analogous instinctive behavior patterns of other animals." He continues: "The social bond embracing a group is closely connected with aggression directed against outsiders. In human beings, too, the feeling of togetherness which is so essential to the serving of a common cause is greatly enhanced by the presence of a definite, threatening enemy whom it is possible to hate."[168] Lorenz proposes that an objective visitor from Mars would "unavoidably draw the conclusion that man's social organization is very similar to that of rats, which, like humans, are social and peaceful beings within their clans, but veritable devils toward fellow-members of their species not belonging to their own community."[169]

While most sociobiologists suggest that this is adaptive behavior and naturally selected for, either because it leads to the survival of the fittest or helps limit population growth, Lorenz has a somewhat different view. Before the invention of weapons, killing another human was difficult, Lorenz claims. They could either run away or elicit pity—behaviors apparently unavailable to rats. In the course of technical improvements, however, "artificial weapons upset the equilibrium of killing and potential social inhibitions. When it did, man's position was very nearly that of a dove which by some unnatural trick of nature, has suddenly acquired the beak of a raven."[170] On this account, humans merely are insensitive to the abstract consequences of killing but not innate aggression. Lorenz proposes these inferences because if there had been the same lethality in the past that we see today, the human species would have become extinct.

Joshua Goldstein, a political scientist who reviews twenty-one hypotheses for why it is virtually always men who go to war, discounts biological accounts of the ubiquity of male soldiers. However, he maintains that biology is a crucial explanatory variable for the fact of war itself:

The interstate system reproduces at the level of large groups the biologically based scripts and dynamics found at the level of small groups. Overall, the international hierarchy resembles a dominance system, fluid international alliances resemble chimpanzee politics, and the tit-for-tat reciprocity studied by international-relations researchers resembles the reciprocal behaviors that enable cooperation in small groups.[171]

Goldstein too naturalizes violence as part of a "dominance system" that humans and chimpanzees alike endorse.

Overlooked by Wilson, Lorenz, and Goldstein are the infinite counterexamples, the preponderance of times and circumstances when groups do not fight, and the numerous individuals who explicitly eschew support for these alliances. Are underpaid human-rights activists working for the American Civil Liberties Union or Amnesty International there because of a mutant gene encouraging them to dive to the bottom of the dominance hierarchy? Should we consider those lawyers who are exceptionally well integrated into the social fabric of the United States—in other words, on the top of the heap—but dedicate their time to penniless Pakistanis held by the U.S. government in a military base at Guantanamo Bay evolutionary mutants? When activists organizing against slavery established the first antiwar movement, was this a symptom of a nineteenth-century extraterrestrial landing?

Goldstein's narrative of war's imperative is imbalanced because he selects on the dependent variable, so to speak, and only considers those cases of leaders urging violence, ignoring the 99 percent of cases when different groups cooperate or compete nonviolently. Goldstein mentions Theodore Roosevelt's belittling of Wilsonian diplomacy—referring to Wilson's policies as "emasculat[ing] American manhood and weaken[ing] its fiber"[172]—as proof that national leaders must convey manly aggressiveness toward others, ignoring the cause of Roosevelt's ire, the internationalist President Wilson, also a powerful national leader. In fact, Wilson became president by defeating Theodore Roosevelt (who was president from 1901 to 1910), whose bellicose foreign policy the electorate rejected. The cosmopolitan, decidedly antinationalist Woodrow Wilson was the prime mover in establishing the League of Nations. Unlike Roosevelt, Wilson gave speeches with the following sentiments: "The same concern for exploitation and injustice within our borders applies to international questions"[173] and "we must shape our course of action by the maxims of justice and liberality and good will, and think of the progress of mankind rather than of the progress of this or that investment."[174] Resisting efforts to have the United States back a coup in Mexico for the purpose of installing a regime more favorable to U.S. business interests, Wilson opposed his own parochial elites:

If American enterprise in foreign countries, particularly in those foreign countries which are not strong enough to resist us, takes the shape of imposing upon and exploiting the mass of people of that country, it ought to be checked and not encouraged. I am willing to get anything for an American that money and enterprise can obtain, except the suppression of the rights of other men. I will not help any man buy a power which he ought not to exercise over his fellow human beings.[175]

For better and worse, Wilson was genuinely concerned with human beings, not U.S.-Americans, dramatically falsifying the claim that because he was the president of "tribe USA," and not all human beings, that he would be indifferent to the rights of anyone else.

The sociobiological defense of war's necessity contrasts not only with the beliefs of many present peace advocates but also with previous comparisons of animal and human behavior. In his 1517 "Complaint of Peace," subtitled "Disavowed and Despised by Nations Everywhere," the humanist Erasmus called on nature to indict, not defend, war:

Even without the aid of reason, loving creatures everywhere assemble in communities, and live quietly together. Elephants gather in herds, pigs and sheep feed in groups, cranes and grackles fly in flocks.... The savagery of lions isn't directed against other lions. One boar doesn't attack another with flashing tusks, the lynx lives in peace with his fellow-lynx.... Only men, who above all other species should agree with one another and who need mutual understanding most of all cannot be united by mutual love in nature (so powerful everywhere else), nor by training, nor by all the advantages to be anticipated from concord, nor even by awareness of the many ends resulting from war.[176]

Without a single DNA assay, Erasmus makes a devastating case against those who attempt to explain warfare as a symptom of innate aggression, one that resonates five centuries later: in those species with intramural competitions for dominance, these are displays among individual animals. Sustained, systemic fighting between separate groups is infrequent,[177] perhaps because geese and ducks do not have marriage registries and other tracking conventions creating hereditary difference and belief in an eternal existence for which they might want to die.

Human beings are capable of ethnocentrism and selfishness as well as empathy. Our present world order legally sustains the former impulse, claiming it is natural, and ignores the latter, which against all odds persists and often dominates. It is true that President Wilson's motive was an earnest Christianity that also has the underside of potential violence in other contexts, but the very possibility of a political leader's discourse challenging nativism is suggestive. If it is only possible to overcome the immortal templates of the nation-state by a religious discourse, then there is nothing especially beneficent in this example. The proposals below, however, begin to suggest an alternative legal framework for nurturing these cosmopolitan proclivities in practices other than those of organized religion.

Citizenship Contingencies

Other evidence at odds with the assertion of birthright citizenship's necessity comes from legal history. Principled political decisions about whom to dignify with rights and needs deserving a government's support vary over time. And even when governments share the goal of advantaging their own people over anyone else, the means to do so also have taken different forms. These variations are consistent with institutions appeasing anxieties about death by providing intergenerational, and therefore eternal, ties—and not with practices advancing rational goals of governance. States have encouraged emigration, discouraged emigration, and attempted to increase foreign-born citizens or decrease foreign-born citizens depending on the political and economic exigencies of the moment. But at no point has any state used any other rule but birth for their main criteria of belonging. At the same time, for as long as these borders have existed they have been crossed and their legitimacy challenged.

MOVEMENT IN EARLY MODERN AND MODERN EUROPE

For the purpose of limiting the burdens imposed by the indigent from the fourteenth to nineteenth centuries, communities throughout Europe and the East required passes.[178] Vagabonds caught twice in England would be branded with an "S."[179] In fact, in early modern Europe it was easier to be without a pass in a parish outside one's domicile if one were a foreigner in the kingdom than if one were a fellow subject. Aliens were usually merchants and therefore perceived as men of means unlikely to impose any financial burden on those with whom they did commerce.[180] Though villages and kingdoms shared similar goals of securing their jurisdictions from enemies and maintaining high revenues—by limiting expenditures on the poor—their border regulations toward this end differed, and communities pursued very different policies of poor relief and maintaining militias. In other words, not only is the notion that what counts as the political unit worthy of protection is akin to one's family historically contingent—sometimes it is a country and sometimes a village—but even within such parameters there is no consensus on the right objectives for membership nor for the policies to achieve similar objectives.

To prevent the equivalent of draft dodgers, Louis XIV forbade subjects from leaving the kingdom without a pass,[181] as did Germany following the French Revolution,[182] Italy in World War I and under Mussolini,[183] and countries in contemporary wars, such as Serbia, Bosnia-Herzegovina, and Iraq. After the French Revolution, the Parliament, worried about aristocrats of dubious loyalty to the new regime moving in and out of France, prohibited titled nobility from emigrating.[184] The government did not want aristocrats as soldiers but feared their regrouping outside the country to plot a counterrevolution. Thus for purposes of surveillance they strived to keep these potential insurgents within French borders. Meanwhile, the revolutionary government solicited the immigration of foreigners, with the proviso that the newcomers were from countries that France deemed to be its allies.[185] In more recent history, one motive for Germany taking the lead in pushing for European unification in the 1970s was the promise of centralized passport data, so that Germany could obtain better information on the movement of potential terrorists.[186] Rather than limit the movement across its borders in order to deny terrorists safe havens, Germany saw a cooperative federated community with good information technologies as a means of enhancing the German state's security.[187]

States' uses of immigration and emigration rules for controlling the size of their populations have also varied. Today there is a widespread belief that *jus sanguinis* (citizenship by descent) is a more restrictive rule than *jus soli* (citizenship by territorial birth) and that both restrict immigration more than a mere residency requirement. Yet when assessing how to increase their tax base in 1818, the Bavarian government switched from residence (Wohnsitzprinzip) to *jus sanguinis* for determining citizenship and thus tax obligations. Henceforth, those born in Bavaria and moving elsewhere were still responsible for paying taxes to Bavaria.[188] John Torpey's history of the European passport explains how states in the late eighteenth and nineteenth centuries used paternal descent to determine membership in reaction against populations that were mobile, cosmopolitan, and splintering the putatively sacral tie of land and blood.[189] Changing the taxation rule meant that although the state's assumption of a connection between *jus sanguinis* and *jus soli* had been falsi-fied, the rule nonetheless still presupposed and insisted that one's birth iden-tity was irrevocably tied to that land.

Whereas Bavaria used *jus sanguinis* for the purpose of increasing reve-nues, England had shifted much earlier, in the fourteenth century, away from *jus sanguinis* to *jus soli*, also for the purpose of increasing its tax base as well as national security. After conquering Scotland, *jus soli* gave the English king dominion over those born to Scottish parents. It also prevented potentially disloyal subjects whose parents had emigrated to France from inheriting En-glish land. Being born outside the realm could signify just the sort of Papist loyalties against which English blood alone could not inoculate.[190]

In keeping with the changing calculations for using *jus soli* or *jus sanguinis* for the same goal of increasing loyalty and tax revenues, governments also use different migration strategies to increase employment. Through the 1790s, the United Kingdom sought to limit emigration because even amid high unem-ployment, the government feared depopulation and the attendant loss of a military reserve and tax base.[191] Yet just two decades later, in 1819, a Parlia-mentary committee on the Poor Laws was "virtually recommending emigra-tion to the working class."[192] The motive was not to increase the relative pros-perity of those remaining but to stave off the labor riots, which at that point were more destabilizing than the potential loss of tax revenues and military manpower.[193]

The above examples are intended for purposes of illustration only and not to elucidate the causes of their variation. This brief, schematic record shows that states sharing general military and economic security concerns have in-stituted different membership and migration policies. Ancestral attachments have been used to imbue a people with a sense of belonging and national pur-pose, but such kinship ties have also been, if not ignored, then episodically and strategically transgressed. Not only do states change their immigration strate-gies, but the borders themselves change. This alone will change a population's nationality, and people living in border zones are very aware of this. The predic-tion by Sidgwick and Walzer was that those who live in border areas would be especially hostile to the infiltrations of aliens and that awareness of a border's fragility would make them anxious. This sometimes occurs. But the opposite occurs as well. Border regions are the very places where past and present bor-der changes and immigration have created diverse, hybrid communities that often are the most adversely affected by, and thus resistant to, the arbitrary borders that slice through their ties of work, neighborhood, and family.

Describing in 1990 the coordinated activities between the local governments of Tijuana and San Diego, Jorge Bustamante, director of the College of the Northern Border, in Tijuana, said, "Washington and Mexico City look at all of this with suspicion, since the feeling in both capitals is that if we understand each other, something must be going wrong."[194] The towns of Columbus, New Mexico, and Las Palomas, Mexico, shared local government and private services, and the mayors and many other families had spouses from the other side of the border. "Everything is international here, including most families," said the mayor of Las Palomas, whose children were attending school in neighboring Columbus, New Mexico.[195]

It was not simmering local resentments but orders from Washington, D.C., that changed the easy trade and movement among sister towns along the U.S.-Mexican border. Speaking to a reporter in 2004, seventy-five-year-old Russell Duncan said, "This border is about as phony as a three-dollar bill." The gunsmith and knifesmith continued: "People cross the border as if it were a bus station. We got illegals, we got drug smugglers, but the only people we're able to keep out is our neighbors and many of these people we're related to."[196] In one case, a border guard caught and sent his own uncle back to Mexico.[197] After noting that the southwestern border of the United States does not unite but often divides families, a reporter observed: "Many American-born children who moved home with their Mexican parents do not come to school in Jacumba [California] anymore. Some families have scattered." It is not local police but national officials making porous cities into militarized outposts. A spokesperson for the Border Patrol stated, "It's unfortunate that American citizens suffer, but we are committed to protecting the nation's borders."[198]

While some in the U.S. Southwest, most prominently the Minutemen, have instituted vigilante border patrols and pressed for police to detain undocumented foreigners for deportation—even passing laws to make it impossible for undocumented residents to work or even rent an apartment[199]—other cities have declared themselves sanctuaries for these residents and encourage them to make use of public services. In Los Angeles and New York, the two largest cities in the United States, city policy is for the police and other officials not to detain aliens on immigration grounds. Los Angeles and San Antonio are major border cities that have elected Mexican American mayors. These demographic and political situations falsify the provincial ethnocultural assertions of Berlin, Walzer, and Rawls.

One reason that border populations understand that the divisions between them are contingent is that they see very clearly the shifting locations of these borders. In the first part of the nineteenth century, Mexico had sovereignty over the entire West, as far north as the present state of Washington. Had it not been for U.S. citizens staking land claims as filibusters, some to preserve plantation slavery, and resisting the sovereign government of Mexico, for whom they were outlaws and terrorists, roughly one-third of the present United States would be Mexican. In the words of Mexicans frustrated with having to deal with old and new restrictions in the U.S. Southwest, "We didn't move, the border did," a comment referring to the previous Spanish and then Mexican sovereignty over this area—not to mention that of the other nations there for hundreds of years earlier.[200]

It is not just San Antonio, Texas, with a large foreign-born population but numerous other major cities with high percentages of foreign-born residents that belie the myth of a homogenous country defending itself against incursions that would make it impure. In Berlin's London, Walzer's New York, and Rawls's Boston, 32, 36, and 27 percent of the populations, respectively, are foreign born.[201] This has not led to ethnic antagonisms and local border guards but thriving metropolises. Immigration has not meant all communities have embraced all newcomers, but these cities offer fluid zones serving as natural experiments that provide some evidence that opening borders creates tolerance and indeed a communal investment in diversity, as well as backlashes and some anxiety. There is little empirical basis for the view that attachments to communities based on ancestral principles are rooted in anything but the worst efforts of a mortal citizenry's self-comfort in the myths and legal infrastructure sustaining the otherwise impractical, irrational nation.

For as long as there have been restrictions on citizenship and free movement, there has been an outcry against these measures. Among the first new laws proposed to the French Revolutionary Parliament in 1789 was free movement to, from, and within France without the use of passports.[202] In 1790, defending this position a writer asserted in *Le Moniteur*: "To allow a man to travel is to allow him to do something that one has no right to deny: it is a social injustice."[203] The German leader of the Liberal Party, Eduard Lasker, a Jew from the east, stated in 1871, "It is a barbarity to make a distinction between foreigners and indigenous [Einheimischen] in the right to hospitable residence. Not only every German, but every human being has the right not to be chased away like a dog."[204] This does not mean that unfolding reason eventually will enlighten people and borders will dissolve, but rather that a political struggle has been occurring, the result of which is not possible to predict. The May 1, 2006, marches and boycott protesting a House bill that would make it a crime to be a foreigner lacking documentation in the United States drew both millions of documented and undocumented immigrants and their birthright-citizenship friends, relatives, co-workers, employers, and employees. A police officer in New York City said, "If I weren't in uniform, I would be marching with you guys. You guys are fighting a good cause."[205] This sentiment has appeared in national-policy goals intermittently as well, not surprisingly from the family of a president whose own nieces and nephews are Latino. On the eve of the September 11, 2001, attacks, President George Bush's major policy goal was establishing a guest-worker program with Mexico, an unprincipled plan to allow agribusiness to hire cheap labor, but the plan was scaled back and ultimately stalled by jingoistic politicians, Republican and Democrat alike, mired in nativism. It will not always be the case that changing border demographics and intermarriage will lead to more liberal border policies. They could, and have, elicited resistance, some violent, as did occur in modern Europe in the late eighteenth and early twentieth centuries, as populations there too resisted and then capitulated to the demographics of internal movement.[206]

If the historical precedent of strongly and deeply felt anxieties about free movement among towns can become a historical oddity, then it certainly seems plausible to imagine that a similar dynamic might occur in the aftermath of eliminating birthright citizenship. Berlin, Walzer, and Rawls do not argue that people should stay put in their cities of origin, but in another time and place they very well might have. Perhaps in the 1530s these theorists would have supported King Henry VIII, who ordered the execution of tens of thousands of vagabonds, meaning anyone traveling outside their parish of birth without documented permission of the king, as this is behavior consistent with fortress cities.[207] And were they to have criticized the sixteenth-century French policy denying aid in Paris to French subjects born outside the city[208] by the standards of present U.S. welfare policies, which provide aid regardless of the time lived in the state or city of residence, their words likely would be treated with the same bemusement that greets today's advocates of open borders among countries. Prior experiences of tumult and then adjustment following the opening of internal borders suggest that within a period as short as one generation following the lifting of our present restrictions, these current ones will seem just as arbitrary and old fashioned as those we find odd in early modern Europe.

HEGEL ELIMINATES THE LIBERAL PARADOX

The only truly coherent defense of birth citizenship remains Hegel's, who never claimed to be a liberal. He admired and even embraced the blood thirst of the nation-state, which he viewed as an achievement of an individuality for a people and for each citizen made possible by civilization, not nature: "War is the spirit and the form in which the essential moment of the ethical substance, the absolute freedom of the ethical *self* from every existential form, is present in its actual and authentic existence."[209] War is not a necessary, instrumental evil to be endured for the sake of defending legitimate governments but a sacred opportunity, a joining with an immortal body politic. The historical record indicates that far from being "human nature," a commitment to kill and risk death on a systematic scale occurs only for a handful of groups. The nation, and the ethnic and racial groups produced through the nation-state's kinship laws, model and generate virtually all systemic, mass violence, which is why Hegel pays homage to the nation-state. He understands that people kill and die in the name of these groups, for honor, for their families, and through the organizations that nation-states generate. They do not do this for any other groups, other than religions (which will be discussed in chapter 8). The family, nation, and religion Freud criticizes as illusions Hegel defends as ethical necessities.

There may be glory in the wars Hegel and his followers relish, but there is no justice or sanity. In other words, the only principled defense of the nation-state is that it provides conditions conducive to a particular variant of recognition and identity, as Hegel suggests regarding the lord-and-serf relationship, where a serf has more freedom than a lord, because the former is not dependent on someone else for labor and because someone with power sees him. Recognition and thus subjectivity follow from relations of domination, according to Hegel.[210] Hegel's allegory implies that this struggle for recognition is only necessary to work out individuality for those living in fear that they cannot produce life from their bodies and that they will die.[211] Psychologically, the lord is the phallic mother and the serf her child, the latter attempting to gain autonomy and recognition through objectification, a result of compensatory infant male fantasies of maternal omnipotence and a boyish lack—specifically that he will never give birth, the most magical of acts in the infant imagination. Hegel's phenomenology is for fragile boys who feel diminished by their fantasies of origins and death—both beyond their biological control but yielding to the force of law, at least in their fantasies. An Hegelian moral ontological commitment to death with honor explains birthright citizenship in a world of compensatory masculine fantasies but not in one where pragmatism, justice, rationality, or necessity are the dominant values.

CHAPTER TWO

ABOLISHING BIRTHRIGHT CITIZENSHIP

ReportIllegals.com provides concerned individuals with a fast and efficient method to report illegal aliens and illegal employers to an agency capable of investigating and prosecuting "undocumented immigrants" and their illegal employers. Our reporting service facilitates the transfer of information from a concerned individual to the proper government agency.

REPORTILLEGALS.COM WEB SITE

"Mexican Immigrants Are the Jews of the 21st Century"

HAND-PAINTED SIGN CARRIED BY PARTICIPANT IN "A DAY WITHOUT IMMIGRANTS" MARCH, MAY 1, 2006, LOS ANGELES

Political theorists discussing the principles that societies ought to use for allocating resources tend to assume a single government and its enemies (for example, Plato's *Republic*, Hobbes's *Leviathan*, and Locke's *Two Treatises*). The use of one static society for the framing of questions about distributive justice is used also by John Rawls in his *The Law of Peoples*. Rawls's goal is a theory of international norms of justice. His "law of peoples" is an ethical guide for a single liberal society: "The Law of Peoples proceeds from the international political world as we see it, and concerns what the foreign policy of a reasonably just liberal people should be."[1] Rawls assumes a closed, liberal society that must be prepared to defend itself from its enemies, support other countries under conditions of duress, and thwart "outlaw regimes." To move beyond the "international political world as we see it," Rawls implies, would be to follow a path dead-ending in utopia. But it is not clear why Rawls draws this line for the unrealistic when it comes to evaluating international institutions. No country, much less his own, has adopted or even seriously considered Rawls's proposals for domestic politics in *A Theory of Justice* (1972). Rawls appears comfortable with a focus on a single country's foreign policy because, as discussed below, he endorses some of the more provincial characteristics of the "international political world as we see it" and not just because of pragmatism.

Cosmopolitan writers also do not account for the nation-state's dialectics. Their substantive critiques of provincialism are illuminating, but the methods assume a universalist framework without contemplating the institutional steps necessary to accomplish the change in mentality necessary for their aspirations to be realized. It may be difficult to contemplate changing laws along the lines proposed here, but it may be even more unrealistic to think that the national commitments characterized here will be abandoned without these changes. Martha Nussbaum's and Jeremy Waldron's cosmopolitan norms, Thomas Pogge's global justice, and Seyla Benhabib's more qualified cosmopolitanism, to name just three of the many theorists doing wonderful work exposing the limits of the nation-state, do not focus on the legal templates creating the present inequalities and violence.[2] They offer bold criticisms and proposals, but the changes necessary for their ideals to be realized may have to be even more radical than those they and other cosmopolitans envision.

One study that appreciates the fundamental challenge that birthright citizenship poses for liberal theory and that does not capitulate to sentiments of nationalism, as do Peter Schuck and Rogers Smith, cleverly extrapolates from Eugenio Rignano's inheritance proposals to suggest a graduated tax on one's citizenship: "revenues generated by the 'levy' on inherited citizenship in an affluent polity would be devoted to specific projects designed to improve the life circumstances of children who are most adversely affected by the legal connection drawn between circumstances of birth and citizenship."[3] Ayelet Shachar and Ran Hirschl do an admirable job of identifying the illiberal economic inequality of birthright citizenship and identifying a possible cure for this, but like most theorists, they continue to accept the unit of the nation-state as inviolable. Taxing citizenship will not ease national attachments but only strengthen the sense that the nation and birthright citizenship determine our initial identities. Even if these lead to economic redistributions, the nation's role in organizing the fundamental experiences of inclusion and exclusion are further materialized and thereby strengthened. State discrimination against or on behalf of those in the economically weaker races, sexes, or, in the case of Shachar and Hirschl, nations both strengthen attachments to the particular identities that pay and reinforce an uncritical sensibility that accepts hereditary distinctions as inevitable features of the political landscape.

The analysis here does not begin with a starting point of inequality within societies or even among them, instead conceptualizing the relation between present state forms of exclusion and the politics of violence and inequality. The very form of the adversarial nation-state, especially its birthright-based membership rules and the legal kinship paradigms sustaining these, are the root cause of systemic violence and inequality within and among political societies. Ameliorating violence and inequality within any particular political society thus requires changing these membership rules. The thinking here is similar to that offered by liberal critics of affirmative action who see the perpetuation of racial categories by the state enforcing redistributive policies as a reinvigoration of invidious classifications whose short-term palliatives will impose long-term harms. But there is a crucial difference. The synchronic liberal critics, looking only at a single country and time period, do not see how race (and ethnicity, caste, clan, and tribe) are sustained by the very form of the nation-state. Trying to end racism by deleting race taxonomies in one state's domestic policies is like trying to end war by one state disarming.

Just as capitalism is a political-economic system and not the result of the aggregated behaviors of individual entrepreneurs, the nation-state system entails oppression by its very design as well. The benign behavior of some capitalists and the episodic bouts of kindness and compassion shown refugees and immigrants by some national communities does not redeem these respective systems. Capitalism and its myths have just such a systemic critique, one that, alas, directs attention away from an equally if not more endemic institutionalized form of oppression, that is, one based on the nation and its kinship rules, including ideologies of ancestry. Just as capitalism creates workers and proletarians out of human beings, the nation-state creates Israelites and non-Israelites, for example, people whose shared mortal condition is obscured by a system that requires difference and a way to create the illusion of certainty for a human condition riddled with doubts.

The discourse surrounding the treason conviction of the French Jewish officer Alfred Dreyfus—used as an example here because of its familiarity—exposes the confusion of the legal categories that produce the possibility of "divided loyalties." National identity's familial form makes one's attachments to it, for example, Dreyfus's Jewish nationality (what we now call ethnicity) seemingly strong, solid enough to potentially trump his civil commitments as a French citizen, even though nationality's roots in kinship also reveal the ambiguities, inventions, and falsifications of lineage to anyone who takes a careful look.[4]

The French journalist Bernard Lazare, attempting to understand the Dreyfus Affair, quotes a Talmudic rabbi, "'Are we perfectly sure,' said Rabbi Ulla to Judah-ben-Ezikiel, 'that we are not descended from pogroms who dishonored the young daughters of Zion after the capture of Jerusalem?'"[5] Or, Lazare writes, perhaps we are descendants of the slaves and other peoples conquered by the proselytizing Jews, of whom he quotes another Talmudic rabbi writing, "Wherefore has God scattered Jews among the nations? To recruit for Him proselytes everywhere."[6] Jews, the paradigmatic example of a supposedly insular group begotten via tribes traced genealogically to Abraham, have been recreated through an amalgam of many disparate groups. They/we changed the lines of descent from patrilineal to matrilineal to reproduce Israelites, a reaction to the depletion of Israelite men in war. Jews, as other nations, have been conquered and have themselves used conquest and taxation as a means of procuring conversion. Freud offers either evidence or wishful thinking that Moses himself was Egyptian.[7] Again, every nation has a similar story equally easy to document. Nations that reproduce by securing membership through carefully codified kinship rules are not protecting discrete lines of genetic descent but the myth of this.

The challenge of group attachments and antagonisms exposed in the Dreyfus case, and all other scenarios that entail animosities among hereditary groups (nationalities, ethnicities, races, clans, and castes) within and among societies, is revealing and destroying presently obscured psycholegal structures through which people who are otherwise largely similar are made to think of themselves as different, not developing abstract principles for distributive justice among fixed groups. The problem with a remedial model of distributive justice is that it recodifies differences that depended on these odd rules for their initial harms, not preexisting, prepolitical differences. If Dreyfus might be a descendant of an enslaved Balkan invader captured and converted by Jews in the Roman Empire, and if that Balkan invader might have had a Gallic ancestor, then the French, using their own national logic, would not be convicting a Jew but a Frenchman or, more accurately, someone who, like the rest of us, has no certain national origin, because ancestors who are purely this or that do not exist. (From what kinship group was the Gallic relation descended? And from which one were they?) The gap between the historical plausibility of this scenario and its appearance to the modern citizen or even scholar as an intellectual puzzle is symptomatic of nationality's naturalization and thus its mystifications. To draw on Hegel's dialectics for a moment, a world that institutionalized through its membership laws contingencies of state membership would shift the phenomenology of ancestry from one of sense-certainty to that of the more subtle shades of perception and understanding. The legal force underlying rules of nationality, in particular their institutionalization through states and other political societies without bureaucracies (for example, tribes), creates the perception of nationality, ethnicity, and race as facts. Removing the legal force creating nationality and its related hereditary groups would allow the contingencies of these affinities to be truly performed and definitively revealed.[8]

STATES WITHOUT NATIONS: FIRST PRINCIPLES

Instead of strategies for improving the nation-state singly or in aggregate, the proposal here is to contemplate a world of states without nations, where people belong because of choice, residence, and commitment. The nation-state provides the façade of fulfillment by manipulating experiences of birth, fantasies of immortality, and honor as victims or victors in war. States without nations would eliminate the legal foundations of these narratives, enabling a popular understanding of the various levels of one's historical, narrative embeddedness in a group or society without feeling reduced to any one of them and enabling the creativity, empathy, and freedom the nation-state suffocates.

Instead of the international system of nation-states, where ancestry or birthplace avail themselves to ventures of vengeance, victimization, or discrimination, being born in San Diego or Tijuana in a world of states without nations might yield attachments to the respective countries no different from the small affinity one has for the hospital where one was delivered. One might appreciate those employees more than the staff of a nearby facility, but one would not regard the actual building where one was born especially sacred, patrol its perimeter to prevent anyone whose parents had not been born there to enter or give birth, or volunteer to kill those who worked in a neighboring hospital for attempting a hostile merger with the hospital where one was delivered.

It is not that one is born here or there that makes a place or land sacred but the sacral myths that render one's birthplace a community totem. New stories of belonging imbuing one's place of birth with the insignificance actually due this random mundane event and discrediting the fantastic and fanatic myths about birth might help liberate us from the craziness of repressing the open secret that differences attributed to birth are impossible and ludicrous, especially as the legitimation for the state. Without being burdened by the fantasies that states need to uphold for sustaining intergenerational differences and myths, they would be free to operate according to norms advocated by Hannah Arendt in her vision of politics, especially her understanding of power bereft of force and violence.[9] Arendt's lofty words are hard to imagine being realized through the mundane workings of present government institutions, but perhaps one example that would not constrain these possibilities might be found in the world of nonprofit organizations, in particular those run on the stakeholder model, whereby decision making is tied to being affected by the outcome.[10] The notion that there is something at stake in the quality of the decision reached is not one that Arendt discusses, but there is no reason not to aspire to this. More importantly, the possibility of building on and developing community through recognizing a variety of voices in the deliberative process is one feature enabled, though by no means required, by such a model. In a stakeholder model of governance, those affected by a decision's outcomes need at least some representation during policy deliberations, and they also may vote on these. Elucidating this combination of participatory self-governance with the provision of concrete benefits, Wendy Sarvassy suggests that what she is calling a feminist vision of social citizenship would be concerned only "partly with achieving new social rights" and also would include the "democratic subversion of a variety of unequal power relations, including those embedded in the bureaucratization process."[11] For instance, a nonprofit drug-counseling clinic would include on its board people who were currently receiving services, although it might also select those who are parents of drug addicts, their partners, and others immediately affected by drug addiction.

If states were more like nonprofits, then perhaps their citizens would be more like nonprofit trustees and members—serving for the public benefit and not for the promotion of their private interests, with providers and recipients, producers and consumers alike, exercising trustee roles on behalf of the overall good of the community's general welfare. This is a goal Rousseau introduces with his idea of the general will,[12] but as Hegel notices, its basis in a particular nation deprives the Rousseauan state any claim to universality.[13] This contradiction between the particularity of the civil religion, depending on birth, and the aspiration to universality is celebrated by Hegel, who points out that history has come down on the side of the former, meaning that the nation has been the crucible for our development as individuals and states. But this is because our institutions have conformed to Hegel's desire for laws mandating membership through intergenerationality, a situation that has prevailed for millennia but can change, as have many other practices.

Conceiving of citizenship as strictly a relationship of governance and not as a prerogative of solidarity based on birth radically shifts how we might think of new criteria for this right. If we accept a very basic assumption that governance should come from decision makers who will make the best judgments, then citizenship rules would assign membership to those who have skills best suited to making good decisions. Rather than view citizenship based on consent as a means of gaining the obedience of individuals, which it has never been,[14] or as a prize for being born in a particular democracy (worth more or less depending on the accident of one's birth), which is what citizenship has been, what if citizenship combined direct action with the space for creative self-governance, an open-source means for government to benefit from those most qualified and interested in offering guidance for rules affecting public order, the public committed to that organization and affected by its rules?

States need to enact useful policies and not just avoid war or corruption. Hence a citizen's desire for promoting the public's well-being is a necessary but not sufficient qualification for participating. It is the nexus between residency and expertise that makes people who have lived only in the United States unqualified to vote in Danish elections. Nonresidents may not be corrupt, but they will be insufficiently familiar with the geography of the area, the political economy, the current resource needs of residents, and so forth to make policy decisions. Because of the tie, albeit imperfect, between living in a place and understanding its practices, residency seems a fair and sensible criterion for establishing citizenship in a state without a nation.

Experiments along these lines have been tried in the past. According to Plutarch, the Roman leader Numa Pompilius attempted to overcome ethnic rivalries in the seventh century B.C. by instituting new societies recognized by law—officially sanctioned groups that would cut across and render useless the old political units that followed from Roman or Sabine ancestry.[15] William Blackstone writes that Numa, to break up the "two rival factions of Sabine and Romans, thought it a prudent and public measure to subdivide these into many smaller ones, by instituting separate societies of every manual trade and profession. These were afterwards much considered by the civil law in which they were called universities, or *collegia*."[16] The Athenian leader Cleisthenes did something similar in the sixth century B.C., when he devised new political districts to crosscut older ones associated with ancestry, an effort that succeeded initially and then failed as new ancestral cleavages eventually developed along the lines of Cleisthenes' political divisions.[17] This is because the regime, though it redefined the unit of ancestry from birth to residency for one generation, did not eradicate marriage and hence the use of ancestry subsequently. It was the continued use of birthright based on these reinscribed lineages— evidence of their indeterminacy and malleability—and not the inevitability of ancestral ties that accounts for the Athenian relapse into the problems Cleisthenes sought to solve. This situation resembles that portrayed by Rabbi Ulla. The rules of descent invoking but not relying on genetic ancestry ground faith in a national identity, one's own as well as others. If Cleisthenes had followed through with his insights, then he would have made future membership entitlements continue to depend on residency and not the newly arranged lines of descent. Likewise, for Numa's Roman experiment to have succeeded, other measures would have been necessary to ensure that the new ties were not simply absorbed into the older ones experienced as hereditary.[18]

To end birthright citizenship, three other measures must be concomitant: (1) free movement among existing states; (2) the prerogative to revoke membership and acquire it in other states if one resides in them long enough to learn their particularities, say, three to five years; and (3) abolition of state-sanctioned marriage, to abolish official lineages transcending mortal lifespans and thereby making families synchronic and not diachronic.[19] In practice, this might mean that when someone who has grown up in France, for example, turns eighteen, that individual could claim French citizenship. This decision would not bind for life—as John Locke proposes, for example—but only as long as she prefers French citizenship over any other.

To continue the example, if this French citizen subsequently decides to live in Syria, she could either retain her French citizenship or, after three years of residence, become a citizen in Syria. This residence would not have to be constant but would require more than six months per year for three consecutive years of residence. Becoming a citizen of Syria would not entail renouncing her French citizenship. Insofar as citizenship denotes prerogatives to judge what is best for a country based on one's experience of that country, there is no reason to privilege the judgment of those currently residing in France over those who have accumulated that expertise but live elsewhere. This is why a few local communities, including in the United States, allow noncitizens to vote in municipal elections and why their countries of origin allow them to vote with absentee ballots. Expertise on France for an expatriate who has settled in the United States, for example, might even be expected to assist new citizens in their ability to advise their new countries of citizenship.

BENEFITS FROM STATES WITHOUT NATIONS

Free movement among autonomous sovereign administrative entities is exemplified in federated countries with decentralized policymaking bodies in their states or provinces. These countries show that it is possible to attend to free-rider problems with mobile populations. Crucially, these administrative units only map onto violent entities when they overlay kinship-based or religious communities, for example, Serbia and Croatia in the former Yugoslavia or Muslims and Jews of Palestine-Israel, and not when they are experienced as purely residential: San Francisco and Los Angeles, Tokyo and Kyoto, and Paris and Lyon are autonomous political administrative bodies with competing interests, but their respective city police forces are not deployed to resolve these.

Federal systems, as might a world of states without nations, allocate burdens among internally mobile populations by using residential status to trigger financial obligations. In order to collect fees for using their roads, for instance, states require that those drivers who have state residency register their cars in that state. Visitors from other states or countries may use their own license plates—reciprocally recognized on behalf of their own travelers to other states and countries—but if one is a resident, then one is required to pay that state's highway fees. The same holds for driver's license requirements, in this case to increase the state's enforcement capabilities. A number of law-enforcement groups have lobbied to allow licenses for undocumented immigrants precisely because this enhances their ability to track them and solicit them for information.[20] The more people with licenses, the easier it is to find offenders. Groups opposing universal access to driver's licenses say they object only to "lawbreakers" receiving licenses—in other words, those in the country without the state's permission.[21] But it is their insistence on denying legal status to immigrants that creates this condition of illegality in the first place. Providing legal status to all residents avoids the tautology of "illegality" and would increase state revenues, as the denial of documentation makes it practically impossible to pay taxes as new residents. The status of legal newcomer avoids these problems.[22]

It may appear that if all borders are opened, those from very poor countries would quickly move to wealthy countries, leading to overcrowding and increased poverty in destination states. Currently less than 3 percent of the global population resides outside their country of birth.[23] Current experiences with newly founded federations suggest that fears of massive dislocations from poor to rich countries are unfounded. The enlargement of the European Union has been a natural experiment in how to allow free movement and maintain stability. By ensuring entering states are provided with financial support for their own universities, hospitals, and other infrastructure, the European Union has seen relatively low rates of migration among states with large differences in wealth and incomes. This suggests that disposable income is a less important influence on migration than receiving necessary services such as health care, education, and economic security. The EU experience is the regional equivalent of the proposal here for a global agency that would provide for similar amenities from the estates of the deceased (discussed in chapter 3). These funds could be distributed on the basis of population, meaning that governments competing for these dollars would pursue investment policies to increase the likelihood their current residents would remain in place, encouraging stability. Making global funds available on a per capita basis gives states an incentive to direct domestic spending toward providing public goods that will encourage residency, including mass transportation, pollution controls, and a government that follows the rule of law.

Some critics speculate that free movement would bring a race to the bottom in providing services, as governments worried about free riders would curtail benefits for everyone. Others worry about open borders based on the assumption that businesses and potential employees will not move to jurisdictions with the higher tax rates necessary for more generous government programs. The libertarians advancing this line of thinking suggest that those places with low taxes (and government) services will actually have a higher standard of living than other places and would therefore be preferred by potential immigrants over those with more government support for infrastructure. Announcing President George Bush's tax policy, the White House states: "Countries with low taxes, limited regulation, and open trade grow faster, create more jobs, and enjoy higher standards of living than countries with bigger, more centralized governments and higher taxes. The United States has led the way in economic performance over the last century because America is a freer country."[24] In other words, one premise held by some opponents of free movement is that those places with relatively high tax collections per capita offer on average a higher standard of living than those places with low taxes per capita, while more doctrinaire laissez-faire thinkers would claim otherwise. For instance, some believe a market-based system is preferable for health-care delivery; others think a single-payer plan provides the highest quality and most efficient public health care. States committed to libertarian policies could enact them and find out if that would increase immigration. Based on current trends, it seems they would fail.[25] The Mexican government's inefficiencies in tax collection do not cause massive flows of millionaires and their savings into Mexico and Mexican banks. Instead, the wealthy leave their wealth in countries that have invested in secure financial institutions and productive infrastructures.

If the wealthy were trying to save money by not residing in places that taxed to support their infrastructures, large numbers of very rich people would live in Nevada and New Hampshire, states with low business taxes and no income taxes. But this is not the case. In 2000, the single zip code of 10021, comprising a few blocks in Manhattan's Upper East Side, included about 43,000 individuals who filed tax returns with an average income of almost $213,000, more filings in this range than for the entire states of New Hampshire and Nevada combined.[26] This contrast is especially intriguing, because New York City has an additional residence tax that goes up to 4.8 percent for income above $500,000.[27] Still, 42 percent of married households in 10021 earned more than $200,000. In Nashua, New Hampshire, just 2 percent fell into this category.[28] The discrepancy says as much about the New York City economy compared to Nashua as it does about tax preferences, but the data show that high tax rates do not deter residence and economic success and indeed may even encourage them, as people are attracted to the collective benefits that result from this.

Moreover, free movement has a dynamic effect. As countries such as Greece and Portugal with previously unstable governments joined the European Union, they attracted higher levels of foreign direct investment, resulting in lower rates of emigration. The capital flows following their integration into the European Union meant more work in these countries, higher wages, and less of an incentive to leave. People do not move for marginally small wage increases. Even in places where the economic prospects are poor and the opportunity costs of movement are very low, people nonetheless remain in their home states. Despite completely open borders in the 1990s for those who were citizens within the European Union, in 1996 only about 5 percent of people living in Western Europe were foreign nationals, of whom two-thirds were European and one-third citizens of states outside the European Union.[29] In Germany in 2005, 2.6 percent of the resident population were foreign nationals from other EU countries. According to analysts of EU migration trends following integration, it would "appear the relative importance of other EU foreigners in EU states is not increasing."[30]

Since their accession to the European Union, virtually all of the residents of Portugal and Greece chose to stay in their places of birth. Although in 1997 Spain's unemployment rate of 20.8 percent was substantially higher than that of Austria (4.5 percent), net migration was from Austria to Spain (for retirement).[31] In 1997, the GDP per capita in Greece was 56 percent that of France,[32] yet relatively few Greeks are economic migrants. Indeed, during the decade *before* joining the European Union, Greece had a 9.7 percent decline in its labor force due to emigration, while after joining the European Union Greece's labor force increased by 12 percent, as Greeks in the 1980s followed the new foreign investments in their country and returned.[33] A study of Euro-Turks asks "What is the first thing you would do if Turkey joined the European Union?" The most common answer: return to Turkey.[34] Available statistics on population mobility show us that not only do people who have legalized emigration options tend to stay put, but even when they move, their decisions are often short term. In the last forty years, since the development of cheap means of transportation across long distances, most people who are economic migrants eventually return to their countries of origin.[35]

To make movement and open citizenship possible does not mean that it will be the preferred or most popular form of existence. As interesting as it may be to speculate about a world unmoored and people cycling through countries at warp speed, it is important to bear in mind that what many people in countries outside North America and Europe long for is not permanent relocation elsewhere but a passport that simply allows them to travel. In places where the passport does not grant easy access to other countries, elites will arrange for extended visas to accommodate giving birth to their children in countries whose passports give them this mobility: their children are raised by their parents in their countries of origin, undistinguished from their peers save for the passports allowing them to move around the world. Changing laws to allow for free movement means that for a very privileged class of people, the numbers of those claiming citizenship outside their place of birth might fall.

OBJECTIONS CONSIDERED

What About the Rights of Ethnic Minorities?

Will Kymlicka, Charles Taylor, James Tully, and others have proposed that ethnic oppression can be limited by government policies guaranteeing the protection of minority rights[36] or by multinational or multiethnic federal governments, such as those of Canada, Belgium, Ireland, and Spain.[37] In addition to their misguided defense of specifically ethnic and national culture, explored below, their claims include unexplored premises that bear scrutiny.

Editors of a collection of essays championing states where the preferences of the majority may be trumped by what they call "minority nations" write:

> Since the nations of a multinational democracy *are* nations, their members aspire to recognition not only in the larger multinational association of which they are a unit, but also to some degree in international law and other, supranational legal regimes. . . . A legitimate multinational democracy runs against the norms of single nationhood, not the norms of constitutional democracy, which are, fortunately for the future, contingently related to the old ideal of a single-nation polity.[38]

Extrapolating from the indeterminacy of the representational units called for by democratic theory, the authors assert that this openness allows for quasi-sovereign, separate administrative bodies united only for purposes of foreign and not domestic policies—although how such an entity might arrive at a single foreign policy is unclear. What if France and England go to war? Which foreign policy would Canada follow, that of French Quebec or that of Anglo British Columbia?

These are not merely hypothetical questions. After Prime Minister Stephen Harper proclaimed the "Québécois form a nation within a united Canada," the *New York Times* published an opinion piece by two social scientists stating: "Anyone who has traveled to Montreal or Quebec City will recognize that Mr. Harper was merely stating the obvious, at least where the term 'nation' is concerned."[39] The editors' use of italics ("nations of a multinational democracy *are* nations") in their introduction and the opinion piece's tautology (Quebec is a Québécois nation because Montreal and Quebec City are in a nation) are poor substitutes for a rational defense of nationality and highlight the phantasmatic character of the nation—its experience as obvious and yet when it is time to define this thing, elusive.

The resurgence of the phrase "national minority" and not "ethnic minority" here heightens the claims to quasi-sovereignty. The first modern international legal reference to "national minorities" was in the treaties establishing the prerogatives of the League of Nations. Attentive to the Versailles Treaty's twenty to twenty-five million newly minted "minorities"—especially Germans and Russians in Poland and the Baltic countries—and because of anti-Semitic laws in Germany, the League of Nations required member states to "accord to all racial or national minorities within their jurisdictions exactly the same treatment and security, both in law and in fact, that is accorded to the racial or national majority of their people."[40] The worry was that absent special protections, national majorities would deprive national minorities of political and civil rights. Newly sovereign countries needed their constitutions to set aside funding and parliamentary seats for their respective national minorities or the League of Nations, at the behest of the United States, would not recognize their governments, and festering territorial disputes would remain.

According to those presently defending laws favoring ethnic or national minorities, strictly majoritarian democracies effectively disenfranchise those belonging to minority cultures and language groups. Francophones and First Peoples in Canada, Flanders in Belgium, Castilians in Spain, and Catholics in Northern Ireland, for instance, would all be at risk if left to devices of a simple majoritarian government. The fear is that without ethnic-minority rights, ethnic groups must face a choice between oppression and assimilation. For example, Turkey limits the airing of Kurdish radio programs, Kurdish schools, and prohibits giving children Kurdish names with letters not found in the

Turkish alphabet. Kurds fight these measures by appeals for minority rights and demands for the eastern part of the country to have greater administrative autonomy.[41] They have largely failed in their efforts.

Elsewhere we see attempts at redress for such a situation effected through either ethnically based minority-rights laws or semisovereign administrative units. The French in Canada residing in Quebec have their own rule of law, as do ethnic minorities in their respective territories of Belgium, Spain, and Northern Ireland. According to the political and scholarly representatives of these minority groups, freedom is only guaranteed "if the nations or peoples have the right to initiate constitutional change and the other members have the duty to enter into negotiations over how to reconcile a well-supported demand [from a minority] with the requirements of unity."[42] Recognition of a minority's "well-supported demands" is the price of the majority's self-determination or freedom, which must be paid to accommodate the freedom of the minority. The justification for such protections seems straightforward: ethnic divisions are lines of fissure that political institutions must respect for their alleged inevitability, popularity, and practical benefits.

The contemporary author who makes this case for the nation most explicitly and at far greater length than Berlin, Rawls, or Walzer is Gregory Jusdanis. In *The Necessary Nation* Jusdanis, who is not especially interested in liberal theory, challenges works by prominent cosmopolitan critics of what Jusdanis calls "cultural nationalism," including Arjun Appadurai, Benedict Anderson, Partha Chatterjee, Michael Ignatieff, and Etienne Balibar and Immanuel Wallerstein. Instead of eliminating the nation, Jusdanis endorses multination states, stating, first, that nationalism is necessary and, second, that nationalism has a modernizing, progrowth imperative that lifts countries from their isolation and backwardness:

> Rather than constituting a compensatory prize of victimized people in search of absent ideals, nationalism acts as a dynamic power, pushing societies into a modern, global world.... Nationalism promotes modernization by reassuring the *Volk* that its way of life will survive because it, rather than the monarchy, the church, or the colonial ruler, now forms the life and structure of the state.[43]

Other than the correlation of capitalism with the rise of modern bureaucracies associated with the modern nation-state, Jusdanis provides no evidence for this bold claim that nationalism is modernizing. His examples are only of the supposed benefits of nationalism—staving off anomie while allowing progress—and he denigrates other scholars for mentioning nationalism's flaws: "One can speak authoritatively of culture, it seems, only if one represents it as an instrument of oppression or imperialism. Or one does not consider it all for fear of essentializing it."[44] Jusdanis claims his "approach to nationalism is historical rather than ethical,"[45] but criticizing others for not agreeing with one's own view on the value of culture seems a fairly pointed normative claim.

Jusdanis's work echoes many common intuitions, even when not so boldly stated. First, Jusdanis falls into the "culture" abyss, asserting that people find culture necessary, but he never defines culture, ignoring equally cultural practices and traditions that occur outside intergenerational forms of being associated with the nation. Thus Jusdanis never contemplates that nations might end but culture persevere, including state cultures separate from national attachments, for instance, the specific enduring cultures of cities such as New York, Paris, and Istanbul—all political administrative units that do not depend on birthright residency requirements and that may even, because of their cosmopolitanism, define themselves in opposition to the rest of their countries' nationals.

In addition to the undefended identification of all culture with the nation, Jusdanis's work contains other empirical and logical weaknesses, again crystallizing intuitions that are widely held even if less clearly articulated. Jusdanis asserts that the modern state of the last three hundred years is the first time groups mapped identity onto territory: "The nation is modern insofar as culture legitimates political sovereignty."[46] This repeats a cliché proliferated by those who equate the commitments of the Westphalian Treaty to the dawn of the nation-state, even though the manipulation of a hereditary culture to sacralize political authority unequivocally has existed for millennia, from the Athenian claims of citizen autochthony to the eleventh-century crown's claim of its English national rights against invaders from Normandy.[47] These were not times of capitalism, and it is thus impossible to correlate the rise of nationalism with the rise of free markets.

Jusdanis's contradiction is the assertion that people have a need to exist in the very nation-states he insists are specific to modernity: "Because groups will continue to identify their well-being with the condition of their culture and rationalize their sovereignty on the basis of their ethnic difference, culture will in the foreseeable future act as a fault line for conflict. . . . Any solution that . . . does not recognize the need people feel for their identities and their connection to the native soil will fail."[48] But if nation-states are modern, then how did human beings survive millennia without them, as Jusdanis claims was the case? How can a need to map an ethnicity onto "native soil" that appeared only in the last three hundred years be innate?

The claim might be made that Jusdanis is contradictory but that nonetheless these national attachments meet deeply felt psychic needs and thus political societies must cope with them. This is James Tully's point. Nations have always existed, he believes, and in constitutional democracies we may devise rules for their legitimate recognition. Tully acknowledges that one might question whether a minority group claiming to represent a national culture is an offshoot or imposter minority invoking the name of this group. Tully also stipulates the impossibility of knowing in advance any particular nation's need for autonomy and recognition and instead relies on procedural rules of democracy for the definition of a nation: majority rule. "A clear majority must come to support a demand for recognition as a nation from a first-person perspective."[49] Such a measure would seemingly ensure the advancement of only those groups with a majority supporting what Tully calls national interests.

Privileging national minorities over all others is tacitly predicated on an assumption that many people's attachments to their nationalities are stronger than their other attachments. But even an archideologist of nationalism such as Jusdanis would concede that some people might feel otherwise. Perhaps they might be moved by cosmopolitans and cosmopolitan culture. Jusdanis acknowledges such global liberals exist—they infuriate him!—and Tully appeals to global liberals by invoking the familiar liberal democratic practice of majority rule. But institutionalizing national minorities is an affront to cosmopolitans and raises questions as to whether Tully's minority-rights criterion discriminates against the cosmopolitan minority.

Tully's arguments appear to eliminate inequities in group power by giving self-identified national groups the means to gain recognition as minorities, but at the cost of a principled democracy that does not a priori instruct its citizens on the most valuable forms of attachment and self-expression. Democratic theorists encouraging minoritarian institutions for intergenerational groups cannot justify why ethnic or national minorities should be entitled to special rights within a dominant group or to special sovereign claims unavailable to other minorities, including cosmopolitans. Some feel much stronger attachments to other features of their identities than to their ethnicities. Battle zones are filled with refugees saying they do not care who is of one group or another. The numbers are impossible to assess, especially in a political system that awards power based on intergenerational or religious affiliations, but in the context of minoritarian arguments, the precise figures are irrelevant. This is one key argument of this book: if political societies did not award power on the basis of intergenerational attachments, over time these attachments would lose their potency and allure.

Using democratic theory to legitimate a majority's hypothetical preference for national minority rights that would trump majority rule is illogical. The a priori recognition of a need for minority rights in some contexts means that any group that does not receive a majority's endorsement to have its rights recognized can claim their minority rights need recognition. Democracy's defect may well be that majorities are tyrannical, but if this is so, it does not provide grounds to award special recognition only on the basis of ethnicity or religion when a majority supports these and not protections for others. What about the minorities of those committed to saving the environment, empowering labor, or advancing the agenda of global peace, for instance, groups that are systematically trounced at the ballot box? Likewise, some groups believe that, as a result of being in a cultural minority, their own ways of being are imperiled under the weight of an overbearing majority's preference. Vegans suffer by being surrounded by leather products. Were vegans granted special recognition, they would ban the leather products that violate their sense of community. Those who share an affinity for full-body tattoos may find it more difficult to be employed than those who have a discreet, small heart on the back of a shoulder blade. Especially when cultural difference is the basis of a group's experience of discrimination, there is no a priori reason to privilege deprivation of, say, one's preferred date for celebrating the Sabbath over infringements on other cultural attachments. If cultural imperialism, that is, the substantive hegemony of certain practices and the obliteration of others, triggers minority rights, and if artists and intellectuals, for instance, are perennially aggrieved and suffer from their society's materialist culture, then a recognition of minority communities' rights would mean that creative minorities alienated by the effects of a mass consumer culture also should be entitled to claim a constitutional minority standing. If majority rule is not a fair decision rule and special minority rights need to be recognized, then there is no deontological reason to infer that majority rule should be used to decide on the representation for a minority and no basis for inferring that national minorities in particular should have these privileges. Having thrown off the constraints of simple majoritarianism, minority-rights advocates invite discussion of which minorities should be favored.

Tully states that freedom requires recognition only of nations, not these other communities: "In multinational democracies, this condition of freedom is met if the nations or peoples have the right to initiate constitutional change and reconcile a well-supported demand with the requirements of unity. If peoples in multinational democracies do not have this right and duty they are unfree."[50] But he provides no grounds for privileging this minority. Why not substitute "cosmopolitans" or "intellectuals" here?

Libertarian and anarchist theories[51] advocating for minorities of one bemoan the burdens of government restrictions that may outweigh the benefits and rights that governments putatively provide. Likewise, the communitarian, nationalist objection to majority rule has no tolerance for anarchist or libertarian individualist objections to sovereignty. This objection instead relies on the mere assertion of the priority of nationalism and provides no persuasive arguments as to how these feelings politically trump attachments to individualism, including the feeling of self-sovereignty and the desire to be left alone altogether. This sentiment was felt strongly enough by one man that he made a statement to this effect and gave it to his town clerk: "I, Henry Thoreau, do not wish to be regarded as a member of any society which I have not joined."[52] A majority may de facto endorse a call for ethnic-minority rights and not those for other groups or individuals, but this does not provide a defense of the principle on which such a majority acts.

In addition to the indefensibility of a constitutionalism that recognizes only ethnic or national minorities, there is a long historical record documenting the unhappy consequences of once weak ethnic and religious minorities gaining such sovereignty: the torture of heretics by a Christianized Roman empire that used to kill Christians for their defiance; the pogroms by the Baltic villages oppressed by the czar, once liberated, against the Jews; the oppression of Arabs by Israelis. Minorities and victims are not static but rise and fall depending on circumstance. What Locke questioned among advocates of religious toleration holds for those pressing the case for ethnic-minority rights. The people who write on behalf of these causes are largely uninterested in the principle but are partisans for their own causes: "Where they have not the power to carry on persecution and to become masters, there they desire to live upon fair terms and preach up toleration. . . . But so soon as ever Court favour has given them the better end of the staff, and they begin to feel themselves the stronger, then presently peace and charity are to be laid aside."[53] Winning sanctification for a minority's protection from an otherwise majoritarian government does not have the effect of promoting toleration but of ensuring the very attachments that lead to violence. Rather than heavy-handed tinkering by constitutional experts to the end of perfectly balancing the political prerogatives of existing ethnic, national, or other interest groups—efforts that ultimately result in resentments and a reaffirmation of cleavages that history shows will often reopen with disastrous consequences—a global framework that alleviates the political pressures of such identities is more just and stable, in the short and long term.[54]

What About Alien Free Riders?

Walzer and Rawls believe that in addition to innate proclivities that justify excluding foreigners, societies have a right to limit immigration for economic reasons. As discussed above, Rawls desires to characterize the "law of peoples" by offering norms for a "realistic utopia," one that attends to the problems of famine and severe deprivation by the requirement of mutual assistance to very impoverished countries, not by eliminating nations, a possibility Rawls does not countenance, or even by allowing free movement, which Rawls explicitly dismisses.[55] However, if Rawls is right that attending to severe deprivation ameliorates the need for migration,[56] then there would be no need for states to impose laws restricting economically motivated movement and no justification for requiring another society's consent for the purpose of crossing boundaries Rawls concedes are arbitrary.

Rawls gives an additional reason for this restriction on movement, so that a people "cannot make up for their irresponsibility in caring for their land and its natural resources by conquest in war or by migrating into another people's territory without their consent."[57] But here he confuses the genuine problem of insuring against free riders, those who would take advantage of the work of others without contributing anything in return, with the situation of the arbitrariness of citizenship tied to birth. Individuals are not responsible for the land-management decisions resulting in the ecological disputes Rawls posits here. Before Rawls personally rejected the cosmopolitan inferences from his work, Joseph Carens wrote:

> Consider the implications of [Rawls's] analysis for restrictions on immigration. First, one could not justify restrictions on the grounds that those born in a given territory or born of parents who were citizens were more entitled to the benefits of citizenship than those born elsewhere or born of alien parents.... One of the primary goals of the original position is to minimize the effects of such contingencies upon the distribution of

social benefits. To assign citizenship on the basis of birth might be an acceptable procedure, but only if it did not preclude individuals from making different choices later when they reached maturity.[58]

That one child is already in a well-to-do country by birth is also a form of free riding so accepted as to go unnoticed by Rawls and most other commentators. We do not view children as "free riders" but as dependents deserving protection. Rather than resort to the pseudosolution of resource allocation by using birth as a proxy for distinguishing between the deserving and the undeserving (in this case deserving and undeserving children), the criteria for deciding on the deserving and undeserving free rider need to be established.

Also, newcomers suffer from their previous circumstances and benefit from new ones only after they move. Not only is it fair for one to pay only when commencing the use of parks, libraries, roads, and so forth, but because such benefits disproportionately advantage one as a child and adolescent, those who move as adults to places with benefits above those of their original countries receive less in return for their contributions than those who grew up there. As mortals, we are especially sensitive to our educational and physical environments when young, and first experiences have continued strong consequences, in contrast with hypothetical creatures who might live forever and therefore have an infinite timeframe for overcoming early obstacles or losing the benefits of initial advantages. Indeed, the period most crucial for the collective benefits and hardships that will determine one's lifespan and wellbeing is that of early childhood, a time when all humans live under conditions over which they have no control. Because of our simultaneous condition of childhood dependence and the long-term impacts of childhood nutrition, health care, education, toxic exposures, and many other factors, collective burdens are an intergenerational debt and form of cost sharing in which one cohort covers for the next. This is a necessary condition; excluding beneficiaries based on place of birth is not.

Absent an intergenerational trustee relationship, land-use planning could extend no more than the remaining years of the youngest person in any venture, perhaps sixty or seventy years at most. No one would even pay lip service to anxieties about radioactive leaks, the effects of deforestation, or budgetary debts and the impact they would have in a hundred years, much less a few hundred years. Although governments vary in their prioritization of the needs of their living constituents compared with those of future generations, no democratic government makes it their policy to burn through present resources as quickly as possible so that those living may benefit exclusively at the expense of future generations with no say in the matter. But why not? These unborn citizens give politicians no money, write no letters, and will never vote for them. Walzer himself notes that there are "certain similarities between strangers in political space (immigrants) and descendants in time (children)."[59] Descendants are strangers because they belong to groups that cannot influence government policies, but they nonetheless are stakeholders. Walzer's formulation here is revealing. An immigrant is already a resident, and perhaps a citizen, and so is not a stranger but a new neighbor. An unborn descendant has no presence in one's life at all. Although Walzer intends by the analogy to make descendants seem perhaps "stranger" than usual, the sentiment further emphasizes Walzer's view of immigrants as strangers.

Similarly, populations unaccountable to citizens and residents in one location may make collective decisions or, to the same end, fail to impose regulations that provide benefits for others unable to participate in these but who bear both their good and ill effects. For instance, people who live in Armenia benefit from flat-screen computer monitors, even though they paid no taxes for their research and development. And one can live in Nebraska and benefit from cheap computers that result from a government that represses unionization in, say, Singapore. Although populist politicians and so-called liberal writers stir up animosity on the part of native residents against newcomers, the far more questionable fault line between the deserving and undeserving lies elsewhere. Most people making use of anything their country of birth has to offer did nothing as individuals to earn this. The eighteen-year-old Californian-born student who is able to obtain a cheap education at University of California–Berkeley is as much a free rider on the last generation's investment in the economy as any immigrant's child.

If Advanced Industrialized Countries with Low Birth Rates Open Their Borders, Won't This Put Heavy Pressures on Land Use and Scarce Resources?

The worry that natural resources will be exhausted through uncontrolled land pressures differs from the free-rider concerns when raised as a matter of stewardship and not unearned individual benefits. Members of the Sierra Club, for instance, have since its inception brought up Malthusian arguments for limiting population growth completely independent of distributive justifications. Since the mid-1990s, the organization began to debate whether it should take a position against immigration into the United States, legal and otherwise. In

1998, a measure proposing that the "Sierra Club reverse its 1996 decision to 'take no position on immigration levels or on policies governing immigration into the United States'" was defeated by 60 percent of the voting membership.[60] Since that vote, anti-immigrant activists in Support U.S. Population Stabilization (SUPPS) have organized to have their members elected to the Sierra Club's Board of Directors, arguing that continued immigration is responsible for the sprawl that has been cutting into pristine environments.[61] "Many environmentalists are not willing to deal with this very important issue," said board member Ben Zuckerman, a UCLA astronomy professor and SUPPS co-founder. "The numbers need to come down. Legal and illegal immigration are at record-high levels."[62] This concern poorly targets the potential offender. It is underinclusive of the most serious environmental threats.

The destruction of forests, the Alaskan wilderness, and pollution of coastlines across the United States are proceeding apace because of profit seeking in mineral rights, oil, natural gas, lumber, and toxic, large-scale agribusiness, not residential settlements of immigrants. Similarly, the threat to the world's water supply is from a combination of corporate excesses and outright plundering. Some agribusinesses waste prodigious amounts of water, to take one example, and other firms are lining up to collect from water-privatization schemes implemented in developing countries by the IMF and World Bank.[63] Immigration limits will not alleviate these harms. Reciprocally, simply by staying in place, residents in the United States are contributing to one of the greatest threats to all life on earth: global warming. It is materialism and consumerism (addressed in chapter 3 and 4), not population movement, that is primarily responsible for wreaking havoc on the planet's ecosystem.

Most economic migrants to the United States are not buying second estates in places such as Idaho, although U.S. citizens are harming the environment this way.[64] Many poor countries have numerous isolated spots of great beauty. What attracts most immigrants is not the possibility of open land or scenic vistas but infrastructures that are readily available in well-developed metropolitan centers. Census data show that new immigrants settle in these areas of high density, the most environmentally friendly places on the planet, at a rate almost twice that of the native U.S. population: 59 percent of all immigrants live in ten metropolitan centers, compared with 31 percent of the general population.[65] If the Sierra Club and other groups are concerned about preserving the environment, then rather than attack the chimera of immigration, they would do better to support cleanly burning renewable energy, mass transit, and green development.

Why Not Allow Free Movement by Choice but Not by Citizenship?

Others have pursued the idea of free movement across borders, rightly observing the injustice of assigning people different risks of poverty and well-being because of birth status. Brian Barry, Charles Beitz, Joseph Carens, Robert Goodin, and Henry Shue are among the scholars who have used Kant or Kantian arguments to claim that individuals are the appropriate unit for evaluating a global system's justice and to ridicule nationalists for their myopic parochialism.[66] Their moral compass has a cosmopolitan orientation, but their analyses are confined to microlevel effects, without accounting for the nation-state's recursive, dynamic consequences. Our most pressing conflicts and sources of inequality follow from the collective identities states require. As long as we are made into the sort of people who design and are designed for affinities and hatreds of kinship, then free movement alone, without eliminating birthright citizenship, may assist individuals seeking to improve their personal situations but will still leave "us" and "them" in a world riven by blood vengeance, family violence, and enduring, pervasive inequality.

Why Continue to Use Current Territorial Boundaries?

If there is no underlying ancestral basis for assigning a governing unit to a particular territory, why not reshuffle borders altogether, perhaps to make them conform with major geological divisions or to pursue more egalitarian divisions in their landmass, water access, and other resources? If it appears unfair for Jane in Oxford to have access to an excellent education that John in Greenland lacks under conditions of birthright citizenship, is it fair for England to have a country with a moderate climate while Greenland must freeze?

These situations are not analogous. "England" and "Greenland" have no special needs separate from those of their inhabitants. Once people live in a state by choice, the borders setting them apart raise questions only about preferences and not fairness. No one worries about whether it is fair that IBM makes computers and McDonalds sells hamburgers, or that peoples' consumption preferences vary, as long as they have their basic needs met. Present borders are arbitrarily mapped onto areas with already established administrative institutions. The problem with today's borders is not that they do not match onto any essentially correct or marginally better units of governance but that they connote attachments of life and death. Borders themselves do not need to be changed, only their role in establishing groups by birth and in restricting movement on this basis.

Why Not World Government?

The approach taken by some of those favoring liberal norms for social justice has been to move from justifications for a cosmopolitan ideology to policy proposals for a single world government. Since 1947 and the revitalization of the United Nations out of the remains of the League of Nations, transnational organizations have pressed for making the United Nations sovereign. For instance, the World Federalist Movement wants the "determination to exercise our rights and responsibilities as citizens of the whole world in order to achieve the high purposes of the United Nations" through "developing world institutions of law by which the world's peoples and nations can govern their relations to assure a peaceful, just, and ecologically sustainable world community."[67]

In one of the first treatises envisioning the cessation of war, Kant pointed out that they tended to be fought on behalf of enriching the power and coffers of the ruling elite. Kant inferred that under conditions of democracy the majority, being uninterested in self-sacrifice, would vote against such causes:

> The reason is this: if the consent of the citizens is required in order to decide that war should be declared (and in this constitution it cannot but be the case), nothing is more natural than that they would be very cautious in commencing such a poor game, decreeing for themselves all the calamities of war. Among the latter would be: having to fight, having to pay the costs of war from their own resources, having painfully to repair the devastation war leaves behind, and, to fill up the measure of evils, load themselves with a heavy national debt that would embitter peace itself.[68]

Crucial for Kant's model is not that democracies do not fight those who share their general values, a common misreading of him as having located a cultural fellowship in voting norms.[69] Rather, Kant thinks that people are rational and that democracies allow such rationality to prevail against the narrow self-interest of dictators. By extension, governments run by such rational actors would understand the benefits of dispute-resolution institutions of a "world republic," as Kant calls it. But this is not feasible: "Under the idea of the law of nations they do not wish this," Kant writes, "and reject in practice what is correct in theory. If all is not to be lost, there can be, then, in place of the positive idea of a world republic, only the negative surrogate of an alliance which averts war, endures, spreads, and holds back the stream of those hostile passions which fear the law"—this being a stopgap plan until states come to their collective senses or until anarchy prevails.[70]

This and other analyses on behalf of world government has cosmopolitan aspirations but misdiagnoses the fundamental cause of war, which is not greed—many organizations are greedy—but group membership narratives that invoke birth and death. It is possible that world government might seem more desirable after nations have been vanquished; however, until this occurs, the wish for world government is surely utopian. Under present circumstances, world government alone may episodically repress violence, but it cannot erase the underlying source of divisions. As long as nation-states remain in their current form, establishing a world government, even if it could be done by the universal assent of sovereign countries at one point in time, would leave in place the templates of national and ethnic difference that have proved so destabilizing for cosmopolitan aspirations. In short, something like the United Nations is an oxymoron and global peace impossible until nations—political societies where membership is based on kinship and birth—no longer exist.

Shocks in Real-estate Values

It is likely that if residents compete on a world scale for a limited number of spaces, the price of real estate in places with great natural beauty and desirable climates will increase. Something like this is already afoot in Greece, Portugal, Spain, and many other places where wealthy northern Europeans are buying vacation and retirement properties, though some locals are doing so as well. The investments are largely in new developments specifically pitched as second homes or retirement destinations, though the environmental effects and the global economic collapse of 2008 are beginning to discourage further building, the former producing a tipping point of growth that renders these places suburban and no longer rustic, thus deterring new residents.[71]

There are a variety of ways to think about this situation. At this point, the problem largely is that of tradeoffs many communities experience, between desires for wealth associated with more growth and lifestyle preferences for less density. A strict libertarian would instruct current residents to obtain better-paying jobs so that they might compete in the market to retain their residences. Yet if we return to the human condition of mortality to help guide our values, then we would see the need for consideration of our embodied fragilities and that these entail the provision of shelter and also stability. Were it the case that we might live forever, then it might make sense to allow, among other random forces, those of the market to play a strong role in shaping where we live. But adjusting to new places is a challenge that requires time to overcome. At a minimum, one must learn new geographies, social and commercial networks, and perhaps a new language and job skills. While doing so, one is literally displaced, awkward, and somewhat adrift, not able to take in the pleasures of friendships and saddled with frustrations of the unfamiliar. The finitude of our existence makes it easy to distinguish the need to live in one place for long periods of time at a stretch—decades and not years—from the fungible preference for a BMW. Even the smallest body needs space in which to realize the fulfillments of residential attachment, of home. Governments inattentive to these needs will fail their constituencies. Attention to the needs and benefits of a stable home does not require any particular housing policy, for example, rent control. But it does burden the possibility of movement with a corollary expectation that people be allowed to meet these needs by relying on governments and not markets.[72] That these attachments to home are significant can be observed by present migration patterns, as returning emigrants tend to be those at retirement age.[73] Economic migrants are sometimes only happy to find themselves in locations with more opportunities to earn money, but they often find themselves making the best of an undesirable set of choices. Other factors influencing these choices are their citizenship status, the social welfare policies of the country where they reside, and the relative purchasing power of their earnings.

Immortal creatures might find it only annoying to make ties in new places and to be temporarily deprived of old friendships. Life being infinite, it would be easy to imagine renewing these connections another time and even in another place, when your neighbor in New York might run into you in Karachi after your five hundred years in London. Similarly, the investments of time and energy put into learning new geographies would be proportionately easier to bear. The year or so becoming familiar with a new place would be a small matter for creatures who live forever, but they are something else for mortals, to whom several years of dislocation is a palpable and significant experience.

Our mortal life cycles mean we spend a portion of our lives as dependents, and studies suggest that during these early years, the need for stability is especially acute. An article by behavioral psychologists summarizes this research:

> All children need stability in terms of both their overall environment and their primary caregivers. Furthermore, there is no evidence that instability benefits children. Permanency planning attempts to maximize stability, particularly regarding the provision of a consistent, safe, and nurturing caregiving situation. Support for the concept of permanency

planning, therefore, arises from the literature on basic requirements for healthy child development.[74]

If parents move, then children will have to move as well, undermining their need for continuity. Thus it is not an unprincipled primordialism for government policies to discourage undesired residential displacement. The sustenance of home meets a legitimate need here and now and differs from a claim based on nativism or heredity, ideas of past and future.

To reflect this tradeoff of the freedom to immigrate and the need for stability, a system of vouchers or other instruments might discount years of residence against other more fungible preferences in areas of rapidly changing density and housing prices. This would only restrict but not prohibit movement to a specific local area and not to a nation-state. People can survive and even flourish without remaining in one place for decades, but those who are displaced against their will suffer at best short-term traumas. People may be willing to trade this for other benefits, but this is an exchange of a different character than most others and one that societies concerned with the mortal citizen might want to prevent people from having to make. This is not a requirement for states without nations but one example of using the norm of mortality for evaluating difficult policy decisions.

What About Persevering Enmities?

Although one set of objections to the proposal to allow people to choose citizenship is that a world of ethnic divisions will be replaced by one of chaos, another concern comes from the opposite direction: the predilections to stay put will leave in place traditional patterns of affiliation and commitment based on nationality, ethnicity, race, kinship and so on, and these will have the same violent outcomes seen today.

Such a prediction is based on two assumptions that bear further examination. First, there is an expectation that sovereign political entities are predisposed to fighting. But, as we have seen, federated systems give us many instances of autonomous cities and police forces that do not use violence against one another. This is not simply because cities are under the control of a unitary sovereign. The Yugoslavian government's sovereignty did not prevent the local police forces in Croatia from organizing to secede. Unlike California, for instance, Croatia was not only an administratively separate jurisdiction. It also had a population whose identity cards registered a different Croatian nationality and religion based on ancestry and not residence. Official kinship groups and not administrative sovereignty predict for violent conflicts.

The second assumption among those who see ethnic conflict as inevitable is that children will fight for the allegiances of their parents. The inference is that when a group includes parents and children, that group is bound to use violence. But children and parents being in the same group does not predict for this, only their being in such a group through membership rules that use legal ancestry. The pattern of children taking after those who raise them does not itself lead to the wild fanaticism enabled by groups that are hereditary by law, not practice. Children of college alumni are overrepresented among those colleges' student bodies, children of professionals tend to be professionals, and children of Knicks fans tend to be Knicks fans. Colleges, occupations, and team affinities, however, are not considered a birthright and do not inspire competitors to commit mass slaughter. Doing something because it is familiar may result in practices resembling those of one's parents: going to college, joining a gang, playing the piano, playing baseball, becoming a doctor. But the very fact that the group makes no promises about birth or death means no sustained, systemic intergroup fighting. With the emergence of states without nations, dictators could not use ethnic honor to garner support, as administrative borders would no longer connote familial or family-like allegiances. As Serbia becomes a country based on choice and not heredity and as states cease to track and produce intergenerational kinship groups, ethnic Serbians and Croatians, for example, created by the kinship rules of respective and arbitrarily established political societies, would vanish over time. Political societies mutate constantly. Of the thousands of political societies that have populated the planet in the last twenty thousand years, only a handful are recognizable today.

States Without Nations Are Boring

Most of the objections above emerge from the belief that states without nations are impractical if not impossible. A different complaint, alluded to earlier, is that a world without nations should be rejected because were such a vision realized the planet would be homogenous and dull, atomized and uncaring.

Against this assertion—by Walzer and Jusdanis most notably, and also critics of neoliberalism—it seems that a rich array of rituals, traditions, and worldviews may not be best preserved by intergenerational communities and even may be harmed by them. Opening a previously national state to all comers should not have the effect of annihilating all that is "French," for instance, but of making Frenchness a lifestyle that anyone can adopt. In fact, there are many indications that people are quite open to this. No pedigree is required to enjoy a croissant and espresso for breakfast or to smoke strong cigarettes in a café while arguing about Sartre and Foucault, regardless of one's current residence. That this is experienced as French has nothing to do with French ancestry but with the reputation of a country, a reputation that does not follow from anything unique to the French government but is a result of randomly accumulated traditions. Just as French culture is carried on by those who are not born French, the traditions of many groups are preserved and even reproduced through the efforts of overtly nonnative research groups and hobbyist experts. Many practices and customs survive because of how they are exported to new places and also adopted by newcomers. Coca-Cola traveling from Atlanta to a village in southern Africa, Indian Yoga practices influencing recreational habits in Berlin, and Chinese acupuncture changing medicine in Santa Monica are all examples of local, national, or regional commodities or practices gaining influence when those partaking are not confined to ancestral groups.

The examples above suggest why it is entirely possible that habits previously considered ethnic, national, in other words, ancestral, would survive in a world no longer organized to prioritize ancestry. Yet even if this is completely wrong, and specifically French or other national rituals lose salience, this is only cause for alarm in a world bereft of any imagination. To worry about the loss of a hereditary culture is to assume that the only way people can exercise ritualistic noncommercial rites is through inherited practices, not reinventions and inventions of other practices. The AIDS quilt, grunge, and community yoga centers are only a few of thousands of examples where people brought together by shared suffering, lifestyle preferences, or recreational or spiritual aspirations establish and continue to honor distinctive memories and traditions. New subcultures that persist over time emerge everywhere, from the gay Olympics to hoop dancing.[75] Eliminating groups whose anxieties about death may require the annihilation of others does not eliminate culture, community, and meaningful affiliations.

Finally, if establishing governance without a national basis would somehow weaken attachments to ancestral rituals, this seems a small price to pay for ending organized violence and freeing resources for more creative pursuits, for sustaining rather than suffocating impulses of empathy whose institutionalization has only been hinted at and whose possible encouragement and sustenance would be at the very least an interesting experiment.

Why Not Eliminate the State Altogether?

The class of laws proposed for elimination would disappear as well were governments to end entirely. Certain strains of anarchist theory provide persuasive critiques of numerous other government-enforced sanctions that constrain freedom and creativity and that are conducive to mindless barbarity beyond those sustaining intergenerational practices and institutions. Mikhail Bakunin, for instance, notes that individuals left to their own devices would never be able to mobilize to cause the death and destruction one sees states producing daily in their wars. Bakunin does not see the nation but the state as causing war and many other harms to body and spirit.[76] Likewise, Barbara Cruikshank suggests that a truly participatory democracy could not, by definition, be institutionalized by a coercive government.[77]

Bakunin's critique is an appealing one, as are anarchist collectives on various scales, including Kronstadt in the early twentieth century, the Catalan villages in the 1930s, and intentional communities established globally from the 1960s through today. Open-source digital communities also exemplify some of these values as well and have been thriving.[78] However, the definition of anarchism based on procedural theories of governance alone is not sufficient to thwart the dangers of nationalism and other exclusions based on birthright. Robert Paul Wolff, for instance, in his book *A Defense of Anarchism*, extends insights from Kant's categorical imperative of a free will to argue against governments using domestic coercion. These governments, however, are expected to raise volunteer armies for purposes that are not only defensive but "include territorial expansion of economic imperialism."[79] This is an excellent example of why political theory might do well to focus on substantive and not deontological reforms. It is true that most of those calling themselves anarchists would take umbrage at Wolff's proposals, but this still begs the question of what counts as anarchism. Rather than a debate over whether a procedural system meets the true definition of anarchism, and rather than worry about whether a particular set of democratic or liberal procedures will result in just policies, the approach here sets out the norms for sane mortal citizens and argues for their implementation regardless of the government in place.

CHAPTER THREE
A THEORY OF WEALTH FOR MORTALS

Percentage of U.S. Americans who paid an estate tax in 2002: 1.17[1]
Percentage of U.S. Americans who favor "doing away with the estate tax": 67.8[2]

WEALTH AND SUSTENANCE

The richest 1 percent of the people in the world own 40 percent of the wealth.[3] Their wealth takes the form of real estate and other expensive tangible goods such as cars and jewelry, as well as stocks, cash savings, and numerous other investment instruments from bonds to venture capital loans. These holdings give people security not because they provide food or shelter but because wealth allows for the purchase of commodities whenever needed. In the United States, the richest country in the world, fewer than one-third of 1 percent are full-time family farmers,[4] and even these farmers produce commercial and not subsistence agriculture.[5]

Financial currency has been crucial to capital accumulation and productivity, but it has also launched zero-sum conflicts over resources and resulted in extreme inequality. John Locke wrote: "This I dare boldly affirm, that the same *rule of propriety*, (viz.) that every man should have as much as he could make use of, would hold still in the world, without straitening any body; since there is land enough in the world to suffice double the inhabitants, [but for] the invention of money, and the tacit agreement of men to put a value on it."[6] Locke believed that if people could possess only the acorns they collected and the corn they grew and not sell them for cash, they would collect only what they needed or could quickly barter for other perishable items. There would be no incentive to take over tracts of land larger than necessary for subsistence, and hence no one would suffer for want of such land.

Locke's hypothesis about the effect of money in a largely agrarian era is not offered to idealize a barter economy or even suggest that the use of money requires dire poverty and inequality. The point of reflecting on how money itself affects wealth is simply to show that mortal humans, unlike gods, have limited immediate physical needs and capacities. Money and inheritance law, discussed below, both incentivize the acquisition of far more than is required to meet basic needs, and both create myths that make it difficult to see their practical effects. Recognition of mortality helps establish a relatively transparent and concrete benchmark for measuring the extent to which certain institutions allow and even encourage individuals to accumulate assets beyond a relatively low threshold.[7] Disagreements may occur over the level of needs conceptualized on the basis of consumption during a single lifetime and the investments in infrastructure over time necessary to sustain these. But whatever these may be, they are much easier to meet than the infinite demand created by the unrestrained hoarding incited by progeny.

One way to see the incommensurability of concentrating massive quantities of wealth among a small number of mortal people is to compare the magnitude of disparities in wealth with those of longevity. Bill Gates Jr. possesses millions of times more wealth than the vast majority of the population but at best will live three or four times longer than the average child born in sub-Saharan Africa.[8] The marginal number of years added for every billion dollars accumulated past a very low threshold is zero. And yet most people in the world lack the personal wealth or support from a government that would protect them from early death.[9]

Wealth that accumulates because of laws guaranteeing currency and producing estates provides the protection during years when, to follow Locke's analysis, squirrel infestations or old age make acorns hard to find. Money makes most items fungible, even when merely denominated and not actually sold. A luxurious home both offers its own pleasures and provides collateral against which one might borrow for additional goods and services, from college loans to vacations. Wealth gives peace of mind. Studies show that a threshold amount of wealth correlates with thriving along a number of dimensions, from educational achievement to political influence to health.[10] Having ten million times more wealth than your neighbor will not lead you to live ten million times longer, but having wealth above a certain amount is protective.

George Simmel describes the "unearned increment of wealth," that is, the ease and even financial benefits that wealth ensures: "The wealthy man enjoys advantages beyond the enjoyment of what he can buy with his money. The merchant supplies him more reliably and cheaply than he does poorer people; everyone he meets, whether likely to profit from his wealth or not, is more deferential; he moves around in an ideal atmosphere of unquestioned privilege."[11] Such social and economic inequality in market privileges would not be possible in a barter economy; it occurs only when money allows the means for vastly unequal accumulation.

The effects of wealth above those of income on human well-being is crucial as an object of analysis because of copious evidence showing not only wealth's importance but also that the distribution of wealth among individuals within and among countries is extremely uneven, far more so than the distribution of income.[12] Globally, the bottom 60 percent owns less than 2 percent of the planet's wealth.[13] And a full 80 percent of the world's population owns just 6 percent of the world's wealth.[14] Wealth also is concentrated within national borders. The United States has between 25 to 33 percent of the world's wealth and less than 5 percent of the world's population.[15] India, with 16 percent of the population, has between 1 and 4 percent of its wealth; China, with about 20 percent of the population, has 2 to 8 percent of its wealth.

Within the United States, wealth also is held unequally. The top one-half of 1 percent owns 25 percent of the wealth.[16] The wealth of 20 percent of all families is somewhere between negative (debt) to $5,000.[17] To some extent, these disparities reflect what economists call "generational effects."[18] One is more likely to consume wealth when one is young, for example, spending one's parents assets or borrowing to pay for college, and to accumulate wealth as one ages. Although virtually everyone is young and grows old, these burdens and benefits are experienced unevenly and are becoming more unequal. In the 1990s, Lisa Keister and Stephanie Moller discovered that "the top 1 percent enjoyed two-thirds of all increases in household financial wealth, and movement into the top segments of the distribution was nearly nonexistent."[19] One indication of this lack of mobility is the relative independence of wealth from income. The correlation of wealth and income is .50 and drops to .26 once income from assets is excluded.[20] Someone with rich parents is going to find it easier to attend private schools and college, an intergenerational transfer that concentrates wealth and poverty through family ties, not income accumulated in lifetime savings.[21] The size, laws, and alternatives to these intergenerational transfers are the focus of this chapter.

WHAT MARX MISSED: THE PERSISTENCE OF FEUDALISM ALONGSIDE CAPITALISM

There is a raging debate among economists as to the role played by life earnings versus intergenerational transfers in the accumulation of wealth. For the most part, this debate occurs under the radar of leftist scholars outside of economics departments and is ignored entirely by critics of neoliberalism. Instead, much of the discussion about economic inequality in the last century has focused on the effects of capitalism on class structure, not the effects of family wealth or inheritance. According to Karl Marx, as productive technologies became more capital intensive, firms would tend to be owned by fewer people and would require ever greater exploitation of their workforces.[22] Only by paying workers less than what they had produced could capitalists accumulate the profits necessary to pay for new, more productive technologies, which were necessary for capitalists to earn more profits and buy more productive machinery to crowd out the competition. Workers would have to submit to these conditions because of the decreasing number of alternative employers in the market for their labor: when Volkswagen merges with Chrysler, for instance, workers lose their bargaining power. Under a condition of what one labor economist termed "monopoly capitalism," the worker would have little choice but to submit to the terms of employment dictated by owners of the ever-decreasing number of firms.[23]

The Marxian explanation of wealth's concentration focuses on firms and workers, not families. Marx was very familiar with the class differences among families but refused to name them as such because he saw them as remnants from a feudal era. For theoretical reasons—the specificity Marx ascribed to the accumulation of wealth under capitalism—Marx dismissed as antiquated political-economic analyses that focused on family wealth or attacked inheritance.[24] And yet it is still idiomatic—and correct—to infer people's class position based on the economic status of their parents and not the child's own relation to the means of production. Knowing that someone is a "trust fund baby" provides more information about her class than learning she waits tables at Denny's.

Marxists and liberals alike who write as though the world has been cleared of laws that guarantee privilege based on birth need to pay more attention to the consequences of family wealth. Lawrence Kotlikoff and Lawrence Summers estimated that from 1900 to 1970, about 80 percent of U.S. Americans' wealth accrued via intergenerational transfers, that is, what children received from their parents, not savings from an individual's accumulated lifetime income.[25] Although they disagree on many findings, economists writing on this topic suggest that intergenerational transfers of inheritance and *inter vivos* transfers comprise approximately two-thirds of individuals' accumulated wealth.[26] Other scholarship suggests that inherited wealth in particular contributes almost all of the assets of extremely wealthy individuals. For instance, C. Wright Mills studied the ninety richest U.S. Americans in 1950 and learned that 93 percent of them had inherited their wealth.[27] Data from the 2006 Forbes list of the four hundred richest Americans shows that 32 percent of them are there because they inherited their fortunes, and this number still underestimates the influence of noninheritance intergenerational transfers. For instance, Bill Gates Jr. would not top the list had he not had the knowhow to invent, patent, and license a PC operating system. But it seems unlikely that he would have been in a position to do this had his father (who was born William Gates III and dropped the suffix in a statement against elitism) lacked the means to send William Jr. to a prep school with an annual tuition higher than that of Harvard.[28]

Due to tax penalties and a lack of reporting requirements for estates under various thresholds, large official datasets on inheritance and *inter vivos* giving do not exist. Economists make their estimates based on a wide number of sources that yield conflicting information, from qualitative and quantitative surveys to models based on hypothetical assumptions. One problem is that the behaviors of most people have little impact on the distribution of wealth, because most people do not own much. However, the public's views are very important: in representative democracies, one looks to these to understand the basis of our inheritance laws. A majority may not be passing on or receiving significant bequests, but in the United States they are supporting laws giving those who do have great wealth the prerogative to control it from the grave. A report by economists using the Survey of Consumer Data in the 1980s suggests that bequests alone accounted for 31 percent of net wealth.[29] This figure is widely cited and accepted by numerous economists studying wealth.[30] This means that the self-proclaimed most mobile, liberal society in the history of the world provides a legal infrastructure ensuring that almost one-third of its total wealth will be distributed as a direct birth entitlement to adult children who, having received a lifetime of *inter vivos* transfers, are the ones best endowed with resources for self-sufficiency.[31] Stephen McNamee and Robert Miller conclude their study of stratification in the United States by writing, "Barring fundamental ideological change, the best practical advice for getting ahead in America remains as it has always been—choose your parents *very* carefully."[32] The same might be said of choosing your place of birth. It is entirely predictable that an international world order that creates segmented labor forces by the artifice of borders would see May Day in the United States shift from a socialist event to a day when immigrant workers press for legalization of their status.

WHY INHERITANCE LAW

Those benefiting from inheritance do so not because they happen to have rich relatives or friends but because they inhabit places with distributive practices burned into legal consciousness on the basis of anxieties about death and fantasies about birth. The impulse behind the laws and practices for distributing wealth when people die consists largely of a presumed shared desire for remembrance and family loyalties and a specifically masculine anxiety about the inability to give birth. There are many expressions of this, of which the scholarly literature on inheritance takes note. Commenting on the nearly universal policy of spouses automatically inheriting estates in the United States and on the failure of even those in unhappy marriages to transfer assets before death, one author explains that this comports with the "desire of most testators to be remembered favorably by their family, friends, and community.

The testator who disinherits his spouse risks the possibility that she will vilify his memory in response. . . . If the testator is worried that the spouse might air . . . real or manufactured dirty linen, he may try to buy her silence by providing generously for her in the will."[33] Another author, attempting to explain why very wealthy people do not avail their intimates of tax advantages by giving away property before death, writes that bequests provide a "limited measure of immortality that cannot be achieved through *inter vivos* transfers at all."[34]

These and more prosaic accounts of inheritance, such as the supposedly natural desire to ensure that one's progeny flourish, reveal that wealth at death is distributed for reasons that are internally inconsistent, harmful (because the distribution of funds from estates would help far more families and children than the preservation of inheritance regimes),[35] and, for the most part, very poorly understood.[36] This chapter makes explicit the inconsistencies in present thinking about inheritance so as to reveal and confront the socially neurotic if not psychotic melancholia that presently guides public policy on estates. The laws and then the political theory texts symptomatic of these melancholic reflexes and the harms they cause will be evaluated below, before a characterization of a more psychologically and materially healthy alternative for distributing resources of the deceased in chapter 4.

Estate Law in the Twentieth and Twenty-first Centuries
THE RULES

It is telling that although each and every person on this planet is fundamentally shaped by the distribution of the wealth of dead people, we have a collective ignorance as to the actual amounts at stake and the rules for how this wealth is allocated. Most countries have laws regulating inheritance that cater to two constituencies. The first is the "dead hand" of the deceased. The second group that inheritance laws favor are relatives of dead people who are presumed to have a right to their accumulated wealth. There are four ways that governments worldwide implement these commitments.

The first is by providing rules and enforcement for executing lifetime preferences about how one wants one's wealth allocated once one's death deprives one of the ability to do this directly. One cannot write a check to a favorite niece from the grave; thus one must rely on the law to ensure that lifetime wishes are followed. Legal trusts have been a fairly recent phenomenon. Immediately after the American Revolution, courts refused to enforce any future acts, including trusts.[37] Law makes it possible for people to enforce from the grave the distribution of their assets, but this is not unlimited.

A second way that governments control estates is by requiring nondiscretionary disbursements for at least a portion of one's wealth to family members, the rules for which vary by country (or state within the United States). This is called a "forced share," and it dates from a time when governments directed how the entirety of estates were disposed, by either reclaiming land for the king or church or by denoting precise terms of its succession in families (for example, all the land would be passed on to the eldest son). Although the forced-share provisions for spouses or children diminish a testator's autonomy, testator wills, so to speak, still loom relatively large, especially if the deceased has no surviving spouse or children. In either case, individual preferences of either the deceased or their heirs would be irrelevant. Regardless of how intensely one might prefer one's entire estate go to the Red Cross and not one's husband, only Georgia's law imposes no minimum requirement on the estate wealth to which one's spouse is entitled.[38] In all other states in the United States, either the entirety or some minimum portion of a married person's wealth will go to a spouse. And in most non-Anglo countries, one's children are also nondiscretionary heirs, in addition to or even instead of one's spouse.

A third way laws redistribute estates is by taxing them, usually at a marginal rate above a fixed threshold. For instance, in the United States this threshold was $600,000 until 2000, when it was increased to $1,000,000; in 2009, the amount exempt went up to $3.5 million, amounts above that being taxed at 45 percent.[39]

Fourth and finally, if one does not leave a will but dies intestate (the case for about half of U.S. Americans),[40] then the state directs the wealth's distribution, which means for the most part that this wealth is distributed to surviving family members. If none are found within the requisite degrees of proximity, the wealth goes to the state. Intestacy rules bear close examination because they express the preferences of the state absent any preference on the part of the deceased, articulating the state's legal narrative in which the family is the means for transmitting capital.

Intestacy

RULES

A brief review of these statutes makes it clear that there is nothing intuitive, much less simple, about using the family as a basis for apportioning estates. To list a few sample variations: in Alaska, there is a complex system of dividing an estate among the surviving spouse and the deceased's parents and children, depending in part if the children are those of the spouse, in which case all wealth goes to the surviving spouse. Or, "one-half of it if the decedent is survived by issue" from another parent to whom the deceased is no longer married. There are also cutoff levels of $200,000, $150,000, and $100,000 for spousal claims, depending on the configuration of surviving parents and children.[41]

Idaho is an example of a state going to great lengths before it claims possession of any property. There are many degrees of surviving relatives who may be delegated shares of the estate: "if a decedent is not survived by a spouse, descendents, or parents, the entire net estate passes to the decedent's parent's descendents (siblings of the decedent). If there are no siblings or descendents of siblings, the net estate goes to the decedent's grandparents or their descendants."[42] A "grandparent's descendents" includes the progeny of two separate couples, one's maternal and paternal parents; all of their descendants as well are among the possible heirs, a search process that requires extensive reliance on marriage certificates and other documents of official kinship ties. This last provision makes it possible for people to receive surprise windfalls from someone who could be a very distant relative.[43]

California, to name a third example of intestacy practices, ensures that the children of a "predeceased spouse" will inherit wealth from the most recent deceased person, even if they are not related:

> If the portion of the decedent's estate attributable to the decedent's predeceased spouse would otherwise escheat to the state because there is no kin of the decedent to take under Section 6402, the portion of the decedent's estate attributable to the predeceased spouse passes to the next of kin of the predeceased spouse who shall take in the same manner as the next of kin of the decedent take under Section 6402.[44]

This baroque rule means that if a man dies without leaving a will, and if his wife at that time who is not the mother of his children later dies without a will, and if she has no eligible relatives and he has children with another woman, then his surviving children would inherit his deceased wife's estate, implying an unbroken tie from his grave to his wealth allowing his children to access what is still presumptively his before it may be claimed by the state.

Regardless of their merits, these laws cannot be construed as natural. Were property rules governing prerogatives to wealth upon the death of its owners based on prelegal conditions, this wealth would revert to the commons and become available to the next individual to claim it either by occupation of some other effort, as John Locke held occurred before governments arose.[45] Also, if inheritance were natural and not historical, its practice would have been in place universally and transhistorically. However, until England enacted the 1540 Statute of Wills, land, in that century the major form of wealth, could not be bequeathed.[46] The sixteenth century would appear to be a very late date for *homo sapiens*, a species with a pedigree of several hundred thousand years, to hit upon a supposedly natural practice.

INTESTACY LAWS' TENSIONS

Intestacy rules are interesting because they give us a pretty clear snapshot of how states use law to materialize kinship relations. Intestacy laws distribute wealth and other material resources in ways that literally give value to kinship ties. When the state designates that the wealth from the estates of people who have not expressed any intentions on the subject—they have not left a will— should go to their spouses, children, parents, and other relatives, this reveals the economic role that law accords the family. Such a decision to prioritize family ties over the well-being of the citizenry is especially striking in democracies. Countries run by aristocracies predictably preserve title and wealth to themselves, but majoritarian legislative bodies acting on behalf of individual preferences might be expected to require that as a first and not last resort all the wealth of those who die intestate would revert to state coffers. That is, since wealth is concentrated, the majority has a stake in having estates escheat to the state. By saying that as a first move wealth goes either to spouse(s) or children (whose proportion varies by degree depending on legal recognition or genetic ties), the state indicates a very strong preference for making family pay.

Intestacy laws by design and function do not passively reflect preexisting preferences. Intestacy laws by definition are reserved to those instances when people either do not have any preferences about what happens to their wealth after they die or, if they have such preferences, do not take legal actions to ensure their preferences are followed. The reasons for intestacy are important, because some commentators assume as a policy stance that the overriding goal of probate law should be to enact the preferences of those who previously owned the wealth that requires distribution once their rights to it cease by virtue of their death. One widely cited law review article on intestacy states: "Intestate statutes should reflect the distributive preferences of intestate decedents" and adds further that "Testamentary freedom should include the right not to have to execute a will in order to have accumulated wealth pass to natural objects of the decedent's bounty"—an objective that the Universal Probate Code also took as its norm.[47]

The goal, therefore, was a law that would match the actual distribution of assets with the supposedly underlying preferences of people dying without a will. This is a strange law. It is inconsistent with policy requirements in other parts of law, where an individual's legally valid statement of intent is necessary to infer intent and consent.[48] When legal documents expressing intent do not exist in other contexts, then the state does not take heroic steps to infer and execute actions on the individual's behalf. Instead, the state refuses to intervene.

Similar to marriage, divorce, adoption, and any other contract, a will is a legal performative.[49] Just as the classic performative "I promise" commits one to a promise, the first-person statement of willing—typically "I, Jane Doe, hereby make this Will"—effects one's will. Indeed, the word itself would suggest that it is even more performative than these other legal actions, which is to say, it is constituted and known as it is performed in a legally specific manner. Absent our legally valid, that is, sometimes notarized, express consent, the liberal state refrains from deciding whether we are truly married, divorced, adoptive parents, or parties to any other contract. Even the rare cases of common-law marriage entail following a practice that a judge in any particular case will have to recognize as an official marriage. And it is telling that marriage would be a possible exception, as it too allows the state to impose a specifically familial status relation on parties who themselves have not explicitly consented to this (for example, the possibility of palimony parasitic on the resemblance between the legal status of marriage and a long-term arrangement of cohabitation).[50]

"A missing will that wills X" is an oxymoron. Attempting to guess the unwilled will is impossible; it is like determining the content of an unstated promise. Asking that the state infer a will to distribute property to relatives in the absence of an existing will that specifically states this, on the grounds that the deceased probably would have preferred this, is like having a state pass laws that automatically marry people who went to the same high school and never married anyone else by age forty, on the grounds that lawmakers can guess their true intentions and have decided that people would prefer such a relationship to being single. If the state presently limits itself to inferring the desire to divorce from the existence of a divorce certificate, and it does the same in other areas of contract law where intent is not clear, then it is strange for the state to do otherwise when it comes to a will.

Oral contracts often are enforceable, but those alleged from putative mental states are not. If property that is abandoned during one's lifetime escheats to the state (not to putative preferred relatives or others), then why impose a different principle for that property abandoned by virtue of death? Probate law by definition is not executing my will but rather performing something very different: executing the will of the state.

One response to the above might be that the ubiquity of intestacy laws using kinship for distributing assets produces implied consent. Perhaps people do not leave wills because they have faith that the state has done just what the American Bar Association desired: pass probate laws to divide estates in the manner the deceased lacking wills would have preferred. And yet in the largest study of intestacy to date, among the 55 percent of people saying they did not have wills, only 45 percent correctly stated how their wealth would be distributed, and only 16 percent of the respondents favored the distribution provided by the intestacy statutes.[51] Of those without a will, 63 percent gave the reason for this as "laziness."[52] This last point is interesting for two reasons. First, for almost two-thirds of those without wills, the distribution of their assets when they die is not that important. Real priorities do not succumb to laziness. Were the consequences of not knowing where one's money would go if one died without a will sufficiently urgent and pressing, then people would overcome their laziness and make wills. Second, it further highlights the extent to which intestacy laws are inconsistent with other state policies on contracts. The failure of people to transfer funds from savings to checkings does not prompt the government to do this in the name that saving money "implies consent" to avoid check-bouncing fees. Rarely does the state intervene to second-guess unexpressed preferences, especially in areas of finance and other important life decisions. In the case of dying without a will, the closest thing to passively accommodating a "non-will" would be for the state to collect the wealth as revenue and distribute it at the discretion of the majority, not to distribute it to relatives to whom the individual was too lazy to bequeath the wealth herself. One reason for the laziness is that most people do not have much to pass on, but intestacy law per se is not simply compensating for laziness. It is making substantive decisions about the allocation of wealth.

Recognizing that intestacy laws are rather odd in principle raises the further question of why it is that the family in particular is the fallback unit for allocating wealth.[53] This is the same question raised by the fact that the United States does not allow complete testamentary freedom. The same authors who endorse the notion that intestacy laws enact an approximation of the deceased's unstated preferences criticize allowing complete freedom in this capacity, as this would "leave the nuclear family unprotected," adding, "wills that do not provide for a 'natural' distribution are disfavored."[54] The quotation marks around the word "natural" seem to concede that a government policy for allocating the wealth of people by laws that are recent—on behalf of people who often do not live in monogamous partnership with the other parent of their children and who are often too lazy to follow social conventions on behalf of their offspring—may not be natural. This in turn raises questions about the meaning and relevance of what is called "natural."

Betraying the highly elaborated and political character of inheritance are the tensions among the four modes by which the state attends to our property after we die (protecting the deceased's choices, a forced share for family members, taxing some of it, and intestacy measures). The intuitions supporting the first approach—a freely determined will—and the second and fourth—forced provisions for relatives—are incompatible. It is logically inconsistent to hold that dead people should be able to determine what happens to wealth after their death because of their respective rights as individuals, on the one hand, and, on the other hand, for the state to act as an agent on behalf of prerogatives earned only by family ties and not individual effort. The only subject position reconciling these two principles is the "gold-digger." She weds the entrepreneurship of the capitalist with the imperatives of marriage law: unlike a person who happened to be born to rich parents or who gained wealth because of the good luck of being loved by and loving a rich person, the gold-digger actually *earns* her inheritance. Admittedly, such a view seems unfair. What about children who work on the family farm? The diligent child caring for his sick mother? We will consider these concerns at some length, but this discussion will be more sensible after we explore the underlying principles supporting these conflicting intuitions about distributing estates of the deceased. The next section considers in detail the individualist, the capitalist, and the familial justifications for present inheritance laws.

THE THREE JUSTIFICATIONS FOR INHERITANCE

Natural Rights and Anarchoindividualist Reasons for Inheritance

The term "anarchoindividualism" is used here to signify the ideology of the libertarian philosopher Robert Nozick, who embraces this description of the so-called moral perspective informing his political theory.[55] Nozick calls his philosophy "anarchist individualism" because he believes in a world of Robinson Crusoes, people who, if the world were perfect, would survive by dint of their own effort alone, without the assistance of a community—much less a state. Nozick concedes the impossibility of such a world but insists that modeling it is useful: "State-of-nature explanations of the political realm *are* fundamental potential explanations of this realm and pack explanatory punch and illumination, even if incorrect."[56] The italics for "are" prompt the following question: is it true that Nozick's, or anyone else's vague fantasies, help us understand existing social relations? Probably not.[57] The reason to initiate an engagement with radical individualist arguments defending property rights based on fairy tales about the state of nature is not because they give us grounded information about our institutions and practices but because these beliefs are prevalent in influential policy circles and because, unlike other conservatives, these libertarians do not concede that property rights are contingent on the government. State-of-nature theories are necessary to consider because people use them for analyses that influence government policy, not because the theories reflect observed behaviors of people in nature.

Nozick offers as his maxim of a rights-based theory of distribution the aphorism "from each as they choose, to each as they are chosen" and includes bequests as a legitimate way to choose and be chosen.[58] While Nozick devotes considerable attention to defending the first part of his proposal, that people choose, he is less forthcoming in justifying the inequality that occurs from being chosen through mechanisms of chance and not effort. He simply asserts that some resources happen to be distributed randomly. This is not a defense of "being chosen" but an empirical statement that laws distribute some wealth randomly. Moreover, because the analysis fails to compare alternative means through which one might be chosen to receive wealth—is it more just or sensible to have this done by parents or by the government?—Nozick's chosen people, so to speak, are not well defended by his theory.

The argument for inheritance rights that would seem to be most consistent with the Nozickian strain of liberalism would be one inferring that the full expression of property rights entails the prerogative or "choice" to determine the transmission of these rights after one dies. The argument takes the form of finding personal enjoyment from current rights to be augmented by the knowledge that one can transfer them to anyone, including selected survivors. Nozick might claim, then, that one benefit of property rights is that they allow individuals the pleasure of imagining disbursement of their assets among family, friends, and charitable organizations, even though they themselves will not experience the results of their largesse.

In making such a claim for bequests, Nozick overlooks the point made especially cogently by the rights theorist Hillel Steiner: justifications for rights, including those of choosing to whom to alienate one's property, only apply to the living.[59] In a real state of nature, dead people can do literally nothing at all. The British common-law authority William Blackstone writes:

> For naturally speaking, the instant a man ceases to be, he ceased to have any dominion: else, if he had a right to dispose of his acquisitions one moment beyond his life, he would also have a right to direct their disposal for millions of ages after him: which would be highly absurd and inconvenient. But [as not allowing inheritance] would be productive of endless disturbances, the universal law of almost every nation has either given the dying person a power of continuing his property, by disposing of his possessions by will or by succession.[60]

This "will" is deceiving, because those who have it do not execute it themselves but expect the state to use its power to distribute assets in ways that dead people cannot do for themselves, a point made by the U.S. Supreme Court when it asserted the constitutionality of estate taxes.[61] If the property earned through my labor continues to be animated as the expression of my personality at the behest of state legal instruments effecting my will on its use, then on what principle might this practice end? If this is justified for two minutes after I die, Blackstone points out, then this justification would apply to two millennia after I die as well, and this would be absurd, a problem the plethora of trusts instantiates (discussed in chapter 7).

Death takes from us the ability to impose our preferences in many ways. Consider a property right to one's job. If a professor's employment contract is violated, then she can sue her employer. But this property right does not allow her to pass on her tenured position to someone else once she dies. The same goes for libel. Living people may sue for libel, but they cannot will a right to their good name to someone else. Many other commercial rights are similarly limited, often explicitly. My "lifetime" warrantees (for example, for a roof, a sink, or a hose) are just that and cannot be extended to survivors. It is the extension of this intuition that laws apply only to the living that initially limited trusts, which for hundreds of years were historicized as a legal and not a natural right. Writing in the eighteenth century, the British legal historian William Maitland said, "If we were asked what is the greatest and most distinctive achievement performed by Englishmen in the field of jurisprudence I cannot think that we should have any better answer to give than this, namely, the development from century to century of the trust idea."[62] The English jurists had to impose a legal instrument for maintaining wealth in families on a population that otherwise would have seen this property revert to the state, an institution that will always precede kinship groups.[63]

Nozick often claims to be following in the footsteps of great Anglo-American individualists, but these writers directly contravene Nozick's belief that the rights of the person should extend past death. Ronald Chester's rich history of U.S. inheritance law and theories reveals a tradition of founders seeking to eliminate the power of testament and leave the disposal of property to the living:

> Paine mirrored Jefferson's belief that the earth belonged to the living, who could change the dead's rights. He wrote: "[No] generation [has] a property in the generations who are to follow. . . . It is the living and not the dead that are two be accommodated. . . . When man ceases to be, his power cease[s] to be with him." Others of his circle, such as Jefferson's personal physician in Paris . . . had urged him that "the dead and those who are unborn can have no rights of property."[64]

Similarly, if it is unreasonable to expect the state to assign someone responsibility to water my flowers, nag my friend to floss, or vote in a particular way after I die, then on what principle is it reasonable for the state to effect my no longer actually existing will over property I used to be able to distribute until death deprived me of this ability as well?

Insofar as the subject whose will is supposedly being followed no longer exists, inheritance laws ultimately require states to act on behalf of a ghost. If one were to give all her wealth to chosen intimates one second before she died, this would be in accordance with a right that differs categorically from that whereby the same person expects the state to follow her will, one second or one million years, after one dies. A natural-rights understanding of property accommodates wealthy individuals distributing their own resources while they live, but after that last breath, the rights-bearing person and hence her rights cease to exist.

In short, the pleasures of one's present property rights that follow from fantasies about what the world will look like when one no longer exists cannot be defended within a libertarian framework. A strict anarchist-individualist position does not see property rights and their pleasures as following from government recognition, but inheritance rights require just this government recognition to be enjoyed. The only Nozickian ontology consistent with inheritance would require that individuals have spirits who somehow survive their hosts' passing, such that these spirits may enjoy the property claims held from when they were embodied in human form. Unless corpses or spirits—or other postdead beings—are demonstrably aggrieved by their former wealth supporting the World Health Organization and joyous about wealth assisting their grandchildren when they die, Nozick's theory lacks an agent who might benefit in death from commitments made while alive.

Capitalist Reasons for Inheritance

A separate argument made today against escheat at death is that wealth going to the state might harm markets and free enterprise. Lacking the ability to pass on wealth might deprive people of the incentives necessary for them to accumulate, which is crucial for capitalism's continued success. This is one speculation about public support for inheritance: most people may not benefit directly but they realize the benefits of a society in which the accumulation of family wealth gives people an incentive to work hard, save, and make productive investments. The empirical reasons for doubting the assumption that bequests motivate savings are discussed below. Relatedly, the effects of taxing income or capital are very different than confiscating inherited wealth. The former taxes (on income and lifetime savings) may deprive people of an incentive to work, on the theory that people are more motivated to earn when they keep all the profits rather than when they share them with the state. But if the state takes what I used to own after I die, then it is death that is depriving me of enjoying my property, not the state. My incentives for earning, saving, and spending are not affected by this, either in principle or in practice. The term "death tax" bandied about in the Untied States by pundits arguing that the estate tax should be eliminated entirely is as plausible as a "death vacation," it being equally impossible to pay taxes or to have a vacation once one is deceased.

Estate taxes also can be envisioned as promoting rather than discouraging hard work: "By taxing estates heavily at death the State marks its condemnation of the selfish millionaire's unworthy life."[65] The sentiment is not that of a fringe communist but was penned in 1894 by Andrew Carnegie, founder of U.S. Steel. In his testimony before Congress urging passage of a 50 percent estate tax, the country's first federal estate tax, Carnegie refuted medieval norms and embraced capitalism:

In monarchical countries, the estates of the largest portion of the wealth are left to the first son, that the vanity of the parent may be gratified by the thought that his name and title are to descend unimpaired to succeeding generations. . . . Under republican institutions the division of property among the children is fairer, but the question which forces itself upon thoughtful men in all lands is, why should men leave great fortunes to their children? . . . Wise men will soon conclude that for the best interests of the members of their families and of the state, such bequests are an improper use of their means.[66]

Confiscating estates gives children of wealthy individuals an incentive to work that they would lack if they simply lived off income from trusts. A society following Carnegie's capitalist ethos might abjure the tax on an individual's income, which, ideally, individuals earn, but capitalism is entirely consistent with wealth at death escheating to the state. Likewise, economist Joel Slemrod observes, "taxing an event probably largely due to luck [i.e., being an heir] has minimal disincentive effects."[67] Carnegie was truly a consistent practitioner of the Protestant ethic and took as his responsibility doing good works for the advancement of his society, not passing on a fortune to his children. Better to be a philanthropist or taxpayer than to encourage profligacy. If his fellow robber barons were too lazy to endow public institutions, as did Carnegie's substantial bequests to libraries and to a center to promote peace and democracy, then he thought their wealth should go to the federal government.

Family Sentiment and Inheritance

A third justification for inheritance, alluded to earlier, is that it fulfills men's needs to protect their children and has nothing to do with either micro- or macroeconomic models of capitalism. This account goes a long way toward apparently explaining legal restrictions on testamentary freedom, intestacy law's prioritization of provisions for family members, and opposition to estate taxes by people who will never pay them. It would be almost a crime against nature, many believe, to stand in the way of using kinship ties for allocating wealth from the deceased. Views expressed just over a century ago by the famous liberal economist Alfred Marshall resonate today:

That men labour and save chiefly for the sake of their families and not for themselves, is shown by the fact that they seldom spend, after they have retired from work, more than the income that comes in from their saving, preferring to leave their stored-up wealth intact for their families. . . . A man can have no stronger stimulus to energy and enterprise than the hope of rising in life and leaving his family to start from a higher round of the social ladder than that on which he began. . . . The chief motive of saving is family affection.[68]

On this model, each preceding generation in a family provides security for the next, stimulating savings and relieving any burdens from the state. To the extent that estate taxes and especially full escheat would seem to stand in the way of fathers' strongest urges to protect their dependent children, impeding inheritance and especially familial heirship would seem to be equal parts misguided and ineffectual.

Marshall was neither the first nor last economist to assert as axiomatic his own fantasies. Just as a 50 percent divorce rate belies the public's belief in the sanctity of marriage, actual saving and giving practices, as well as attitudinal survey data, refute Marshall's expectations about the motivations for saving. First, 75 to 90 percent of the very small portion of elderly people whose estates are large enough to trigger taxation once they pass away do not avail themselves of any *inter vivos* gift giving.[69] Among these, just a few make transfers up to the allowable amount. One of the rare direct studies of *inter vivos* giving finds the median level for gift giving in a group with resources that would trigger an estate tax is $900 annually[70]—even though transferring up to the $11,000 annually allowable would reduce the tax burden on their heirs. If one accepts the model that parents' saving and spending patterns should be devoted to passing wealth to their children, then it would seem that saving the entire transfer of assets until death taxes progeny for parental hoarding. Granting that parents would not want to give away wealth they need to support themselves in old age, and assuming people tend to be optimists—guessing they will live two years longer than they do—a study suggests that their estimates alone are not sufficient explanations for their reluctance to make larger *inter vivos* transfers.[71] Consistent with this is other research showing that individuals without children have the same dissaving behaviors as individuals with children, suggesting that family sentiment is not affecting the rate at which the elderly spend down their savings, including selling family homes and spending these profits.[72] A bumper sticker seen on recreational vehicles says as much: "Retired—Spending My Children's Inheritance."[73]

Other evidence of the discrepancy between the ideology of familial urges and individual-level motives comes from a focus group of high-net worth people in their fifties. When asked by researchers to name their savings goals, none of them mentioned amassing wealth for heirs.[74] Economists note also the diminished savings of the elderly, for which they do not compensate by purchasing more life insurance: "If the elderly were concerned that the forced annuitization of their wealth would lower their bequests, they would fully or partially offset it by purchasing additional life insurance," but these purchases have "actually declined as a fraction of their total resources."[75] Recent large-scale surveys of savings motivations yield similar results. In response to a question asking them to list their savings motives, 5 to 8 percent of all individuals and 12 percent of retired U.S. heads of households mentioned lifetime and bequest saving on behalf of their children and grandchildren,[76] responses similar to those given in Japan.[77] This data from over four thousand families is inconsistent with the savings motives Marshall asserts. He would be especially shocked to hear that the only comment referencing inheritance during the focus-group discussion of savings among the high-net worth individuals was a woman who said, "When I die, my daughter's reaction is going to be, 'Mother's dead? That's too bad. Where's the jewelry?'"[78]

Interestingly, in the same large-scale survey in which only a handful volunteered they were intentionally saving for their estates, when individuals were asked a specific question about the importance of saving for a bequest, almost 50 percent said this was an "important" or "very important" reason for saving.[79] The disparity between what people gave as their savings motives when asked an open-ended question and their responses when specifically prompted to comment on bequests indicates how the hegemonic discourse of family sentiment may elicit what might be termed the "right answer" yielding the wrong facts. In many areas of family norms, what most people believe occurs, what they say others ought to do, and what people really do and think themselves may differ, sometimes quite radically. This is not simple hypocrisy but is symptomatic of the specific incongruity between the national, familial myths told to provide psychic comfort, on the one hand, and our experiences of daily life—where more people list saving for a vacation than their children's education—on the other.[80] Nonetheless, studies still cite this higher figure on the bequest motive and then express puzzlement over the inconsistency between this response and people's actual inheritance behaviors.[81]

None of the individual studies cited above on end-of-life saving, giving, and bequest behaviors are conclusive. Others suggest that individuals do attempt to enlarge their children's estates by avoiding taxes, saving, or avoiding dissaving.[82] Even if it is impossible for experts to assess the validity of contradictory claims,[83] the mixed data and inferences are revealing. In the face of at best in-conclusive evidence on parental behaviors and attitudes, public policy none-theless reveals an unambiguous, categorical commitment to accumulating and concentrating wealth based on family ties. Perhaps, if we can understand the reason for the specific disparities between family myths, family practices, and the most practical and equitable possibilities for settling estate wealth, it might be possible to approach the discussion of laws regulating these activi-ties with more insight.

JOHN LOCKE: EARNING LIFE AND RESPECT BY PAYING ONE'S DEBT TO MOTHER

A Theory of Property Rights and Inheritance

To understand the tensions within and among the theories, laws, attitudes, and behaviors of distributing the deceased's property, I want to offer a close reading of a text that not only crystallizes these competing approaches quite clearly but is also partly responsible for them. In his *Two Essays on Govern-ment*, John Locke embodies so-called liberalism's ideological amalgam of Noz-ick, Carnegie, and Marshall noted above. Giving voice to all their impulses—of individual rights, capitalist imperatives, and familial (and national) devotion—Locke's richly elaborated political and psychological concerns reveal the deeper substrate giving rise to these apparently disparate feelings in Locke, and, I believe, many others. Having at hand a single text that voices these themes and is for many a touchstone of liberal theory reveals the politics and logic that resonate in today's inheritance rites.

Specifically, Locke's text vividly lays out the sexed economy of reproduc-tion: boys grow up into men who pay back their mothers for giving them the gift of life by providing economic security for their own progeny, a story that includes the aspiration of leaving a bequest. As is the case with many gifts, this one reaps more benefits for the potential donor's psyche than for that of the recipient. The paternal monopoly of wealth necessary for this fantasized payback to occur not only deprived women of financial autonomy but still leads to a concentration of wealth far more systematically harmful to the vast majority of children than even capitalism itself. The result is the psychic com-fort that law gives fathers—who enjoy the social status of provider incommen-surate with their actual economic abilities—alongside a legal structure de-priving most children of meaningful security in such necessities as health care, education, housing, electricity, and indoor plumbing.

Tensions in attitudes about inheritance appear in Locke's views on inheritance, as they do in U.S. law. Locke thinks it is a natural right for fathers to leave their estates to their children, but he is ambiguous on whether receipt of an estate is also a reciprocal right of the child and thus imposes an obligation on the part of the parent. Locke also leaves unresolved whether the state is obligated to enact intestacy laws, making no mention of them. Locke clearly states that intergenerational transfers of inheritance are natural and ought not be impeded by government, even though he holds no similar absolutist views for other property relations. For those property relations except inheritance, Locke maintains that once political society is established, the simple prerogatives of majority rule should prevail, even if the taxes and other entailments might encumber rights otherwise absolute in the state of nature.[84] The natural right to property one has in the state of nature does not exist in political society, while the putatively natural distribution of estates through patrilineage is seemingly inviolable.[85] Locke provides no overt explanation as to why property one earns is open to taxation and even confiscation while an estate inherited from one's father is quasi-sacred and off limits from the government. But his subtexts are revealing.

As Jeremy Waldron has pointed out, Locke's views on inheritance are rather unexpected.[86] What finally impedes Locke's theory from being read as a wholehearted endorsement of the possibility of majorities redistributing wealth are not his views about individual property rights—even though Locke is no Nozick—but Locke's analyses of maternity, fathers, and reproduction, all of which culminate in his beliefs about inheritance. When making the case for inheritance, Locke, particularly in the *First Treatise*, blurs a sharp line he otherwise recognizes between the prerogatives of natural law and the obligations of positive law, belonging, respectively, to the state of nature and political society once it is formed by its members' consent. In the passages on inheritance, Locke assigns rights not to the grass that one has cut, as he does in the *Second Treatise*'s passages on synchronic property rights in the state of nature,[87] but, effectively, to grass cut by one's father. That Locke begins with the father's obligations, not the son's rights, suggests that the father is the main protagonist Locke's narrative seeks to protect.

Waldron suggests these patriarchal justifications for inheritance are at odds with the conventions described in the *Second Treatise* of acquiring property through one's labor:

If a right of property is essentially *earned* by an individual [as Locke seems to believe], then one would expect that right to die with the man who earned it. To vest the earner's right in somebody else as a result of his death would amount to the creation of an *unearned* right of property.... Succession, therefore, would undermine the justification of property entitlements on the basis of labor.[88]

When it comes to inheritance, when families enter the picture, Locke offers a set of rules markedly different from those for individuals in civil society. Waldron writes, "All this contrasts markedly with the designation of Locke's political and social philosophy as the philosophy of 'possessive individualism.'"[89] Locke's theory of property rights never did sustain the "possessive individualist" caricature,[90] but Waldron is pointing out that Locke appears to support Carnegie's view of how property is legitimately acquired but then contradicts this by sustaining Alfred Marshall's views.[91]

In his passages on inheritance, Locke collapses positive law with natural law, preempting a majority from passing laws limiting the rights of children expecting to inherit their fathers' estate: "Nature appoints the descent of their property to their children, who thus come to have a title, and natural right of inheritance to their fathers goods, to which the rest of mankind cannot pretend."[92] Although inheritance practices in England during this period were deeply enmeshed in legal requirements and had numerous restrictions on bequeathing land, in particular, Locke represents inheritance practices as a natural extension of paternal lifetime duties toward their offspring:

> Men being by a like obligation bound to preserve what they have begotten, as to preserve themselves, their issue come to have a right in the goods they are possessed of. That children have such a right is plain from the laws of god, and that men are convinced, that children have such a right, is evident from the law of the land, both which laws require parents to provide for their children.[93]

First, the obligation is creating the right, and not vice versa, which is unusual. Locke opens his discussion of inheritance by mentioning the father's obligations, first emphasizing the paternal desire to protect, one that reciprocally suggests not only these rights of inheritance but a broader array of paternal roles and privileges.

Second, the laws of England in 1689 set only lifetime, not posthumous, obligations of child support. And the laws of primogeniture directly contravened the supposed obligations Locke describes, requiring all wealth to go to the eldest son, often resulting in other children being left penniless. Locke, a bachelor with no children, also was not writing based on his own practice of supporting children. In sum, Locke's effort to forestall the government's role in the family—forestalling intervention in bequests—draws from a set of myths about the family that lead him to policy preferences that differ from the norms he uses to evaluate governments controlling the actions of individuals, businesses, or any other nonfamily unit. Locke allows for a majoritarian government to legislate property relations that are experienced as among individuals—we give up rights we had in nature—but government cannot intrude in relations experienced as familial, that is, intergenerational transfers of wealth, even though it is the government effecting these bequests.

Locke's inheritance narrative is sex specific, as well. In keeping with the norms of seventeenth-century British common law, daughters might inherit property, but they are not the ones who might bequeath it. A daughter's property became that of her husband. Unmarried women might own and distribute property if there were no sons. This last caveat notwithstanding, inheritance decisions within families remain solely the responsibility of fathers, according to Locke. This is an especially curious state of affairs because Locke, in several passages, proclaims that mothers are due as much honor from—and have as much authority over—their children as fathers.[94] Why does not Locke honor mothers by recognizing their authority to disburse the family's assets? On what basis is Locke defending the father's role as the exclusive head of the household in this matter, when he explicitly states that fathers are of little consequence in the "begetting" of children and that paternal authority does not give them political authority, including that of violence against his wife, which is the prerogative of a magistrate?[95]

Locke's intuitions on these questions map nicely onto those of Alfred Marshall and others assuming paternal obligations to children. Pursuing Locke's thought in more detail here may suggest insight into the tensions between these commitments and those Locke also claims to have for a majoritarian, representative government, one that could be predicted to be more hostile to the concentration of wealth such familial deference requires.

The Family Debt
Modern law enshrines the nuclear family as a site of economic security. This is paradoxical because the result of this is a concentration of wealth that makes most families financially insecure. Intergenerational transfers confined to families are consistent with widespread, extreme poverty; its perseverance is

not because of its effectiveness in promoting the general welfare. So why does it provoke such strong defenses on the part of so many who not only will not benefit from it but actually pay high opportunity costs by not having access to wealth from alternative legal arrangements for estates?

One way to understand the structures that result in our present outcomes is to observe how the nuclear family and its intergenerational transfers perform a drama of debt, what sons owe mothers and can never repay.[96] Inheritance regimes do not exist to promote individual rights, capitalism, or paternal sentiment but rather boys' feelings of powerlessness vis-à-vis the birth narratives explained to them and adult males' compensation for this early psychic wound.

There are hundreds of texts to which one might turn to support this analysis,[97] but in addition, one sees the pattern of sons' debts to mothers being repaid by the reproductively challenged but financially well-endowed bequesting father in Locke's texts.[98] The mechanism for repaying this debt is realized in laws that establish husbands as the father of their wives' children and also establish paternal prerogatives to control familial wealth posthumously.

The basis of men's desires for "fame and memory" in posterity is a fascinating psychological complex, and Locke's influential ideas about property rights reveal these otherwise tacit fantasies. "It might reasonably be asked here," Locke writes, "how come children by this right of possessing, before any other, the properties of their parents upon their decease." He explains this arises because:

> God planted in men a strong desire . . . of propagating their kind, and continuing themselves in their posterity, and this gives children a right to inherit their possessions. Men are not proprietors of what they have meerly for themselves, their children have a title to part of it, and have their kind of right joyn'd with their parents, in the possession which comes to be wholly theirs, when death having put an end to their parents use of it, hath taken them from their possessions, and this we call inheritance.[99]

The natural impulse of "continuing themselves in their posterity" is imbricated in an extremely naturalized fashion with inheritance practices. Fathers may not be able to author birth (God does) or give birth (mothers do this), but they can care for their children materially and thus fulfill the ambition to be connected to posterity through patrilineage, passing along his name and his wealth. Inheritance is necessary so sons can discharge the debt "owed" to their own mothers. Unable to give birth themselves, men give property and impose their names.[100]

This perspective on men's reproductive lack is at odds with commentary since Pythagoras that gives primacy to the male "principle" in contrast to the otherwise shapeless "matter" females contribute. Interestingly, Locke was clearsighted enough to reject this specious analysis, itself a symptom of pregnancy envy, and offered a much more straightforward framework for evaluating the relative sexed contributions to birth, prioritizing the actuality of labor over fantasies about powerful semen.

Locke scorned the idea that genetic contributions played any significant role in repaying this debt: "What father of a thousand, when he begets a child, thinks farther than the satisfying his present appetite? God in his infinite wisdom has put strong desires of copulation into the constitution of men, thereby to continue the race of mankind, which he doth most commonly without the intention, and often against the consent and will of the begetter."[101] Men are focused on sex, not children. This is not so for mothers who, regardless of their sexual desire, are responsible for a child's birth. Hence, Locke says, the child *owes* more to the mother:

> For no body can deny but that the woman hath an equal share, if not the greater [of authority over children], as nourishing the child a long time in her own body out of her own substance. There it is fashion'd, and from her it receives the materials and principles of its constitution; and it is so hard to imagine the rational soul should presently inhabit the yet unformed embrio, as soon as the father has done his part in the act of generation, that if it must be supposed to derive any thing from the parents, it must certainly owe most to the mother.[102]

Having disrupted the myth that man contributes the form to the otherwise soulless matter of the mother's egg, Locke states that the child's main debt for his life is owed to his mother.

Just as labor determines property rights in the state of nature—and not who has the most guns (the Stuarts)—labor, not genes, determines parental ties to children. Thus, Locke explains, a father's relation to his children is contingent in ways that the mother's is not:

Nay, this *power* so little belongs to the *Father* by any peculiar right of nature, but only as he is guardian of his children, that when he quits his care of them, he loses his power over them, which goes along with their nourishment and education, to which it is inseparably annexed, and it belongs as much to the *Foster-Father* of an exposed child as to the natural father of another: so little power does the bare *act of begetting* give a man over his issue, if all his care ends there, and this be all the title he hath to the name and authority of a father.[103]

The "name and authority of a father" comes from nurturance and education, not "begetting."

Locke repeatedly uses a language of debt in describing the meaning of fatherly responsibilities. If the father puts the "tuition of his son in other hands," then the father has "*discharged* [the son], during that time, of a great part of his obedience both to himself and to his mother." But, Locke continues, "all the duty of honour, the other part, remains never the less from them both; *nothing can cancel that....* Nor can any man *discharge* his son from honouring her that bore him . . . whatsoever gratitude can oblige a man to, for the *highest benefits* he is naturally capable of, be always *due from* a son to his parents." This does not lead to the father's absolute authority, "however it may become his son in many things, not very inconvenient to him and his family, to *pay* a deference to it."[104] And, continuing to describe the parent/child relation as one of debt and payment, Locke writes: "A man may *owe* honour and respect to an ancient, or wise man; defence to his child or friend; relief and support to the distressed; and gratitude to a benefactor, to such a degree, that all he has, all he can do, cannot sufficiently *pay* it."[105]

In sum, mothers, and fathers give children the "highest benefits." Sons are responsible for actual payment to their sons (or fathers), whereas daughters repay mothers by giving birth. Boys cannot discharge their debts by repaying parents directly but, Locke believes, redeem themselves by supporting their own progeny. Although here Locke substitutes the son's debt to his father for the debt owed the mother. Even though the main debt for life is to one's mother, Locke says that fathers' support of their children is payback to their own fathers, not mothers, who have in like manner supported them: "having been done in obedience to the same law, whereby he received nourishment and education from his own parents, this score of education received from a man's father, is paid by taking care, and providing for his own children."[106] This elision of the mother erases the debt's origin—the maternal birth that requires that sons contribute to their children's financial wherewithal—and performs the exclusivity of the law of the father, the man whose only certain, that is, legal, access to children is through marriage and not biology, discussed in chapter 5.

The instantiation of men's repayment of debts to their mothers in law is important. It means that everyone is co-opted into the script of paternal relevance through marriage and family wealth. The effect of these relations as codified differs from a scenario of men who, absent kinship rules, might informally desire to distribute wealth to children. Men may save and support children regardless of laws granting them the juridical status of father. Laws enhancing paternal status and not obligating fathers to commensurate responsibilities reflect perfectly that the law of the father is compensatory to his inability to give birth; its function is to massage a wounded masculine psyche, not to impose obligations on men to support children, a goal that would be best met by the redistribution of wealth through government institutions and not its hoarding in families. The status of a legal father is categorical, regardless of their children's well-being. The possibility of reproducing through law a semblance of oneself that reproductive biology alone seems to deny men is visible in a variety of practices familiar to Locke, and indeed to us today, especially via the convention of the family name.

A 1565 English probate order provides an example:

> By the continuance in the name of the Boynton [Andrew Boynton] intended to exclude all females from inheriting this land and to place it in the heir's male; for a female changes her surname into her husband's name and loses her fathers name, whereas the male continues his first name. . . . Also by establishing the inheritance in the heir's male having the name of Boynton, Andrew would thereby obtain fame and memory with his posterity.[107]

The possibility of remembrance is allocated specifically to fathers, who have their name and identity in posterity institutionalized through law.[108]

If property in the *Two Treatises* has any value, it is not because it affirms individuality but because it interpellates men into kinship relations. Were it not for inheritance, Locke tells us, men would be incapable of participating in the sustenance of the human race, which requires the different-sex life partnership and property relations institutionalized through marriage.[109] Inheritance law materializes the family as a financial institution, albeit one ineffective at supporting most dependents. Not only does inheritance concentrate wealth, but even the few who benefit from it do so long after they are dependents. Children coming into bequests are rarely minors. If they happen to be born into wealthy families, the wealth they obtain does not provide security against an Oliver Twistian life in the poorhouse but rather gives them a second or third house or more disposable wealth in their fifties to sixties. The absence of any mention of debt to the mother in passages pertaining to inheritance, coupled with the higher significance Locke accords women in the bearing of children, is consistent with property claims as the prerogative of the masculine subject, the one sexed as such by responses compensatory to the inability of giving birth. Only a psychological wound such as this (Bruno Bettelheim calls pregnancy envy the "symbolic wound")[110] can explain why a legal regime that is avowedly individualist and majoritarian would enshrine rules that violate both principles and deny genuine economic security to a population's dependents.

G. W. F. HEGEL: INHERITANCE AS ETHICAL IMPERATIVE

Inheritance as a Building Block for Family and Nation

The arguments on behalf of inheritance reviewed here reveal little self-awareness about their internal tensions and inconsistent phenomenologies of family in practice, ideologically and institutionally, or legally. There is, however, another defense of familial inheritance that, although less prevalent and ultimately unpersuasive, is at least logically consistent and self-conscious. Inheritance, which makes no sense as a means of guaranteeing individual rights, protecting free markets, or providing family security, does have coherence when understood as Hegel describes it: how the nation-state makes family matter so that it may interpellate its members into a larger, national economic project.[111] Hegel writes: "The family, as person, has its real external existence in property; and it is only when this property takes the form of capital that it becomes the embodiment of the substantial personality of the family."[112] Inheritance is a crucial means to this, as confining wealth to the family makes our familial attachments necessary. Hegel prefers that inheritance be confined to one's spouse and children and bemoans the testamentary freedom associated with the modern state, as this introduces caprice threatening to family wealth: "The so-called family of friends which testamentary disposition brings with it may be admitted only in defect of members of the family proper, i.e., of spouse and children."[113] Attempting to justify melancholic longing and provide it a political theory, Hegel is a modern thinker whose analysis of inheritance most accurately summarizes how inheritance is required by and contributes to the strength of the nation-state, the family, and the individual these institutions produce. His work defends many of the impulses connecting micro- and macrolevel interpersonal political and personal relations in ways that prompt strong disagreement from Marxists as well as liberals.[114]

Hegel believes that when capital accumulates in families,[115] not just in firms or individuals, and is institutionalized as family wealth through the conventions of inheritance, then modern citizens self-consciously embrace identities of nationality, race, religion, and family roles.[116] They do so precisely because these commitments are not the result of their individual beliefs and actions.[117] Hegel celebrates this. Citizens who come into their identities and also their wealth through a family membership denoted by official kinship rules will feel most grounded in their families. How kinship rules do this will be explored in chapter 4, but their impact on inheritance is clear. The family in a society that requires that wealth must pass through kinship ties will elicit more loyalty than a family in a society providing security through other institutions, for example, the government.

The nation-state needs the family, Hegel explains, because this is how the nation receives its imprimatur as something given, certain, joined by birth. One joins the nation, from the Latin *nasci* (birth), by birth into a family, experienced as being born into a nation.[118] The family, which Hegel emphasizes exists dialectically with the nation and does not precede it, helps citizens feel connected to others who share a family tie to the same nation. Just as children materialize the ties of husband and wife and make the legal existence of their marriage seem natural, according to Hegel, inheritance also materializes the ties between children and parents.[119] Children have a literal investment in family stability. If they alienate their parents, they may lose their inheritance.[120] This does not mean that children are overtly conscious about a quid pro quo between appearing affectionate, on the one hand, and receiving an inheritance, on the other.[121] Rather, the awareness of the family as a possible source of financial sustenance cements ties in ways that are subtle.[122] This juridical family does not produce actual affection and economic security, but it nonetheless induces a strong belief that the family is the political unit responsible for providing these.

It is precisely law's tacit assignments, using inheritance and kinship to create a nation by rules for distributing wealth, that result in the tensions between a sensibility of the family as a source of affection and security and the reality of its resentments (the mother resentful of a daughter supposedly looking forward to her mother's jewels), passive neglect (parents who do not shelter their wealth from taxes through *inter vivos* transfers), and the inequalities occurring because most people do not have families that might deprive them in these ways.

The patriarchal family Hegel admired so greatly arose and persisted, he believed, because of an ethical, not biological, teleology of human development realized through the development of the modern state.[123] Although one may question the high esteem in which Hegel holds this modern family, his arguments on its behalf (other than his analysis of its metaphysics, a distraction avoided in this discussion) are illuminating. Although Hegel's endorsement of the status quo he observed is troubling, his analysis of the family as a political-economic institution empowered by the state provides a far more helpful characterization of the family's functions and the structures in which inheritance is imbricated than do more current popular theories defending and attacking inheritance.

A Critique of Hegel's Inheritance Analysis

The two dominant critiques of present intestacy laws and inheritance norms—individualist and utilitarian—have already been mentioned. Bequests are illiberal because rich parents cannot be earned; they are antiutilitarian because present inheritance practices leave most people badly off. As opposed to inheritance's less logical defenders, however, Hegel acknowledges these points. Hegel was not interested in justifying either individual choice, as were the social contract theorists Hegel attacked, or producing the greatest happiness for the greatest number of people, the dogma of the mid- and late nineteenth century. Rather, Hegel wanted to explain and enhance the state-nation as a nation-state, which he took to be the rational goal of any sound philosophy. He wanted to show how the rules that turn us into communities experienced as natural do this, and he wanted to explain why, nonetheless, we are not conscious of the law's work and experience our intergenerational attachments as prepolitical. Hegel's challenge, whereby he shows that inheritance helps place the nation-state on solid ground, is thus not contravened by evidence on inheritance as illiberal, antiutilitarian, or even outright unfair. Hegel's defense of inheritance can be refuted only by showing either that inheritance weakens the nation-state (and this is untrue) or by confronting his nationalism directly, the tactic taken here. Hegel believes the nation-state is composed of family units of internal domination (on the basis of sex) and that in their outward relations with other nation-states these hierarchical units also pursue domination toward the end of distinction. Hegelian nation-states are ipso facto nationalist, racist, and driven to war. Hegel is useful in providing a clear description of the choice we face. If we want a world in which hundreds of millions will die in war and face unnecessary poverty in the name of particularism, then inheritance should be defended. If not, then it and the other institutions Hegel defends toward this end need to be changed.

CHAPTER FOUR

ABOLISHING INHERITANCE

Amount spent lobbying to eliminate the estate tax by Alice Walton (daughter of the founder of Wal-Mart): $3.2 million[1]
Annual budget for Citizens for Tax Justice (2005) (country's largest progressive tax organization): $101,963[2]

DISTRIBUTING ESTATES TO MEET BASIC NEEDS

Current Proposals

The combined wealth of the richest two hundred billionaires was $1,135 billion in 1999, which was more than the combined wealth of one-third of the world's population: roughly two billion people who own close to nothing.[3] Confronting this vast unequal distribution of wealth, scholars have pursued a variety of policy proposals. These seek either to redistribute all wealth or to reconceptualize the subject positions that might benefit from inheritance by moving away from the "family paradigm," discussed below, and expanding the definition of kinship.

A well-known proposal for redistributing wealth is through a special wealth tax, as has been implemented in many European countries. The results of this have been inauspicious. The rich been moving their capital to countries without this tax (a problem that would be avoided were the tax imposed universally, as is proposed here for the collection of estate wealth), and they claim that it stifles their work and investment incentives. They also hide this wealth.[4] Supporting basic needs by eliminating inheritance avoids the problems that occur in taxing the wealth of the living. As discussed in the previous chapter, there is no evidence that eliminating inheritance reduces entrepreneurship—the charge against a wealth tax—and a global policy would make it impossible to shop for tax havens. Before turning to how this proposal might be implemented, two other alternatives for alleviating poverty and more fairly distributing wealth deserve consideration.

One suggestion that has captured the imagination of pundits, especially outside the United States, is a currency transaction tax (CTT), first proposed by James Tobin in 1972 as a means of reducing currency fluctuations and then taken up anew in the 1990s, with some arguing for a transaction fee as a vehicle to collect funds for economic development. The practical problem is that the number of targeted transactions has fallen sharply between 1998 and 2001, as the result of the introduction of the euro, among other changes.[5] Economists in the early 1990s had predicted potential revenues of $50 to $180 billion annually,[6] but more recent data have lowered these estimates.[7] A further difficulty is that without other political reforms, most of these funds would go to the domestic budgets of relatively prosperous nations and not impoverished ones.[8]

In a separate initiative, Bruce Ackerman and Anne Alstott propose equalizing wealth in the United States by having the state give citizens $80,000 when they "reach early adulthood."[9] This amount would be reclaimed by the government from an estate, provided any exists, when the grantee dies.[10] There are several difficulties with this proposal, beginning with the corollary closed borders and nativism that the authors stipulate.[11] Such a windfall through nationality ratchets up the sanctity of birthright and further materializes the nation. A second problem is that the program is inflationary and would not achieve its stated objectives, even at the first infusion. Each young U.S. citizen who receives tens of thousands of dollars would be competing with millions of other young adults similarly positioned for the same goods and services. It is impossible to increase savings and therefore demand without also increasing prices. In this inflationary scenario, those relatively better off before the $80,000 windfall still will have the upper hand. Finally, the authors' avowed individualist stance—they prefer to give money to individuals and not invest in collective resources—avoids the root problems of health, education, and security faced in the United States and other countries that lack government-supported infrastructures for health, the environment, and education. For instance, citizens of European countries have less private wealth but spend less of their GNP on national health care than the United States.[12] They are healthier and live longer.[13] If a citizen receives $80,000 but spends $500,000 over her life on health insurance, then she is worse off than her counterpart in Europe who receives no grant but benefits from government funds invested in health care.

The "stakeholder" approach fails to grapple with the underlying problems leading to inequality and only addresses the symptom. In a similar vein, another proposal is to extend the definition of family to include larger kin and friendship networks. In this attempt to better approximate the decedents' intentions than the present family paradigm,[14] the norm still participates in the fantasy of testator immortality discussed in chapter 3.[15]

The microeconomic proposals to provide wealth to young adults or to broaden the circle of heirs sidesteps the ontology of mortality and provides only meager and ad hoc, individual-level transfers insufficient to eliminate extreme inequality and poverty. As long as accumulation is institutionalized as the goal and function of the family, and not the global community, the result will be intergenerational attachments that result in provincialism and its deadly consequences, as well as unearned wealth and inescapable poverty. If Hegel is correct in observing that the transmission of wealth materializes ties between the giver and the recipient, so that the heir feels a debt not only to her family but also to the state that guarantees that wealth remains in the family, then perhaps the collection and disbursement of wealth through a global humanitarian aid agency would be a good way to materialize feelings of cosmopolitanism.

MATERIALIZING COSMOPOLITANISM

Research suggests that support for distributive arrangements is more easily garnered for specific programs and not vaguely defined government goals. In her study exploring the estate tax in particular, economist Lee Ann Fennel shows how new discursive frameworks to support increasing the percentage of the estate tax are more likely to succeed if the programs funded by the transfers are specifically named: "People who might be reluctant to contribute to a general pot of money for doing random . . . vaguely good things might well contribute money to provide assistance to a particular starving child, or to supply building materials to volunteer workers constructing homes for the poor in one's hometown, or to add books to their alma mater's library."[16] This also holds true for estate taxation. A study of NES survey data on tax policy attempting to explain the perplexing widespread support for the Bush administration's tax-cut policies found that "most Americans supported tax cuts [including those of the estate tax] because they largely failed to connect inequality and public policy."[17] U.S. Americans cared about increasing inequality in wealth but did not see the relation between this phenomenon and tax policy.

When it comes to foreign aid, U.S. Americans tell opinion researchers that "combating world hunger should be a very important goal of U.S. foreign policy," and "84 percent say they favor food and medical assistance to people in needy countries, with only 12 percent opposed."[18] Seventy-four percent support aid for poor countries to help with their economies. Although most governments tailor aid to suit their strategic priorities,[19] most publics say "aid should go to needy countries that would use it well rather than being used to promote narrow national interest."[20] Another study states: "In most cases, the overwhelming [public] support for foreign aid is based upon the perception that it will be well spent on remedying humanitarian crises."[21] In short, people in wealthy countries would like their governments to do more to help the poor, but states follow parochial, national interests instead.

One way to envision translating the support for helping poor elsewhere into an institutional plan would be a postnational version of the United Nations, a global agency that would have as its sole purpose the collection of the wealth of dead people to be distributed for providing everyone with basic health care, nutrition, housing, clean water, electricity, and education, all budgeted and funded transparently. These goals are the ones expressed in a number of important global treaties and United Nations documents. They have not been enacted, and indeed they receive little discussion in any political arenas in the United States, but they are unquestionably the norms expressed by current multilateral and international groups and governing bodies. Specifically, Article 25.1 of the Universal Declaration of Human Rights proclaims that "Everyone has the right to a standard of living adequate for the health and well-being of himself and of his family, including food, clothing, housing and medical care and necessary social services, and the right to security in the event of unemployment, sickness, disability, widowhood, old age or other lack of livelihood in circumstances beyond his control." Another global treaty, the International Covenant on Economic, Social, and Cultural Rights—ratified or acceded to by 108 states—affirms the right to housing. Article 11.1 of the covenant declares that:

> The States Parties to the present Covenant recognize the right of everyone to an adequate standard of living for himself and his family, including adequate food, clothing and housing, and to the continuous improvement of living conditions. The States Parties will take appropriate steps to ensure the realization of this right, recognizing to this effect the essential importance of international co-operation based on free consent.

In addition to these two sources, both the United Nations Declaration on Social Progress and Development (1969) and the United Nations Vancouver Declaration on Human Settlements (1976) also recognize a universal right to adequate housing.[22] In 2000, 180 countries supported the UN Millennium Declaration's goal of worldwide "freedom from want."[23]

The evidence from public attitudes and governmental treaties suggests consensus on the desirability of the world's inhabitants receiving health care and provision for other basic needs, including clean water, sanitation, electricity, education, nutrition, and housing, all goods associated with numerous UN reforms. As opposed to individual-level disbursements, centralized investments in key sectors may yield significant, dynamic benefits. For instance, a report describing the harms caused by contaminated drinking water indicates that water purification alone "explains half the mortality reduction in the United States in the first third of the 20th century."[24] Preventing these norms and policies from being realized have been funding shortfalls and paralyzing fears of inefficiencies and corruption. These last challenges are not specific to the developing world but face all governments to some degree. It is not common for a theoretical proposal to provide details on such matters, but the radical difference between present arrangements and the principles advanced here suggests it would be useful to be somewhat concrete in explaining a new vision for redistributing global wealth.

Characteristics of a Global Provisions Agency (GPA)

A GPA receiving only wealth from estates of the deceased would have at its disposal, in the first generation of its existence, hundreds of trillions of dollars. In 2004, approximately $275 trillion was transferred from estates to heirs in the United States alone.[25] Inheritance is theft. Inheritance is the government allocating from the commons tremendous resources on behalf of an hereditary or chosen few, who are given title to vast sums of unearned wealth. Once estates of the deceased lose their state protections, private trusts of the descendants of John D. Rockefeller, King George V, Mayer Amschel Rothschild, Prince Alwaleed Bin Talal Alsaud, or Sam Walton would no longer be passed on to their few children and used for mansions, jewelry, racehorses, and so forth—or hoarded in first-world banks, strengthening their countries' currencies and making low interest rates available to their citizens. Instead, that wealth could be dedicated to projects including building electrical grids and decent plumbing for the one-third of the world's population that lacks drinking electricity and clean water, as well as for education, health care, and other necessities decided on a regional basis.

There is certainly a special windfall that the first GPA would receive, but unlike the appropriations by communist regimes, wealth from estates is renewable, so to speak. Having benefited from previous generation's contributions to infrastructure, each cohort also would produce wealth that, when they died, would be available for socially beneficent ends. Such investments have well-documented dynamic consequences that would enhance further accumulation. Solid economic infrastructures consequent to the provision of basic amenities enable the development of consumer markets, and this increases productivity. For instance, the UN Human Development Report estimates forty billion hours a year are spent collecting water in sub-Saharan Africa each year, equivalent to "a year's labor for the entire workforce in France."[26] Such an investment is not zero sum but will stanch the waste of productivity lost from current policies for distributing wealth: "allowing the water and sanitation deficit to continue would cost roughly nine times more than resolving it."[27] The World Health Organization estimates the total economic benefits from halving the number of households without water and sanitation is $38 billion.[28] With these and other investments, over time there would be more income, savings, and eventually more wealth to be reinvested in social infrastructure when people die.

For a suggestion of the possibilities of such a GPA, consider that while the value of transfers through estates only in the United States in 2004 was estimated at $275 trillion, the estimated cost for providing safe sanitation and water worldwide is at most $30 billion annually.[29] Overall, relying on calculations made by the Millennium Development Report, it would cost at most $500 billion annually to meet their goal of eliminating fear from want.[30] This would leave substantial funds for expanding and improving infrastructure and education that would increase the world's health and productivity far above the levels obtained from current policies, which restrict wealth's distribution to the whims of a small number of those with estates.

There can be little disagreement from liberals with either the principle that wealth concentrated by birthright among a privileged few is unjust or with the desire to make the planet's population healthy and educated. The questions most likely to be raised here would be addressed to implementation of these new programs. Why would a GPA do better than present practices, which may not eliminate inequality but at least provide some measure of security for some people? Would a GPA lead to massive corruption or inequities different from but no improvement over those resulting from the present distribution of wealth through nations and families? Might not a GPA run roughshod over people's preferences, if those running the GPA have goals and priorities at odds with provision recipients? What might be the relationship between a GPA and states without nations?

The means to distribute wealth most consistent with the principles informing citizenship for mortals is to collect and distribute wealth on a per capita basis, so that states would have an incentive to invite settlement. Such a plan encourages governments to provide socially, ecologically, and financially hospitable environments, to attract new residents, in much the same ways that states or provinces currently compete for national funding in federal systems on the basis of population. To institutionalize the goal of citizens understanding their attachments to the GPA, it might allocate aid proportionate to populations directly to nonprofit organizations, including but not limited to local governments, and would not micromanage the programs. Each country would have its own GPA representatives and a self-contained board for making grant decisions. In short, the GPA might run according to principles similar to present nonprofit grant-making organizations. The main difference between present grant-making organizations and a GPA is that the former are not representative of all stakeholders, whereas for the latter, regional-board memberships might be determined by a combination of lottery, election, and government appointments. The variety of constituencies involved would guarantee representativeness, transparency, participation, and also convey the benefits of wealth's distribution through this institution and not rich families.

The notion of eradicating inheritance may seem implausible, but it is in keeping with the antifeudal ideology of the country's founders. In abolishing inalienable estates, the North Carolina legislature held in 1784 that they only "raise the wealth and importance of particular families and individuals, giving them an unequal and undue influence in a republic, and prove in manifold instances the source of great contention and injustice."[31] These criticisms hold for the legal, hereditary concentration of wealth as well, as this also favors the concentration of power in certain families and removes incentives for productivity from the beneficiaries. The early republicans abolished entail and primogeniture, but not inheritance, though their analyses and some of their preferences would seem to support this.[32]

Collecting GPA Funds

The challenge of collecting wealth accumulated over an individual's lifetime has no single, foolproof solution. But most of the difficulties posed for a GPA exist for present governments seeking estate or gift taxes from wealthy people who attempt legal and illegal means to hide this wealth. Present tax and financial-transaction laws also accommodate a number of scenarios envisioned in a world without inheritance: surviving friends and relatives who inhabit homes in the name of deceased; business partners whose livelihoods depend on their ex-partner's capital remaining invested; and survivors, with or without the foreknowledge of the deceased, attempting to cheat by hiding from the government transactions giving them title and possession of estate wealth without taxation. These and many other tax-resistant strategies have provoked the development of legal instruments. Below is an extrapolation from present practices to envision how a GPA might function.

HOUSING

Because most people's wealth is accumulated as their homes, and because most estates are left to spouses, a strict confiscation of wealth could have the effect of evicting many elderly women from their residences. Under current law, spouses are protected from such actions by a combination of tax and marriage law. But citizenship for mortals means that the government would not select a particular kinship arrangement to extend its perpetuation as a nation, that is, marriage, and therefore would not codify "spouses" or privilege this relation over others. Copious research has shown the incommensurability of laws privileging the marital relation with actual housing patterns and support systems (discussed in chapter 5). Citizenship for mortals would begin with these facts and establish policies consistent with them and not the fantasies nurtured by the nation-state bent on reproducing its putatively particular people. Distributive norms that eliminate inheritance and marriage would result in extending government support to vastly larger numbers of people than currently benefit from the birthright protections presently in place and would easily accommodate those with monogamous two-parent family lifestyles as well.

Any discussion of first-world family living arrangements needs to occur in a context recognizing the tremendous disparity in the quality of housing available to elderly people worldwide. Nearly 100 percent of older people who live in Europe and other industrialized countries occupy "conventional housing," compared with 1 to 3 percent of older women in most African countries.[33] One simple way to address this inequality and at the same time avoid traumatic dislocations is that those wanting to remain in residences owned by the deceased could pay either rent or mortgage to the new legal owner, the GPA. In some cases, the deceased might have arranged an *inter vivos* transfer of part of the title (presently occurring in most countries via estate and marriage law), so that the surviving partner or other resident would absorb only that proportionate remaining cost. If the deceased had transferred the entire title to surviving occupants, then at death the GPA is not involved. The GPA would absorb only the estates of the deceased; it has no claim to gifts transferred before death. For those remaining in housing transferred to the GPA, the funds from their rent or mortgages, if they choose to purchase the home, would go to the GPA budget and be used to invest in housing stock in areas that lack conventional housing. If the occupants decided to live elsewhere, the GPA would sell the home and retain the proceeds.

If the surviving inhabitants cannot afford rent for their home, then they would be in the class of those needing subsidies for their housing costs, and the GPA would partially or entirely finance the surviving occupant's housing. Rich people would no longer receive an additional unearned windfall in the form of housing wealth, and those who could not afford housing as a result of a partner's death, or for any other reason, would receive a housing subsidy.[34] In other words, GPA funds collected from their housing rentals or mortgages would not be a "redistribution" of wealth from the deserving rich to the lazy poor but reflect each generation's new, initial distribution of property rights. After the person with title dies, there is no party with rights from whom the government is actually taking the property, only a collection of assets and things over which, absent current family law, no one has legal title. Alternative conventions for the distributions of this wealth at death are perhaps unfamiliar, but they are no more inherently prone to confusion or abuse than those relying on the family paradigm. If a GPA paradigm were instantiated, the legal frameworks and practices most likely would become as normal and eventually seem as natural as those presently used.

PERSONAL MEMENTOS

The character of property at death emphasized so far has been largely practical and financial. But mortals leave behind other objects, including those with little market value, including mementos that survivors cherish as touchstones for passionate memories, either of a specific event or the deceased's general presence in their lives and on the planet. Mortals deserve societies in which the wealth of the deceased is distributed to prioritize the needs of the living and not to serve fantasies and anxieties about death, but mortal citizens who survive the death of an intimate also realize their existing attachment to the deceased's memory in relationship to things. The analysis here is not to serve the interests of a radical libertarianism but to sustain rational and not psychotic forms of mortality. The unit of analysis is not the abstract individual but the mortal citizen, a person born into a web of intergenerational sustaining institutions that provide a feeling of history and a capacity for narratives of various attachments. The ontology proposed here to respect this derives from Nietzsche's and Arendt's depictions of individuals and larger groups existing by the stories they tell, framing themselves between a past and a present, one that will inevitably contain signified objects of place, people, time, and also things. The persistence of a place, in other words, anchors thought, even when its significance is contingent and variously crafted and expressed. A memory of a life's journey is sustained by the material presence of these places, even if one never returns. There is a feeling of permanence in the world, especially in contrast with the transience of our own time in it. This sense of quasi-permanence—as ancient Pergamum and contemporary New Orleans ebb out to sea—helps provide a feeling and experience of worldly familiarity, even as the stories we invent about these environs may be strange to each other. A visitor's memories of Istanbul are not the same as those of a lifelong resident, but both believe there is something relatively concrete about Istanbul's geological, demographic, and historical existences.

The possessions of someone deceased may be experienced similarly to those of place. Memories, feelings, and thoughts of another awaken through an infinite variety of objects: a small picture framed twenty years ago, the deceased's rings, watch, an old sweater. These might have little market value and therefore pose no pragmatic distributive problems. In other cases, a GPA could accommodate the need for anchoring memory and feeling as well as the need for a fair distribution of wealth by setting a price ceiling under which survivors could lay claim to small reminders. In the event more than one person desires the object, it could be distributed by a lottery.

Yes, these attachments also follow from feelings of melancholia. Provision made for their expression as a desire for personal mementos and not for national memorials can be justified because the former do not have any associations with mass, systemic violence and the latter do. The aim of proposing laws consistent with citizenship for mortals is not to limit melancholia at the level of individual emotional engagements but to restrict its appearance to just these private realms. According to Freud, melancholia is the "morbid internalization of the loss of a loved person, or of some abstraction which has taken the place of one, such as a fatherland, liberty, an ideal, and so on."[35] The word is from the Greek *melin*, meaning black or dark, and *khole*, meaning bile.[36] Quite literally, it is the condition of not being able to digest something that is dead, of being made uncomfortable by this failure of the excretory process. Melancholia as a social phenomenon was first discussed in detail by the British author Robert Burton in his *Anatomie of Melancholia* (1628). There he quite cheerily reflects on his own disquisition as a symptom of being afflicted by the subject of his study: "I writ of melancholy, by being busy to avoid melancholy."[37] In keeping with the synechdocal impulse since Plato, Burton finds that the disease thrives in certain institutions as well as individuals: "I undertook at first that Kingdoms, Provinces, Families, were melancholy as well as private men.... Where [a population] be generally ... contentious, where there be many discords, many laws, many lawsuits, many lawyers ... it is a manifest sign of a distempered melancholy state."[38] Peter Goodrich takes Burton's point much further, exploring how all law is a symptom of melancholia: "The legal tradition embodies the melancholic soul of a private nation afraid not simply of others but, in analytic terms, primarily of itself and its emptiness, its stupidity and lack of thought."[39] The notion here seems to be that the ancient origins on which law depends for its authority are a form indigestion. To put this in Nietz-sche's terms: the past is dead but still inside us, keeping us from fully experiencing all that is new and truly nourishing.

That legal narratives require history and that this may be deadening certainly is true, and that enduring melancholia for long periods of time is unhealthy also seems correct. But the tropes above suggest that the nation and the family are the vehicles for melancholia's worst symptoms. If the goal is to eliminate mass, systemic violence and extreme inequality, then the nation and its history, including its form of legal history, are intolerable. But this does not require eliminating melancholia as an individual psychological condition, a goal that may not be obtainable. Melancholia as a private affair seems inevitable and will be different degrees of painful and cathartic, dark and visionary. This is part of the human condition. It may be repressed, sublimated, and experienced through a variety of different rituals. Its psychic power, however, does not require that our melancholia, including its ancillaries of nation, race, religion, and family structures, must exercise sway over the disbursement of resources (and over the rules for citizenship, marriage, and land possession) when their influence over legal domains causes such harms.

The only small problem that mementos pose for a GPA is when they have a large exchange and not just personal value. If I am so deeply attached to Aunt Jane that I must have her Rolls Royce because driving it reminds me of our weekly outings, then either the principle of the needs of the living may trump my attachment to this experience of Aunt Jane or I must pay for it through the same system of either outright purchase, mortgage, or rent from the GPA described in the cases of homes and businesses. It is true that this will impose hardship on those who lack funds to pay for these memories, but in the case of the Rolls Royce, the emotional impact is presumably far less than that of the anguish and loss that five thousand mothers watching their children die from starvation would feel, which could be prevented by the $100,000 collected from that car's sale.

SCOFFLAWS

Under any regime in which individual contributions are required to sustain the organization, some people will cheat. The main government mechanisms for prohibiting this are punishment, ostracism, and surveillance. A GPA, because it is a financial institution and not an institution with its own monopoly on the legitimate use of force, would be unable to ensure compliance by threat of punishment. It also could not obtain compliance through banishment, as the United States presently attempts by deporting resident aliens convicted of crimes.[40] Some people, especially those who might connive securing great fortunes, might calculate an overall utility to living elsewhere with their wealth over remaining in their present state of residence if it would pose great tax burdens. The final mechanism of surveillance in modern bureaucracies generally is done by the agency itself collecting, maintaining, and monitoring its records on a regular basis. For a GPA lacking any enforcement capabilities, this is not an option, as people simply might not register and could not be punished for their omissions.

The GPA could coordinate with state governments to collect funds by using another mechanism that governments since at least ancient Athens have used: the bounty hunter. Individuals who are not government employees can be induced to report violations of civil and criminal codes in exchange for a reward. This is already the case for tax fraud. In the United States, those who provide the IRS with information on tax cheats receive 15 percent of the amount recovered.[41] Enabling such a system for the GPA would not require that individuals leave open to public view all their financial records, but it would require a database in which residents of any country were registered. When one's death is reported, the government of legal residency would publicly announce the death and encourage the collection of assets by a small transaction fee paid to the financial institutions or individuals presently possessing the wealth (either as currency, stock certificates, other titles, or the goods themselves), with a slightly larger fee paid going to the state governments in which the deceased last resided, to enlist their cooperation with a GPA.[42] Today, when individuals die, estate lawyers contact their banks and so forth to request the assets be transferred to an escrow account; a GPA would do something similar.

Those institutions or individuals failing to cooperate would be subject to penalties from their state governments in the event they held the wealth themselves, as is the case today. Larger estates would be especially easy to locate: regardless of the regime in place, when Bill Gates Jr. passes away, the IRS will be sure to pay close attention.

Certainly there might be cheaters who will go uncaught. While this is unfair and undesirable, if the cheating were on a small scale, for example, a handful of institutions or individuals failing to report wealth, it would affect very few people and be little cause for concern. If it is widespread, then the relative distributive unfairness of an ineffective GPA compared with present inheritance practices is an empirical question: it is easy to imagine that the friends and relatives of those who would steal from an estate will be more numerous and less advantaged than the relatives and friends of the rich deceased person. Best to devise plans to minimize cheating and increase confidence in the GPA, but potential corruption does not doom a GPA any more than this possibility (and reality!) has harmed inheritance.

Finally, the proposal to eliminate the violence and inequality from inheritance's bolstering of the family and nation does not speak to the violence and inequality caused specifically by capitalism. But it is not clear that capitalism's worst excesses are caused by free markets or prevented by them. The global economy has known only the free movement of capital, not the free movement of labor. It seems apparent that the worst forms of violent capitalist exploitation, including de facto slave labor in places such as the Dominican Republic, could not be maintained if workers could leave the country.

Many large businesses and Wall Street favor free movement for instrumental and ideological reasons, as Marx predicted, so it is ironic to find it is a Jewish family business running a kosher meatpacking company fighting to erect barriers against foreign workers, which Marx pointedly did not predict. Marx's "On the Jewish Question" (1843) suggests that the liberal German citizenry had misplaced fears about particularism. Rather than be worried about Jews in Germany behaving as a separate ethnic, national, or religious group, Germans should worry about Jews as a special economic class, the bourgeoisie. And yet the Rubashkins as U.S. Americans, and not as capitalists, are trying to stave off recognition of their employees' successful unionization drive. Agriprocessors, the Rubashkin business, is claiming that the voting workforce included undocumented workers of Mexican ancestry. Agriprocessors filed a lawsuit stating that these workers cannot be allowed in unions.[43] In other words, when labor won through democratically passed laws protecting workers, the Rubashkins decided to give up its fight against labor as a universal class and to fight Mexicans as a particular class.

Marx's materialist analysis begins by arguing that capacities and needs are produced by new means of production. He guessed that the tendency of new technologies toward requirements of ever greater capital accumulation would tend toward their increasing capital's centralization. He did not anticipate that new technologies might make capital's decentralization also a possibility. In other words, as productivity from the exploitation of previous generations is accumulated in new means of production, they become increasingly cheaper. A calculator in 1970 embodied a much higher proportion of labor power than one today, and the same goes for computers and cars, all of which make their ownership more available to a broader spectrum of individuals, increasing competition for the labor that might create objects with exchange values. Rubashkin's strategy of fighting Mexican labor as nationals is one that Marx thought capitalists in general and Jews in particular were too smart to pursue. By discouraging Mexicans from entering the United States for employment, the Rubashkins are decreasing the availability of labor and thus increasing its price, something very similar to what racists in the South did when they discriminated against African Americans despite this being against the economic interests of white Southerners.[44] Although it is true that the best way to mitigate slave labor is with open borders, the best way for Agriprocessors to keep labor prices down and to fight against unionization is to draw from a large labor pool. Legalizing alien workers would be the quickest way to diminish the bargaining power of labor unions across the United States, just as it would be the most direct means of enhancing labor power in Mexico: the possibility of free movement threatens the efficacy of violence against unionizers who may pursue jobs elsewhere.[45] Moreover, with the elimination of inheritance, perhaps Rubashkin would feel less compelled to exploit his workforce, because the profits he accumulated from it would be redistributed to a GPA after his death and thus be used to help poor people everywhere and not his heirs.

To summarize some of the salutary effects of free movement on labor markets does not mean that all problems can be left to free markets. The argument here is that once certain needs are taken off the bargaining table and afforded to people regardless of income or family background, including those for health, education, and housing, then markets, including labor markets, probably do ensure the fairest, least coercive, and most equitable means for allocating income and other resources.

Long-term Dynamic Effects

The family paradigm for inheritance, while neither a universal nor natural reflection of prelegal preferences, has been very successful in using wealth to influence individual-level aspirations. Parents appease their fears of mortality as they orbit trajectories established by law, including its rules and expectations for wealth flowing through family ties. Eliminating the gravitational force field of inheritance law might have other consequences extending beyond the new possibilities of wealth's distribution.

For example, those people motivated to accumulate wealth to pass onto their children might be more responsive to other individuals and groups beyond their own families. All things being equal, no one prefers a world of child slavery, polluted air, or global warming. These events are externalities of a profit motive in an economic universe of superaccumulation. There is no worldly incentive to seek profits of $10 billion instead of $5 billion, and thus eliminating inheritance also may eliminate an important context for the exploitation of strangers. Perhaps some will seek to accumulate extraordinary wealth because they see business as a game and more makes them feel as though they are winning. For those whose acquisitiveness is motivated by a family paradigm, its disappearance would perhaps reduce the incentive to make a personal fortune and therefore also decrease the desire to maximize worker exploitation and cut other corners that harm people in order to create enormous profits. Rather than requiring new, repressive, and most likely ineffective global institutions, eliminating inheritance does away with one of the incentives to accumulate from exploitation and environmental degradation wealth that cannot be consumed in one lifetime and cannot be left to one's children.

CHAPTER FIVE
THE LAW OF THE MOTHER

Despite the feminist protestations, the man remains inferior in pro-
creation: he cannot bear children. Any special access to the child
must be granted to him by the woman. She must acknowledge the
man's paternity and only the woman can acquire sexual affirma-
tion by feeding the infant at her breast.

GEORGE GILDER, *SEXUAL SUICIDE* (1973;

AN ANTIFEMINIST MANIFESTO)

In the last century, marriage has changed more than any of the other institutions discussed in this book.[1] Some measures have expanded marriage's
reach, for instance to same-sex couples. Some decouple social welfare benefits
from marriage, giving assistance to mothers and other dependents directly,
regardless of the legal household to which they may or may not belong; in re-

sponse, some new laws, including state constitutional amendments, have been directed toward maintaining marriage's restrictive definition.[2] Despite the contentions surrounding marriage—not to mention the wide variety of the ways people raise children (at least half outside different-sexed, monogamous married couples who are genetically related to their children)—the public has not witnessed an open debate about the desirability of state-sanctioned marriage per se. This chapter surveys the terms of debate over marriage in the popular media and the academy and then explains the actual laws that these controversies are responding to and shaping. The specific narratives defending marriage deserve comment because the most fervent advocates for heterosexual marriage come from epistemological traditions holding each other in contempt: Bible-thumping fundamentalists opposing stem-cell research, contraception, and advocating intelligent design do not usually find themselves on the same policy page as the atheist descendants of Charles Darwin. That such committed antagonists converge nonetheless to defend the nuclear family—despite these traditions' mutually exclusive doctrines—is one indication of marriage's strong hold over the popular imagination.[3]

The review of differently problematic stories insisting on marriage's importance for Western civilization and the human species leads to a proposal to eliminate state-sanctioned marriage and other legal conventions inciting fantasies of paternal authority and hereditary lineage.[4] Chapter 6 revises a proposal made by Martha Fineman and explores the custodial prerogatives of birth mothers, who may invite any other woman or man, including the sperm donor, to join them as parents. With the elimination of marriage, fathers, but not men parenting, also would come to an end. Evidence from multicountry studies discussed below suggests that marriage and other legal proxies for establishing paternity are harmful and even fatal. Instead of fixed kinship rules, chapters 5 and 6 suggest that states implement measures providing for children's developmental needs by guaranteeing health care and education, as well as by enforcing family contracts initiated by mothers. The goal of these two chapters is to decouple myths of genetics and the nuclear family from practical and principled models for allocating the burdens and privileges of childrearing.

THE DEBATE

Marriage law is being contested worldwide, though the specific rules at issue vary by country. In 2006, Spain angered the Catholic Church by joining Belgium, Canada, and the Netherlands in legalizing same-sex marriages;[5] citizens in the United States have voted in twenty-five states to outlaw recognition of same-sex marriage;[6] and Iran is contemplating new laws for temporary marriages.[7] Marriage practices are not idle controversies. In 2006, the FBI put the leader of a polygamy sect on its "Ten Most Wanted" list, meaning that the attorney general ranked thwarting multiple marriages as a roughly similar priority to catching serial murderers and Osama bin Laden.[8] Unlike immigration and inheritance, where the debates in scholarly and popular media track rather closely, the main terms of debate about marriage in the mainstream media among groups holding restrictive, inclusive, or abolitionary views differ quite substantially from their respective counterparts in the academy. Current examples of marriage's radical changes in the last fifty years (especially no-fault divorce, same-sex marriages, and serial monogamy) failing to produce the end of civilization so-called traditionalists had hyped previously might suggest precedents useful for dissuading those anxious about ending marriage entirely. But the stickiness of certain assumptions in the face of this and other evidence, discussed below, indicates why such a rational conversation is so difficult.

Popular Arguments

CONSERVATIVES

In the United States, popular defenses of the different-sexed marital unit as the basis of an intergenerational family tend to rely on one of three rationales. The first is a utilitarian, social welfare argument. The absence of marriage today leaves as the only default legal alternative families with single mothers, and some commentators assert this is responsible for poverty: "Children raised by both biological parents are significantly healthier, happier, and better adjusted emotionally than kids raised by single parents of either sex. They are less likely to live in poverty or engage in violent crime or sexual promiscuity."[9] Same-sex marriages are said to have these undesirable results as well.[10] Those who want to restrict marriage to two different-sex parents also apply their pragmatic criticisms to polygamy. An article describing the crackdown on polygamy leader Warren Jeffs states that the government is concerned about the "impact that the group's practices . . . are having on the most vulnerable within the sect, particularly children and women . . . according to some medical experts, intermarriage in polygamous relationships has led to severe birth defects in an unusually high number of children."[11] In short, anything other than two-parent, heterosexual marital families raises health and social welfare concerns.

A second defense of the different-sexed marital family is based on morality. In his speech supporting the 1996 Federal Defense of Marriage Act, restricting marriage to a man and a woman, Senator Robert Byrd said: "If same-sex marriage is accepted . . . [this] would be a catastrophe. Much of America has lost its moorings. Norms no longer exist. We have lost our way with a speed that is awesome. . . . Let us defend the oldest institution, the institution of marriage between male and female, as set forth in the Holy Bible. Else we, too, will be weighed in the balances and found wanting."[12] The current marriage laws in the United States come from the Bible, and changing these is a sign of moral corruption that the government should avoid at all costs.

Finally, defenders of the marital status quo appeal to "the obvious." Marriage by definition is between a man and a woman for purposes of procreating. Period. Dictionaries are enlisted. On their Web page "The Marriage Debate," the conservative Heritage Foundation cites Black's Law Dictionary: "Marriage . . . is the civil status of one man and one woman united in law for life, for the discharge to each other and the community of the duties legally incumbent on those who association is founded on the distinction of sex."[13] To change this would be akin to legislating that a "child" refers to someone between the ages of five and eighty—in other words, to abuse language in a way that offends common sense.

PROGRESSIVES

The social movements and organizations pressing to make marriage more inclusive have many of the same values held by those defending the status quo, but they differ on the facts. Both camps prize marriage, but same-sex couples and polygamists press the case for opening marriage to them as well. The pragmatists pushing for expanding marriage argue that children of same-sex couples do just as well as children of different-sex couples and that all children deserve the same benefits regardless of their parents' relationships with each other. According to the wealthiest same-sex rights organization, the Human Rights Campaign, based in Washington, D.C.: "One thing that both sides of the marriage issue can agree upon is that marriage strengthens families. Children are more secure if they are raised in homes with two loving parents who have a legal relationship with them and can share the responsibility of parenthood."[14] Moral and even religious arguments are also enlisted by those seeking legal recognition of their family relations. The Christian Web site biblicalpolygamy.com offers various exegetical examples from the Bible, under the Web site's logo "Polygamy Really Is Biblical!"

Those pressing to expand marriage share with their more parochial counterparts the belief that the past is a useful guide for present decisions on important policies. Progressives merely differ on the relevant precedents. The same sex–marriage advocates argue that the value of increasing liberty and equality is more of a core tradition in the United States than the specific exclusionary rules of marriage: "The general story of our country is movement toward inclusion and equality. The majority of Americans are fair. They realize that exclusionary concepts of marriage fly in the face of our national commitment to freedom as well as the personal commitment made by loving couples."[15] Marriage once was defined as between people of the same race. Laws prohibiting miscegenation were struck down on the grounds that marriage was a fundamental right, and, contends Evan Wolfson, director of Lambda Legal Defense, the most prominent gay- and lesbian-rights organization pressing change through the courts, this same right should be established for same-sex couples, as it was in 1968 for mixed-race unions.[16] Assisting Lambda's cause, and challenging the conservatives who use dictionaries to constrain marriage to its supposedly real meaning of one man with one woman, is the Canadian edition of the Oxford Dictionary, which has responded to the country's legal changes by changing its definition of marriage to the "religious or civil union of two people" and which also "recognizes that marital unions not validated by some governments are nevertheless marriages."[17]

Academic Debate
PROGRESSIVE SCHOLARSHIP

Themes from the public debate appear in some scholarly fora, but the terms of debate are very different. While major feminist and gay-rights organizations, as well as other progressive allies, support same-sex marriage, many established scholars have presented evidence leading them to propose abolishing marriage altogether. Drawing on research showing that marriage oppresses women, harms children and parents, unjustly distributes resources, privileges heterosexuality, excludes foreigners, or lacks imagination and is boring,[18] they have amassed a very persuasive case against any state, especially one holding itself as liberal, imposing one specific kinship practice and prohibiting others. Their evidence on the harms marriage causes has not been covered by the mainstream media. No talking heads, even on the PBS News Hour, debate whether marriage gives special rights to heterosexuality, as Lisa Duggan has argued;[19] enforces racist ideals and inequality, as Nancy Cott and Patricia Hill Collins have pointed out;[20] or goes too far in domesticating gay culture,[21] to name just three of the many rich, fascinating critiques informing the scholarly discussion of marriage.

Neither do television audiences in the United States hear from Foucauldians complaining that those in the abolitionist camp are giving too much weight to this legal status. Marriage law often does not overtly oppress straight women or, in some jurisdictions, even same-sex people, leading Heather Brook to write:

> If marriage is no longer necessarily grounded in the requirement that marriage is the (*de jure* or *de facto*) union of one man with one woman, it no longer seems to have very much to do with either counter-sexist or counter-patriarchal critiques. . . . Similarly, the counter-patriarchal feminist assertion that marriage is implicated in . . . sexual domestic violence against women must be squared with two factors: first, that women who deliberately choose not to marry but live instead in *de facto* relationships are also subject to such sexual violence; and second, that gay and lesbian relationships are by no means immune from similar problems.[22]

The power/knowledge nexus of marriage law in the past was uncertain, while marriage law now is ambiguous and might even empower same-sex couples in those places allowing same-sex marriage. The Foucauldian lesson is that law in general[23] and marriage law in particular can neither curtail freedom nor produce it, an implicit and explicit goal held by many challenging either marriage's exclusions or its very existence.[24] Thus, Foucauldians resist emphasizing this legal status and suggest analyzing nongovernmental openings for transgression. The work of these various scholars seeking to queer the family and nation by inviting a reconsideration of marriage receives little popular attention, although the group Beyond Marriage seeks to change this.[25]

CONSERVATIVE SCHOLARSHIP

The conservative critique of marriage in universities also has a different emphasis from that in popular venues. Large research universities tend to be unfriendly to analyses overtly drawing on religious dicta. Marriage conservatives in the academy think the law is an important means of crafting social behaviors but defend their position on the basis of evidence they claim to find in the field of sociobiology, an evolutionary framework explicitly rejected by their populist promarriage counterparts who, after their work to ban same-sex marriage, devote their remaining time to campaigns to ban evolutionary theory from high-school textbooks. Popular conservatives support the image of the family that sociobiologists claim to find in nature even as these same conservatives reject the method that academics use to sustain their family-policy preferences.

According to the revised 2000 edition of E. O. Wilson's famous and widely used textbook:

> The building block of nearly all human societies is the nuclear family. The populace of an American industrial city, no less than a band of hunter-gatherers in the Australian desert, is organized around this unit. In both cases the family moves between regional communities, maintaining complex ties with primary kin by means of visits (or telephone calls and letters) and the exchange of gifts. During the day the women and children remain in the residential area while the men forage for game or its symbolic equivalent in the form of barter and money. The males cooperate in bands to hunt or deal with neighboring groups. If not actually blood relations, they tend at least to act as "bands of brothers." Sexual bonds are carefully contracted in observance with tribal customs and intended to be permanent.[26]

Chapter 28, coming at the end of a long textbook climbing the evolutionary tree and explaining animal social behaviors at each branch, implies that the alleged frequency of the nuclear family in other species proves its utility for those other species as well as for humans.[27] The sociobiologists have faced many challenges in finding data to support assertions, alas, echoed elsewhere as though they are empirically accurate. These views will be discussed in more detail below, because on college campuses these sociobiological assertions, especially rooted in genetics, strongly influence students, who privilege information gleaned in their "hard" science courses over the "soft" lessons in the humanities and social sciences.

MARRIAGE INCONSISTENCIES

Before further evaluating the marriage debate, it will be useful to clarify the present laws that constitute its possibilities, exclusions, restraints, and divisions, in part because this information is not what the sociobiologists say it should be. Marriage law varies across countries and among states. There are numerous facets of marriage law affecting thousands of daily transactions, from controlling immigration to inheritance. The focus of this chapter is on the role that marriage and emerging supplementary policies plays in ascertaining paternity, and thus these are the specific rules studied for the six randomly selected countries.[28] In Afghanistan and other communities governed by Islamic law, paternity follows from marriage, unless there is a lack of cohabitation, in which case the child is considered fatherless: "a father may not acknowledge as his offspring the fruit of illicit relationships (walad al-zina); so, for example, the child of an unmarried free woman cannot be claimed by the man who begot him. Such a child would be traced back to his mother alone and would be called a child of fornication."[29] This is precisely the same policy that has prevailed under Christian regimes for millennia,[30] and it resembles those in many African countries today, though with an additional convention of bridewealth: "By paying bridewealth (termed "lobola" among the Xhosa) to a woman's natal family, a man obtains rights over her and her offspring, and undertakes certain corresponding duties. In this way the woman and children are incorporated into his patriline and the wife's guardian forfeits his claims to them, though he retains residual rights of guardianship for the rest of her life."[31] At the same time, some countries are allowing paternity designations outside marriage, including one in this sample, Honduras.[32] However, paternity here and elsewhere is for the purposes of assigning child support and does not provide reciprocal claims to custody, a topic discussed in further detail below.

The contingency of so many marriage rules, from the number of wives to age of consent to the degree of consanguinity in establishing incest restrictions, contrasts sharply with its consistent effects as a template producing two affinities that are impossible without marriage or some form of kinship rules, including assignments of paternity from acknowledgement or DNA tests. The practices and attachments that kinship rules under any regime enforce are not necessary for raising children[33] and, from the point of view of the state, serve only to further a membership regime that alleviates anxieties about birth, on the one hand, and death, on the other.

The rules described below characterize the intergenerational group with which the individual is connected in such a way that his[34] group's immortality enables fantasies of his own as well. And marriage creates fathers, people with legal rights to children based on at least one of two equally tenuous ties: legal or genetic. Marriage rules vary in their particulars, but some functions are constant; their universality establishes the institution's transhistorical and cross-cultural meanings:

1. Kinship rules are universal and require marriage.
2. Marriage requires a political society, be it a tribe, a clan, or a state, specifying what counts as a marriage, and is not possible in a "state of nature."[35]
3. Marriage instantiates men's ongoing ties to specific children, regardless of genetic relations or a mother's preference for the person with whom to raise her child. Absent kinship rules characterizing patrilineality, men would be unable to leave their initials on a family tree.[36]
4. Marriage allows political societies to maintain their integrity as distinct intergenerational communities.[37] Membership in a particular family typically provides individuals with membership in a larger tribe, nation, ethnicity, race, and so forth.[38]
5. The rules for marriage vary across political societies and time, as do many but not all of the meanings associated with the institution.

Marriage rules do not require wives' legal subordination to husbands or even that marriage must exclude gay and lesbian couples or polygamous ones. Marriage law in the United States does displace other models of ensuring security for citizens, but even this is not something marriage per se requires. European states allow for marriage and provide substantial welfare benefits based on one's status as a citizen, regardless of marital status.[39]

Marriage Produces the Law of the Father and the Nation
HOW FATHERS ARE MADE

Although marriage is used differently in different contexts, it inexorably brings about two dynamics of harm. Both follow from, as well as indicate, the origins of marriage rules in unsettled questions about life and death. Lacking clear answers to concerns about "Where am I from?" and "Can I make babies?" boys develop stories that compensate for feelings of powerlessness and inadequacy, an analysis I develop elsewhere and summarize in this section.[40] To answer these questions, boys and girls reduce the complexity of their existence to the problem of pregnancy and birth, an experience with which they are familiar.[41] Toddlers do not understand the complexity of intergenerational care. That humans are born at all, leaving aside our emergence from the abdomen of another human being, appears to them, and perhaps is, truly magical and incomprehensible. Boys develop pregnancy fantasies and have strong reactions when they are told that they cannot have children but must be satisfied with their roles as husbands and fathers. Girls never experience this early insult. As a result, boys and men compensate for their wounded egos—they fantasize they must endure a permanent condition of physical inferiority—by developing compensatory narratives and legal rituals. The one with the most overriding influence and that causes the most harm is marriage.

That pregnant women must be secured by men in matrimony, from the Latin *matrix*, womb, institutionalizes the paranoia of a masculinity anxious about men's inability to give birth and therefore intent on controlling those who do give birth. Experiencing a role in reproduction sustains their fantasies of power over birth as well as death, since the womb's possibility of giving life suggests its power to prevent life as well. The fact of the infant's emergence from the womb entails the possibility of not emerging, a possible nonexistence where the womb also is seen as a place of engulfment and suffocation, a tomb.[42] In sum, to grapple with the reality that boys cannot give birth, they develop compensatory fantasies about the penis's power and political practices that assume the same ontological status as maternity: the law of the father.

The phrase "the law of the father" often resonates as a vague term of art used by psychoanalytic theorists drawing on Sigmund Freud's or Jacques Lacan's views about the inherent importance of the penis in establishing relations of authority in the family and then in political spheres as well. Feminist and queer theorists use this phrase in similar contexts but challenge the anatomically fixed, sexed authority of the paternal penis by emphasizing authority's plasticity occasioned by the supposedly more metaphorical "phallus."[43] The critique of the law of the father in this chapter rejects both Freudian and queer theories stipulating the penis/phallus as powerful. The only reason men need kinship rules and to elevate genetic information to mythic status is because the penis itself is lacking in its ability to physically give them children. Men need laws for this, either on the books in modern states or as kinship rules in preliterate societies, laws giving men the paternal power that their penises, indicating their lack of uteruses, deny them.

The law of the father does not come about because of anything inherently powerful in men, but the opposite. Fathers are like the Wizard in L. Frank Baum's *The Wizard of Oz* (1900).[44] As the motto of the father's custody rights Web site Fathers-4-Justice.org states, "Every father is a superhero to his children." Precisely because paternal authority is premised on fantasy and illusion—real superheroes are childless and do not exist outside fiction—those inhabiting these roles can do so only anxiously. George Gilder, advocating a return to a more patriarchal society in the face of the feminist social movement in the 1970s, admits this: "The male sexual repertory . . . is very limited. Men have only one sex organ and one sex act: erection and ejaculation. Everything else is guided by culture and imagination. Other male roles—other styles of masculine identity—must be learned or created. In large part, they are a cultural invention, necessary to civilized life but ultimately fragile."[45] The result Gilder seeks is reinforcement of masculinity in a variety of ways, especially marriage law.[46] But his own formulation would suggest at best that men harmlessly pretend to have the power they secretly believe mothers have ("this gives the man a position in wedlock to some extent commensurate with the woman's"),[47] while at worst they abuse the power of their invented roles—compensating to hide their equally fantasized weakness and fragility.

Once the law of the father has been established, then individual men do not personally create positions of paternal authority but fall into them, so to speak, as did Oscar Zoraster, whose balloon labeled "OZ" happened to crash in a place with the same name as his initials.[48] The inhabitants of Oz, misunderstanding the coincidence, ascribed to Oscar Zoraster, O. Z., supernatural powers on the basis of the signifier alone. In the chapter "The Discovery of Oz, the Terrible," after Toto knocks down the curtain, Oz explains, "I found myself in the midst of a strange people, who, seeing me come from the clouds, thought I was a Great Wizard. Of course I let them think so, because they were afraid of me, and promised to do anything I wished them to."[49] Oz assumed the role with more and less confidence, fearful and arrogant: nervous that his humanity, his mortality, would be noticed but also hopeful that he could preserve the reverence afforded him by way of his supposedly magic feats.

Just as Oz's wizardry was established by popular proclamation and without careful consideration of its criteria—there is no storyline with a fussy inhabitant of Oz asking, "why do we think that having letters on a balloon that match our city's name means the person flying this is special?"—the crafting of kinship laws, earlier and today, also occurs absent open, rational discussion. When such conversations do emerge, they usually exclude mention of men's reproductive humiliation, Gilder's revealing manifesto notwithstanding. The result is that fathers inhabit roles that demand dishonesty. The requisite duplicity is not willful but habitual, and it influences other family dynamics.

Like the wizard, fathers also compensate for their own illegitimate claims to authority by creating fear out of threats and violence. Gilder writes:

Throughout the literature on feminism . . . there runs a puzzled complaint. "Why can't men be men and just relax?" The reason is that, unlike femininity, relaxed masculinity is at bottom empty, a limp nullity. While the female body is full of internal potentiality, the man is internally barren (from the old French *bar*, meaning man). Manhood at the most basic level can be validated and expressed only in action.[50]

Toward the end of the book, Gilder actually references the "compensatory aggressiveness of the male,"[51] not unlike the frightening magic tricks Oz performed to maintain his authority. Such conditions make it very difficult for those who are not fathers to even look for a curtain. The novel relies on the luck of Dorothy and her friends to explain why they and no one else noticed Oscar. People running from devilish monkeys, witches, and poppy fields often lack the wherewithal to contemplate the bigger picture and how we—those fleeing our fears—may be creating them. Pointing out that the current rules establishing paternity result in scenarios of anxious and compensatory authority does not mean that sexed mortals are doomed by anatomy. Adult men can establish healthy, legitimate, caregiving relations with children, but only as parents, discussed below, and not fathers.

HOW NATIONS ARE MADE

A second reason to abolish marriage is that marriage creates the iconic family tree that results in unfair and irrational inheritance practices (discussed in chapters 3 and 4) and interpellates people into their intergenerational affinities of nationality, ethnicity, race, caste, and clan—those groups enlisting commitments to kill and die (discussed in chapters 1 and 2). It may appear that the fact of birth alone generates these affiliations, but this is not the case. First, these groups do not depend on vagaries of self-assertions of membership or individual recruitment but reproduce through state documents, all referencing a person's recorded ancestry. Absent marriage records, the story of origins would be as obviously haphazard, subject to fakery, invention, and obfuscation as critics of nativism assert occurs at present.[52] The difference is that these would be experienced as the legal conventions they are and not as innate. Marriage laws presently create believable fictions of purity or mixture,[53] implying clearly designated lineages that can be accumulated and accounted for, a false statement of our originally and eternally uncertain, layered, hybrid origins that recurs at any given point in history. From Moses's Egyptian origins, pointed out by Freud, to Bertolt Brecht's Mother Courage, who says that the patchwork ancestry of her sons makes it difficult to know which army they might support, our nationalities are entirely contrived by political rules, especially marriage. The unexamined conventions of marital designations and family trees are so successful that people see only one or perhaps a hybrid of a few generations, not the actual confusions marriage law seems to eliminate. This narrative also misleads, by suggesting earlier groups are themselves homogenous. Even if Freud is correct about Moses's ancestry, there are no pure Egyptians from whom Moses and the Levites emerged, only a collection of kinship groups that became more permanent because of their written, especially legal, inscriptions over time.[54]

A tribe and a nation-state both provide the rules for what counts as a legitimate family. Without a political society in the form of a preliterate society or a bureaucratic state, there are no rules for marriage and thus just copulating individuals and their randomly raised progeny, not families. Such groups not only determine who will be a member during their lifetimes but also imply that all their members may share a future beyond the grave. Membership in an intergenerational group, because it presumably will never die, reassures some that they too will live on indefinitely. In the meantime, as we have seen, nations expect us to kill and die for that vision, and many do.

At this point, it should be clear that marriage is a bad idea because it harms us through the invocation of the father and the nation. But a case might be made that although the national and other intergenerational myths that marriage law generates have harmful consequences, these are offset by the many practical benefits marriage provides in our daily lives, as referenced by many social scientists and the popular press. There are many assertions about the utility of the institution that appear to be empirical, but if we look at the sociology of the institution today, as well as its historical harms, a different picture emerges. Usually, scientists are committed to research agendas with hypotheses that can be falsified. But sociobiologists attempting to shore up the patriarchal family reject this method:[55] patriarchal families are used as evidence on their being selected for through evolution, and nonpatriarchal families are used as evidence that people are deviating from natural selection.[56]

Marriage: Facts and Myths
SOCIOBIOLOGY'S FAILED PREDICTIONS
In the United States, the country Wilson claims to be characterizing, about half of those over fifteen are unmarried, and among those married, only 21 percent conform with Wilson's statement of what is normal: a household with

a sole male wage earner.[57] Overall, only 10 percent of U.S. adults fit his definition of normal. And, almost half the children in the United States will not be raised by two parents who are genetically related to them.[58] The very scenario sociobiologists claim will not occur—because genetic fathers desire to stay with their own children to protect their gene pool and because individuals supposedly have little interest in supporting nongenetically related progeny—has been a fact of life here and worldwide for quite some time.[59] Wilson has not overlooked a small exception to his model; he has misrepresented the main object of his analysis. Although one may expect such an empirical error from a casual social commentator, for an esteemed natural scientist to invent such "facts" in the very field of his expertise speaks volumes to the role ideology plays in mainstream analyses of marriage and family. It also highlights the urgent need for analyses and policies that emerge from how we live and not how Wilson would like us to live.[60]

In keeping with this ideology of the family, Wilson and other sociobiologists assume the wage-earning father and his brood a scene of domestic harmony. For the past two decades, forerunners of the socioevolutionary method, Martin Daly and Margo Wilson, have urged readers to accept "(i) that genetic relationship is associated with the mitigation of conflict and violence in people, as in other creatures; and (ii) that evolutionary models predict and explain patterns of differential risk of family violence."[61] Their results have been disputed on methodological grounds and for their lack of generalizability. Methodologically, the Daly and Wilson studies are flawed because they rely on officially reported, aggregated household data that they themselves do not authenticate. Richard Gelles and John Harrop, who found the same risk of child abuse by stepparents as genetic parents in a large, randomized study where the actual child-adult relationships and outcomes were known, hypothesize that the different results might be explained by the fallibility of homicide reporting data: "child homicides that would increase the likelihood that cases from intact middle and upper class homes would be labeled accidents and cases in single-parent, stepparent, and/or poor homes would be labeled homicide."[62] This hypothesis is borne out in three other studies.[63]

In Sweden, the main risk factor for childhood homicides was living with just one parent: "Children with one stepparent and one genetic parent do not run a greater risk [of homicide] when compared with children living with two genetic parents."[64] And a study in Finland found that of the filicides between 1975 and 1994, 62 percent were committed by the genetic mother, 33 percent by the genetic father, and 4 percent by a stepfather, although more than 4 percent of children lived with stepfathers.[65] Wilson and Daly run into trouble not only in the literature on human families but also in the literature on nonhuman reproduction. For instance, a study coauthored by Daly acknowledges that quite frequently birds will be raised by adult birds who are not genetically related, including species that can distinguish its own from other progeny.[66]

Not only do nongenetic families prove stable and healthy environments, but genetic ones can be treacherous. When a father in England stabs his fourteen-year-old daughter to death for dating a non-Muslim, then slashes his own throat and jumps out a window, it is hard to fathom how this is preserving anyone's gene pool.[67] In fact, such paternal rage against a daughter is directed at the weakest family member, not an outside aggressor, thereby complicating the simplistic, one-dimensional dynamics that evolutionary psychology ascribes to insiders and outsiders.

True, the proportion of all genetic parents killing their children is fairly small, but the percentage of parents attacking children is not, and the proportion of all violent deaths among children, especially infants, at the hands of their parents is high and in some places, including the United States, climbing.[68] "Although the public may believe that biological parents are less likely to kill their own offspring," the authors of a medical article on child-abuse mortality observe that "we found they accounted for 63 percent of the perpetrators of fatal child abuse" and they suggest that biological parents should be "especially targeted in prevention efforts."[69] This advice is at odds with hypotheses about how the family naturally selects for its genetic longevity. Well-recognized doctrines of group honor that condone killing one's children if they violate a certain code go unmentioned in Wilson's description of modern hunter-fathers supporting their families to protect their genetic investments.

Wilson's patriarchal-breadwinner model of the family is also inaccurate as empirical description. When such families exist, they tend to be those with the most violence. A metastudy of ninety societies concluded that "wife beating occurs more often in societies in which men have economic and decision-making power in the household [and] where women do not have easy access to divorce."[70] Interestingly, whereas Wilson's genetic account would predict that men would not harm pregnant wives, as that would endanger their progeny, the data show that intimate-partner violence is responsible for a great deal of maternal mortality: "A recent study among four hundred villages and seven hospitals in Pune, India, found that 16 percent of all deaths during pregnancy were the result of partner violence.... Being killed by a partner has also been identified as an important cause of maternal deaths in Bangladesh and in the United States."[71]

Partner abuse results in a multitude of harms, not just broken bones and bruises. The World Health Organization has linked "functional disorders of irritable bowel syndrome, fibromyalgia, gastrointestinal disorders, and chronic pain syndromes . . . with a history of physical or sexual abuse."[72] As one might infer, there is also evidence that such abuse leads to depression, phobias, and a "heightened risk for suicide and suicide attempts."[73]

According to international studies, marriage, far from inoculating women against male violence, actually puts women at increased risk of abuse: "In many cultures women, as well as men, regard marriage as entailing the obligation on women to be sexually available without limit,"[74] meaning that far from protecting them from male sexual advances, marriage in some contexts, including the United States, deprives women of the prerogative of refusal available women who are unmarried.[75] In some societies, the "cultural 'solution' to rape is that the woman should marry the rapist," and some countries even have laws that "allow a man who commits rape to be excused of his crime if he marries the victim,"[76] meaning that marriage does not protect women from rapists but gives rapists legal sanction. Many societies put forth double standards, as when "extramarital sex is punishable by law when practiced by wives, but it is not punishable when practiced by husbands."[77]

Self-proclaimed purists in social evolution might contend that the pattern of marriage protecting males' sexual access to women, while unfortunately hurting women, at least may increase the number of children born to them.[78] But not only does domestic violence prove harmful for mothers, it is also lethal for fathers' genetically related progeny as well. A study in León, Nicaragua, found that "children of women who were physically and sexually abused by a partner were six times more likely to die before the age of five than children of women who had not been abused. Partner abuse accounted for as much as one-third of deaths among children in this region."[79] These data strongly suggest that male violence is actually being directed against the very population that social-evolutionary theory would predict would be safest from abuse: the physical and emotional caretakers of a genetic father's children.[80]

In Turkey, 62 percent of mothers, almost all of whom were married, reported beating their children.[81] The scholars reporting this believe that this is a consequence of patriarchal families.[82] "Authoritarian parental styles . . . characteristic of patriarchal societies commonly prescribe aggression as both a preventive and a corrective measure."[83] If the analysis is correct, and married women learn to use violence from their husbands, then these children would be safer in single-parent homes than in married households. The social institution of the married family, and especially the family Wilson idealizes, does not seem to be protecting wives and mothers against violence but contributing to it.

Bearing out the individual-level ethnographic data, a comparison among countries indicates that those with higher rates of illegitimacy and divorce, in other words, countries in which marriage is not obligating sexual partners to lifelong monogamy, are those where child abuse is lowest.[84] Once more, this is precisely the opposite of patterns that a sociobiological model would lead one to predict. In the United States, there has been a significant decline in the levels of intimate-partner violence, from ten in every thousand women in 1993 to five in every thousand women in 2001. Still, intimate-partner violence, almost all of which is men harming women, is responsible for 20 percent of all crimes reported against women in the United States and up to 60 percent in other countries.[85] At minimum, present data suggest that a high prevalence of illegitimacy and divorce accommodates low rates of child abuse. And there is no evidence that marriage or being reared in a household where the child is genetically related to both parents prevents violence against children.

PROMINENT FAMILIES IN HISTORY: MYTHS AND FACTS
The discussion above indicates ways that the family today, across cultures, is not a space of guaranteed safety. Still, questions might be posed about premodern families. Misnamed "traditionalists" believe that the maladies depicted above result from deviations from the Wilsonian norm, bringing on a social disease. Women's rights, the "gay agenda," and even, ironically, teaching evolutionary theory are blamed for the family's decline. Thus it is important to reach further back in time to see whether other more beneficent family structures prevailed, from which present ones mistakenly deviated. Although common child-rearing practices merit attention, this section focuses on the most powerful and therefore most famous families in the world, because they are, or should be, familiar and there is no a priori reason to expect they would be less nurturing than poor families, and indeed there is good reason to think the opposite.

The history of elite families suggests that they too are not conducive to tranquility, nurturance, or even the survival of paternal genes. Against the frequent claim that the family is the foundation of the kingdoms that gave rise to our present countries and thus the original and natural basis of all order, consider the thousand-plus years of the Eastern and Western Roman Empires, where being a member of the ruling family was to increase by some an exponential amount one's risk of violent death at the hands of another member of one's own family. The following is a distillation of information with which Wilson, Daly, and other sociobiologists were surely familiar yet ignore. The iconography of famous families is not overflowing with images of sentimental affection but is memorable for fathers such as King Lear and sons such as Oedipus and historical husbands such as Henry VIII and wives such as Loretta Bobbitt, hardly the happy households Wilson's evolutionary theory depicts. His failure to acknowledge these facts is consistent with a quasi-psychotic form of denial.

Consider perhaps the most important historical figure in the rise of Christianity, second only to Jesus, and the obliteration of his family drama from the collective memory. Freud's theory of the Oedipal complex—a depiction of the family as riven by intergenerational sexual competition and violence—often strikes people as ludicrous, and, indeed, it is based on a Greek drama, not political history. But Freud did not invent the biographical details of the son of his father's stepdaughter,[86] who ordered his second wife and the eldest son of his first wife executed because they were lovers.[87] The man who did this was Emperor Constantine, best known for establishing Christianity as the official religion of the Roman Empire. A somewhat dry and decidedly unpsychoanalytic history of Byzantium observes that just after Constantine had his son and wife executed, Constantine's mother/stepsister Helena "probably as a sort of family penance . . . left on a pilgrimage to the Holy Land to distribute alms and to build churches on the sites of Christ's birth and ascension,"[88] and Constantine issued the first edict against infanticide.[89] Thus the cult of the son replaced the earlier pagan gods and their discord, becoming for the first time official state doctrine.

Freud does not discuss these details of the founding of Christian civilization, but what happened is uncannily close to what Freud intended as allegory—a rivalrous son, a vengeful father—but the plot takes a slightly different twist. In fourth-century Rome, it is not the son feeling guilty about killing his father and establishing an almighty Father, as is the case in Freud's description of Oedipus as well as the primal horde establishing God. Constantine the father survives, but guilt leads him and his mother to reject thousands of years of Roman gods and instead establish an empire committed to the perpetual veneration of the Son.[90]

Constantine's family drama enacts a pattern of betrayal and death within royal families that threatened and ruined many others until the empire's demise. This example, and there are numerous others in royal families throughout Asia, Africa, and Europe, not to mention the Hebrew Bible,[91] contradicts two fundamental tenets of sociobiologists: first, the incest taboo, and second, the selective imperatives to protect one's genes. That these examples of mayhem come from high-status groups means that they should be taken especially seriously. From an evolutionary perspective, those in a group whose political status isolates it from others, who are dependent on one person (the emperor), and who have much at stake (inheriting a kingdom) have special incentives and abilities to follow kinship and religious edicts so as to guarantee an orderly succession of authority. Yet even here the family comes up short. When brothers vying for monarchical control kill each other, virtually the same genes are destroyed.[92] In the case of Constantine, not only did he kill one son, but his own death occasioned further family fighting, resulting in the "massacre of Constantius I's [Constantine's father] descendants and adherents."[93] Consistent with old-fashioned individual selfishness, this scenario falsifies the "selfish gene" model of selection. Constantine's place in founding "Western civilization" should have meant more publicity for his own scandalous family relations. If children grew up knowing the actual events in the family lives of their icons, perhaps societies would come to question their faith in the rules producing these travails.

The above statistics and stories of family violence and misery are very incomplete portraits of family life. We all know that families can also be places of tremendous warmth and intimacy, but the ideological strength of scenes such as those in the peaceful animal families in the dioramas at the American Museum of Natural History[94] far surpasses their prevalence in our households and histories. Objectively surveying the promise held forth by the so-called traditional family, it is impossible to see how anyone could meet the burden of proving the extravagant claims offered on behalf of its contributions to the happiness and well-being of its members. Likewise, widespread ignorance of the nuclear family's frequent and dramatic failings is confounding. If the different-sexed genetic unit in the United States cannot survive more than 50 percent of the time even when it is supposedly the cornerstone of this society, instituted by fiat in federal and state laws and reinforced in a range of important cultural activities from religion to mass entertainment, then imagine how such an allegedly natural practice might fare without these incentives.

It is possible that the paternal prerogatives from marriage may fail tests of utilitarian calculations and evolutionary predictions but nonetheless be sound public policy. Our laws follow from background assumptions of norms, especially rights, based on longstanding commitments to beliefs in justice and fairness, even when they violate recommendations that a utilitarian or natural scientist might make. A rights-based doctrine of paternity might point out that the legal status of "husband" protects the rights to children that men earn by virtue of paternal DNA used in human reproduction. Those who convey genes to eggs through their sperm have insisted that this act yields a *de facto* paternity that should be recognized *de jure*.

That judges and legislators might award custody based only on a sex act—an activity that in itself is more likely to be considered "dirty" or taboo than sacred in puritanical countries, including the United States—indicates a disposition privileging genetics over all other human connections.[95] Moreover, technical changes allowing for accurate paternity testing seem to have given new legitimacy to the father's rights movement,[96] and this is bioscientific knowledge that is demanding legal recognition.[97] Courts are not moving en masse from the standard "best interest of the child" criterion—resulting almost always in maternal custody—but in popular discourse, and sometimes in law and in courtrooms, genetic ties may be decisive. Custody claims based only on paternal DNA are rarely successful, but sometimes they prevail,[98] and courts regularly impose child-support payments on this basis.[99] If the "fathers' rights movement" successfully institutionalizes its goal of presumptive custody rights based on DNA,[100] this will not only affirm odd practices and norms that harm children, but the new faith in genes will reinforce faith in the myth of blood ancestors in whose name one should kill and die.

A major assumption underlying the notion that genetic contributions should yield custody rights is that a man's sperm contains something that is uniquely his and that by virtue of contributing this to create an embryo he deserves recognition and rights we normally call paternity. "'You just can't lie to kids,' said Lowell Jaks, president of the Internet-based Alliance for Non-Custodial Parents Rights. 'The truth is that this or that man is or is not his or her biological father, period. It is a basic part of your identity.'"[101] The same supposedly holds for the woman who contributes DNA from her ova, resulting in a "surrogate" mother, suggesting that the real mother is the one with the eggs. However, details of genetic transmission support neither of these claims.

Insistence on parental status based only on one's genetic contribution not only contravenes much of the current admittedly ad hoc and contradictory family law; it also is illogical.

The genetic contributions from a particular inseminated egg contribute little to the biological distinctiveness of progeny beyond species specificity.[102] Heritable characteristics importantly unique to each of us flow from a much deeper gene pool than that of paternal sperm and eggs. Our DNA comes from thousands of individuals going far back in time, with genes subject to mutations at every stage, even during pregnancy, based on the uterine environment.[103] If DNA contributions form the basis for parental custody rights, then earlier ancestors also have legitimate claims as well.

To be true to the logic of genetic prerogatives, one would need to trace out various recombinations and decide which ones contributed most to the characteristics of a particular child. If, because of the hazards of gene expression, the most important changes occurred in mutations and recombinations of a paternal grandmother, should she be the father? Relatedly, since an embryo's genetic expression is partly a result of the uterine environment, would the mother's consumption of pickles and the resulting acid environment mean that the woman who made the pickle also should have parental rights? The cucumber farmer?

Indeed, the environment codes individuals in ways that are at least as constitutive of variations as parental genes. All sorts of symbols, not just those of DNA, materially determine behaviors and personalities. Any armchair ethnologist can observe that differences among us depend more on language, art, forms of technologies, and political institutions than on variations in our DNA.[104] A child brought up in Athens in 500 b.c. would be far more different from a direct genetic descendant in 2007 than she would be from her Persian or Egyptian counterpart living in the same epoch, and all of them would be scored as morons on a modern IQ test. If the contributions of one person's DNA are indeterminate or do not shape progeny more than many other influences, then custody claims based on genetic similarity are invalid. Moreover, even if paternal DNA per se did contribute to the child's individuality, is this a good reason to grant custody rights?

The belief that passing on identity-shaping information gives rise to legal rights and responsibilities over the information recipient (a child) requires analysis. Caregivers may teach a child to speak, read, and otherwise endow her with a language, shaped of course by that person's idiosyncratic inflections and word choices, the books selected, and so forth. Is this permanent and indelible imprinting of the child's cognitive abilities less constitutive of her individuality than paternal DNA? Ninety-nine percent of human DNA is identical; the variation within competency in native languages is much higher. And the actual language spoken shapes one's development and personality— a native Chinese speaker, regardless of any other biological characteristics, will experience the world somewhat differently than a native English speaker.[105] Does it follow that the person who passes on language skills should have custody rights? If giving a special code to someone that makes possible their existence as a unique human being is not sufficient for awarding the language donor custody rights, then we need to look further for why genetics per se is presumed to authorize paternal custody rights (and obligations) based only on DNA.[106]

Another possibility might be that conveying DNA is more than passing on information but involves time and thought. Lockean theory about the state of nature stipulates that property rights flow from labor;[107] perhaps intercourse could be envisioned as a form of labor that produces rights to children. But as we saw in chapter 2, Locke dismisses male ejaculation as anything more than a passing pleasure.[108] On Locke's analysis, awarding custody rights for conveying DNA would be like bestowing a Pulitzer Prize for delivering the newspaper.[109]

This also appears to be the view taken by U.S. courts in contexts where researchers' rights to biological organisms produced from DNA are at stake. In a case where a man who had his spleen cells used for cancer research sued for a share of the patent rights, the California Supreme Court wrote: "The subject matter of the Regents' patent—the patented cell line and the products derived from it—cannot be Moore's property.... Federal law permits the patenting of organisms that represent the product of 'human ingenuity,' but not naturally occurring organisms.... It is this *inventive effort* that patent law rewards, not the discovery of naturally occurring raw materials."[110] If the Supreme Court denies a share in patent rights to the patient whose spleen cells were used to cultivate the cancer samples manufactured and sold to tens of thousands of research laboratories on the grounds that the patient contributed no intellectual work in proliferating the cells, then it seems unlikely that supplying genetic matter through sexual intercourse would meet the court's threshold criterion of "human ingenuity." If any man is anxious about the results of his ejaculate being realized in the creation of another person, that man is at liberty to use contraception or to restrain from having heterosexual intercourse, just as the court ruled that the spleen patient was at liberty not to have his operation by a surgeon who might make use of cancerous DNA cells.[111]

Some might object to the analogy. A patient's spleen cells are not people and thus lack the need for legal recognition of their origin. It is unfair for children, this argument might go, to be deprived of a relation to the person who transmitted half of their DNA. However, children's biological needs do not seem to require a relation to genetic parents. To survive, children need nutrition, shelter, and emotional intimacy, none of which require a narrative or legal arrangements distinguishing genetic parents from any others. That any specific adult performs these tasks is not a consequence of genes unique to that individual but, legally or informally, occurs when one or more adults take care of, or, we could say, adopt, a helpless creature who has no say in the matter. For the dependent infant, the existence of a few mutations in DNA that she may or may not share with her caregiver is completely irrelevant.

In sum, past arrangements for intergenerational care have relied on narratives that assuage anxieties about death and feelings of powerlessness brought on by the inability to give birth. Men's specific psychic histories lead to a special investment in those institutions that produce children with "their" lineage. Ensuring these arrangements, as Gilder observes, is compensatory. The laws created for this purpose not only fail the children in whose name they are ostensibly being promoted, but the larger social and narrative conditions perpetuated by state-sanctioned kinship rules lead to divisions and hostilities that cause great damage. Law's interventions to sustain bodies whose biology means different levels of dependence over one's lifetime have been hypocritical. Previous experiments with marriage have failed; perhaps new policies for managing care over generations deserve consideration.

CHAPTER SIX
ABOLISHING MARRIAGE

FEMINIST INTERVENTIONS

In recognition of how kinship rules have failed to promote the flourishing of family members and instead tended toward their harm and even death, feminists have authored a range of proposals for alternative laws and practices.[1] Their visions for the most part emerge from a somewhat different critique of the heterosexual marital family than that pursued here. But they have offered alternatives that focus on the pragmatic challenges of childrearing and to this end have developed some fascinating and useful ideas.

Perhaps the boldest reconceptualization of the family was undertaken by Shulamith Firestone, proposing the development of technologies to liberate women from childbearing as a prerequisite to sex equality (similar to Marx's stage of full industrialization prerequisite to communism): "Pregnancy is barbaric, the temporary deformation of the body of the individual for the sake of the species."[2] Firestone envisioned new means of reproduction, for example technologies for fetus incubators, so that women would be spared the "tyranny of reproduction."[3] Catharine MacKinnon, also invoking a Marxist framework, suggested the state pay women for their reproductive work, including child-rearing.[4] Meanwhile, those writing from psychoanalytic backgrounds allowed for maternal pregnancy but reconceived the distribution of early childhood care. Rather than women being paid, Dorothy Dinnerstein, Nancy Chodorow, and Jessica Benjamin proposed that fathers shoulder child-care responsibilities that at least equal those of mothers.[5]

Influenced by these earlier writers, and seeking a legal arrangement that would recognize the specificity of the mother-child tie without limiting this to mothers, legal theorist Martha Fineman's *Neutered Mother* (1995) suggested eliminating marriage as a state-sanctioned contract and proposed legal mother-child dyads instead, thus tailoring kinship law to the specific goal of raising healthy children and away from the vague purposes and effects of current marriage law. The mother-child dyad, not the marital couple, would be the unit understood as the "caregiving family...entitled to special preferred treatment by the state."[6] Rather than legislate sexual relations, the state should intervene only in the relations between the mother, who does not have to be a woman, and the dependent child:

> Single mothers and their children and indeed all "extended" families transcending generations would not be "deviant" and forgotten or chastised forms that they are considered to be today because they do not include a male head of household. Family and sexuality would not be confluent; rather, the mother-child formation would be the "natural" or core family unity—it would be the base entity around which social policy and legal rules are fashioned.[7]

In many European countries this already is the case, where state support goes directly to mothers and children regardless of marital status, but welfare policy in the United States has been moving in a different direction.[8]

Fineman states that anyone, men included, could in her scheme apply for consideration as a child's mother, but nonetheless critics have faulted her for this terminology's putative exclusionary meanings. Fineman's mother-child unit challenges analyses that treat paternity and maternity as equivalent. Her work is especially useful because grounding a jurisprudence of parental custody on attributes specific to the mother invites attention to the unique subject position of pregnancy, the specific activity for which current marriage rules are such devastating symptoms. This is not a point stressed by Fineman; indeed, she deflects any inferences from anatomy to custodial responsibility. However, the difference between a nine-month pregnancy and the casual transmission of DNA from sperm, and the difference between pregnancy and any other care or support, warrants a conceptual acknowledgement that Fineman, Fineman's critics, and many feminist theorists fail to provide. This chapter suggests that the subject position of the pregnant mother is the one with the *de facto* status of "real parent" and that this provides the only rational basis of *de jure* custody rights for that child, though these may be alienated.

PREGNANCY *SUI GENERIS*

Birth mothers uniquely devote intensive, constant, long-term labor to reproduction that neither fathers nor anyone else provides, a point suggested in the discussion in chapter 4 of work by John Locke. If Locke is right—that sperm itself does not give men any rights to the fetus—and if custody decisions must be made at birth, then the only person who has earned the prerogative to initiate these is the pregnant mother. It is precisely in reaction to this possibility, and before that to men's uncertainty of any role in reproduction, that men initiated marriage.[9] Thousands of years after the first marriage, Firestone's disembodied technologies for reproduction have not come to market, and uterine pregnancies remain the only means for humans to reproduce. Nonetheless, despite numerous changes in laws displacing antiquated views of women's limits and capacities, the law of the father, which privileges either legal or genetic parents, remains hegemonic, and the subject position of the pregnant mother remains in the legal shadows. The only way to release men, women, and children from the roles scripted to establish and maintain the father is to expose the man hiding behind the legal curtain of fatherhood, allowing him the mortal prerogatives of parenthood and not the unrealistic authority and knowledge unique to the father. And the only way this is possible is by erasing the equivalences that law establishes between those who are pregnant and anyone else.

Those opposed to the potentially restrictive sex-role implications that seem to follow a line of reasoning emphasizing the specificity of pregnancy might respond that although only birth mothers are pregnant, nothing about this act precludes establishing pregnancy's equivalences with other activities, say, contributing time or money in childraising.[10] But are these apt comparisons? Is it sensible to consider pregnancy as just one more form of nurturance, one that is equivalent to, for instance, driving a child to soccer practice, saving money for her college education, or even waking up late every night to bring a bottle? The felicity of such analogies between pregnancy and subsequent support for children depends on whether we agree that the physical risks, excruciating pain, and uninterrupted dedication to the task of pregnancy can be equated with the cumulative labors invested in other life-sustaining enterprises.

Analogizing pregnancy with other support, especially financial support, confronts some stumbling blocks. First, the equivalence evokes the idea of blood money. If we take offense at flesh as collateral, then we might wonder at the Lockean schema whereby fathers provide education and inheritances to pay off the debts sons owe their mothers. In this scenario, a woman's flesh and blood—her contribution to the fetus—is exchanged for the financial consideration that adult males pay to compensate for their own births.[11] Pregnancy requires one's entire body be at the beck and call of another human twenty-four hours a day for several months. Pregnancy also entails substantial risks of permanent injury, long-term illness, and even death, not to mention the often excruciating pain of labor. Cumulatively, severe hemorrhaging (10.5 percent), sepsis (4.4 percent), eclampsia (3.2 percent) and obstructed labor (4.6 percent) mean that 22.7 percent of all pregnancies impose serious health burdens on the mother.[12] Pregnancy also is responsible for heightened long-term risks of other serious illnesses, including thrombosis, diabetes, and liver dysfunction. Worldwide, in 2000 about 529,000 women died due to their pregnancies, at a rate of four hundred for every 100,000 live births, meaning a total lifetime risk of pregnancy-induced mortality of one in seventy-four.[13]

Along these lines, some commentators have pointed to the risk of pregnancy and the judiciary's reluctance to enforce "Good Samaritan" laws as an argument for abortion rights.[14] But analogies to hypothetical unconstitutional Good Samaritan laws for organ donors—suggesting that criminalizing abortion would be like requiring kidney transplants of unwilling donors—do not hold, either. Not only would obligatory self-sacrifice be held unconstitutional, but governments discourage doctors from even allowing such exchanges: "It shall be unlawful for any person to knowingly acquire, receive, or otherwise transfer any human organ for valuable consideration for use in human transplantation if the transfer affects interstate commerce."[15] The point of the analogy is not that sexed labor should always be prohibited, one feminist critique of prostitution,[16] but that the very particular harms and risks expected of pregnant women are so enormous that, absent the imperative for species reproduction, liberal societies would be discouraging pregnancy altogether.

The purpose of this discussion is not to discourage women from becoming pregnant but to ensure that its immense psychic importance and physical burdens are openly acknowledged and not repressed. Using present norms and laws as guidelines for our assessments of legitimate exchanges, it is simply not possible to successfully effect the compensation for which the marital subject positions of "husbands" and "fathers" strive. The present tacit legal recognition of pregnancy as *sui generis*—USC 42 section 273 (b) prohibiting compensation for organ donation has never been used to prosecute women marrying and bearing children in anticipation of their own financial security—merits explicit institutionalization.[17]

Eliminating the Father by Eliminating the Law of the Father
Confining "mother" to the person who gives birth, not the egg donor when she is not pregnant,[18] gives due weight to the distinctive, incommensurable work and risk that pregnancy entails. Curtailing custodial rights[19] and obligations[20] claimed through parental genomes affects two classes of people regarded as parents today: women whose eggs are carried by another woman would no longer have any claim to custody on this basis, and, more significantly, the claim to paternity based only on DNA would play no legal role in custody decisions, including that of the mother to contract with other parents to raise her child or children. With "mother" as the legal term for the woman who gives birth and "parent" the legal term for those contracting to raise a child, the "father" as a subject position would be eliminated altogether, a consequence that reconfigures not only particular families but, at least as significantly, refashions the sexed psychic life ordered by kinship rules from those that artificially elevate men's power and authority to those that recognize men's actual commitments to and support of particular children.

Kinship Priorities for Children
Implementing a kinship system recognizing the unique importance of maternity to reproduction suggests other considerations as well. The objectives guiding the following legal proposals for state support and contracting

rules alternative to marriage echo many of the concerns of contemporary legislatures, but without narratives promoting the marital heterosexual dyad. The purposes of the following proposals are:

1. To provide children and their mother or parent(s) the resources necessary to support children's physical, emotional, and intellectual needs.
2. To make viable long-term relations between a child and a child's mother or parent(s).
3. To allocate the privileges and responsibilities of child care equitably and, as a corollary to this, to recognize the special relation of pregnant mothers to the children they bear.
4. To promote kinship laws with narratives not conducive to mass, systemic violence.

Were those using the rhetoric of "family values" concerned primarily with the well-being of children, then the first policies they would advocate would be health- and child-care programs ensuring that children and their caretakers receive high-quality services, not ballot initiatives precluding the possibility of same-sex marriages.[21] Likewise, lesbian and gay groups invoking "family values" to assist their children would be protecting more children directly if they focused on improving social services for all citizens regardless of their marital status or that of their parents. It is parochial and ineffective to press for marriage as the means to guarantee children's security. Citizens deserve a feeling of security because they are human, not because of marriage to someone with good benefits, a good apartment, or assets one may inherit if that person dies—the traditional arguments for why same-sex couples deserve marital recognition.[22] In short, the instrumental benefits desired by many promarriage advocates should be pressed on behalf of all citizens too physically weak or mentally fragile, regardless of age, to be responsible for their own security, because all human beings need and therefore deserve care regardless of their marital status or that of their parents.

From Marriage Law to Kinship Contracts

Marriage rules not only instantiate the harmful law of nations and fathers; they also aspire to intergenerational forms of being that are impractical, unrealistic, and therefore guarantee at best disappointment and often deep anguish. In particular, the rule that marriage should last for life establishes a norm that is difficult to implement and not necessary for the purpose of raising children, which is why many marriages end when children leave the house and why legal obligations to child care end at the children's age of majority.[23] While a support system providing intergenerational, mutual support over life is one possible happy outcome from families, this need not be the goal of the family's legal structure. The rules of any government policy should be narrowly and clearly drawn to suit the desired outcome. For childrearing, this means accomplishing the objective of ensuring that at least one adult will support each child until the age of eighteen, a point at which she can be assumed to be physically, emotionally, and mentally capable of supporting herself.[24] From a child's point of view, the need for the family to be stable and nurturing decreases over time. Most people can survive and flourish even if their parents do not devote themselves to ensuring this after they are eighteen years old; this may not be true for children who are younger.[25] The calculus leading to the proposals below gives heavy weight to family stability, whatever form that family takes, but does not ignore tensions that arise in any social setting, especially such a demanding one as the family.

The desire for family relations to last for a lifetime differs from a child's survival needs. Conceptually, there is a point at which considerations of parental discord trump the "best interests of the child." In practice, that point will depend on the particularities of the situation. The possibility of a threshold age of eighteen for dissolving the legal family by no means requires that families dissolve their emotional and other ties; it merely ends their legal responsibilities, and even here the agreements may be revisited with a new contract. But in no case should adults who commit to raising a child be able to depart from this commitment before the child is eighteen.

By lowering the expectation of what parenting contracts entail, so that they meet the standards of current criminal law and social norms,[26] the result will be realistic goals, giving parents an incentive to stick it out rather than leave in despair. The provisions in such parenting contracts should be substantial minimum commitments to provide for a child's physical, emotional, and intellectual needs. Under a system providing for health care and other needs, poorer families would have far fewer burdens for childrearing than exist under current laws in countries such as the United States, which do not provide for universal health care.

The policies offered below target achieving substantive goals of child care rather than managing adults' psychic disturbances, as is the case for current kinship rules. These policies are not immune to violation, just as current family laws may be disobeyed. However, because these alternatives are more flexible than rules giving rise to our current childrearing roles, they may be far less likely to be broken. They are also conducive to inviting people to form families through a range of encounters, not just sexual ones, and therefore may enrich other relations by allowing for this potential to develop while at the same time lessening the pressure on sexual ones.

POLICY PROPOSALS

1. Health services would be universally available, and health-care workers would receive wages comparable to other high-status professionals.
2. Child-care support services would be universally available to supplement parenting needs, at wages comparable to those paid to other high-status professionals.
3. Every child has one mother: the person who gave birth to him or her.[27]
4. Every child would have one or more parents. For purposes of legal custody, a parent is someone, including a mother, who adopts a child alone or in a group of two or more.
5. The adoption would be a legal commitment to caregiving until the child is eighteen years of age. Ending this contract made with one or more other parents without meeting the conditions is a civil violation triggering a child's legal ability to seek financial compensation via a guardian *ad litem* at a universal level per years remaining before the child turns eighteen. Minimum amounts would be established by regional bodies of the GPA; higher levels might be agreed to among those in a particular kinship unit.
6. The mother would be entitled to determine the child's additional parents, if she desires. She fulfills this responsibility either by (a) signing an enforceable contract acknowledging that she is adopting the child by herself; (b) by forming a larger group to legally adopt the child, possible at any point; (c) by finding another adult or group that will sign this contract within three months of birth; or (d) requesting that an officially sanctioned adoption agency perform these activities so that by three months the child will have at least one parent. As under current law, no money other than transaction fees can be charged for the purpose of executing adoption contracts.
7. All adoption contracts will require minimum adult commitments to child care.

8. All families receive per-child annual fees from a provisions agency for that child's support.

9. Marriage is a purely private activity, receiving no recognition as a legal status by any government agency.

Taken together, the above proposals would directly accomplish the child-rearing objectives mentioned above, which would seem to attract agreement across the political spectrum. (One would be hard pressed to find a critic advocating a family policy designed to increase children's chances of being malnourished, unsafe, and stupid.) Many unhappy couples stay together because they love their children and want to support them. The major difference between current family policies and the recommendations above is that the former attempt to meet these objectives through mediated, confusing, and unfounded religious aims or genetic fantasies. If, as a purely private matter, some or even many people continue to make commitments on the basis of these myths, no policy proposal here prohibits this, but this would be a purely private affair.

A new model of family life, one that severs the raising of children from the traditional kinship group, would be good for children and their parents and a benefit for all adults. As Fineman has pointed out, currently people who seek intimate relations are faced with the confounding task of finding qualities in a romantic partner also suitable for a parent. Separating the two roles clearly removes some pressure from sexual relations. However, far more importantly, the legal norm that any two or more people can be parents together and form a family regardless of genetic or biological ties institutionalizes a potential connectedness among all of us. Not the person one is dating but perhaps a colleague or the person one meets in line at the supermarket could be the perfect parent. Enlarging the scope of potential parenting partners and acknowledging a broader community as potentially family can only deepen all our connections.

CHAPTER SEVEN
ABOLISHING PRIVATE LAND RIGHTS
Toward a New Practice of Eminent Domain

I set out on this ground which I suppose to be self-evident, "that the earth belongs in usufruct to the living"; that the dead have neither powers nor rights over it.

THOMAS JEFFERSON, LETTER TO JAMES MADISON (1789)

I'm buying land . . . 'cause God's not making more.

OPRAH TO DONALD TRUMP, ON "OPRAH" (APRIL 8, 2004)

The proposal to prohibit private ownership of land differs from the previous three proposals to abolish well-established laws.[1] First, public ownership of land already exists to a large extent, under the universal rubric of "eminent domain." Second, land ownership today does not follow in any obvious way from the conventions of family appearing in the previous chapters. Family ties today by law bestow nationality and inheritance, and marriage law produces families, but land rights per se do not appear to require intergenerational or birthright entitlements. One *may* own land through an inheritance or gift from relatives, but save restrictions on land ownership by non-nationals in some countries and customary law in others, discussed below, in the United States and other postindustrial societies one may own land irrespective of any family laws or narratives. The first three proposals set out to abolish laws that create hereditary commitments, and the last one embraces the intergenerational political communities oriented toward conserving the land. Presently, eminent domain is tainted by its association with protecting a specifically national homeland, and public land ownership principles are abrogated by countervailing commitments to individual land rights. This chapter describes present laws regulating land use and explains how they might be reinterpreted in a world of states without nations. An explicit injunction against the nominal appearance of private land ownership recognizes that the earth, unlike other forms of potential property, holds a special place in the life of mortals and is necessary to preserve for mortals, for the sake of their posterity and also their past. Without a sustainable habitat, the human species and its history vanish together.

The practices of nationality, inheritance, and marriage indicate a so-called liberal public's warm embrace of practices inconsistent with the liberal ethos— a form of subconscious hypocrisy, one might say. But the apparent contemporary doctrine of land rights in Europe and especially North America, contrariwise, appears to hew not only to a legal but also an ideological path that is precisely what one might expect to see in capitalist societies. There is strong public sentiment on behalf of birthright nationality, inheritance, and marriage based on melancholia and fantasies of an unbroken narrative stream that an individual joins as a result of ancestry. In contrast, the doctrine favoring a strong defense of private land rights has numerous hard-nosed libertarian proponents and individualist fictional myths for them to circulate. Today's land-rights theory—unlike the theories of birthright citizenship, inheritance, and marriage—has a vibrant liberal individualist folklore, beginning with arguably the first British novel, Daniel Defoe's *Robinson Crusoe* (1719).

The Robinson Crusoe who animates examples in Robert Nozick's libertarian classic *Anarchy, the State, and Utopia* (1974) and is an occasional protagonist in hundreds of articles and monographs by economists speculating on the acquisitive individual[2] does not bump into an Englishwoman with whom he starts a family that becomes a colony and leaves descendants in perpetuity, a fictive choice Defoe might have made as credibly as having Crusoe take a slave named Friday. Rather, Crusoe is cast as the individual in the state of nature, a phantasmatic icon unconstrained by myths of family and country. Crusoe ignores his parents' entreaties against taking treacherous voyages and, after his third shipwreck, is lying in a hammock reading the Bible and sipping mai-tais, so to speak. When Crusoe eventually returns to England, Defoe devotes exactly one sentence in the entire first-person novel to narrating how Crusoe began a family and then abandoned his dying wife and their three children:

> In the meantime, I in part settled myself here; for, first of all, I married, and that not either to my disadvantage or dissatisfaction, and had three children, two sons and one daughter; but my wife dying, and my nephew coming home with good success from a voyage to Spain, my inclination to go abroad, and his importunity, prevailed, and engaged me to go in his ship as a private trader to the East Indies; this was in the year 1694.[3]

The next sentence is about that voyage with his nephew.[4] By Crusoe leaving England at the moment at which the person most dependent on him needs him the most, Defoe draws a character whose independence has no limits, and he entertains a callous cruelty by showing the ease with which one might deny a wife her deathbed comfort and continue one's pursuits, not alone, but with another self-sufficient man, his nephew (or, earlier, Friday).

Economists use a cartoonish version of the Robinson Crusoe narrative: him alone on an island. The omitted details compromise the story in some ways (Crusoe is not alone) and fail to use it to full effect in others. Libertarians might take delight in the fact, for instance, that Crusoe's financial success results from his plantation investment in Brazil, a country far from his patrimony.[5] Crusoe's wealth is not inherited but is a consequence of resisting his father's advice and making a shrewd investment in the land of another country, a clear break from the national, inheritance, and marriage narratives reviewed previously. As an archetype for the principle of land's alienability, Crusoe's story seems to suggest a break from intergenerational narratives and commitments that birthright citizenship, inheritance, and marriage all sustain. Likewise, other stories of land rights in social science texts also center on choices and conflicts among individuals, not intergenerational communities. In the language of cognitive dissonance, land's apparent alienability is inconsistent with intergenerational commitments and therefore might make land's private ownership seem consistent with the theme of "citizenship for mortals." But as the rules below make clear, individuals who would appear to have private land rights, including fictional protagonists, are embedded in legal narratives of the sovereign doling out rights in abeyance to the intergenerational state burnishing its national myths and dreams.

CURRENT STATUS OF LAND RIGHTS

Eminent Domain

Under virtually all doctrines of sovereignty, the nation-state has the prerogative to determine the land rights and uses of territory within its borders. One text reviewing comparative land rights begins: "Land is a fundamental resource of the nation state. Without land, without territory, there can be no nation state. Housing, agriculture, natural resource use, and national security concerns are all based upon land management and use."[6] As a consequence of the government's special interest in land, its regulation since antiquity has produced a different regime of individual prerogatives or rights than is accorded other forms of property, giving individuals the right of usufruct but not possession. This right to use land is only one among the three rights considered by modern commentators to comprise the full package of property rights.[7] Absent the additional right to exclude others from its use and to alienate it at will by contract, one's right to land may be significantly diminished relative to full property rights in moveable goods.[8] The prerogative of a political community to regulate land use is true not only of countries with pasts rooted in the European monarch's control of the "the realme,"[9] but it has prevailed in non-European contexts as well, from Russian czars and Chinese emperors directly owning the land worked by serfs to customary practices in Africa, where land-use decisions were and still are in some places made by tribal chiefs.[10] In many countries today, land cannot be held as property, but rather individuals are given long-term, lifetime, or familial leases by the state, discussed below.

Kelo and the Debate on Eminent Domain

The topic of land rights received renewed discussion in the United States as a result of the mobilization of libertarian legal-rights foundations that took up the case of Suzette Kelo, who challenged the right of the city of New London,

Connecticut, to seize her property in exchange for just compensation, as provided by the Fifth Amendment of the U.S. Constitution.[11] These groups were able to take a boilerplate legal question about eminent domain, one that had facts remarkably similar to those in precedents of other cases empowering the government to use its powers of eminent domain to turn property over to private developers,[12] and to have their case come close to overturning these precedents. Reinforcing a long string of laws and Supreme Court decisions promoting the government's use of its powers of eminent domain, the Court in a five-to-four decision reaffirmed the broad latitude accorded local governments to make these determinations.

As a result of a public poorly informed about U.S. legal history and the meaning of property rights, libertarian think tanks and legal foundations were able to turn *Kelo*'s loss in the Supreme Court into a stunning public relations, and eventually legislative, success story. State and local assemblies across the country—and even Congress—have passed counterintuitive bills designed to limit the discretion of representative bodies to infringe on individual property rights. According to one legal scholar,

> during the year following Kelo, legislatures in twenty-eight states passed bills addressing eminent domain, twenty-four of which were enacted, one of which was awaiting signature of the governor, and two of which were vetoed by the governor. In the November 2006 elections, ten states, Arizona, Florida, Georgia, Louisiana, Michigan, New Hampshire, Nevada, North Dakota, Oregon, and South Carolina, passed constitutional amendments or citizen initiatives limiting their states' abilities to use eminent domain. Measures in California, Idaho, and Washington addressing eminent domain and regulatory takings failed.[13]

Many of these amendments advance a legal norm at odds with the *Kelo* standards for "public benefit," but their actions are moot: there is no mandate that state assemblies or city councils must use eminent domain, on the one hand; on the other, these bills do not constrain future legislative bodies that want to use eminent domain from changing the law and pursuing their development projects.

The easiest way for legislative bodies to appease their citizens' concerns about eminent domain is to forestall exercising it. The Supreme Court did not condemn Kelo's land; that was done by the city of New London. Those legislative bodies and constituencies uncomfortable with asserting prerogatives that the Supreme Court finds the Takings Clause gives them can assuage their worries by not exercising the prerogative of eminent domain. If someone has a disdain for eating meat and refuses to do so, they do not need laws passed to prevent them from eating meat. As a Connecticut legislator pointed out to his colleagues as they were passing a bill to constrain eminent domain from being used to increase property taxes, they themselves had voted to condemn Kelo's land when they appropriated the funds for the redevelopment project.[14]

If at some point these assemblies and city councils reverse their position and decide to use eminent domain, and if the next Suzette Kelo decides that she too wants to remain put, they can easily revoke the laws they passed in the aftermath of *Kelo* and continue to take property with just compensation for public benefit, including those benefits derived from rezoning for industrial parks.[15]

Regulatory Takings and Eminent Domain

In a nearby arena of legal doctrine, another line of analysis dedicated to enhancing individual land rights in the United States has been developing in the last two decades. One reason that the groups pushing to expand individual rights against the government's prerogative of eminent domain felt so empowered to press Kelo's cause, despite numerous decisions against them on the case specifics, was a changing legal climate on property rights instantiated in the sphere of property-rights disputes: a cause its enthusiasts call "regulatory takings."[16] Regulatory-takings jurisprudence requires government to compensate property owners when legislation decreases the value of their property. Richard Epstein, who inaugurated this line of reasoning in the mid-1980s, sees those externalities of government land policies that decrease land values as a "taking," a political-economic theory laying bare the inanity of attempting to individualize the burdens of policies necessary to make a common world mutually habitable.[17] For this market approach to work, governments not only would have to be able to accurately assess the harmful micro impacts of major long-range policies well into the future, but they also would have to do something more implausible: assign costs or user fees to those individuals benefiting from their policies. This would put the government in the odd position of charging its residents for those policies that are most beneficial. If a green belt is established, then Epstein's argument entitles developers whose subdivisions will not come to fruition as a result of a prohibition on new building to be compensated, but it does not require existing homeowners to pay a higher property tax in exchange for the added pleasures the green belt provides them—and it especially would not be able to individualize the various payments, as some people love being near nature and others will be disappointed that the plans for the new mall were cancelled. Markets cannot price outcomes for political undertakings that simultaneously change the living situation for large numbers of people who may not even know their preferences and, especially, the long-term consequences of the decisions. In fact, when these decisions are undertaken as a result of market pressures, as when corporate interests compete through either the legal bribery of campaign contributions or illegal graft to pressure legislators, the results have been disastrous, from global warming to special set-asides for favored contractors.

The theory underlying regulatory takings has been extensively criticized for being impractical, costly, unfair, unjustified, and unprecedented.[18] However, the Supreme Court has gone on record embracing this principle, at least in part. In *Lucas v. South Carolina Coastal Commission* (1992),[19] Supreme Court Justice Antonin Scalia authored the majority's decision[20] stating that when a non-nuisance regulation reduced a piece of real estate to a zero valuation, then this was the same as a "taking" and required "just compensation": "Total deprivation of beneficial use is, from the landowner's point of view, the equivalent of a physical appropriation."[21] The decision is surprising for reasons of fact and law.

First, the Court seems to make a factual error when it states that a gorgeous piece of beachfront land, from which the owner, David Lucas, may use his property rights to exclude others and which he may transfer to others, could be said to have no "beneficial use" simply because he cannot build a house on it.[22] The South Carolina Coastal Commission (SCCC) did not prohibit Lucas from sheltering himself and others on the barrier island, only from building permanent structures. A private campsite on a Carolina barrier island is something many people would love to own, which means that the barrier island, even after the SCCC decision, has "beneficial value" greater than zero.

Second, the logic of the SCCC rule prohibiting building is very much rooted in nuisance theory and hence by Scalia's parsing is not obviously a "taking," a point Scalia himself concedes when he acknowledges the broad scope of actions potentially justifiable by nuisance theory.[23] If a bar's noise violates the city's noise levels and is shut down for this, it cannot sue for lost revenues. Building permanent structures in a hurricane zone is a nuisance to the citizens of the state of South Carolina, who are forced to subsidize efforts to assist the island's inhabitants in the event of a sudden storm likely to be life threatening in that vicinity. The Scalia decision suggested that the state does not have to compensate for using its police powers *as long as they are consistent with the background principles of its public law*. James Burling explains: "In other words, even though a regulatory action may be justified under the police power, if it proscribes a use that has not already been proscribed under the state's background principles, then just compensation must be paid when the economic impacts are severe enough."[24] Background environmental law in that region has imposed numerous restrictions on coastal building and hence meets this standard. Similarly, nuisance regulations cover everything from failing to have a building conform to aesthetic standards in the neighborhood to noise pollution. Homeowners who are charged with clearing brush near their homes cannot pass the gardener fees for this on to the city government.

It seems inconsistent, then, to allow homeowners charged with safe building practices to pass on the costs of following these regulations to the government as well. The courts seem to agree: "after *Lucas*, courts have been reluctant to find a nuisance merely upon the government's assertion of such, unless the finding of a nuisance can be justified under the state's traditional law of property."[25] The broad scope that the courts continue to afford nuisance theory maintains longstanding norms in this country's history. John Hart points out that the *Lucas* decision was an anomaly and break with historical precedents from the early republic: "Because American landowners were not entitled to use their land for any noninjurious purpose at the time of the Constitution, a central premise of Pennsylvania Coal—that landowners' use rights are 'seemingly absolute' under the Constitution—is wrong."[26]

From Early U.S. Land Rights to Current Myths About Early U.S. Land Rights

In his essays on the practice of eminent domain when the states were British colonies and as members of a new republic, John Hart, writing against the *Lucas* decision constricting the government's exercise of the Takings Clause, shows that the *Kelo* decision is entirely in line with the founders' philosophy of eminent domain. The early courts and lawmakers in the United States endorsed a broad set of powers for the federal government that might infringe on individual property rights:

> Riparian land was subordinated to the policy of promoting economic development that would benefit the public. Farmers who owned wetlands were obliged by local majorities of their neighbors to have their

lands drained and to contribute to the costs of drainage. Other farmers were obliged to participate in coercive fencing projects. The public interest in the development of mines and metal production was given precedence over the wishes of affected landowners. Some landowners were prohibited from selling their interests in land. And legislatures sometimes enacted statutes declaring that owners of unimproved land must improve or occupy such lands or forfeit title.[27]

The government "coercively promoted uses of private land that were viewed as conducive to the community's well-being" and did not always compensate for this.[28]

In the early days of the republic, politicians did not envision the U.S. government as a major land owner but instead prioritized distributing large tracts of land to families for the purpose of creating a "stable society whereby broad-based land ownership would provide individuals with a stake in the economy and provide a check on the scope of government."[29] Programs to allow the wealthy to buy tracts of unlimited size were replaced by families receiving at no cost title to 160-acre tracts of land.[30] Some form of property rights to land were intended, but they were limited. They are granted as the state positions itself as the legitimate author and guarantor of these rights and as the state performs the absurdity of giving an exchange value to land.[31] Unlike other property, the government saw land rights as a matter of public and not purely private interests.

Both of these tacit statements on the state's eminent domain became more explicit over time. In 1891, the U.S. government stopped giving away its land. Congress gave the president the authority to turn untitled land into a reserve that would be managed by the federal government, establishing the trend of its acquiring and leasing hundreds of millions of acres.[32] And yet this is not the history of property rights realized in the American imagination, which persists in a view of strong individual property rights misattributed to John Locke. Newspaper editorials and letters to the editor regarding the *Kelo* case were littered with references to Locke's theory of property rights and his place in the pantheon of American founding ideologists. In a letter to the editor, a Pittsburgh resident writes:

> John Locke, whose writings are the foundation of our Constitution, wrote that of the specific powers granted to government, the most important is the protection of private property. The recent Supreme Court

ruling regarding eminent domain (*Kelo v. New London*) and the burdensome property taxes imposed by local governments shows how far we have strayed from the intents of the Founders.[33]

Columnist George Will writes: "Locke, the most important intellectual progenitor of the American Revolution, held that property rights exist prior to government, to which people submit to secure their property."[34] Will is not alone in this sentiment.[35]

Richard Epstein is perhaps the author most responsible both for this view among neoclassical economists—that Locke believed in a strong defense of individual property rights against a regulatory government—and for the association of Locke's values with those of the early republic. In his book, Epstein frequently invokes Locke to support a capacious understanding of the rights that the Fifth Amendment's takings clause affords individuals: (1) "Locke was emphatic in his emphasis that individual natural rights including rights to obtain and hold property are not derived from the sovereign but are the common gift to mankind."[36] (2) "The second point in Locke's argument is that the organization of the state does not require the surrender of all natural rights to the sovereign. [After one leaves the state of the nature,] the sovereign no longer controls the surplus."[37] (3) Epstein refers to Locke's "prohibition against the taking of private property by the 'supreme power' of the state."[38]

Epstein's claims are part of an old echo chamber imputing to Locke values he never held and that cannot be found in his texts. He does not cite passages from Locke but references Robert Nozick's *Anarchy, the State, and Utopia* (1974), a text that, as discussed in chapter 2, also asserts, without references to specific passages, libertarian positions rooted in Locke. Elsewhere I have shown that Locke's "Second Treatise" does not sustain the common view of him as defending property rights as natural rights after people have entered political society. Rather, Locke separates the natural rights people have to property in the state of nature, where they find themselves under the illegitimate assertions of sovereignty by the Stuarts, from the prerogatives of the state to limit those rights once people consent to enter political society.[39]

The one participant in the Kelo controversy who correctly understood the relevance of Locke's thinking was Claire Gaudiani, president of the New London Development Corporation and president of Connecticut College: "Going back to John Locke, the concept of private property, after due remuneration, being transferred to public benefit is a longstanding tradition in the United States."[40] Gaudiani understood Locke's view that political societies condoned by majority rule would be governed solely by positive law, and that this included land rights. According to the *New York Times*, Gaudiani had "led the redevelopment effort and is largely credited with persuading Pfizer to put its new research headquarters on a formerly polluted site. Her husband, David G. Burnett, is a Pfizer executive, the director of Pfizer Research University."[41] A paradox symptomatic of the unintended consequences of the so-called representative democracy in the United States is that a member of the power elite running New London would quote an advocate of "the people's" sovereignty to support government prerogatives. According to Locke, Suzette Kelo is not a victim—in political society we lose natural rights we had in the state of nature—but the wife of the Pfizer executive presiding over the council making land-use decisions favoring her husband's corporation also does not realize that Locke's proposal for a majoritarian government was for protecting "the people."

EMINENT DOMAIN COMPARISONS

Many countries do not allow even the fiction of private property, or they do so only at the margins. The governments of China and several countries in Africa own all land outright. Israel owns 92 percent of the country's territory.[42] In England, 40 percent of the territory is "registered common land," of which 80 percent is "privately owned," although the "common land" designation requires a right of thruway, thereby undercutting the prerogatives of restricting access and use, which are two of the three main privileges associated with property rights.[43] Thus property rights in a good deal of English real estate are not complete ones. In the United States, the federal government owns outright 28 percent of the territory, most of which is under the control of the Bureau of Land Management and available for use through long-term leases to farmers, ranchers, and mine companies,[44] leading one neoclassical economist to observe: "Given the general support provided to the private ownership of assets of all kinds in the U.S., public ownership of nearly one-third of the land is an anomaly."[45] In truth, the anomaly is that a country that has protected its prerogative of eminent domain and has almost one-third of its land publicly owned nonetheless would have so many believing that their government supports unfettered private ownership of assets.

Further suggesting the extent of government land ownership and practices of eminent domain is that the six randomly selected countries whose laws on nationality, marriage, and inheritance have been reviewed in previous chapters also reflect these norms:

AFGHANISTAN: Land rights for natives unclear. Foreigners in Afghanistan are not allowed to own land but can lease for up to ninety-nine years.[46]

DEMOCRATIC REPUBLIC OF CONGO: All the soil and subsoil is owned by the government.[47]

HONDURAS: Foreigners cannot purchase land larger than a quarter-acre or that includes the coastline.[48]

MONACO: The government owns controlling interest in the Société des Bains de Mer, which runs the largest casinos and hotels, occupying the major area of the principality,[49] meaning that the government effectively owns not only most of the land but also most of the businesses.

SENEGAL: The government owns land rights, with rural lands (95 percent of the country) managed by local officials according to customary practices; increasingly, land rights are being alienated by individual contracts, and this is leading to many problems.[50]

ZIMBABWE: The government owns the land and issues ninety-nine-year leases.[51]

Other states have roughly similar laws, although these are under discussion among many African countries. In Eritrea, the land is owned by government, with lifetime "usufructary rights to citizens whose predominant means of income is the land, regardless of race or clan."[52] Countries with intermediate levels of restrictions on using and alienating property include Ethiopia,[53] Kenya,[54] Rwanda,[55] and Zambia.[56] Swaziland has two regimes of title, freehold (no restrictions) and Swazi National Land (cannot be sold).[57] Lesotho prohibits land's alienability.[58] In Nigeria, land is inherited patrilineally.[59] In Mozambique, land belongs to the state,[60] in Tanzania to the president,[61] and in Uganda land title is held by the "citizens of Uganda."[62] South Africa has eminent domain but no alienability limitations.[63]

The status of international laws governing property rights is murky and, as in the cases of the previous chapters, endorses as "rights" government prerogatives causing the very harms against which the United Nations ostensibly was established to protect.[64] According to Article 17 of the United Nations Universal Declaration of Human Rights (1948): "(1) Everyone has the right to own property alone as well as in association with others. (2) No one shall be arbitrarily deprived of his property." As is the case with most of the Universal Declaration, the text is a "common standard of achievement for all peoples and nations," and is not a "universal human right enforceable under Article 56 of the Charter."[65] In addition, the charter's language begs the question of what counts as property. Many states define land specifically as something that cannot be owned by private individuals. If land cannot be privately owned, it is not property, and therefore no subject or citizen would have their property rights denied by laws giving governments exclusive title to land.[66] Moreover, international law allows sovereign countries to take private property for public use.[67]

LAND RIGHTS IN THE AGE OF NATION-STATES

Governments own land because, in addition to the internal administrative functions served by a government's ability to control land use, land ownership materializes a country's national specificity. There are many indications of this across countries. To establish unsettled land as U.S. territory, the early postrevolutionary U.S. government gave private land rights to U.S. soldiers and prohibited them from selling the land, as the legislators "thought that contested territory would be better defended by veterans than by the land speculators who might offer to buy up their rights."[68] Colonial South Carolina required land owners to live on their properties deeded from the crown as a device for declaring sovereignty over lands held by Indian nations. According to a 1716 act of South Carolina, the "well peopling of any country not only enriches it in a time of peace, but also strengthens it in a time of war and whereas the Yamosees having forsaken the said large tract of land, it is highly reasonable that the same lands should be applied to the publick benefit of this Province."[69] The same act, according to Hart, stated that the Indians were in a "war ... against us" and had "gone over to the French and Spaniards."[70] The U.S. "Trading with the Enemy Act 1970" allows the government to seize property owned by aliens from enemy countries during war or a state of emergency.[71] In other words, regardless of any individual property owner's personal political beliefs or if the U.S. government first and foremost sees that person as an enemy, her property is potentially forfeit.

Reciprocally, most countries have a variety of laws regulating land ownership by foreigners, including denying this right altogether.[72] According to a 1999 survey of these laws, a "common provision permits only nationals or citizens to own land, either at all, or free from restriction. For example the Constitution of Lithuania originally provided that only the State and natural persons of Lithuanian nationality could own land. An almost equally common provision is that foreigners may not own land."[73] In the United States, several states, including Indiana, Iowa, Missouri, and North Carolina, prohibit foreigners from owning agricultural land or any real estate.[74] Some countries that prohibit foreign ownership of land make an "exception for those who acquire lands by hereditary succession,"[75] an exception proving the rule that kinship laws defining friends and enemies currently underlie key institutions of government prerogative. The relatives of one's nationals may not be citizens, but nonetheless they are not considered completely outsiders.

Countries also assign land rights based on ethnic differences within countries. For example, 90 percent of the land in Fiji is reserved for putatively indigenous Fijians.[76] In Papua New Guinea, customary groups "own nearly 99 percent of the territory," and these landowners can "only sell 'their' land to another group member. Foreigners cannot become part of such groups."[77] In Africa, many countries allow only "natives" land rights in specific regions.[78] Importantly, these policies do not reflect long-held practices of the so-called natives but are hangovers from colonial lawmakers who throughout Africa used modern bureaucratic rules to impose the same national segregation abroad that they were using in Europe. Karol Boudreaux describes how in Nigeria

> the British government required those on the land to apply for occupancy permits. . . . This system placed limits on the ability of outsiders to move into northern areas. It also had the effect of creating segregated areas of "strangers," or Sabon Garis. Settlers were those people whose relatives had been in the area longer than "non-indigenes" or "strangers." Non-indigenes were granted fewer legal rights than settlers. This differential access to land, to local government services, and to political representation created tensions throughout northern Nigeria— tensions that remain to this day.[79]

This is a telling example of how groups worldwide may be created by fiat but over time, incentivized by habit and instrumental rewards, become "natural" or "native." The families that happened to have been residing in a particular region of northern Nigeria longer than others were there through happenstance and are no more deserving of land rights on grounds of indigeneity[80] than Angelenos born in Los Angeles are more deserving of land rights in Los

Angeles than Angelenos born in New York City—or Mexico City, which was the seat of government for Los Angeles until 1848.

As an unsurprising consequence of these laws, individuals experience land conflicts as rooted in ethnic differences and not greed and self-interest, as some political scientists and economists suggest.[81] For instance, Boudreaux describes the 53,000 killed in a civil war in Nigeria between 2001 and 2004 as not an ethnic or religious conflict but an economic one: "In areas where farmers are predominantly settled Christians and cattle herders, originally from the north, are mainly Muslim, an impression can be created of 'religious' or 'ethnic' tension. But in reality the root causes of the violence are political and economic—a competition for fertile land."[82] Boudreaux believes that the many land-rights restrictions mean that violence is the only way for newcomers to occupy land, and that if there were open markets in land titles, these disputes would not exist.

Boudreaux's narrative about land disputes reveals information that once more shows how family law and inheritance congeal national and ethnic attachments, and it undermines his emphasis on the economic basis for the conflicts. Boudreaux reveals how the British transferred rights to land in the north and prevented from moving there those who did not have ties in the area at the time the British claimed it as theirs. It seems fairly obvious that Boudreaux has captured the results of a natural experiment as to whether artificially imposing legal distinctions that follow kinship lines will create ethnic differences. The answer appears to be "yes."[83] After Britain arbitrarily initiated the zero point of "indigenes" and established legal territorial and kinship boundaries indicating those who were not indigenes, people suddenly belonged to different ethnic groups.

So why is Boudreaux insisting that his is a story about markets and not ethnic groups (the religious differences map onto ethnic ones)? Perhaps it is because Boudreaux has the common belief that there are "real" and "artificial" ethnic groups. That he noticed the legal conventions creating the different kin cleavages in the north does not make the "indigene" groups created through them any less ethnic than every other national, ethnic, racial, and caste division that has ever existed.[84] It is logically possible for groups to have precisely overlapping occupations and ethnic ties, so that every herder is Muslim and every farmer Christian, and for the violence to be that of herders against farmers, with the clan ties merely incidental. However, if occupation were a factor influencing systemic mass violence, then one would expect to see an example of civil wars between herders and farmers elsewhere with no overlapping ethnic differences. Or even a civil war between different job sectors: real-estate firms in hand-to-hand combat with financial companies over building ownership in Manhattan. No evidence of such conflicts exist. Instead, world history reveals widespread correspondences between war and intergenerational affiliations, not jobs. Since people elsewhere have never organized to systematically kill thousands based on affiliations that are not intergenerational or religious, the incitement of an ethnic difference for the purpose of land ownership appears to be a significant cause of this violence, not generic self-interest.[85]

The fighting is not unlike that at the end of *Robinson Crusoe*. Defoe's Crusoe, driven to escape ties of family and nation, ends up imbricated in them. In the novel's last sentences, Dafoe has Crusoe return to his island, where he arranges marriages for his compatriots and is witness to their wars: "how three hundred Caribbees came and invaded [the Englishmen], and ruined their plantations, and how they fought with that whole number twice, and were at first defeated, and one of them killed; but at last a storm destroying their enemies' canoes, they famished or destroyed almost all the rest."[86] It is not insecurity due to fighting among individuals but the invasion by Caribbees of the English, after the English of South America, that imperils land rights.

THE IMPERIALISM OF PRIVATE PROPERTY AS A CONCEPT?

Some critics blame "the West" for the land-rights problems in Africa discussed above, suggesting both that the administrative regimes of ethnic difference culminated in today's violence and that the West's individualist creed also contributed to Africa's strife. The conventional approach for describing land rights is through a Eurocentric chronological and geographical history that begins with Roman law and develops into the property-rights regimes of contemporary European and North American free-market countries, where land supposedly may be freely alienated at will. Commentators contrast these practices with countries that are "slower" or follow customary law in many African, Asian, and South American states. For instance, in his description of Mozambique's Land Law, based on "customary African law," Kendall Burr begins with a description of "Western" law:

> Property is commonly understood in the Western world as an abstract "bundle of rights." The three most important rights in the bundle are

generally considered to be: (1) the right to use property; (2) the right to exclude others from one's property; and (3) alienability, or the right to transfer one's property by sale or by gift. Capitalism requires alienability as a crucial stick in the bundle, on the theory that property will be most efficiently maximized if a private market permits it to be transferred to those who value it the most.[87]

Burr contrasts this with the 1997 Land Law of Mozambique that "embraces customary African law" and is "faulted for depreciating land value" and failure to "comply with the human right to property as understood in international law."

Just as the preceding chapters noted tensions, contradictions, and paradoxes in the narratives of citizenship, wealth, and family reflected in the so-called liberal tradition, land-rights narratives also do not have neat boundaries and consistent stories. First, parts of northern Africa and North African peoples were major constituents of the Roman Empire, calling into question the putative "Western" character of Roman property laws. Thagaste in modern Tunisia was where St. Augustine grew up in the fourth century, just as other Roman political and religious leaders made their homes in cities in modern Libya, Egypt, Tunisia, and many other ports around the Mediterranean— pieces of the Roman Empire on par with those of any other region. Historically, Rome's achievements are in part African ones, and vice versa.[88] Second, the substantive sentiments authors associate with a specifically African "cosmogony" are not unique to that region. Keba M'Baye summarizes the "African conception of land": "Neither the land, nor the sky, nor the sea, the pillars of the universe and shelters of the ancestors, can belong to man. All the lands together make up the patrimony of the community, having been put at men's disposal by God, to enable them to subsist, and so that the race can survive."[89] The earth does not belong to mortals: they use it at God's discretion.

Such a view is precisely that held by such a quintessential "Western" thinker as John Locke. Attacking the connotations of eminent domain being used by Robert Filmer in "Patriarcha" (1681) to legitimate the rule of the Stuarts, Locke writes:

The most specious thing to be said, is, that he that is proprietor of the whole world, may deny all the rest of mankind food, and so at his pleasure starve them, if they will not acknowledge his sovereignty, and obey his will. If this were true, it would be a good argument to prove, that there never was any such *property*, that God never gave any such *pri-*

vate dominion; since it is more reasonable to think, that God, who bid mankind increase and multiply, should rather himself give them all a right to make use of the food and raiment, and other conveniences of life, the materials whereof he had so plentifully provided for them; than to make them depend upon the will of a man for their subsistence.[90]

In the nineteenth century, British political economists also insisted that land was different from other property, and therefore the sacredness of individual property rights was less than that of land. John Medearis suggests that John Stuart Mill "contended that the land itself, unlike many forms of property, was never a product of labor. 'When the "sacredness of property" is talked of, it should always be remembered, that any such sacredness does not belong in the same degree to landed property,' Mill argued, continuing: 'No man made the land.'"[91] African and European political communities may differ in their interpretation and rules among and between themselves, but it seems that the range and terms of discussion are ontologically similar and mutually comprehensible. This should not be surprising, because the Christianity so influential on Locke's thinking is not a Western ideology but has its roots in Mediterranean Asia. (Bethlehem is not in Europe, and neither is Iznik, the modern Turkish city where Constantine signed the Nicaean Creed and gave his imprimatur to a Christian religion for the Roman Empire. So for purely nominal reasons, Christian ideology is not originally and purely Western.)

In practice, land in Europe has been alienable by individuals only relatively recently, and it was previously controlled by rules similar to those of African customary law. In sum, land rights in most countries, including the most liberal, are first oriented toward protecting putative natives thought specific to that nation-state. As a result of land divided in association with nationality or ethnicity, disputes over boundaries result in systematic, mass, violent death. If land divisions and property rights were associated with any other group differences, they might precipitate conflicts, but it appears that these would involve weapons of persuasion and economic sanction, not machetes or cluster bombs.

MARKET BENEFITS OF PRIVATE LAND RIGHTS?

The narrative so far emphasizes the origins of land law in the prerogatives of the state and has shown the origins of eminent domain and other land laws in concerns about materializing and defending the nation. However, it is still plausible that the property rights currently misconstrued still might provide benefits presently denied under current regimes of eminent domain—indeed, this is the claim of the libertarian law firms representing plaintiffs in the takings cases discussed earlier. This section reviews some of the economic advantages and disadvantages associated with private land rights, concluding that their mixed record suggests a basis other than market efficiencies is necessary for evaluating their form and content.

Land Rights Encourage Productivity

The consensus of neoclassical economics is that clearly delineated individual property rights in all investments are crucial to incentivize work. Robert Ellickson, illustrating this principle's relevance to land cultivation, offers examples drawn from early settlements in colonial America, where land rights initially were held in common and then transferred to individuals as private property. Ellickson quotes Captain John Smith, an early settler of Jamestown:

> When our people were fed out of the common store, and laboured jointly together, glad was he could slip from his labour, or slumber over his taske he cared not how, nay, the most honest among them would hardly take so much true paines in a weeke, as now for themselves they will doe in a day.... To prevent which, Sir Thomas Dale hath allotted every man three Acres of cleare ground.[92]

This is a clear illustration of Mancur Olsen's discussion of "free riders" in the *Logic of Collective Action*.[93] As long as people do not see instrumental benefits from their work, they are likely to let others do the tasks, harming the collective and its individuals.[94]

Clear property rights not only encourage hard work, but free-market economists believe that it is the best means for ensuring good land stewardship. The supposedly classic statement of this principle is attributed to Garrett Hardin's work.[95] The

> tragedy of the commons . . . in the Hardin example is an environmental outcome that results from an inadequate specification of property rights to the environmental services of the pasture. Access to grazing services is open to all. The open-access outcome is an inefficient use of the pasture, because it leads to a lower level of meat and milk production than would be possible with a smaller number of cattle.[96]

This is not exactly the problem Hardin found, as will be discussed below, but the view that common ownership fetters productivity using this interpretation of Hardin's work has numerous adherents.

A contemporary example of the dynamic suggested in the Hardineseque scenario above seems to follow from the U.S. Bureau of Land Management's policies, which sets the terms and length of leases for lands owned by the federal government. As a result of the changing priorities of that bureau, new presidents, and Congress, holders of grazing permits cannot be sure about their long-term leasing rights. Gary Libecap writes that "with permit insecurity, private investment in improvements, such as fences and wells, is reduced, and the motivation to overstock increases."[97] Conversely, there have been shocking revelations of oil companies off the coast of Florida and mining companies throughout the United States striking sweetheart deals with federal agencies to which private corporations would never agree.[98]

But property rights, including to land, also cause problems that the proponents of the "tragedy of the commons" worldview overlook. Hardin's *Science* article is a much more compassionate and thoughtful piece than its invocation by neoclassical economists would suggest. Used as a citation to justify property rights of all sorts, Hardin himself is not persuaded of their utility in many contexts. The essay would be more aptly titled, "The Tragedy of the Commons for People with Property Rights." In Hardin's essay, property rights are not solutions, but he suggests they contribute to the tragedy of the commons. His paradigmatic example of grazing described above only poses a problem if land is held in common *while individuals have private rights to their herds*. (If herds also are held in common, then, as we saw, neoclassical economists would worry about slackers, which would be bad for productivity but would not lead to overgrazing.) Similarly, Hardin's solutions do not require more property rights and market solutions but often appeal to an inventive use of regulations.

For instance, noting the degradation of the national parks, Hardin suggests entrance policies based on a lottery, a proposal now in place.[99] And he writes: "Our particular concept of private property, which deters us from exhausting the positive resources of the earth, favors pollution. The owner of a factory on the bank of a stream—whose property extends to the middle of the stream—often has difficulty seeing why it is not his natural right to muddy the waters flowing past his door."[100] Finally, Hardin in 1968 was one of the first to point out the inability of markets to prevent the pollution of what he calls pleasure. As a result of property rights to a store: "The shopping public is assaulted with mindless music, without its consent. Our government is paying out billions of dollars to create supersonic transport which will disturb 50,000 people for every one person who is whisked from coast to coast 3 hours faster. Advertisers muddy the airwaves of radio and television and pollute the view of travelers."[101] Hardin was not arguing that the commons needed to be privatized but that faced with existing regimes of private property rights, the commons was in trouble.[102]

Hardin's warnings echo concerns by the federal government in the late nineteenth century. The government, faced with the prospect of a corporate takeover of the country's land rights, decided to assume stewardship of public lands. In 1886, the chief of the Division of Forestry stated a principle diametrically opposed to the privatization norms popular today:

> The forest resource is one which, under the active competition of private enterprise, is apt to deteriorate. . . . The maintenance of continued supplies as well as of favorable conditions is possible only under the supervision of permanent institutions with whom present profit is not the only motive. It calls preeminently for the exercise of the providential functions of the state to counteract the destructive tendencies of private exploitation.[103]

In light of the development and killing of old-growth forest on privately held lands, the concern proved prescient.

In addition to land conservation, government ownership of land may protect against poverty in developing countries. In an article urging Nigeria to follow the land-reform policies of Eritrea, with the government owning land instead of customary patrilineage or individual land rights, Natasha Robinson explains that government ownership best protects the poor, especially women. Her study on the policy choices presented under pressure to enhance land rights in Africa suggest they may yield undesired consequences: "Land titling in Kenya has resulted in heightened inequality, landlessness, and rural-urban migration."[104] Robinson encourages policymakers in Nigeria to hold off implementing similar policies: "The right to sell does not seem as appealing when it is accompanied by the possibility of more landlessness, urbanization, and economic disparity."[105] Private, alienable land rights would quickly lead to the concentration of land ownership, and customary law would prevent women from having land rights. Kendall Burr writes, "Land markets encourage land concentration even though economic theory predicts that smaller landowners are more efficient."[106]

Note that land rights for usufruct are alienable and therefore provide avenues for capital accumulation even absent the occupant's outright ownership. Robinson writes that Nigerian women presently unable to obtain credit "could use their plots of land or their crop yields as collateral."[107] This is important, because it challenges the neoliberal model of development whereby the concentration of land rights leads to greater productivity and industrialization. The capital from renting out government-owned land is then available to be used for nonagrarian ventures. This way everyone has access to funds that can be accumulated by selling land-use rights, leading to a more equitable distribution of wealth than in countries where individuals' capital from land ownership leads to the increasing concentration of wealth and further inequality. And of course many African governments that own the land do not lease it but manage it through state companies that extract oil and minerals or supervise national parkland for sustaining a tourist industry.[108]

A world-systems analysis, sensitive to the interdependence of markets and the ease of capital's penetration of the Third World, also seems to support government ownership of land. It is this understanding that has led Mozambique's public and their democratically elected representatives to continue their support of the government's land ownership.[109]

What About Government Corruption and Stupidity?

One objection to the proposal for land to be owned by the government might be that governments have their own poor record when it comes to land management. For example, the U.S. government has rendered vast portions of its territory uninhabitable and contaminated its groundwater by creating and disposing of radioactive waste. Problems are emerging across the country, from strawberries and salmon with tritium in Washington State to cancer clusters near nuclear research facilities.[110] In the 1970s, Navajos began exhibiting strange cancers and defects in their corneas and bones.[111] The initial verdict was that these had genetic causes, their frequency being symptoms of so-called in-breeding. It was about sixteen years after the first reporting of symptoms to the public health authorities that an environmental health officer investigated for radiation poisoning: as a result of uranium mining twenty years earlier and the failure to contain its seepage, the water had radioactive contamination thousands of times above the government's safety level.[112]

This is one of thousands of examples in which government officials either beholden to people with strong financial interests or to political superiors with secret and deadly agendas—to allow citizens to contract cancer rather than take responsibility for poisoning people—fail to meet the stewardship responsibilities envisioned by the chief of forestry in 1886. In developing countries, in addition to graft and bribery among elites, as in the North, elections themselves may be bought, literally. Studies on Latin American and Asian elections suggest widespread vote buying. Fred Schaffer writes: "In Thailand, 30 percent of household heads surveyed in a national sample said they were offered money during the 1996 general election. In Taiwan's third largest city, Taichung . . . 27 percent of a random sample of eligible voters reported in 1999 that they had accepted cash during previous electoral campaigns."[113] Democracy has become another victim of the market. Instead of the tyranny of the majority, the minority will buy their domination over the rest. If this occurs, land policies will continue to reflect the short-term instrumental preferences of those funding candidates and not the long-term interests of mortal citizens.

Absent elections, in the interest of enhancing national wealth, the Chinese government has been using its ownership of land to remove inhabitants and pave the way for international development: "Since the end of the 1990s, cities have become accustomed to selling the best locations to foreign investors and commercial developers. . . . The main reason is that selling land is the most expedient way to increase local GDP. In recent years, local GDP has become an overwhelming standard for assessing the ability of the local officials."[114] Criticized as an example of eminent domain's harms, the facts suggest that it is state capitalism and nationalism—the country's short-term GDP goals and not the long-term well-being of its citizens—in concert with the acquisitiveness of foreign banks, venture capital, and real-estate firms that determine these results from eminent domain. Private wealthy landlords make the same decisions the Chinese government is making and, for the right price, also use local police to evict long-term tenants obstructing lucrative property sales.

African governments are notorious for corruption, a reputation that has made it difficult to attract foreign investment. A review of efforts over the last thirty years to fight corruption is a depressing read:[115] "In most countries not only are police forces seriously underresourced in the face of crime rates that are rising generally, but they may be susceptible to corruption themselves. Given that much corruption is consensual and hence hard to detect and to prove, and given that its investigation may be politically sensitive, it would not be surprising if the police devoted their efforts elsewhere."[116] Equally harmful is the absence of government and its replacement by warlords, another major challenge facing many countries in Africa.[117]

CONCLUSION: LAND RIGHTS FOR MORTALS

Arendt was writing about the inability of racists and rioters in the late 1960s, as members of a society bereft of a public culture, to understand their long-term interests, but the following passage from *On Violence* also speaks to why land-use decisions should not be made privately. Taking the parochial example of a landlord-tenant dispute, Arendt writes, "Self-interest is interested in the self, and the self dies or moves out or sells the house; because of its changing condition, that is ultimately because of the human condition of mortality, the self qua self cannot reckon in terms of long-range interest, i.e., the interest of a world that survives its inhabitants."[118] This is true for all political endeavors, but the insight bears special weight when it comes to decisions about the earth. Neoclassical economists recognize that land rights pose problems for mortals—their rational-choice model means individuals lack an incentive to care for objects they will not use—and believe that these problems are addressed by laws that protect inheritance. Robert Ellickson writes: "the preeminent advantage of an infinite land interest is that it is a low-transaction cost device for inducing a mortal landowner to conserve natural resources for future generations."[119] Ellickson explains that absent this convention, people, especially as they age, would tend not to make improvements on their property: "The fee simple in land cleverly harnesses human selfishness to the cause of altruism toward the unborn, a group not noted for its political clout or bargaining power."[120]

It is plausible that government ownership of land will continue to be plagued by conflicts to which there is no single solution. Nonetheless, the government's outright ownership of land remains preferable to a mystifying legal arrangement that empowers individuals and families to believe that the land is theirs when it ultimately remains the government's. The fee-simple arrangement Ellickson references is no more than the right of an estate holder to bequeath rights to his estate, normally without restrictions on the heirs. Therefore, Ellickson's assumption that this method of conveying wealth in land is inherently advantageous provokes the same questions raised about the assumptions favoring present inheritance laws. It is not at all obvious that a fee simple does anything other than guarantee that after people who have a title to land die, someone who did not work or pay for the title will possess it and the wealth it entails at the exclusion of others[121] and, depending on the terms of the will or trust, dictate land-management practices undesired even by the heir.[122]

Private land rights are inconsistent with the norms of citizenship for mortals. Those moveable possessions over which we have rights have different qualities. Ellickson writes: "The most fundamental features of a land surface are: immobility; uniqueness of location; infinite duration (relative indestructibility); lack of natural boundaries; ascertainable neighboring surfaces; and suitability for multiple uses."[123] Land is unique in other ways as well. Destroying one's car deprives one the benefits of driving, at least that car, and imposes small externalities on one's contemporaries and future generations by increasing the individual's global footprint, provided she replaces the car. But the costs imposed on someone in a future generation by dumping toxic chemicals, destroying historical buildings and archaeological objects, strip mining, and felling old-growth forests, to name a few harms that unfettered land rights enable, are not incurred by the owner and may even be avoided by her contemporaries. The species now extinct due to strip foresting on land owned by private corporations took a few generations to vanish. This is why land, and not all property, is inappropriate for individual ownership.

Giving individuals the rights to own and inherit land in the name of productivity, as Ellickson proposes, is also inconsistent with the condition of mortality, because it instrumentalizes the earth. In her book *The Human Condition*, Hannah Arendt writes eloquently about many themes inspiring the work here, including the belief that people need a shared world that is not a tool for increasing their wealth or a toy that they might destroy with their nuclear weapons (or their research). In despair she writes: "Still bound to the earth through the human condition, we have found a way to act on the earth and within terrestrial nature as though we dispose of it from outside, from the Archimedean point. And even at the risk of endangering the natural life process we expose the earth to universal, cosmic forces alien to nature's household."[124] Concerned about the instrumentalities of consumerism, communism, and the cold war, Arendt explored the possibility of people establishing meaningful lives through knowledge of something permanent and indestructible that they shared for the sake of being. Government ownership of land in a world where movement is not restricted would accomplish the Arendtian objective of materializing citizens' attachments to the earth and to a shared community, and not subject land to the instrumentalities of the market.

DELIBERATIVE POLITICS: A CODA

A citizenship associated with the important prerogative of controlling land use where one lives materializes membership and duties in ways that would provide the attachments Hegel envisioned through family and national ties. The understanding that one's individual existence is materially based on a larger political body to which one belongs concretizes the loyalties and commitments to that group. However, present structures of government in most countries do not realize the potential commitments and benefits of a politically committed citizenship but rely on the loyalties of a pathological nationalism, a confusion of the politics of friends and enemies with the politics of aesthetics, justice, and economics. There are ways other than nativism and religion for people to join in communities (discussed in chapter 8).

There are methods for controlling land and other state-owned resources by citizens that can replace the political processes parasitic on institutions that develop as a result of the rupture between birthright citizenship's passivity and the norms of action expected by those who believe in participatory self-governance. The goal of this project is to focus on substantive policies consistent with citizenship for mortals and not on a theory of rules that will guarantee fairness or justice. Current institutions are badly failing the goals of self-governance and need reform so that mortal citizens will not only eliminate war but also be able to realize the pleasures of state membership absent nationalism. It is possible that without the materialist values institutionalized by inheritance and private land ownership—incentivizing acquisitiveness instrumental to more acquisitions—political institutions will develop that express different values as well.

To this end, this section briefly sketches some possibilities for integrating ways that local communities could decide on land use and grant lifetime permits that cannot be revoked by subsequent committees except by supermajority. The basic questions concern the size of the relevant community for which decisions will be made and the character of the group making these land-use decisions. The proposal for land-use districts no larger than thirty thousand persons follows from this being the threshold number of inhabitants required for a congressional district when the U.S. Constitution first passed.[125] It is a number that the massification of government has left far behind, with congressional districts now including upward of 800,000 residents. Thirty thousand inhabitants was initially a minimum number, because the framers assumed there would be ongoing populist pressures for small districts, which they feared would lead to faction and chaos. It never occurred to them that the public would be so complacent as to allow the dilution of government accountability to its present levels. If the U.S. population had the same level of representation now as residents had in 1790, there would be about nine thousand members in Congress, not 435. The figure of thirty thousand proposed here as the size of a land-use district not only has a historical basis in English parliamentary government but also seems a reasonable number for the problems of zoning and land use: it would give people control over their immediate living environments and not put them in the position of making decisions that will not affect them.

The problem with using the government to allocate land rights resembles that facing other challenges of collective action. If "the people" are going to ensure that government will act equitably, then it would appear that they would need to develop oversight strategies, so that land policy in representative democracies is not determined by the wealthiest campaign contributor.

James Krier's work challenges the "free-market environmentalism" Garrett Hardin's work engendered,[126] even though Hardin's own work does not support this. Nonetheless, Krier points out that the "tragedy of the commons" comes from the challenges in ensuring that governments working on behalf of the commons do so fairly, and this is a problem with or without strong property rights: "What Hardin neglected is a point taken from modern political theory: The public has to coerce the government to coerce [the public], and to do this the public must organize. Yet an inability to organize, or coordinate, is the problem to begin with."[127] This observation should be the starting point of political theory in the aftermath of democracy's numerable failings, and it is tempting to reduce the problems raised in these pages to practical, egoistic failures of self-governance. As long as government and the citizenry are at best incompetent and at worst corrupt, it may seem odd to justify their ownership of land or anything else. Instead of faction checking faction, the government kleptocracy perseveres.

Wendy Brown offers a widely shared belief that the contemporary failings of the U.S. government is due to market values eclipsing those of justice and other public norms:

> As neoliberalism converts every political or social problem into market terms, it converts them to individual problems with market solutions.... This conversion of socially, economically, and politically produced problems into consumer items depoliticizes what has been historically produced, and it especially depoliticizes capitalism....

[Neoliberalism] produces the citizen on the model of entrepreneur and consumer.[128]

Yet there are unexpected tensions between the protagonists Brown sketches and the actions imputed to them. The consumers and entrepreneurs Brown describes would reject not only the government's nationalism but also its fraud and theft. If there really were a market mentality dominating government and civil society, then Iraq would not have been invaded, the Securities and Exchange Commission would have responded in 1999 to the documentation of Bernard Madoff's hedge-fund fraud (and not in 2008, when his pyramid scheme collapsed), and the banks would have been allowed to fail, just as the neoliberal International Monetary Fund had ordered in the 1980s for banks in South America and Africa. No serious neoliberal economic model would have sustained Vice President Cheney's "one percent doctrine," whereby a 1 percent chance of a serious terrorist attack was the trigger for aggressive and illegal CIA, military, and detention-camp actions unconstrained by either rational budgeting that would assess the opportunity costs of these investments or by an assessment of the heightened risks from possible reactions to these measures (for example, Al Qaeda's use of the Bush administration's torture policy to recruit new members).[129]

Brown accurately identifies a neoliberal discourse popular in a number of venues, but if neoliberal policies and values were actually institutionalized, then the rhetoric would not have been effective in stripping the government of its ability to stop finance fraud and negligence. Real neoliberals would not have been fooled by slick sloganeering into overlooking how the market was being betrayed by old-fashioned corruption easily hidden by, and sometimes overlapping with, old-fashioned nationalism.

Jonathan Simon points out that it is victimization and fear of the other, not market rationality, that have been influencing political mobilization and policy making in the United States: "Crime victims are in a real sense the representative subjects of our time. It is as crime victims that Americans are most readily imagined as united."[130] Simon emphasizes that the legislation on behalf of crime and terrorist victims is "deeply racialized" and that its proponents are largely "white, suburban, [and] middle class."[131] Instead of a public mobilizing for health care, education, and a clean environment, the public worries about crime and terrorism, another iteration of Michael Rogin's demonology.[132]

None of this is to suggest that self-interest does not interfere with sound policy making and its implementation, but only that the problems this poses are not unique to this epoch nor best understood as the implementation of market rationality. Land-use decisions being handled by small groups of citizens on a local level may be tainted by self-interest, but the political practice itself may perhaps provide possibilities for reimagining government decision making. Empowering residents to make land-use decisions has the potential to blend the qualities of passive and active citizenship. To borrow from Hegel for a purpose he would oppose, deliberating for the purpose of just decisions balancing short- and long-term interests and commitments substantiates the value of citizenship.

In Arendt's effort to conceptualize a citizenship concerned with the public good, she writes that the "'public good' . . . is indeed the common good because it is located in the world which we have in common without owning it. Quite frequently [the public good] will be antagonistic to whatever we may deem good to ourselves in our private existence."[133] There are echoes of an early Christianity underlying this appealing but somewhat naïve statement about the common world. Those making decisions about the earth who live in political societies can do so only because of property rights established by positive law. Arendt discredits the notion that the government owns the land—it is in common, with no one owning it—possibly because she believes that any hint of ownership thwarts civic-mindedness. But highlighting the public's ownership of land and ability to decide on its uses substantiates citizens' ethical ties to the state. It connects passive citizenship's qualities—membership by residence and express consent—with those of active citizenship—as members make decisions on the land they inhabit with their neighbors. Such ties might be strengthened by land-use decision-making procedures that borrow from what is arguably the world's least corrupt political institution: the jury. Members might be appointed to these anonymously on the basis of a local lottery, much as how members of U.S. grand juries are selected.[134] The terms of the land juries might be for somewhere between two to four years, with staggered terms to allow for the accumulation of an institutional memory, and members could be compensated on a per diem basis, reflecting the body's power and status. A few positions to run the jury's staff and organize their business might be filled by election among each jury, in much the same way that criminal juries elect forepersons. The size of each land jury might range between twenty and forty members.[135] As a whole, these characteristics conform with the most respected of all U.S. government decision-making bodies: the trial jury,[136] an institution for which Arendt also expressed admiration,[137] for the reasons mentioned above.

One of the chief reasons for eminent domain (that is, the ability of a government to secure land for its own nationals and against invaders) rests on the very nativist beliefs this book questions. With the passing of nationality, a result of ending laws producing birthright citizenship and marriage, the state no longer would be premised on the myth that it embodies a specific intergenerational people existentially distinct from others. Hence governments directly owning the land would no longer sacralize the country's territory and would allow resident citizens without parochial hereditary agendas to control land use, a way to reconcile the relatively short lifespan of the individual with the potential immortality of the planet and the political institutions governing its maintenance.

CHAPTER EIGHT
RELIGION AND THE NATION-STATE

For to know thee is complete righteousness, and to know thy power is the root of immortality.

WISDOM OF SOLOMON 15:3

Affective fascination with a world thought to be unworthy of it may help to ward off the existential resentment that plagues mortals, that is, the sense of victimization that descends upon the tragic (or absurd or incomplete) beings called human.

JANE BENNETT, *THE ENCHANTMENT OF MODERN LIFE* (2001)

RELIGION AND SYSTEMIC VIOLENCE

Elsewhere I have compared the narratives of birth and death in religion with those of the nation,[1] but without reference to the violence associated with religious causes. That violence is important to reflect on, because if religions operate separately from nation-states and perpetrate mass, systemic violence through their own promises of immortality, then abolishing the legal narratives inducing violence perpetrated in the name of national hereditary attachments will still leave open the possibility of religious violence. This chapter suggests that while religious groups do exist separately from nation-states, their means for recruitment, affinities, and antagonisms associated with mass, systemic violence are largely dependent on hereditary groups and not the deeds of individuals acting on the basis of their singular beliefs. Whether in alliance with or opposed to a specific hereditary group, individuals who die and kill for a religion know they are participating in intergenerational narratives of ethnicity, race, clan, caste, or nation and not only doctrinal differences of faith, especially when the violence is on a large-scale and persistent. After reviewing the relation between religious groups and mass, systemic violence, this chapter suggests an alternative appeal for a paradoxical embodied ecstasy, the possibility of finding joy in the mundane, in life itself. The chapter concludes by mentioning a deformed version of this: the rampant failures of modern states to abide by the rule of law, a psychotic effort to refuse the world and its limits, to affirm an ethics of death instead of pleasure.

There are three modes of relation between religions and nation-states: (1) religions rooted in particular nation-states; (2) religions associated with substate ethnicities or other hereditary groups, for example, clans; and (3) religions that maintain no formal or informal ties to states. The first two are the most common religious forms of being, and they are the ones associated with systemic, mass violence. Absent the *telos* of a national form of being, the third mode of religion, existing without the goal of achieving political sovereignty, may result in ad hoc violence but seems not to be associated with the violence of war or imperialism. These three modes do not correspond directly to specific religions. The same religion may, as in the various Christian empires, exist in different modes, even in the same period. Christianity began as a movement commemorating the end of the world, including states, and about three hundred years later became a state religion. But even as Constantine established the Roman Empire as Christian, many Christians (and pagans) rejected this. Large sects of Christians practiced their devotion to Jesus and the God of the New Testament with no regard for the emperor's interpretations.[2]

National and Sovereign Religions

Of the three modes of religion, the ones that seem associated with the most violence are those religions most true to themselves when they are the official spiritual belief of one or more nation-states that have proclaimed support for these gods and not others or that nominally determine the law for their own sovereign rule. The mark of this mode of religion in its first guise is the belief that its members are born into the group and do not convert. The paradigmatic example of this type of religion is Judaism. According to the Hebrew Bible, being a descendant of Abraham is a necessary but not sufficient condition to be saved by God. Individual Israelites may or may not adhere to God's commandments, and suffer the consequences, but only the Israelites are in a position to redeem God's decision to choose them and not another nation:

> "And I will make my covenant between me and you, and will multiply you exceedingly." Then Abram fell on his face; and God said to him, "Behold, my covenant is with you, and you shall be the father of a multitude of nations. No longer shall your name be Abram, but your name shall be Abraham; for I have made you the father of a multitude of nations. I will make you exceedingly fruitful; and I will make nations of you, and kings shall come forth from you. And I will establish my covenant between me and you and your descendants after you throughout their generations for an everlasting covenant, to be God to you and to your descendants after you. And I will give to you, and to your descendants after you, the land of your sojournings, all the land of Canaan, for an everlasting possession; and I will be their God." And God said to Abraham, "As for you, you shall keep my covenant, you and your descendants after you throughout their generations."[3]

The nation will be produced through Abraham's patrilineage, and successive generations will covenant in perpetuity. Even when they do not perform their covenants and other duties to God correctly, they are still Israelites, whereas the other nations are, in the Hebrew Bible, God forsaken. This was an extremely common mode of religion in antiquity, before non-nationally rooted religion took root. The restrictive character of birthright rules for membership meant that those religions allowing conversion (including Judaism in some periods)[4] attracted far more members than those where membership was through descent (another reason to question whether other cultural practices are best preserved by a closed hereditary nation as opposed to more inclusive groups).

Among the religions seeking converts are Christianity and Islam, both manifesting at times political institutions characteristic of the second variant of a state religion. Instead of the religion being bestowed on a nation, some religious groups may attempt to establish themselves as a sovereign political body and create their own rules of kinship and intergenerationality. The religion is not a separate nation but rather creates separate sovereign institutions that absorb national groups. Whereas in the Hebrew Bible God selects one nation, in the Koran, many nations are given the option to choose God: "And certainly We raised in every nation an apostle saying: Serve Allah and shun the Shaitan. So there were some of them whom Allah guided and there were others against whom error was due; therefore travel in the land, then see what was the end of the rejecters."[5] The passage implies at least recognition that populations are organized nationally and will be recruited on this basis, even as it acknowledges that not everyone in a nation will make the correct choice. But all nations are eligible. This mix of empire and the doctrine of conversion led Christianity and Islam on the path to becoming world religions. The Catholic Church and the Islamic Caliphate both used their control of marriage as well as armies to secure their rule. Groups with national religions, such as the Greeks and Jews, could take in as co-religionists members from conquered territories, especially if they were slaves, but generally they were more interested in maintaining their specificity than in sharing their gods.

Hereditary, Tribal, or Ethnically Rooted Religious Conflicts

Religions in their hereditary modes exist through hereditary templates of the nation-state and kinship rules but do not use sovereign institutions for recruitment. This is the most common mode of violent religious groups today. Examples include the Sunni and Shiite conflicts in Iraq and the tensions throughout the Middle East; the fighting among Muslims, Catholics, and Orthodox Christians in the former Yugoslavia; battle lines between Christians and Muslims in Nigeria; and a simmering civil war for the past several decades between Muslims and Christians in parts of the Philippines.[6] In all of these conflicts, the religious cleavages do not arise from the aggregation of individuals who separately adopt rival religions. Rather, they reflect the attachments to tribes, clans, or ethnic groups that at some point in the murky past had a leader with political authority who for reasons of coercion, choice, or other inducements aligned that hereditary population with a particular religion or religious sect. The conflicts among these groups are therefore impossible to distinguish from hereditary groups with common religions. It is true that individuals from one hereditary group may cross over and adopt the religion of another, but these examples are infrequent. The main cleavages of fighting among religions are when their memberships overlay kinship groups. As an example of the general predominance of these kinship attachments over religious ties in matters of warfare, consider the large number of deaths from the U.S. Civil War, World War I, and World War II, all of which had divided Catholics and Protestants on both sides of the battle lines and, in the two world wars, had most Muslims aligned with and not against a Protestant power. This last alliance cannot be explained by a mutual desire to kill Jews, as the Protestant British and Protestant Germans behaved quite differently. Instead, it was the explicit goal of Jewish settlers from Europe to establish a national homeland that would appeal to the devout and nondevout world Jewry that turned Jews into the object of national and not religious warfare on the part of the various religious and tribal communities that Jews were displacing as well as nationalizing in Palestine.

The religious conflicts of the sixteenth and seventeenth centuries in England, France, and Ireland also took this form. The Catholics not only were presumed to follow the orders of the papacy, a sovereign entity, but they also were suspected of being loyal to England's archenemy, France. Likewise in Ireland after the Civil War (1641–1647), the Protestants were largely the English who had settled there and expropriated the Catholic landowners, so that their respective descendants were ethnically marked. Before the Civil War, Catholics owned 59 percent of the productive land. After the Protestant parliamentary army won and expropriated that land to pay for the cost of the war, Catholics owned about 9 percent of the land.[7] A historian writes of the difficulties in deciding whether the term "Anglo-Irish" or "ascendant Protestant" more accurately referred to the post–Civil War colonialists, a group that was simultaneously ethnic and religious.[8]

In his tome on Christian imperialism, Forrest Wood documents numerous examples of various European nation-states and the United States drawing on religious doctrine to justify war against other countries, even Christian ones, such as Mexico.[9] The difference between one country's Protestant and another country's Catholic associations provided another layer of justification for conquest. Wood argues that Christianity constitutes a racist religion, but this is not convincing in light of the extensive evidence of Christianity's central role in slavery's abolition, not to mention more contemporary invocations of Christianity in liberation theology and progressive social movements. Instead, Christianity and other religious discourses have in some times and places provided additional resources via their appeals to immortality for motivating mass, systemic violence among hereditary groups already predisposed to this.

Religions Without Sovereignty or Heredity

Finally, there is the mode of religion that has no ties to state officialdom or hereditary groups. The Merriam-Webster Dictionary states for its first two definitions that a religion is: "1a: the state of a religious <a nun in her 20th year of *religion*>; b (1): the service and worship of God or the supernatural."[10]

Religious groups without ties to the state, nation, or other hereditary groups, as a result of practices or rituals in observance of their faith in a god or the supernatural, may act in ways that their governments consider illegal. It is possible that this might lead to a clash of loyalties such that in the name of their god and eternal salvation for their souls, these individuals will die and kill. The episodic examples of this pass under the rubric of "cults."[11] Recent examples of deaths instigated by cults, for example, the followers of Jim Jones, David Koresh, and Marshall Applewhite and Bonnie Nettles (the leaders of Heaven's Gate), include individuals who were at least as religiously devout as are members of world religions. The murders and suicides within these communities transpired because of the members' faith that their souls would find salvation. The thirty-eight suicides of Heaven's Gate members in 1997 was occasioned by the passing of the comet Hale-Bopp, which followers believed was concealing a spaceship that would take their souls from the earth, which was about to be annihilated.[12]

The suicides of the Heaven's Gate adherents all appear to have been performed with members' advance consent and were not associated with physical violence inflicted on anyone else. For this reason, they posed no threat to the political sovereign and did not—would not—prompt mass violence.[13] The murder-suicides at Jonestown and the Koresh compound, on the other hand, exemplify Hobbes's concern about the devout. Jim Jones ordered a Jonestown inhabitant to kill Congressman Leo Ryan and his delegation in Guyana,[14] David Koresh's followers resisted and killed FBI agents,[15] and both groups eventually committed murder-suicide within their compounds because they had faith in the afterlife and distrust of the present.

These examples suggest that although hereditary groups may select religions and fight in their name, religions alone may be sufficient to sustain systemic, mass killing. Thus, eliminating laws constitutive of nationality, inheritance, and marriage may remove some inducements to act on the basis of superhuman fantasies that are destructive of life on earth—but as long as people are afraid of dying, religions will proliferate, as will the violence and death they seem to allow, if not demand. But there is more to these stories and those of other religious communities.

RELIGION AND (DIS)ENCHANTMENT

One thread running through the narratives of members of all religious communities is despair over the condition of the earthly city, so to speak. Augustine and Marshall Applewhite had different cosmologies, but they both believed in Jesus, that humans had polluted the planet morally and materially, and that bodily death was the threshold into eternal freedom, a beginning and not the end. Religious enclaves—a prerequisite for the organization to perpetrate mass violence—attract people who do not have faith in this world, perhaps with good reason.

The point being developed here is quite different from the interpretation of Marx's claim that "religion is the opium of the people"[16] to mean that religion allows people to endure daily suffering as cogs in the capitalist machine in the hope that something better awaits them in the next life. Not only did Marx have a slightly more complicated understanding of religion in mind, but such an analysis fails to acknowledge that religion in its essential form rejects the material world that makes capitalism possible. It is not a palliative that allows workers to carry on but a way of being directly opposed to capitalism.

Perhaps the reason that religion's antagonism to capitalism often is misunderstood is that it is read through the work of another theorist who tried to reconcile theology with economic theory to account for the apparent persistence of Christianity in an age of capitalism. Distortions of religious texts to suit the imperatives of greed occur in all ages, at which point the ideologies are pseudoreligious. In his analysis, Max Weber confused just such pseudoreligious worldly instructions on accumulating wealth in the name of Protestantism or Calvinism with practicing Christianity as a religion.[17] Religion per se does not encourage hard work and material gain for the sake of a soothing afterlife, much less for its own sake. Rather, religion encourages a breaking away from the daily grind of job, family, the body. The martyrs, the celibate, and the devout who flagellate their backs with iron chains, wear shoes with broken glass, and don hairshirts are hard to square with Weber's cadre of entrepreneurs reinvesting wealth to buy their way into God's grace.

According to Weber, Protestantism and Calvinism are religions whose doctrine reconciles people to working on behalf of the material world when, by definition, any ideology that does this is not religious but purely secular. People turn to religion to withdraw from the world. Again, this is not to ignore the many religions that refer to material incentives in their recruitment efforts, including contemporary evangelicalism, but to stress that in these guises the claims are capitalist or consumer ideologies dressed up as religion and nothing more. Those who follow such ideologies, regardless of what they call themselves, will not systemically kill or risk death, because their materialism binds them to the world as strongly as their atheist counterparts. So regardless of what they are called, the religious adherents who may persist and authorize violence in the name of their faith are the ones who have withdrawn from society.

Why have they done this? Can it be changed? Marx writes:

Religious suffering is, at one and the same time, the *expression* of real suffering and a *protest* against real suffering. Religion is the sigh of the oppressed creature, the heart of a heartless world, and the soul of soulless conditions. It is the *opium* of the people. The abolition of religion as the *illusory* happiness of the people is the demand for their *real* happiness. To call on them to give up their illusions about their condition is to call on them to *give up a condition that requires illusions*.[18]

Marx does not present religion as an ideological trick played by those with power on those who lack it but rather as a thwarted effort at soulfulness and real existence in a material world that makes this impossible.

Marx sees the deprivations of capitalism's alienation from the means of production and its pointless exchange cycles, and perhaps the oppression from earlier economic systems, as the culprit that drives people to religion. But as long as there has been oppression from economic relations, there also has existed real alienation, a word whose German meaning (das Fremde) similarly conveys foreignness. For religions that seem to be separate from the nation-state, of which Christianity is the purest and largest example,[19] faith appears to provide the potential to achieve community and immortality through universality and not, as the nation requires, through particularity. Moreover, when religion implies encounters with the divine, it promises as well what Jane Bennett describes as "enchantment" and then refigures as an ethical imperative for contemporary social justice.[20]

Perhaps a world that treated mortals as mortals—and thus enabled a world with which to be enchanted and not escaped—would not require fantasies of death and the afterlife. Bennett writes of enchantment that is nonreligious and nonconformist, the ecstasy of Dionysius: "Enchantment is a mode of lively and intense engagement with the world. . . . Enchantment consists of a mixed bodily state of joy and disturbance, a transitory sensuous condition dense and intense enough to stop you in your tracks and toss you onto new terrain . . .":[21] in other words, the opposite of the religious believer's rejection of this world, at least if that religion is quietist, dogmatic, and conformist.

At the same time, religions have been able to draw on selected materialist values that do not flow from consumerism or the work ethic. Religious missionary groups, from Christians to Muslims to the Hare Krishna, do not extol hard work for the sake of consumer goods or for profits to earn yet more profits, but they do commit themselves to materially improving the condition of the communities to which they reach out. If religions can gain devotees by offering enchantment and demonstrating their ability to care for basic needs, then perhaps states might do the same and nurture mortals coming to grips with their mortality, instead of encouraging its escape. As Bennett describes it, an ethics of enchantment is not naïve distraction from serious political crises. Rather, much of politics is a naïve effort to distract mortals from the fear of death.

THE RULE OF LAW FOR FRIENDS AND ENEMIES

So far we have seen that religion, while promising universality, may be used in the service of the particular, with deadly ends. Moreover, religion, which appeals to a desire for enchantment, in truth is a symptom of alienation. Marx writes: "It is the immediate task of philosophy, which is in the service of history, to unmask self-estrangement in its unholy forms once the holy form of human self-estrangement has been unmasked. Thus, the criticism of Heaven turns into the criticism of Earth, the criticism of religion into the criticism of law, and the criticism of theology into the criticism of politics."[22] Marx is criticizing the Hegelian conception of religion as a manifestation of Geist and is revealing its legal, political character as a complement to state ideology. This

Hegelian, state form of religion is always ready for violence. Usually, this is a result of orderly procedures, but it may also occur through an undisciplined, extralegal, violent deification of the state independent of its worldly ties. This is the Hobbesian state, whereby government becomes God and lacks accountability to mortals.

The most recent manifestation of the state's unaccountable use of violence occurred in the responses to the attacks by Al Qaeda on the Pentagon and World Trade Center on September 11, 2001, when the international community's commitment to the rule of law worldwide, never a sure bet, faltered significantly: warrantless detentions of immigrants who had been residing in and outside the United States; a "preemptive," that is, illegal, invasion of Iraq; an Israeli- and U.S.-backed coup overthrowing a democratically elected government in Palestine;[23] Egyptian government arrests of opposition political leaders;[24] genocide in Sudan;[25] arrests of journalists in Somalia;[26] dictatorships in countries from Burma/Myanmar to Zimbabwe; and fraudulent elections and opposition harassment in Ethiopia.[27] The list is not, alas, exhaustive, but merely exemplifies cases where the rule of law has been abandoned. In this context it may seem a little strange to prioritize theorizing the abolition of birthright nationality, inheritance, marriage, and private land rights and not to focus on unresolved problems of self-governance—that is, how to make sure that government will follow the law.

And yet, if one follows the recent trend of thinking among neoconservatives as well as their critics now turning to Carl Schmitt's analysis of the "state of emergency"[28]—when elected and even unelected political actors sanction the illegal use of force a public will accept and perhaps desire—we see that it is the imperatives of the so-called foreign threat that legitimates, if not motivates, these sovereigns and their citizenries. In each of the cases above, not to mention Nazi Germany, hereditary national or ethnic differences or religious differences either within or among countries legitimated the suspension of law. In the case of Germany, it was the nationalist resentment of the Versailles Treaty signed in surrender to foreign powers and the scapegoating of Jews and communists (both caricatured as foreign invaders) that led to the street fighting and collapse of traditional parties that set the stage for the Nazis to take power.[29] Today, anxieties about actual and pretextual Islamist militants are legitimating government lawlessness.[30]

This is the world of Schmitt, in which "friends" forge military alliances and fight "enemies," with little regard to the niceties of law, but what Schmitt and those on the Left who admire his insights fail to appreciate is that this perverted Hegelianism is not the inevitable point of "the political." It is merely the current habituation of the state to misshapen psychological imperatives, specifically the human inadequacies and weaknesses in the face of birth and death.[31] Schmitt's critique of Kant and the League of Nations in "The Concept of the Political" is identical to the attack Hegel made in *The Philosophy of Right*, which Schmitt himself acknowledges.[32] And Schmitt's idealization of an existential commitment realized in risking one's life to kill enemies[33] is a restatement of Hegel's citizen-warrior, whose very identity depends on the perpetuation of his nation. Schmitt writes: "War is the existential negation of the enemy," and "there exists no rational purpose, no norm no matter how true, no program no matter how exemplary, no social ideal no matter how beautiful, no legitimacy nor legality which could justify men in killing each other. . . . If such physical destruction of human life is not motivated by an existential threat to one's own way of life, then it cannot be justified."[34]

It really is impossible to understand this without being familiar with Hegel's thoughts on the ways that citizens achieve their individuality through identification with the nation-state, culminating most particularly in the willingness to annihilate those from other nations, to kill and sacrifice themselves in war. The difference between Schmitt and Hegel is that Hegel imagined that the unification of God, nation, family, and the individual through the state would inevitably result in a meaningful and rule-bound ethics, whereas Schmitt was so craven as to deny the relevance of this and to imagine the state could, in its appropriation of violence, become divine in itself.

It is Schmitt's notion of "the political" as a justification of violence that defines the national commitments that posed the problems Hannah Arendt explored in her account of Adolf Eichmann's trial and in many other places in her oeuvre. Arendt and her interlocutors have led the way in showing the existential possibilities in very different ideas about "the political" from those proposed by Schmitt. In the same vein, the proposals here are part of what I take to be a project of critical theory to carefully analyze structural constraints with an eye to overcoming them and, as well, to hold out more positive possibilities: what Bennett calls enchantment and perhaps what Arendt, in a less exuberant register, calls thinking, an attitude that finds a quiet joy in the here and now.

Appendix
METHODS FOR AN OPEN SOCIETY

No doubt the spirit of Hitlerism won its greatest victory over us when, after its defeat, we used the weapons which the threat of Nazism had induced us to develop. But in spite of this, I am today no less hopeful than I have ever been that violence can be defeated.

KARL POPPER, "UTOPIA AND VIOLENCE" (1947)

One of the points on which I feel sympathy with Marxists is their insistence that the social problems of our time are urgent, and that philosophers ought to face the issues; that we should not be content to interpret the world but should help to change it.

KARL POPPER, "PREDICTION AND PROPHECY IN THE SOCIAL SCIENCES"
(1948)

It is really strange that human beings are normally deaf to the strongest arguments, while they are always inclined to overestimate measuring accuracies.

ALBERT EINSTEIN, IN "LETTER TO MAX BORN" (1952), QUOTED IN PAUL FEYERABEND, *AGAINST METHOD* (1975)

The rule or craft of "valid induction" is not even metaphysical: it simply does not exist. No rule can ever guarantee that a generalization inferred from true observations, however often repeated, is true. . . . Induction, i.e., inference based on many observations, is a myth. It is neither a psychological fact, nor a fact of ordinary life, nor one of scientific procedure.

KARL POPPER, "SCIENCE: CONJECTURES AND REFUTATIONS" (1953)

WHY A METHODS APPENDIX?

Personal experience with the futility in trying to engage colleagues across fields with methods questions leads me to save this discussion for a section where it will satisfy interlocutors who, fairly enough, wonder about my selection of theories and evidence, without distracting readers from the more important epistemological project of elaborating what I hope are insights worthy of further investigation. The placement of this discussion also signals frustration with the hollowness of the antimethods methodology scholarship[1] when it produces only claims about methods and not knowledge.[2]

The intellectual history of social science methods is not as straightforward as some may imagine. Before detailing my own commitments, I want to untangle some epistemologies from the political milieu of their advocates. I do so because the approach I am using is ecumenical, but not thoughtless, about its criteria for knowledge, and I want to map some prevailing assumptions to help orient readers as to where I stand. To do so, I discuss tacit beliefs that we think we share or reject with our friends and adversaries, respectively, but may not.

RECONSIDERING THE THEORY-AND-METHOD DEBATE

One of the most familiar and enduring twentieth-century divisions in research approaches in political science is between what Sheldon Wolin calls the "the methodist" and "the theorist,"[3] a dichotomy that seems to hold for the social scientist and humanist more generally. The division states a disciplinary rupture, the nuances of which Emily Hauptmann thoughtfully renders in what she calls a "local history" of Berkeley's political theorists' alienation from political science.[4] But, like the divisions in the Berkeley political science department, these have more to do with different political agendas vis-à-vis the cold war—and, today, the even more ad hoc distinctions of Left and Right—than with thoughtful, substantive disagreements about research methods.

The Politics of Karl Popper and His Adversaries

The key figure in this debate is an Austrian philosopher of science, Karl Popper, the man whose name is iconographic for asserting a demarcation between scientific and nonscientific knowledge claims. Many social scientists believe they are adhering to the methods principles laid out for natural scientists by Popper in his *Logic of Scientific Discovery* (1934)[5] and that by doing so they are producing knowledge. According to Popper, for a claim to count as scientific knowledge, it has to be falsifiable, tested, and the tests must be reproducible. Assertions not meeting these criteria might be true, but truth and knowledge are not the same, a point resembling the one Immanuel Kant made by distinguishing the noumenal (reality in itself) from the phenomenal (its appearance to human minds). Kant suggested that philosophers confine inquiry to the latter. Popper, influenced by Kant, also emphasizes a difference between *scientific knowledge* (theories subject to falsification that are provisionally verified), which is possible, and *knowledge of the truth* (assertions based on either scientific experiments or a nonscientific method), which is not. Popper provided a demarcation for claims that might contribute to scientific knowledge, that is, the ones adhering to his method, from all other observations, regardless of whether they might be truthful. Few publications in the humanities would meet Popper's threshold for this definition of knowledge. But at least Popper acknowledged that some work in the humanities was intellectually fruitful, whereas according to Popper's criteria, virtually none of the most influential studies in the contemporary social sciences would count either as knowledge or even as interesting. Popper was brutal about the equivalent in his time, as we shall see below, and would have regarded the work of today's most feted economists, political scientists, and sociologists as pointless counting.

Popper's writings are one of the best sources for thinking about how to construct a research agenda that encourages both imagination and the ability to convey insights to others so they can be intersubjectively assessed. His insights have been ignored by those who think they are adhering to his method and by those who are following his lead without knowing it. The person most at fault for this confusion is Popper himself, who rooted his epistemological commitments in his political worldview. Popper, similar to Jewish émigré philosophers across the political spectrum, including Hannah Arendt, was a fierce opponent of the Soviet Union. His book *The Open Society and Its Enemies*, written in the early years of World War II, asserted parallels between Hitler's Germany and Stalin's USSR. According to Popper, in claims that appear throughout his oeuvre, "historicism and the myth of destiny" are not just found in the "chosen people" mentality of Israelites and Nazis but appear among Marxists as well, not to mention Freudians and Adlerians.[6] But Popper says Marxists are his special concern: "My analysis of the role of prediction and prophecy could . . . be described as a criticism of the historical method of Marxism."[7] Popper acknowledges that others, including Hegel, also use this method but writes, "Nevertheless, I have decided to speak as if Marxism were my main or my only object of attack, since I wish to avoid the accusation that I am attacking Marxism surreptitiously under the name of 'historicism.'"[8] Popper, who dedicates the collection of essays in which these passages appear "To F. A. von Hayek," observes a correlation between nonfalsification and Marxism and therefore asserts that the way to Marxism's epistemological and thus intellectual comeuppance would be by way of Popper's theory of scientific investigation.

The result was that those who agreed with Popper's anticommunism said they were using his method even when they were not. And those who rejected Popper's political mission appeared to think it necessary to reject his epistemology, even if the attacks were largely ad hominem and the substance of the disagreements hard to see.[9] In fact, Popper and Arendt share some significant influences and positions. Their work is heavily influenced by Kant's ethics and politics; both were highly critical of Karl Marx, communism, and the Soviet Union; both wrote major books on the parallels between Nazism and the Soviet Union (as did Frederick Hayek);[10] and both were very critical of nationalism in any form, including Jewish nationalism. Indeed, in their own ways, both Popper and Arendt were committed to the project of critical theory: they drew on Kant to ridicule the inductivism and positivism that became characteristic of behavioralism and stressed that violence was the enemy of political community. It seems that Popper was dismissed by leftist scholars more because of his association with the cold-warrior, free-market academic circle at the University of Chicago and less because of his epistemology or political theory, key elements of which were embraced by Arendt, a political theorist admired by portions of the Left. As a result, today's social scientists fail to see that Popper's method does not accommodate their research, and humanists have not taken advantage of its possibilities for framing a rational critique of prevailing social norms.

The following points from Popper are consistent with the Frankfurt School's rejection of behavioralism, are useful for exploring the possibility of knowledge for social change, and are beacons for considering the theories advanced in this book. First, Popper is contemptuous of probability studies and all predictive work in the social sciences. Second, according to Popper, knowledge is provisional and can never be proven true. And third, Popper was extraordinarily sensitive to the importance of theories derived from the imagination or intuition, any source other than simple empiricism, for generating new discoveries.

Confusing Popper with Behavioral Social Science

The story about Popper's actual epistemological commitments is at odds with the expectations for the father of the natural scientific method, the one revered by those who swear by their datasets and reviled as a banal "methodist" in the well-known essay by the political theorist Sheldon Wolin:

> There are inherent limits to the kinds of questions which the methodist deems appropriate. The kind of world hospitable to method invites a search for those regularities that reflect the main pattern of behavior which society is seeking to promote and maintain. Predictable behavior is what societies live by...hence their structures of coercion, of rewards and penalties, of subsidies and discouragements, are shaped toward producing and maintaining certain regularities in behavior and attitudes.[11]

Wolin is right to see these sentiments in the norms advocated by his colleagues in political science at Berkeley. But this is because they are hacks and not because they are following Popper's scientific method.

Consider the following passage from Popper's *The Logic of Scientific Discovery*: "I think that [induction] is not needed; that it does not help us; and that it even gives rise to inconsistencies. Thus I reject the naturalistic view. It is uncritical. Its upholders fail to notice that whenever they believe themselves to have discovered a fact, they have only proposed a convention. Hence the convention is liable to turn into dogma."[12] Popper understood the implications of this for the social as well as the natural sciences. His criticism of Marxists for inferring from their assumptions about present observations insights about the future are equally if not more relevant for conservative political scientists of this era as well. Popper dismissed the notion that the "task of the social sciences is fundamentally the same as that of the natural sciences—to make predictions, and, more especially, historical predictions, that is to say, predictions about the social and political development of mankind,"[13] explaining that "long-term prophecies can be derived from scientific conditional predictions only if they apply to systems which can be described as well-isolated, stationary, and recurrent. These systems are very rare in nature; and modern society is surely not one of them."[14] Indeed, Popper frequently makes the obvious point that history is contingent and its possibilities open ended, exactly what is not the case in the natural world or that of the world constructed by so-called social scientists.

Popper would have no patience with so-called social scientists' addiction to statistics and probability, which he finds useless for making scientific claims even about nature. When so-called social scientists offer a hypothesis producing an independent variable having a .4 correlation with the dependent variable, then they believe their theory has been verified (for example, the studies of civil war by James Fearon and David Laitin[15] discussed in the introduction). And yet the variation in the outcomes of the regression equations may mean that many of the observed cases directly falsify the theory, as is the case in the work by Fearon and Laitin. According to Popper, this means that the theory needs to be discarded: "Instead of discovering the 'probability' of a hypothesis we should try to assess how far it has been able to prove its fitness to survive by standing up to tests."[16] Popper resembles Stephen Jay Gould[17] in his condemnation of probability as a scientific method: "If you cannot verify a theory, or make it certain by induction, you may turn to probability as a kind of 'Ersatz' for certainty."[18] When the apple falls one million times out of one million, we verify Isaac Newton's theory of gravity. Newton turned the observation of things falling into an example of something that his imagination expanded into a theory of gravity. Newton's theory of gravity makes a very basic point, yet the significance of this inviolable pattern was crucial for advancing theories of physics. If the apple landed on the ground only 40 percent of the time under controlled conditions, then Newton's theory of gravity would have been falsified. This is the situation for virtually all work published in today's journals of so-called social sciences. However, most of the claims made in these pages can be verified as easily as the apple falling. Here are two of the basic ones: (1) every single society in world history and today has kinship rules,[19] and (2) every single war has been conducted on behalf of an intergenerational or religious group.[20] Moreover, the theories that have been used to explain current institutions of violence and inequality do not bear up under scrutiny: sociobiological theories do not explain kinship rules; models in the so-called social sciences theories do not explain war. This book uses evidence to falsify dominant causal narratives by leading social scientists.

Second, unlike the so-called social scientists, Popper does not believe in timeless certainties about human nature, be they those of the Marxist, Freudian, or the rational-choice theorist. Popper, like Feyerabend, looks at the history of science and does not see eternal truths but provisional theory that may be verified at one point and then replaced, as "subsequent negative decisions may always overthrow it."[21] Theories may count as knowledge for long periods of time, but, Popper continues, "I never assume that by force of 'verified' conclusions, theories can be established as 'true,' or even as merely 'probable.'"[22] As mentioned earlier, the distinction that Popper develops is not truth versus belief but scientific versus unscientific knowledge claims. Hence Popper does not say Freud is wrong but that Freud's work is solipsistic and does not allow for intersubjective standards of analysis. In fact, at various points Popper suggests that intuitively he finds Freud's claims persuasive and even attempts to complement Freud's analyses by writing that "most neuroses may be due to a partially arrested development of the critical attitude" in early childhood.[23] If people were not so neurotic, Popper suggests, they would be more amenable to the scientific method. The difference between the skeptical postfoundationalist and Popper is that the former does not insist on intersubjective understandings that make the author's claims intelligible to her audience, while Popper takes this as a starting point for developing norms of rational conversation, an enterprise that shares commonalties with the work of Jürgen Habermas, albeit Popper lacks the teleological dogma, discussed below, that so frustrate Habermas's colleagues in critical theory. By insisting that scholars be responsive to questions about their claims and not simply behave as artists creating new visions that the audience must take or leave, Popper is promoting a discourse that is more democratic and antielitist than the ad hoc claims advanced by so-called social scientists and political theorists.

A commitment to rationality is about extending conversations, not foreclosing them. Paul Feyerabend, who studied with Popper, does not seem to understand this:

To those who look at the rich material provided by history, and who are not intent on impoverishing it in order to please their lower instincts, their craving for intellectual security in the form of clarity, precision, "objectivity," "truth," it will become clear that there is only one principle that can be defended under *all* circumstances and in all stages of human development. It is the principle: *anything goes.*[24]

Although his ostensible target here is Popper, the attack seems off the mark. Feyerabend's work, despite his worst efforts, reveals commitments to reason and clarity. And Popper is not proposing that scholars must uniformly follow his method. Popper writes: "I do not care what methods a philosopher (or anybody else) may use so long as he has an interesting problem, and so long as he is sincerely trying to solve it."[25] Anything goes, as long as the research is interesting, which generally would preclude the work of Wolin's methodists. Popper is especially open minded when it comes to generating the ideas for research. Inventing a theory does not, Popper says, "call for logical analysis nor to be susceptible of it."[26] Inspiration, intuition, and years of study are all suitable theoretical sparks.

Finally, Popper and Feyerabend agree in principle on the central finding from Thomas Kuhn's sociology of science: theories that have been falsified will remain dominant for long periods of time; theories that may come to be verified later may early on in their invention be falsified because of poor heuristics, techniques, or other errors.[27] Popper describes scientists since antiquity trusting their imagination over impoverished dogmas and quotes Galileo praising Aristarchus and Copernicus "precisely because they dared to go beyond this known world of our senses: 'I cannot,' he writes, 'express strongly enough my unbounded admiration for the greatness of mind of these men who conceived [the heliocentric system] and held it to be true . . . in violent opposition to the evidence of their own senses.'"[28] Feyerabend concurs in this, pointing out that Galileo could not address concerns that perpendicular falls without swerves appeared to falsify Copernicus's theory, quoting Galileo: "It is, therefore, better to put aside the appearance, on which we all agree, and to use the power of reason either to confirm its reality or to reveal its fallacy."[29] It is not even clear that Feyerabend's provocative claim that Galileo's scientific victories depended on his qualities as a "propagandist"[30] would trouble Popper, who understood Galileo's struggles against the preconceptions of his contemporaries. If a propagandist is someone who propounds his own well-contemplated theories against the proven dogmas of the moment, then Nietzsche and Popper alike would seem to support this.

REAL DISAGREEMENTS AND THEIR IMPLICATIONS

The serious methodological and not ideological difference between Popper and Feyerabend is one of focus; they are largely providing complementary views of knowledge formation. Popper wants more falsification and Feyerabend wants to make sure that knowledge claims in falsified theories are not ruled out definitively. Popper takes this last point as a truism—hence his recognition of Copernicus's accomplishments—but Popper is more concerned with the false generalization of particular observations than he is with the false particularization of observations that might be generalized with validity.

Popper worries that Marx might see one example that fits his prediction and announce confirmation that his theory would hold true everywhere. Feyerabend is concerned that the prejudices of an epoch might lead to a theory's erroneous falsification and dismissal. Both concerns are valid, and they are not mutually exclusive. They emblematize the condition of inquiry into meaningful and difficult research questions.

The Falsification of Popper's Epistemology for Anticommunists

The enmities between Popper and many of his critics are not rooted in irreconcilable methodological commitments, but the formal claim to methods disagreements are based on political differences. And yet the political commitments do not lead in directions that Popper and Feyerabend—and Wolin and the behavioralists—imagine. Popper does not appreciate the extent to which his own anticommunist worldview was a justification for the use of violence and repression of at least the same scale and intensity as seen in the Soviet Union's actions in the name of Marx. Naomi Klein writes:

> It was the Chicago Boys' vision of a total country overhaul that appealed to [Pinochet's] newly unleashed ambition, and, like Suharto with his Berkeley Mafia, he immediately named several Chicago grads as senior economic advisers.... [Pinochet] called them the *technos*—the technicians—which appealed to the Chicago pretension that fixing the economy was a matter of science, not of subjective human choices.... This mutual claim to be taking orders from higher natural laws formed the basis of the Pinochet-Chicago alliance.[31]

The inspirational figure for the Chicago School? Popper's hero, Hayek:

> Much of this Puritanism came from Friedrich Hayek, [Milton] Friedman's own personal guru, who also taught at the University of Chicago for a stretch in the 1950s.... According to Arnold Harberger, a longtime professor at Chicago, "the Austrians," as this clique-within-a-clique was called, were so zealous that any state interference was not just wrong, but "evil.... It's as if there is a very pretty but highly complex picture out there, which is perfectly harmonious within itself, you see, and if there's a speck where it isn't supposed to be, well, that's just awful ... it is a flaw that mars that beauty."[32]

The results of this fervor were policies implemented regardless of the harms caused to the target populations. In chapter after chapter, country after country, Klein documents the Hayekians's Platonic vision of the good and true coming undone by the actual effects of Friedman's policies. Describing the effect of the Chicago School policies in Argentina after the 1976 military coup, Klein writes:

> Once again, the human impact was unmistakable: within a year, wages lost 40 percent of their value, factories closed, poverty spiraled. Before the junta took power, Argentina had fewer people living in poverty than France or the U.S.—just 9 percent—and an unemployment rate of 4.2 percent. Now the country began to display signs of the underdevelopment thought to have been left behind. Poor neighborhoods were without water and preventable diseases ran rampant.[33]

Friedman's theories were being falsified and, as is often the case in the social sciences, the methodists refused to believe this. They insisted something must be wrong with how the policies were implemented: "Like all fundamentalist faiths, Chicago School economics is, for its true believers, a closed loop. . . . It follows ineluctably that if something is wrong within a free-market economy—high inflation or soaring unemployment—it has to be because the market is not truly free. There must be some interference, some distortion in the system."[34] In the face of their policies' failure, the model must be preserved; the people could be sacrificed. Instead of treating these episodes as experiments falsifying their theories, the Chicago School embraced Frances Fukuyama's story of free markets as the "end of history,"[35] a narrative relying on the very Hegelian methodology Popper loathed.

Klein does a remarkable job of explaining how the International Monetary Fund and World Bank spawned death squads from Chile to South Africa, as kleptocrats pursued loans in exchange for wiping out the voices opposing radical privatization. Klein's argument is that torture and violence were necessary to impede the normal functions of democracy so that dictatorships might implement Friedman's programs. Elected politicians accountable to majorities would never impose these policies, and thus the democratically elected leaders from Argentina to Guatemala had to be assassinated and replaced by juntas. Or the majority could be disenfranchised altogether, as was the case in South Africa.[36]

Even more ironically, the protégés of Popper's anticommunist hero Hayek relied on the use of the most insane and brutal form of epistemology ever invented: torture and brainwashing. In 1963 the CIA, fearful of Chinese mind control, produced a manual for the purpose of achieving this result themselves. The purpose of the MKUltra program was "not to research brainwashing (that was a mere side project), but to design a scientifically based system for extracting information from 'resistant sources.' In other words, torture."[37] The reverse engineering of Chinese brainwashing techniques led to the U.S. appropriation of these practices. Communist and laissez-faire ideologues alike are susceptible to dogma and to the violence that it may entail.

This was exactly the epistemological-political scenario that Popper most feared. But he thought Marxism was the only culprit: "The view that it will be the task of the revolution to rid us of the capitalist conspiracy, and with it, of opposition to social reform, is widely held; but it is untenable. . . . For a revolution is liable to replace old masters by new ones. . . . The theory of revolution overlooks the most important aspect of social life—that what we need is not so much good men as good institutions."[38] The Chicago Boys' coups were arguably worse in this regard, because they would have even less of a popular base than a revolution. Popper thought democracy the best political process and defined it as the "type of government which can be removed without violence,"[39] the opposite of how the governments that implemented the Chicago School policies gained power. Why did Popper overlook the ideological fervor of Hayek's acolytes and the possibility that revolutions might be inspired by their free-market fanaticism and not Marxian theory? Perhaps, because of his own prejudices and friendships, Popper did not see that a chosen people could be happy gathering together as such under the auspices of either Marx or Hayek. In other words, Marx and Hayek were not substitutes but supplements for the chosen people, who remained unchanged in their national and religious commitments. The Nazis vilified Jews for being communists and capitalists. The Zionists who came to Palestine settled under the banners of Marx as well as Hayek, but they united to throw out the non-Jews. In the end, it was Jews, communists or capitalists, who would be sent to the death camps and always the Germans who were organizing this. Yes, the Nazis targeted non-Jewish communists, but even here the agenda was driven by nationalism. The friend of my enemy (the Russians) is my enemy, a dynamic Carl Schmitt documented contemporaneously with the Nazi party's ascendance to political power.[40] China and the Soviet Union were nationalists first and communists second.[41]

This depiction of national attachments driving violence is not the story Klein seeks to advance. Hers is a narrative of neoliberal zealots pressing their view of market equilibriums by any means necessary. But here, too, another dynamic is evident in the nationalist agendas to which these respective visions were tied. The United States hated communism because it was Russian, that is, un-American; it did not hate Russia because it was communist.[42] Michael Rogin's work on demonology makes this point, as he describes Ronald Reagan's anticommunism as based on nationalism and a paranoia about Russia: "'Russ Imperialism Seen by Veteran' ran the headline over a 1950 story in the *Los Angeles Times*,"[43] Rogin writes, and describes Reagan as a "statist" who supported a "global, interventionist foreign policy" and had no patience for isolationism.[44] Rogin also describes the nationalist demonology of the cold war more generally, in language that seems prophetic:

> The alleged menace of international terrorism provides the rationale for these executive actions [of domestic surveillance]. The Soviet state is accused of directing small bands of terrorists, mostly from the Third World, to commit acts of political violence.... By merging savages (from the first moment in American political demonology), revolutionaries (from the second moment in American demonology), and Soviet agents (from the third), the theory of international terrorism also encapsulates and brings up to date the entire history of American countersubversion.[45]

Just as Popper overstates the identification of state violence with Marxists, Klein misapprises the contribution of neoliberal theories per se to governmental violence.

As Rogin points out, the

> Soviet Union replaced the immigrant working class as the source of anxiety, and the combat between workers and capitalists ... was replaced by one between Moscow's agents ... and a state national-security apparatus.... [The] free man and the military state are not two alternative poles in American ideology, nor are they merely a recent symbiosis. Their marriage goes back to the beginning.[46]

The ideological fervor on behalf of the free man in American lore, from the Jacksonian wilderness to the Friedmanian adventurism abroad, has been tied to his nationalism and militarism. In an essay that documents specifically anti-Russian prejudices by cold war–era filmmakers, Rogin suggests that the attachment to liberal or neoliberal rhetorics is based on a U.S. psychohistory that, in its embrace of demonization and violence, is irrational and not based on economic ideology per se.

More directly contravening Klein's analysis is the evidence that countries spanning world history and geography have used torture for reasons that have nothing to do with neoliberalism. Klein does not discuss noneconomic motives for torture and state violence, because focusing on the nationalism invoked by the various political and military leaders who are Hayek's and Friedman's free-market advocates in Chile, Argentina, Brazil, Poland, and Russia is not good for Klein's 1990s antiglobalization agenda. Klein comes out of the anti-NAFTA, anti-GATT, anti-WTO movements, which were advancing the very parochial, nationalist commitments of the juntas who were torturing people.

This is not to say that so-called indigenous peoples protesting in Seattle favored torture or any other policies of the death squads, but it is to say that the belief in a native people that should be protected from outsiders was also an ideology the Nazis shared and that in less dramatic circumstances appears in political contexts worldwide. The examples of groups victimized by nationalism becoming violent perpetrators of nationalism, discussed in the introduction and chapter 1, are legion and persist regardless of the economic ideology in vogue. In 2007, Vladimir Putin's party, in charge of a government responsible for targeted assassinations, received 61 percent of the Russian vote[47] because he had been bellicose in defying the United States on Russian defense (withdrawing just before the election from a treaty that would have limited the Russian army's presence near European borders); his renationalization (not privatization) of oil; and his feeding bigotry against non-Russian residents,[48] for which they would be rewarded by the invasion of Georgia. In other words, in Russia and elsewhere, including the United States, warmongering leaders maintain the power to implement their economic plans when they violate the rule of law because of nationalist fervor among majorities relinquishing the citizenry's civil rights and not because the government is threatening them.

Perhaps the most conclusive evidence that neoliberalism requires the nation and not vice versa has been the U.S. federal government coming to the aid of the Milton Friedman–trained scions of finance. Political theorist Shlomo Avineri writes: "Economics 101 in universities in the West, and in Israel [where

Avineri lives], will now have to listen to other voices, and finance ministers will not be able to say, 'for example, in America....' The unbridled market has proven itself to be a god that failed."[49] The trillions of dollars being borrowed and printed on the credit of the federal government prove that having a former CEO hold a cabinet position is good for one's business, and the ease with which this occurs shows the identification of the Goldman Sachs–Wall Street neoliberal ideology with the national interests of the United States. Capitalism itself is branded American. And when capitalism suffers so unequivocally and demonstrably, then America, too, has an image problem.

One way to bring together Klein's persuasive account of the state robberies that required extreme violence with the nationalism that accompanied this is to refuse to use the Chicago School's language of liberalization altogether. As Klein points out, the main thrust of the plans was privatization. Proudhon's aphorism, "property is theft," when inverted, holds as well: Thievery depends on private property. As Kant would appreciate, that is how thieves keep their loot. Kleptocracy has nothing to do with liberalism. Instead of a compatibility between liberalism, neo- or otherwise, and nationalism—Klein's ostensible narrative—Klein's is a story of nationalism and force, assisted by a lie that these were outcomes of open markets and choice. If only these reforms really were liberal, and not the expression of U.S. military priorities determined by its cold war with Russia—as well as the nationalism and greed motivating the repressive forces in other countries as well. Klein's book opens with the CIA's mobilization against Soviet Russia, but it then fails to show how the facts she discovers mark largely nationalist and not economically driven pathways toward violence.

METHODS IN STATES WITHOUT NATIONS

The theories and empirical examples here are designed to help imagine a new path to replace those on which many seem pathologically stuck, regardless of rational evidence. The claim is not that these alternatives are necessary or even likely but simply that they are worthy of consideration. To advance my substantive arguments, I draw on Popper's suggestions as well as Kant's and Arendt's ideas about judgment and, especially relevant for the explorations of this book, what Alessandro Ferrara calls the "force of the example."[50] Ferrara uses this phrase to characterize the idea of reflective judgment developed by Kant and elaborated by Arendt. Kant writes:

The reflective judgment which is compelled to ascend from the particular in nature to the universal, stands, therefore, in need of a principle. This principle it cannot borrow from experience, because what it has to do is to establish just the unity of all empirical principles under higher, though likewise empirical, principles, and thence the possibility of the systematic subordination of higher and lower. Such a transcendental principle, therefore, the reflective judgment can only give as a law from and to itself.[51]

Popper, too, believes that knowledge cannot be generated based on experience but first needs a more general aesthetic principle or theory. Popper says more about where this theory does not come from (inductivism) than how the imagination he credits with new theories arrives at these new ideas, but here it seems that Arendt's work on Kant is complementary.

Ferrara writes that Arendt develops ideas about the imagination to explain the cognitive interplay between the particular and the general: "it is the imagination—'the faculty of making present what is absent'—that evokes in our mind examples that might apply to our case. . . . It does so by means of providing schemata for cognition and *examples* for judgment (79-80). A schema, in the case of cognition, is 'an image for a concept,' a tangible instantiation of the concept."[52] Ferrara goes on to explain the circularity in this approach—one cannot recognize an example of something until one has a schema, but the schema depends on knowing the right example—by suggesting that Arendt develops ideas about an intersubjective validity that the example enables through communication and does not reveal in itself: "*exemplary* validity is best understood in terms of *creating* an example rather than *applying* an example. . . . Identifying an action as exemplary in the latter sense means to 'bring to a concept' the uniqueness or particularity of it."[53] Examples are used in this text not only to falsify the theories backed up by inductive regression equations but also to elucidate new understandings of hereditary and religious attachments and their disavowed alternatives. The analysis leading to the suggestion to eliminate four laws rests on claims that can be debated based on procedures of falsification and validation but that also appeal to Ferrara's description of reflective judgment.

This does not mean that such a debate is dispositive. Popper himself was forced to admit, in a reply to a critique by Einstein, that falsification using conceptual systems from incorrect theories may not be valid. This concedes a significant question about Popper's method, one Feyerabend raised as well.

Only after the owl of Minerva has landed does one know whether a theory has been falsified because it was wrong or because the investigator's heuristics or measurement tools were not up to the task and therefore could not yield accurate observations. But only if the theory is provisionally accepted can there be an effort to create the right tools for assessing it.

Nonetheless, just because Popper's theory does not overcome the objection that early tests of Copernicus's ideas falsified them—and early tests of Einstein's theory of relativity falsified it as well—does not mean that his insights are pointless. First, the work in this text conforms with Popper's instruction against using crude induction. The theories leading to this analysis are borrowed from political, anthropological, and psychoanalytic theorists, not induction. Second, unlike the Marxist and Freudian theories to which Popper objected, the claims here are not predictions about inevitable trends but *falsifications of such predictions made by so-called positive social scientists* and then alternative hypotheses with provisional but not conclusive tests. I never state that the elimination of birthright citizenship, or the other three laws rooted in fears of mortality, is inevitable, much less that I can prove this. I only show how this is possible. I also do not state that I have a theory proving that eliminating birthright citizenship will eliminate mass, systemic violence and inequality. I have a hypothesis that this is the case, and I have initial tentative evidence that confirms this. Mostly, this book provides evidence that disproves the claims and theories that legitimate the status quo. Although the terrain of investigation is that of the modern society that Popper finds so inhospitable to prediction, this does not mean that modern society is a poor place to make informed, tentative experiments, for precisely the reasons quoted from Popper in this appendix's epigraphs. The ideas in this book are part of a broad-based effort that Popper lauds: philosophers trying to rid the world of political violence. Finally, I agree wholeheartedly with Popper (and Arendt): the "chosen people" mentality makes people stupid.

Habermas believes much of the above as well, but his teleology is hard to countenance. It is not utopian to explore alternative political institutions likely to improve on our present ones, but it is utopian to expect that rationality will suddenly dominate the terms of institutionalized political debate, the Enlightenment's inevitable trajectory. One problem is that Habermas's theory has no room for the unconscious. The substantive proposals this book explores are necessary to confront specific attachments leading to the melancholic familial, national, and religious attachments that Freud describes, the ones that enable institutions that realize the worst in the unconscious and perpetuate repression and oppression, and paralyze the possibility of their succession. Unlike Habermas, I do not believe rationality is a historical imperative; it is rather a possibility, if there is sufficient consciousness raising.

By contrasting archaic lifeworlds based on kinship with the values of the modern state, Habermas misstates findings from political anthropology, including its historical analyses.[54] Habermas writes: "In societies based on kinship, institutions protected by taboos form a site where cognitive and normative expectations merge and harden into an unbroken complex of convictions linked with motives and value orientations."[55] Habermas believes that the "modern situation of a predominantly secular society"[56] stands in contrast to this, and that here "law claims to be rational because it guarantees liberty."[57] Habermas writes as though Kant and not Hegel has channeled the modern state, proposing that the value of individual liberty is democracy's highest goal and that this demands rational debate: "Either the legal order remains embedded in an encompassing social ethos and subordinate to the authority of a suprapositive or sacred law (as in stratified societies and absolute states of early modernity), or else individual liberties are supplemented by rights of a *different type*, rights of citizenship that are geared no longer to rational choice but to autonomy in the Kantian sense."[58] But what about the stratified societies of late modernity, where kinship rules and intergenerational transfers, not individual earnings, determine our disparities in wealth? What about the birthright rules for membership in modern societies?[59] What about a cadre of U.S. presidents and political leaders ruling the country in the name of Jesus? In light of the last century, marked by genocides and nuclear bombs—in which rationality was no more than the old game of figuring out technologies to best obliterate one's enemies—and the new one, distinguished by the "Long War" and a reinvigorated territorialism, Habermas's insistence that his Kantian, procedural, discourse preferences in politics are an inevitability and not a possibility seems out of touch.[60]

The method—an experimental inquiry appealing to reason—and content of my project are connected. Acknowledging the persistent importance of the unconscious in shaping our political institutions does not require believing its effects are inevitable. It is not reasonable simply to tell people to think rationally because theirs is a modern age that expects this. But that does not mean that political theorists cannot assist in promoting rationality, for the sake of rationality and not history. New ways of imagining our laws and legal political bodies scripting and changing the current embodiments and divisions of family, nation, and religion are crucial for allowing rationality to emerge. Rationality is necessary for setting a new example, but it also may require examples for its emergence. Consistent with the idea developed in chapter 2, that procedural justice may need substantive justice, is the notion that a vivid image of legal arrangements consistent with the condition of mortality may be necessary to catalyze the rationality necessary for institutionalizing these new forms of being and thinking. The critical theory advocated here rejects as an epistemology of change the instrumental materialism of the Left and the Right as well as phenomenologically normative theories pleading for implementation because they are ethically superior. Instead, the hope is a Nietzschean and Arendtian one that new examples may inspire critical reason.[61]

Acknowledgments

This book has benefited from numerous provocative interlocutors in a variety of venues. The main ideas were fleshed out when I was teaching at Istanbul Bilgi University, where I was blessed with some very special friends, colleagues, and students. I am especially grateful to Soli Özel, who made my time in Istanbul possible. Murat Bovovalı (the editor of the Turkish translation of John Rawls's work) and Murat Özbank (the editor of the Turkish translation of Jürgen Habermas's work) gave me their feedback on these ideas in their early form, Ayhan Kaya shared his fascinating research in progress on Euroturks and Europeans in Turkey cited here, Emre Gönen provided European Union data, and Alan Duben wrote detailed comments on an early version of the introduction. For their friendship and comments, thanks also to Feride Çiçekoğlu, Celil Erdoğan, Gazi Erçel, Zeynep Gambetti, Serhat Güvenç, Mehmet Kutan, Cynthia Madansky, and Abdullah Yilmaz.

For thoughtful comments and editing suggestions on a substantial portion of the manuscript, I am deeply indebted to Gordon Babst. I also appreciate the advice on portions of the book from Mary Coffey, Dalton Conley, Richard Falk, Amy Goldstein, Laura Green, Philip Green, Sally Haslanger, and Juliet Williams. Thanks to John Seery for his helpful suggestions, inspiring the book's subtitle, and much more.

Others whose friendship and collegiality provided an intellectual and political community that made this work possible include Hany Abu-Asad, Rebecca Baron, Ali Behdad, Aaron Belkin, Randy Cohen, Rosemary Comella, Marianne Constable, Elizabeth Daniel, Jodi Dean, Nazli Durlu, Hilel Elver, Samera Esmeir, Jill Frank, Michael Froman, Nancy Goodman, Terri Gordon,

Edin Hajdarpasic, Sarah Hogarth, Adele Horne, Susan Lehman, Michael Ludwig, James Martel, Don Reneau, Christine Schoefer, Charity Scribner, Jacques Servin, Seki Tatlic, and Armin Wulf.

This book developed in conjunction with an online digital project expressing the ideas in this work, commissioned by the Tate Museum Online from Natalie Bookchin and myself. For their work on agoraXchange (phase I http://www.agoraxchange.org), a site for developing an online community and game for states without nations, I want to thank Natalie and the curator of the Tate's digital installations, Jemima Rellie. Zeljko Blace, an artist and curator based in Zagreb, has supported and exemplified agoraXchange and its aspirations in Europe since 2003. I also want to thank the talented individuals who contributed work designing, programming, or hosting agoraXchange: Ayhan Ates, Ana Carvalho, Jeff Crouse, Eric Goldhagen, Doug Goodwin, Katherine Hill and Marko Moretti of FDTdesign, Susanne Lang and Florian Schneider of kein.org, and David Ross. Thanks also to the University of California at Santa Barbara's Instructional Development office, and especially George Michaels, executive director, for financial support. And thanks to Robert Nideffer, director of the Game, Culture, and Technology Lab at the University of California at Irvine.

Many, many thanks to the conveners and participants who have supported this project, including by asking tough questions that helped me understand potential objections and engage them in the book. These include the Multimedia Institute in Zagreb, the Center for Art and Culture and the Media Center in Sarajevo, Peter Goodrich and his students at Cardozo School of Law, Jeremy Waldron and the Philosophy Symposium at Columbia University, and Lisa Ellis and the Political Theory Workshop at Texas A&M, where Russell Muirhead helpfully paraphrased one of my critiques of prevailing policies executed in the name of liberal values: "Liberalism's great; let's try it sometime."

Flora Sanchez, Jenna Reinbold, and Aerin Murphy provided assistance and were supported in part by University of California research funding. Thanks also to Rebecca Musselman for the book's indexing.

Laura Green has my gratitude for her care and attention in discussing every stage of the book's development, from the proposal to the cover design.

Finally, I was lucky indeed to have found a wonderful press and series as a home for this project. I am extremely grateful to Wendy Lochner at Columbia University Press and Amy Allen, the editor for the New Directions in Critical Theory series, for their support and suggestions. Many thanks as well to Assistant Editor Christine Mortlock and to Robert Fellman, for careful copy editing. And thanks also to the outside reviewers for astute comments and for pointing out where my analyses needed more evidence or explanation. That I received advice and assistance from so many quarters means that I was fortunate for the opportunity to learn from experts generous with their time and thought but does not mean that they have assented to any of the book's theses.

Notes

PREFACE

1. The articles on Eichmann's trial first appeared in five issues of *New Yorker* in 1963 and provoked international controversy. Arendt's response to this was "Truth and Politics," which also first appeared in the *New Yorker*. Arendt's Eichmann articles, slightly revised, appear in Hannah Arendt, *Eichmann in Jerusalem: A Report on the Banality of Evil*, rev. ed. (New York: Penguin, 1965).

2. Arendt, *Eichmann in Jerusalem*, 44.

3. Theodore Herzl, *The Jewish State* (New York: Dover, 1988). Herzl draws up specific plans for the Jewish Company, "modeled on the lines of a great land-acquisition company ... founded as a joint stock company subject to English jurisdiction." The company will "first of all convert into cash all vested interests left [in Europe] by departing Jews." The company will make a profit because the "newer, more beautiful, and more comfortably fitted [estates] ... will cost the Company comparatively little, because it will have bought the ground very cheaply" but sold the land in Europe at a high price (98–100). Herzl also envisions funding from Christians eager to rid Europe of Jews (122).

4. Arendt, *Eichmann in Jerusalem*, 44, also remarks on the "Transfer Agreement" between the Nazi authorities and the Jewish Agency for Palestine allowing Jews to emigrate to Palestine with their physical property.

5. Arendt, *Eichmann in Jerusalem*, 61, quoting from Jon and David Kimche, *The Secret Roads: The "Illegal" Migration of a People, 1938–1948* (London, 1954).

6. Elisabeth Young-Bruehl, *For the Love of the World* (New Haven, Conn.: Yale University Press, 1982), 355–378.

7. Hannah Arendt, "Zionism Reconsidered," in *The Jew as Pariah: Jewish Identity and Politics in the Modern Age* (New York: Random House, 1978), 140, 131–163.

8. Arendt, "Zionism Reconsidered," 162, continues: "Only folly could dictate a policy which trusts a distant imperial power for protection, while alienating the good will of neighbors. What then, one is prompted to ask, will be the future policy of Zionism with respect to big powers, and what program have Zionists to offer for a solution of the Arab-Jewish conflict?"

9. Arendt, "Zionism Reconsidered"; see also "Herzl's State Fifty Years Later," in *The Jew as Pariah*.

10. Arendt, "Christianity and Revolution," *The Nation* (September 1945): 288, quoted in Young-Bruehl, *For Love of the World*, 227.

11. The history of Zionist collaboration with the Nazi expulsions has been well documented by the most authoritative account of this period, Raul Hilberg, *The Destruction of European Jewry*, 3rd ed. (New Haven, Conn.: Yale University, 2003). Arendt relies heavily on this text.

12. For an excellent history of the internecine struggles of American Zionism, see Thomas Kolsky, *Jews Against Zionism: The American Council for Judaism, 1942–1948* (Philadelphia: Temple University Press, 1992).

13. Michael Hardt and Antonio Negri, *Empire* (Cambridge, Mass.: Harvard University Press, 2000).

14. Karen Tumlin, "Suspect First: How Terrorism Policy Is Reshaping Immigration Policy," *California Law Review* 92 (2004): 1173–1239, esp. 1228; Mathew Coleman, "Immigration Geopolitics Beyond the Mexico-U.S. Border," *Antipode* 39 (2007): 54–76, esp. 60.

15. *A Bill to Provide Comprehensive Immigration Reform and for Other Purposes*, S Res. 1348 and 1639, 110th Cong.

16. Jacqueline Stevens, "Senator Harry Reid Reveals True Attitude Toward Immigrants," http://stateswithoutnations.blogspot.com/2007/06/s<->1639-democrats-fall-asleep.html.

17. http://mccaskill.senate.gov/record.cfm?id=275718.

18. http://tester.senate.gov/News/record.cfm?id=275460.

19. S Res. 1639, 110th Cong., Title VI, Section 922.

20. S Res. 1639, 110th Cong., Title VI, Section 922.

INTRODUCTION

1. Eric Partridge, *Origins: A Short Etymological Dictionary of the English Language* (New York: MacMillan, 1959).

2. John Seery's rich exploration of death in canonical political theory has highlighted some of the ironies in death narratives, deliberate or unintended. He interprets the Myth of Er at the conclusion of Plato's *Republic* as an arch, ironic reminder that there are no simple incentives to behave justly. Seery's work mining themes of mortality has influenced my own a great deal, to wit my use of his title for my subtitle. John Seery, *Political Theory for Mortals: Shades of Justice, Images of Death* (Ithaca, N.Y.: Cornell University Press, 1996), 74–75.

3. Plato, "Apology" [c. 399 BC], in *Collected Dialogues of Plato*, trans. Benjamin Jowett (New York: Bollingen, 1961), 128c.

4. The full passage reads: "If I say, now, when, as I conceive and imagine, God orders me to fulfill the philosopher's mission of searching into myself and other men, I were to desert my post through fear of death, or any other fear; that would indeed be strange, and I might justly be arraigned in court for denying the existence of the gods, if I disobeyed the oracle because I was afraid of death: then I should be fancying that I was wise when I was not wise. For this fear of death is indeed the pretence of wisdom, and not real wisdom . . . since no one knows whether death, which they in their fear apprehend to be the greatest evil, may not be the greatest good." Plato, "Apology," 128c.

5. Hobbes, *Leviathan* [1651] (London: Penguin, 1985), chap. 15.

6. For a review of the literature documenting cross-cultural practices of pregnancy envy, see Jacqueline Stevens, "Pregnancy Envy and Compensatory Masculinities," *Gender and Politics* 1 (2005): 265–295.

7. For an anthropological account documenting hundreds of rituals and laws indicating pregnancy envy, see Bruno Bettelheim, *Symbolic Wounds: Puberty Rites and the Envious Male* (New York: Collier Books, 1962).

8. Hannah Arendt in several places describes the constraints and possibilities of natality's and mortality's dialectics, including their realization through nations and empires as well as political action. For a further discussion of this, see Jacqueline Stevens, *Reproducing the State* (Princeton, N.J.: Princeton University Press, 1999), 270–273.

9. Stevens, *Reproducing the State*.

10. Stevens, *Reproducing the State*, 236–275. I agree with Martha Nussbaum's equality approach to understanding the First Amendment's Free Exercise and Establishment clauses but would suggest that this is because religious freedoms are always about group rights, not individual conscience. I also disagree with her belief that U.S. jurisprudence has struck a balance between religion and nonreligion. *Liberty of Conscience: In Defense of America's Tradition of Religious Equality* (New York: Basic, 2008), e.g., 23.

11. The Correlates of War Project at the University of Michigan has numerous databases for researchers to download and use in their regression analyses. The Web site also contains links to articles published using this database. Perhaps the most influential work by economists using these datasets has been done by Paul Collier and Anke Hoeffler, "Greed and Grievance in Civil War," CSAE Working Paper 2002-01 (2002), http://www.csae.ox.ac.uk/workingpapers/pdfs/2002-01text.pdf.

12. James Fearon and David Laitin, "Ethnicity, Insurgency, and Civil War," *American Political Science Review* 97 (2003): 75–90.

13. Christopher Cramer, "*Homo Economicus* Goes to War: Methodological Individualism, Rational Choice and Political Economy," *World Development* 30 (2002): 1845–1864.

14. Laurie Nathan, "'The Frightful Inadequacy of Most of the Statistics': A Critique of Collier and Hoeffler on Causes of Civil War," Crisis States Research Centre, University of Capetown, No. 5 (2005), http://www.crisisstates.com/Publications/dp/dp11.htm; Bethany Lacina and Nils Petter Gleditsch, "Monitoring Trends in Global Combat: A New Dataset of Battle Deaths," *European Journal of Population* 21 (2005): 152.

15. Daniel N. Posner, "Measuring Ethnic Fractionalization in Africa," *American Journal of Political Science* 48 (2004): 849–863. See also a devastating critique of ELF by Fearon: "Ethnic and Cultural Diversity by Country," *Journal of Economic Growth* 8 (2003): 195–222. Nonetheless, due to the authors' scholarly credentials and the compatibility of their thesis with neoliberal paradigms, these studies have attracted media interest and attention from the U.S. foreign-policy establishment. The Web page for the Stanford Center sponsoring research by David Laitin and James Fearon lists their appearances on national news programs and Congressional testimony. See http://cisac.stanford.edu/news/cisac_civil_war_experts _influence_policy_debate_on_iraq_20061213/.

16. Agamben's pairing of Foucault's biopower with Hobbesian announcements of sovereignty's sovereignty and Arendtian critiques of state violence give Foucauldians a lens to see state violence that Foucault's method would otherwise obscure, and this may explain why some theorists find Agamben's critiques illuminating.

17. Agamben, *Homo Sacer: Sovereign Power and Bare Life* (Stanford, Calif.: Stanford University Press, 1995), 143.

18. Plato, *Republic*, trans. Paul Shorey (New York: Bollingen, 1961), book 5.

19. W. V. Harris, "The Theoretical Possibility of Extensive Infanticide in the Graeco-Roman World," *Classical Quarterly* 32 (1982): 114–116; Cynthia Patterson, "'Not Worth Rearing': The Causes of Infant Exposure in Ancient Greece," *Transactions of the American Philological Association* 115 (1985): 103–123.

20. Sarah Pomeroy, *Goddesses, Whores, Wives, and Slaves: Women in Classical Antiquity* (New York: Schocken Books, 1975), esp. chap. 7.

21. Plutarch, "Lycurgus," http://classics.mit.edu/Plutarch/lycurgus.html.

22. Plutarch, "Lycurgus."

23. Andrew Stewart, "Imag(in)ing the Other: Amazons and Ethnicity in Fifth-Century Athens," *Poetics Today* 16 (1995): 588. For a thorough background on Athenian myths of autochthony and the marriage policies this produced, see Nicole Loraux, *Children of Athena* (Princeton, N.J.: Princeton University Press, 1993).

24. R. J. Rummel, *Death by Government: Genocide and Mass Murder since 1900* (New Brunswick, N.J.: Transaction, 1994), 45–75.

25. Rummel, *Death by Government*, 11.

26. By "nation," I mean any group experienced as the hereditary past, present, or aspirational group of a political society. For details see Stevens, *Reproducing the State*, 102–171.

27. This work and *Reproducing the State* draw extensively on the analyses of the nation, state, and family in Hegel's *Philosophy of Right*, trans. T. M. Knox (Oxford: Oxford University Press, 1952); and *Phenomenology of Spirit*, trans. A. V. Miller (Oxford: Oxford University Press, 1977). For an insightful study of the politics of recognition in Hegel, see also Patchen Markell, *Bound by Recognition* (Princeton, N.J.: Princeton University Press, 2003).

28. Quoted in Joachim Fest, *Hitler*, trans. Richard and Clara Winston (New York: Harcourt Brace Jovanovich, 1973), 369.

29. Helmut Heiber, *Hitler's Lagebesprechungen* (Stuttgart, 1962), 126–127; quoted in Fest, *Hitler*, 665.

30. Brown, *Life Against Death*, 102.

31. Freud's is a pseudohistory of civilization and an unsystematic and often indefensible analysis of the causes of family strife. Nonetheless, Freud's accounts make brutally clear the hypocrisies of his age and ours.

32. Sigmund Freud, "Civilization and Its Discontents" (1930), in *Civilization, Society, and Religion*, ed. Albert Dickson, trans. James Strachey (London: Penguin, 1991), 274–275.

33. Freud, "Civilization and Its Discontents," 49; Sigmund Freud, "Thoughts for the Times on War and Death" (1915), in *Complete Psychological Works of Sigmund Freud, Standard Edition*, ed. and trans. James Strachey (London: Hogarth Press, 1955), 14:278–279.

34. Freud, "Civilization and Its Discontents," 274.

35. Freud, "Thoughts for the Times," 275–300.

36. Freud, "Moses and Monotheism" (1939), in *SE* 23:3–137.

37. Freud, "Why War?" (1933), in *SE* 22:197–221.

38. For an analysis of Freud's ambivalence about the biological and cultural basis of nationalism, see Jacqueline Stevens, "Sigmund Freud and International Relations," *Journal of Law, Culture, and the Humanities* 2 (2006): 201–217.

39. Freud believed that the three instincts we all share are for incest, cannibalism, and a "lust for killing." Realizing that cannibalism seemed out of place, he said this was only because cannibalism alone seems "universally proscribed" and to have been "completely surmounted," while "incestuous wishes can still be detected behind the prohibition against them" and "killing is still practised, indeed commanded, by our civilization." In other words, that just cannibalism seems "wrong" here only underscores a tacit agreement with the accuracy of his other claims, regardless of whether one accepts what he says about cannibalism. Freud, "Totem and Taboo" (1913), in *SE* 13: 1–161.

40. Freud, "Totem and Taboo."

41. Freud also saw the destruction of chieftains and kings rooted in men banding together to overthrow as adults the fathers they endured as children as the basis for Judeo-Christianity: "If the Son of God was obliged to sacrifice his life to redeem mankind from original sin," Freud wrote, "then by the law of talion, the requital of like by like, that sin must have been a killing, a murder. Nothing else could call for the sacrifice of a life for its expiation." Freud, "Thoughts," 292. Freud believed that men projected their own fantasies of killing their father into a religious script, giving all men an omnipotent father whom they revered and also desired to kill. Freud explained, "since the original sin was an offence against God the Father, the primal crime of mankind must have been a parricide, the killing of the primal father of the primitive human horde, whose mnemic image was later transfigured into a deity." In short, out of guilt and anxiety over killing the tribal father, men established a religion, Christianity, in which there was another father, God, who exacted retribution by killing his son, Jesus. The new god was a father who was all-powerful and whom they could not kill. Freud, "Thoughts," 293.

42. Freud, "Civilization and Its Discontents," 338.

43. Rummel, *Death by Government*, 15.

44. R. J. Rummel, "Democracy, Power, Genocide, and Mass Murder," *Journal of Conflict Resolution* 39 (1995): 3–26.

45. Earlier studies of war documented only the deaths of combatants or those directly related to battles, e.g., civilians killed by missiles. More sophisticated epidemiology makes it possible to estimate other less immediate mortality rates from war's well-known consequences of disease, poverty, and forced migration. This leads researchers to claim that war has "profound consequences for public health." E. G. Krug, Linda Dahlberg, James Mercy, Anthony Zwi and Rafael Lozano, eds., *World Report on Violence and Health* (Geneva: World Health Organization, 2002), 217; citing J. Goodhand and D. Hulme, "From Wars to Complex Political Emergencies: Understanding Conflict and Peace-building in the New World Disorder," *Third World Quarterly* 20 (1999): 13–26; and Jennifer Leaning, Susan Briggs, and Lincoln Chen, "Introduction," in *Humanitarian Crises: The Medical and Public Health Response*, ed. J. Leaning et al. (Cambridge, Mass.: Harvard University Press, 1999), 1–11.

46. D. Levinson, "Family Violence in Cross-cultural Perspective," in *Handbook of Family Violence*, ed. V. B. Van Hasselt et al. (New York: Plenum, 1988), 435–455; cited in Krug et al., *World Report on Violence and Health*, 100.

47. For a broader discussion and references, see chapter 3. Genetic parents have more opportunities than others to kill their children, but that they should take advantage of these opportunities is not predicted by idealized nuclear family narratives or by evolutionary biological theories.

48. Richard Stern, "The Power of Faith," *International Herald Tribune*, letter to the editor (July 10, 2004).

49. This book focuses on religion. For a critique of religion, including its violence, see Christopher Hitchens, *God Is Not Great: How Religion Poisons Everything* (New York: Twelve, 2007), esp. 15–36.

50. Amy Wolf (director), *Deliver Us from Evil*, 2006.

51. Wolf, *Deliver Us from Evil*. In addition to having paid $245 million to date in California alone, the Los Angeles Archdiocese is attempting to settle years of litigation by paying $60 million to adult survivors. Other settlements include $25 million in the Louisville Archdiocese, $22 million in the Tucson Archdiocese, $16 million in the Milwaukee Archdiocese, and about $3 million in the Alaska Archdiocese, which is selling property to settle its lawsuits. The following sources for the data above were obtained from Lexis-Nexis: Gillian Flaccus, "Partial Settlement Close in LA Clergy Abuse Cases" (September 30, 2006); Ashbel Green, "$36 Million Church Fund Off-limits in Bankruptcy," *The Oregonian* (July 21, 2006); Associated Press, "Louisville Archdiocese Settles Last of Sex-Abuse Cases," (April 22, 2006); Associated Press, "Anchorage Diocese Sells Property to Cover Lawsuit Expenses" (September 27, 2006). A Los Angeles District Attorney pursuing criminal charges against priests who molested children says the local archdiocese resembles the Mafia. Cardinal Roger Mahoney was charged with aiding and abetting a felon for his role in paying priests to leave the country to evade prosecution. September 9, 2006, personal communication with District Attorney; John Spano, "Suit Says Cardinals Aided Pedophile Priest," *Los Angeles Times* (September 20, 2006), http://www.latimes.com/news/local/la-me-abuse20sep20,1,233357.story.

52. United Nations Development Program (UNDP), *Human Development Report 2002*, 30, http://hdr.undp.org/reports/global/2002/en.

53. UNDP, *Human Development Report, 2000*, http://hdr.undp.org/en/reports/global/hdr2000.

54. UNDP, *Human Development Report, 1998*, 49, http://hdr.undp.org/en/reports/global/hdr1998/.

55. UNDP, *Human Development Report, 2002*, 21.

56. Majid Ezzati, Alan D. Lopez, Anthony Rodgers, Stephen Vander Hoorn, Christopher J. L. Murray, and the Comparative Risk Assessment Collaborating Group, "Selected Major Risk Factors and Global and Regional Burden of Disease," *Lancet* 360 (2002): 1347–1360.

57. BBC, "Rwanda: How the Genocide Happened" (June 7, 2001), http://news.bbc.co.uk/2/hi/africa/1288230.stm.

58. Jon Elster, "Motivations and Beliefs in Suicide Missions," in *Making Sense of Suicide Missions*, ed. Diego Gambetta (Oxford: Oxford University Press, 2005), 258. In the parable, the scorpion kills a frog carrying him across the river, thus dooming both of them, and as an explanation says, "it's my nature."

59. Bonnie Honig, "Ruth, the Model Émigré: Mourning and the Symbolic Politics of Immigration," *Political Theory* 25 (1997): 113.

60. Michael Rogin's work on "demonology" describes the mobile character of irrational, national paranoia. *Ronald Reagan, the Movie, and Other Episodes in Political Demonology* (Berkeley: University of California Press, 1987).

61. Excerpted in *New York Times Magazine* (June 15, 1913), http://query.nytimes.com/mem/archive-free/pdf?res=9E07E1D6143FE633A25756C1A9609C946296D6CF.

62. Sigmund Freud, *The Future of an Illusion* (1927), trans. James Strachey (New York: Norton, 1989), 40.

63. For a rich historical description of Christianity's impact on U.S. slavery and the subjugation of Native Americans and Mexico, see Forrest Wood, *The Arrogance of Faith: Christianity and Race in America from the Colonial Era to the Twentieth Century* (New York: Knopf, 1990).

64. E.g., David Held, *Democracy and the Global Order* (Stanford, Calif.: Stanford University Press, 1996); Saul Mendlovitz and Burns H. Weston, eds., *Preferred Futures for the United Nations* (New York: Transnational Publishers, 1995).

65. Peter Hunt, *Slaves, Warfare, and Ideology in the Greek Historians* (Cambridge: Cambridge University Press, 1998); Joseph Vogt, *Ancient Slavery and the Ideal of Man* (Cambridge: Cambridge University Press, 1975); William Westerman, *Slave Systems of Greek and Roman Antiquity* (Philadelphia: American Philosophical Society, 1955).

66. Hammurabi's Code, #32, from *Ancient History Sourcebook: Code of Hammurabi, c. 1780*, trans. L. W. King, http://www.fordham.edu/halsall/ancient/hamcod.html.

67. Ehud Toledano, *The Ottoman Slave Trade and Its Suppression, 1840–1890* (Princeton, N.J.: Princeton University Press, 1982).

68. Kevin Bales, *Disposable People: New Slavery in the Global Economy* (Berkeley: University of California, 1999).

69. http://iraqbodycount.org.

70. Vogt, *Ancient Slavery*, 42.

71. Toledano, *Ottoman Slave Trade*, xiv.

72. *American Heritage Dictionary*, 4th ed. (Boston: Houghton Mifflin, 2000).

73. The Israelites called the Canaanites "servants of servants" and believed their descendants "condemned to perpetual bondage." After Babylon was destroyed, Israel's "former oppressors were to become their slaves." Solomon exacted slavery from those Canaanites spared during war. Davis, *Slavery in Western Culture*, 63–64; citing Genesis 9:25, Isaiah 14:2, I Kings 9:21. The ancient Greek word for slave is *doulos*, from the verb *deo*, to bind, and does not fit this pattern.

74. Hammurabi's Code, #32.

75. Hammurabi's Code, #32.

76. Hammurabi's Code, #32.

77. Hammurabi's Code, #32.

78. Hammurabi's Code, #280.

79. Plato, *Republic*, book 5, line 471a.

80. Davis, *Slavery in Western Culture*, 47.

81. For an account of slavery's demise, see Stevens, *Reproducing the State*, 177–195.

82. Susan Reynolds, *Kingdoms and Communities in Western Europe, 900–1300* (Oxford: Oxford University Press, 1997).

83. Davis, *Slavery in Western Culture*, 33–34. See also 47, 52, 53.

84. Davis, *Slavery in Western Culture*, 34.

85. Hobbes, *Leviathan*; John Locke, *Two Treatises on Government* (1689) (Cambridge: Cambridge University Press, 1960).

86. Vogt, *Ancient Slavery*, 42.

87. Joseph Nevins and Mizue Aizeki, *Dying To Live A Story of U.S. Immigration in an Age of Global Apartheid* (San Francisco: City Lights, 2008).

88. For an analysis of the similarities between the stigma of homelessness and statelessness, see Kathleen Arnold's rich and insightful *Homelessness, Citizenship, and Identity: The Uncanniness of Late Modernity* (College Park: Pennsylvania State University Press, 2004).

89. Thomas Pogge, "Recognized and Violated by International Law: The Human Rights of the Global Poor," *Leiden Journal of International Law* 18 (2005): 717–745.

90. CIA World Factbook, http://www.cia.gov/cia/publications/factbook/geos/sl.html.

91. This directly recalls the Nuremberg laws prohibiting those without state papers from full economic and political rights.

92. "Project to ID Bodies Found at Borders," *Washington Times* (October 1, 2001).

93. Marc Cooper, "12 Die on the U.S. Border: A New Season of Death Begins," *Nation Online* (May 25, 2006), http://www.thenation.com/doc/20050606/cooperweb.

94. Oliver Harvey, "Entering the Promised Land," *The Sun Online* (September 19, 2006), http://www.thesun.co.uk/article/0,,2-2006430362,00.html.

95. UNDP, *Millennium Development Goals Report* (2005), 9, http://www.un.org/docs/summit2005/MDGBook.pdf.

96. Somini Sengupta, "No Relief from War in African Refugee Camps," *New York Times* (May 19, 2003).

97. Steven Greenhouse, "Congress Looks to Grant Legal Status to Immigrants," *New York Times* (October 13, 2003). In France it was estimated there were 400,000 undocumented immigrants in 2001; there are about one million a apiece in Britain, Germany, and Greece. In Spain, "44,841 illegal immigrants were deported, expelled, or refused entry" and in Austria in 2001, 48,659 inhabitants were told to leave for want of documentation. Reuters, "The Breakdown: Where Migrants' Journeys Began, and How They Are Faring in the European Squeeze," *New York Times* (April 28, 2002).

98. Jeffrey Passel, "Size and Characteristics of the Unauthorized Migrant Population in the U.S." PEW Foundation (March 7, 2006), http://pewhispanic.org/reports/report.php? ReportID=61.

99. For an excellent discussion of the illegal alien and "alien citizen" in U.S. history, see Mai Ngai, *Illegal Aliens and the Making of Modern America* (Princeton, N.J.: Princeton University Press, 2004). For an overview of the legal definitions of a U.S. citizen and national, see Linda Bozniak, *Citizen and Alien: Dilemmas of Contemporary Membership* (Princeton, N.J.: Princeton University Press, 2007). For a legal ethnography of the harms caused by border enforcement, see Susan Coutin, *Nations of Emigrants: Shifting Boundaries of Citizenship in El Salvador and the United States* (Ithaca, N.Y.: Cornell University Press, 2007).

100. Steven Greenhouse, "Foreign Workers at Highest Level in Decades," *New York Times* (September 4, 2000).

101. Anthony DePalma, "Farmers Caught in Conflict Over Illegal Migrant Workers," *New York Times* (October 3, 2000).

102. Peter Stalker, *No Nonsense Guide to Immigration* (London: Verso, 2001), 34.

103. Kwok Yenni, "On Hire to the Cruelest Bidder," *South China Morning Post* (June 7, 2000).

104. Neil MacFarquhar, "After the War: Refugees; Iraqis in Iran: Unwanted in Both Countries," *New York Times* (June 12, 2003).

105. MacFarquhar, "After the War."

106. Raul Hilberg, *The Destruction of European Jewry* (New Haven: Yale University, 2003).

107. Francisco Balderrama and Raymond Rodríguez, *Decade of Betrayal: Mexican Repatriation in the 1930s* (Albuquerque: University of New Mexico Press, 1995). A government report documented the systematic violation of the rights of U.S. citizens based on racial profiling during this period: National Commission on Law Observance and Enforcement, *Report on the Enforcement of the Deportation Laws of the United States* (Washington, D.C.: GPO, 1931).

108. Jacqueline Stevens, "Thin ICE," *The Nation* (June 23, 2008). Chapter 1 describes some of these practices in more detail.

109. Stevens, "Thin ICE," and "States without Nations," http://stateswithoutnations.blog spot.com.

110. Vogt, *Ancient Slavery*, 32; see also 92, 168, 187.

111. The slave rebellion itself yields the same paradox: the national difference that led to enslavement also prevented the slave's liberation, as combat emerged among the slaves based on their different origins. Vogt, *Ancient Slavery*, 72.

112. Vogt, *Ancient Slavery*, 92, 168, 187.

113. Thomas More, *Utopia* (1513) (Cambridge: Cambridge University Press, 2002).

114. Giovano Pontano (1426–1503), discussed in Vogt, *Ancient Slavery*, 193–194.

115. Malcolm Goggin, "The Courts, Interest Groups, and Public Opinion About Abortion," *Public Behavior* 15 (1993): 381–405.

116. John Curran, "Vermont Gay Marriage Debate Tamer This Time," *USA Today*, http://www.usatoday.com/news/nation/2008-01-13-3932657192_x.htm.

117. Will Lester, "Acceptance of Gay Marriage Has Grown Since 2003 Decision," *The Berkshire Eagle* (July 13, 2005).

118. Paul Carrier, "Group Drops Antigay Effort," *Morning Sentinel* (Augusta, Maine) (June 20, 2008), http://morningsentinel.mainetoday.com/news/local/5170407.html.

119. http://primary2000.sos.ca.gov/returns/prop/00.htm; "Gay Marriage Ban: A Tale of Two Votes," *Los Angeles Times*, http://www.latimes.com/news/local/politics/cal/la-2008election-prop8prop22,0,6153805.htmlstory.

120. "A new vision for how Americans can work together to prevent the epidemic of violence now raging in our society has emerged from the public health community. This vision arises from the recognition that, by any measure, violence is a major contributor to premature death, disability, and injury. Fundamental to this vision is a shift in the way our society addresses violence, from a focus limited to reacting to violence to a focus on changing the social, behavioral, and environmental factors that cause violence." James Mercy, M. L. Rosenberg, K. V. Powell, C. E. Broome, and R. L. Roper, "Preventing Violence," *Health Affairs* 12 (1993): 7–29.

121. Krug et al., *World Health*, 17. In 2002, the *British Medical Journal* devoted an issue to war's public-health consequences. See especially Christopher Murray, Gary King, Alan Lopez, Niels Tomijima, and Etienne Krug, "Armed Conflict as a Public Health Problem," *British Medical Journal* 324 (2002): 346–349.

122. Murray et al., "Armed Conflict."

123. Benjamin Coghlan, Richard Brennan, Pascal Ngoy, David Dofara, Brad Otto, Mark Clements, and Tony Stewart, "Mortality in the Democratic Republic of Congo: A Nationwide Survey," *Lancet* 367 (2006): 44–51.

124. Les Roberts, Riyadh Lafta, Richard Garfield, Jamal Khudhairi, and Gilbert Burnham, "Mortality Before and After the 2003 Invasion of Iraq," *Lancet* (2004): 7.

125. Coghlan et al., "Mortality in the Democratic Republic of Congo," 51.

126. Martha Nussbaum, "Patriotism and Cosmopolitanism," in *For Love of Country*, ed. Joshua Cohen (Boston: Beacon Press, 1996), 3–20.

127. Habermas makes this point in numerous texts, including *Between Facts and Norms: Contributions to a Discourse Theory of Law and Democracy* (Cambridge, Mass.: The MIT Press, 1996), especially his concluding chapters emphasizing the European Union as a symptom of cosmopolitan reason's inevitability.

128. Amy Allen, *The Politics of Our Selves: Power, Autonomy, and Gender in Contemporary Critical Theory* (New York: Columbia University Press, 2008), 3.

129. Allen, *The Politics of Our Selves*, 21.

130. Foucault is clearly the absent presence in this review of scholars influencing contemporary political theory. I explain why I find his approach to history and sovereignty not especially useful in *Reproducing the State* and also "On the Morals of Genealogy," *Political Theory* 31 (2003): 558–588.

131. See Hannah Arendt, *The Human Condition* (Chicago: University of Chicago Press, 1958); and *Between Past and Future* (New York: Viking Press, 1968). See also Elisabeth Young-Bruehl, *Hannah Arendt: For Love of the World* (New Haven, Conn.: Yale University Press, 1982).

1. THE PERSISTENCE AND HARMS OF BIRTHRIGHT CITIZENSHIP IN SO-CALLED LIBERAL THEORY AND COUNTRIES

1. Daniel Bell, *The End of Ideology: The Exhaustion of Ideas in the Fifties* (New York: Free Press, 1960).

2. Francis Fukuyama, *The End of History and the Last Man* (New York: Free Press, 1992). This book, initially widely endorsed, has since been refuted, including by the author himself.

3. This boilerplate claim associated with liberalism is made by every putative and self-proclaimed liberal from John Locke to John Stuart Mill to Robert Nozick.

4. For a partial list of emigration rates by country, see World Population Prospects 2002, http://www.esa.un.org/unpp. Between 1995 and 2000, fewer than one-hundredth of 1 percent of the population of Africa emigrated to another continent. Europa World, http://www.europaworld.com.

5. These six countries were selected from an alphabetized list. It includes the first and last countries, as well as three spaced at even intervals between these. The rules for these countries are as follows:

AFGHANISTAN: If either parent is a citizen. If one marries someone who is a citizen. If one has lived in Afghanistan for five years naturalization is possible. U.S. Office of Personnel Management (USOPM), "Citizenship Laws of the World," (March 2001), citing the Official Gazette of the Ministry of Justice for the Republic of Afghanistan (March 19, 1992), http://www.opm.gov/extra/investigate/IS-01.pdf.

CONGO, REPUBLIC OF: If either parent is a citizen. If one is a woman and marries a man who is a citizen. If one is adopted by a citizen of Congo. If one has lived in country for five years naturalization is possible. USOPM, "Citizenship Laws of the World," 55, citing the Congolese Civil Code and the Special Law on Congolese Nationality.

HONDURAS: If one is born in Honduras. If one is born outside Honduras and one parent is a Honduran citizen. Naturalization is possible if one is born in Central America and has lived in Honduras for one year; one is Spanish or Spanish-American and has resided in Honduras for two years; anyone who has resided in Honduras for three years; person who has married Honduran citizen. USOPM, "Citizenship Laws of the World," 91, citing the Honduran Constitution.

MONACO: If parents are married and one is a citizen of Monaco. Citizenship may also be obtained by a foreign woman marrying a Monegasque man; or if one has resided in the country for ten years after the age of twenty-one. USOPM, "Citizenship Laws of the World," 136, citing the Acquisition of Monegasque Nationality (January 1, 1987).

SENEGAL: If one's father is Senegalese or if one's mother is Senegalese and one's father is unknown; or one may marry and apply for citizenship; or if one has legally resided in the country for at least five years and is of good moral character. USOPM, "Citizenship Laws of the World," 171, citing the Code of Nationality (1960, amended in 1989).

ZIMBABWE: If born to a father who is married to one's mother and she is a citizen of Zimbabwe, or if born to a mother who is a citizen of Zimbabwe. Child adopted by citizens of Zimbabwe may be granted citizenship by registration. One is eligible for citizenship if one marries a citizen of Zimbabwe. Residence and naturalization are possible after five years of residence for: Persons possessing skills required but not available in the country. Aged parents and close dependents or relatives of resident citizens. Persons willing to invest capital in Zimbabwe. USOPM, "Citizenship Laws of the World," 219, citing the Constitution of Zimbabwe.

For a survey with general information, see Jules Coleman and Sarah Harding, "Citizenship, Justice and Political Borders," in *Justice in Immigration*, ed. Warren Schwartz (Cambridge: Cambridge University Press, 1995), 18–62.

6. Nicole Gaouette, "Worker Rules Called Likely to Hurt the Economy," *Los Angeles Times* (August 11, 2007).

7. Gaouette, "Worker Rules Called Likely to Hurt the Economy."

8. United States Congressional Budget Office (USCBO), "Immigration Policy in the United States" (2006), 4, http://www.cbo.gov/ftpdocs/70xx/doc7051/02-28-Immigration.pdf.

9. USCBO, "Immigration Policy," 4.

10. USCBO, "Immigration Policy," 5.

11. USCBO, "Immigration Policy," 5.

12. USCBO, "Immigration Policy," 5.

13. USCBO, "Immigration Policy," table 2, "Numerical Ceilings and Admissions, by Immigration Category," 8.

14. USCBO, "Immigration Policy," table A-1, "Requirements for Naturalization," 18.

15. USCBO, "Immigration Policy," 18. Historian Will Durant wrote, "War helped to make slavery, and slavery helped to make war." Will Durant, *Our Oriental Heritage* (New York: Simon and Schuster, 1951), 20; cited by James Lee Ray, "The Abolition of Slavery and the End of International War," *International Organization* 43 (1989): 405.

16. The columnist continues, "In September, the Annenberg Public Policy Center released a poll showing that only two-thirds of Americans could identify all three branches of government; only 55% of Americans were aware that the Supreme Court can declare an act of Congress unconstitutional; and 35% thought that it was the intention of the founding fathers to give the president 'the final say' over Congress and the judiciary." Rosa Brooks, "An SAT for Citizenship: Natural-born Citizens Should Take the New Naturalization Test for Immigrants—and Be Deported If They Fail," *Los Angeles Times* (December 8, 2006).

17. Questions most of my U.S.-born college students could not answer included: "How many amendments does the Constitution have?" and "Name your U.S. Representative." Some are vague, e.g., "Why do we have three branches of government?" (checks and balances? a fear of democracy?) and others reminiscent of game-show material, e.g., "Name two national U.S. holidays." http://www.uscis.gov/portal/site/uscis/menuitem.5af9bb95919f 35e66f614176543f6d1a/?vgnextoid=dcf5e1df53b2fo10VgnVCM1000000ecd190aRCRD/l.

18. See note 5, above.

19. CIA World Factbook, http://www.cia.gov/cia/publications/factbook/geos/sl.html.

20. Ayhan Kaya, personal communication, based on his research on ethnicity in Turkey. Two anecdotal cases illustrate this. A German citizen married a Turkish citizen and moved to Istanbul in 1988. Two years later they divorced. She continued to live in Turkey and sought citizenship. After her application was refused or "lost" twelve times, she stopped trying. Every three months she leaves and reenters Turkey to maintain her legal visitor status. Likewise, a Turkish colleague's uncle married a British woman, whose application for Turkish citizenship was also "lost" annually.

21. Christian Joppke, "How Immigration Is Changing Citizenship: A Comparative View," *Ethnic and Racial Studies* 22 (1999): 629–655.

22. The number of feminist engagements with liberal theory during this period is enormous. The most prominent critic of liberalism during this period is perhaps Catharine MacKinnon, whose attacks on liberal theory emphasized its passive protections of male power. Under the guise of neutrality and equality, liberal theory and law justified men's sexual exploitation of and violence against women. *Feminism Unmodified* (Cambridge, Mass.: Harvard University Press, 1987). Another strain of "difference feminism" also emerged during this period. Inspired by Carol Gilligan, *In a Different Voice* (Cambridge, Mass.:

Harvard University Press, 1978), these authors urged women to find their own approaches for conflict resolution and not assume as universal schemas for moral reasoning approaches specific to a supposedly masculine psychology.

23. Carole Pateman, *Sexual Contract* (Stanford, Calif.: Stanford University Press, 1988).

24. Susan Okin, *Justice, Gender, and the Family* (New York: Basic Books, 1989).

25. Sigmund Freud, "Totem and Taboo" (1913), in *Complete Psychological Works of Sigmund Freud, Standard Edition*, ed. and trans. James Strachey (London: Hogarth Press, 1955), 13:1–161.

26. One text in particular stands out: Hilal Steiner, *An Essay on Rights* (Cambridge: Blackwell, 1994). For a good example of applying liberal theory to intimate relations, see Jeremy Waldron, "When Justice Replaces Affection: The Need for Rights," *Harvard Journal of Law and Public Policy* 11 (1988): 625–647.

27. John Locke never referred to himself, his work, or the work of anyone else as "liberal." The connotations of the concept are rooted in the work of John Stuart Mill, especially his essay on free speech *On Liberty* (New York: Penguin, 2006).

28. In their studies of U.S. citizenship, W. E. B. Du Bois, Michael Rogin, Rogers Smith, Alexis De Tocqueville, Howard Zinn, Ari Zolberg, and many others have pointed out that the nativism and racism running through U.S. immigration policy is at odds with other overt commitments to political equality. Much of what is called liberal theory and justifies these exclusions is not actually liberal.

29. Johann Gottfried Herder, *Philosophical Writings*, trans. Michael N. Forster (New York: Cambridge University Press, 2002).

30. For a rich discussion of the tension in Berlin's work between his liberalism and his nationalism, see Joan Cocks, *Passion and Paradox: Intellectuals Confront the National Question* (Princeton, N.J.: Princeton University Press, 2002), esp. 99–110.

31. Isaiah Berlin, *Crooked Timber of Humanity* (New York: Random House, 1990), 261.

32. Avishai Margalit and Joseph Raz, "National Self-Determination," *Journal of Philosophy* 87 (1990): 440.

33. Margalit and Raz, "National Self-Determination," 448.

34. Margalit and Raz, "National Self-Determination," 447.

35. For a similar critique of the gap between liberal attitudes toward Constitutional change in other practices and the Supreme Court's refusal to budge in challenging the illiberality of immigration law, see Howard Chang, "Immigration Policy, Liberal Principles, and the Republican Tradition," *Georgetown Law Journal* 85 (1997): 2105.

36. For a critique of Walzer's views on family and membership, see Jacqueline Stevens, *Reproducing the State* (Princeton, N.J.: Princeton University Press, 1999), 5–9. See also Howard Chang, "Cultural Communities in a Global Labor Market: Immigration Restrictions as Residential Segregation," http://law.bepress.com/alea/16th/bazaar/art28.

37. Michael Walzer, *Spheres of Justice* (Cambridge, Mass.: Harvard University Press, 1983), 39.

38. Walzer, *Spheres of Justice*, 38–39.

39. Henry Sidgwick, *Elements of Politics*, 4th ed. (London: MacMillan, 1929), 309.

40. Uday Mehta, *Liberalism and Empire: A Study in Nineteenth-century Political Thought* (Chicago: University of Chicago, 1999). For an overview on discussions of Mill and Sidgwick's racism, see Bart Schultz, "Mill and Sidgwick, Imperialism and Racism," *Utilitas* 19: 104–130.

41. John Stuart Mill, *Considerations of Representative Government*, ed. J. M. Robson (Toronto: University of Toronto Press, 1977), in *Collected Works*, vol. 19, chap. 16, p. 546, quoted in Rawls, *The Law of Peoples* (Cambridge, Mass.: Harvard University Press, 1999), 23, note 17.

42. Rawls, *Law of Peoples*, 23, note 17.

43. Freud, "Moses and Monotheism" (1939), in *SE* 23:8.

44. This is not to overlook that descent and race have played a role in eligibility for joining this community but to point out that other criteria predominate.

45. Coleman and Harding, "Citizenship, Justice, and Political Borders," 50.

46. Sidgwick, *Politics*, 311.

47. Sidgwick, *Politics*, 386.

48. Sidgwick, *Politics*, 387.

49. Joseph Carens, "Aliens and Citizens: The Case for Open Borders," *Review of Politics* 49 (1987): 258.

50. Locke, "Second Treatise," §122, in *Two Treatises on Government* (Cambridge, Mass.: Cambridge University Press, 1960).

51. Peter Schuck and Rogers Smith, *Citizenship Without Consent: Illegal Aliens in the American Polity* (New Haven, Conn.: Yale University Press, 1985), 8.

52. Schuck and Smith, *Citizenship Without Consent*, 94.

53. Ayelet Shachar and Ran Hirschl, "Citizenship as Inherited Property," *Political Theory* 35 (2007): 280.

54. Shachar and Hirschl, "Citizenship as Inherited Property," 275–276.

55. Calculation based on estimate that approximately 400,000 Mexicans move to the United States annually, from a population that in 2005 was 107,029,000. United Nations Population Database, http://esa.un.org/unpp/p2kodata.asp.

56. Ronald Dworkin, *Taking Rights Seriously* (Cambridge, Mass.: Harvard University Press, 1978). Arguments about a right to exclude strangers from a sovereign territory or control a national culture by using birthright as the membership criterion are discussed below.

57. For a review of major databases for war mortalities and the different methods of counting war casualties, see Bethany Lacina and Nils Petter Gleditsch, "Monitoring Trends in Global Combat," *European Journal of Population* 21 (2005): 145–166.

58. R. I. Sivard, *World Military and Social Expenditures* (Washington, D.C.: World Priorities, 1993); and Carol Bellamy, *The State of the World's Children* (New York: Oxford University Press, 1996). Cited in Barry Levy and Victor Sidel, "The Impact of Military Activities on Civilian Populations," in *War and Public Health*, ed. Barry Levy and Victor Sidel (Washington, D.C.: American Public Health Association), 149.

59. Monty Marshall, comp., "Major Episodes of Political Violence, 1946–2006" (last updated September 18, 2007), http://members.aol.com/CSPmgm/warlist.htm.

60. Rauschning, *Gesprache mit Hitler* (Zurich, 1940), 129, quoted in Fest, *Hitler*, trans. Richard and Clara Winston (New York: Harcourt Brace Jovanovich, 1973), 680. Thanks to Richard Koenigsberg for bringing this passage to my attention.

61. "Pro Patria Mori!: Death and the State," in *The Morality of Nationalism*, ed. Robert McKim and Jeff McMahan (Oxford: Oxford University Press, 1997), 233.

62. Hegel writes: "It is a popular view in modern times that the state is a contract of all with all." But, Hegel points out, whereas contracts are at will, "the spontaneous choice of the persons . . . with the state it is different. An individual cannot enter or leave the social condition at his option, since everyone is, by his very nature a citizen of a state." *Philosophy of Right*, trans. T. M. Knox (Oxford: Clarendon Press, 1952), §258.

63. Birthright Israel organizes groups of Jewish teenagers to spend a summer in Israel. During their visits, students are encouraged to move to Israel, join the Israeli army, and overtures are made for Jews to provide other forms of political and economic support for Israel from their native countries if they decide against relocating. http://birthrightisrael.com.

64. John Locke, "Second Treatise," §19. Kant accepts this premise but in "Perpetual Peace" (1795) challenges its necessity by proposing a worldwide federated government of republics.

65. Tamir, "Pro Patria," 229.

66. Tamir, "Pro Patria," 229.

67. George Bisharat details the role that law plays in the history of the Palestine-Israel conflict, noting that "its legitimating function may be chiefly, if not exclusively, among those proximate to the centers of social and political power." "Land, Law, and Legitimacy in Israel and the Occupied Territories," *American University Law Review* 43 (1994): 467.

68. Carl Schmitt, *The Concept of the Political* (Chicago: University of Chicago Press, 2007), 48.

69. Ellen Kennedy, *Constitutional Failure: Carl Schmitt in Weimar* (Durham, N.C.: Duke University Press), 110.

70. Michael Kearl and Anoel Rinaldi, "The Political Uses of the Dead as Symbols in Contemporary Civil Religions," *Social Forces* 61 (1983): 699.

71. Robert Hertz, *Death and the Right Hand* (London: Black, 1965), 77; quoted in Kearl and Rinaldi, "Political Uses of the Dead," 699.

72. Kearl and Rinaldi, "Political Uses of the Dead," 699.

73. Alex Markels, "Showdown for a Tool in Rights Suits," *New York Times* (June 15, 2003); Augustine Ikelegbe, "The Perverse Manifestation of Civil Society: Evidence from Nigeria," *The Journal of Modern African Studies* 39 (2001): 1–24. Iklegebe shows how political groups that may seem to be organized along the lines of interest groups reiterate ethnic alignments. These ties also manifest in how government leaders maintain order and allow for the group loyalties adumbrated by Schmitt.

74. There are datasets purporting to measure the relative impact of ethnicity compared with other variables associated with war or civil war, but these miss the big picture: we have the entire history of the world as a dataset showing that absent past, present, or future attachments experienced as either hereditary or religious, people may die and kill at most in the dozens but never in the thousands, much less millions. For a review of this literature, see Stevens, "The Correlates and Laws of Mass Violence," http://www.jacquelinestevens.org/CLMassViolence.

75. For a discussion of the mutual effects of foreign policy and health, see Colin McInnes and Kelley Lees, "Health, Security, and Foreign Policy," *Review of International Studies* 32 (2006): 5–23.

76. Hazem Adam Ghobarah, Paul Huth, and Bruce Russett, "Civil Wars Kill and Maim People—Long after the Shooting Stops," *American Political Science Review* 97 (2003): 189–202.

77. United Nations, *Millennium Development Goals*, 9. Drawing on International Rescue Committee methods for estimating the ratio of battle deaths to total war-related deaths, epidemiologists estimate total deaths from conflicts in selected African countries as two million in the Sudan (1983–2002), one to two million in Ethiopia (1976–1991); and 2.5 million in the Democratic Republic of Congo (1998–2001). Lacina and Gleditsch, "Monitoring Trends in Global Combat," citing L. Roberts, *Mortality in Eastern DRC: Results from Five Mortality Surveys* (New York/Bukavu: International Rescue Committee, 2000), 159; Lacina and Gleditsch, "Monitoring Trends in Global Combat," table 4, p. 159. This last figure was revised to 3.9 million for 1998–2004 in a more recent *Lancet* study. Benjamin Coghlan, Richard Brennan, Pascal Ngoy, David Dofara, Brad Otto, Mark Clements, and Tony Stewart, "Mortality in the Democratic Republic of Congo: A Nationwide Survey," *Lancet* 367 (2007): 44.

78. Ghoborah, Huth, and Russet, "Civil Wars Kill," 189.

79. Elisabeth Skön, Wuyi Omitoogun, Catalina Perdomo, and Petter Stålenheim, "Military Expenditure," in *Armament, Disarmament, and International Security*, SIPRI Yearbook, 2005 (Oxford: Oxford University Press, 2005), http://yearbook2005.sipri.org/ch8/ch8/.

80. The amount is still low by the standards of developed countries with universal health care ($3,000–$3,500) but the impact of this increase would be a significant one. World Bank Data and Research, http://devdata.worldbank.org/hnpstats/cd.asp.

81. William Connolly, "Discipline, Politics, and Ambiguity," *Political Theory* 11 (1983): 326–327.

82. Table 1-1, "National Defense Budget Estimate for 2007" (March 2006), defenselink.mil/comptroller/defbudget/fy2007.

83. Karen Brooks, "Illegal Immigration's Give-and-Take: Study—Their Taxes Lift State but Services Drain Counties," *Dallas Morning News* (December 8, 2006).

84. Bruce Russett and Joel Slemrod, "Diminished Expectations of Nuclear War and Increased Personal Savings: Evidence from Individual Survey Data," *American Economic Review* 83 (1993): 1022.

85. An overview of the investment challenges facing war-torn regions can be found in Tony Addison, "Reconstruction from War in Africa: Communities, Entrepreneurs, and States," in *CSAE Conference 2001: Development Policy in Africa*, Centre for the Study of African Economies, University of Oxford (March 29–31, 2001), http://www.csae.ox.ac.uk/conferences/2001-DPiA/pdfs/Addison.pdf.

86. For an analysis of how the Bush administration "literalized its 'war' on terrorism," see Kenneth Roth, "The Law of War in the War on Terror," *Foreign Affairs* (2004), http://www.foreignaffairs.org/20040101facomment83101/kenneth-roth/the-law-of-war-in-the-war-on-terror.html.

87. Hannah Arendt, *Eichmann in Jerusalem: A Report on the Banality of Evil*, rev. ed. (New York: Penguin, 1965), 171.

88. "International Migration Policies in a Changing World System," in *Human Migration: Patterns and Policies* (Bloomington: University of Indiana Press), 221; quoted in John Torpey, *The Invention of the Passport: Surveillance, Citizenship and the State* (Cambridge: Cambridge University Press, 2000), 162. Mark Tushnet offers a different take on the exit option, speculating that if the citizens of dictators leave, then there will be no one to attempt regime change. Still, recent evidence suggests regimes falling apart from within when their populations exit, a revolution from above that is far less bloody and more desirable than a civil war.

89. A U.S. State Department document states: "The disposition of those detained in the October 29 arrival will spur further migration if they are released into the U.S. Such treatment would create a perception in Haiti of an easing in U.S. policy with respect to admission of migrants. For this reason, the Department of State strongly recommends that the 216 migrants (207 Haitians, 9 Dominicans) from the boat which reached Key Biscayne on October 29 be detained while they undergo processing." Interim Decision #3488, April 17, 2003, cited as 23 I&N Dec. 572 (A.G. 2003), http://www.usdoj.gov/eoir/efoia/bia/Decisions/Revdec/pdf DEC/3488.pdf.

90. *U.S. Cuban Adjustment Act* (1996), uscs.gov/graphics/services/residency/caa.htm.

91. A journalist wrote at the time, "Today, many of those fleeing Haiti say their hopes now rest with Clinton's recent attempts to force the nation's military leaders to step down. Says

Steven Forester, a lawyer with Miami's Haitian Refugee Center: 'Haitians don't want to come here. They want their president back.'" Michael Rezendes, "A Policy Lost at Sea; Worldwide Requests for Asylum Swamp the Immigration System," *Boston Globe* (July 10, 1994).

92. Elisabeth Rosenthal, "China and U.N. Meet on North Korea Immigrants," *New York Times* (June 28, 2001).

93. Sabrina Tavernise and Robert Worth, "As Iraqis Flee, Few Are Gaining Sanctuary in U.S.," *New York Times* (January 2, 2007).

94. J. Widgren, "Multilateral Cooperation to Combat Trafficking in Migrants and the Role of International Organizations," Eleventh IOM Seminar on Migration (October 1994); cited in John Salt and James Clark, "International Migration in the UNECE Region: Patterns, Trends, Policies," *International Social Science Journal* 52 (September 2000): 323.

95. Vincenzo Ruggiero, "Trafficking in Human Beings: Slaves in Contemporary Europe," *International Journal of the Sociology of Law* 25 (1997): 232. For a discussion of historical differences and similarities in slavery, see Joel Quirk, "Trafficked Into Slavery," *Journal of Human Rights* 6 (2007): 181–207.

96. UNICEF, "Trafficking in Human Beings, Especially Women and Children, in Africa" (2005), 15–16.

97. John Salt, "Trafficking and Human Smuggling: A European Perspective," *International Migration* 38 (2000): 48.

98. Salt, "Trafficking and Human Smuggling," 48.

99. Michael Kamber, "Shame of Imported Labor in Kurdish North of Iraq," *New York Times* (December 29, 2007).

100. Kamber, "Shame of Imported Labor," A6.

101. For the political and psychological paradoxes of immigration restrictions, see Bonnie Honig, *Democracy and the Foreigner* (Princeton, N.J.: Princeton University Press, 2001); and Ali Behdad, *A Forgetful Nation: On Immigration and Cultural Identity in America* (Durham, N.C.: Duke University Press, 2005).

102. UNICEF, "Trafficking in Human Beings," 18.

103. UNICEF, "Trafficking in Human Beings," 18.

104. Editorial, "In Praise of Huddled Masses," *Wall Street Journal* (July 3, 1984).

105. For details of the immigration debates over S Res. 1348 and S Res. 1637 in 2007, see "States Without Nations," http://blogspot.stateswithoutnations.com.

106. "In Praise of Huddled Masses," *Wall Street Journal* (July 3, 1984).

107. Brooks, "Illegal Immigration's Give-and-Take."

108. Brooks, "Illegal Immigration's Give-and-Take."

109. David Card, "The Impact of the Mariel Boatlift on the Miami Labor Market," *Industrial and Labor Relations Review* 43 (1990): 250.

110. Howard Chang offers a good survey of key texts in this literature in "The Economics of International Labor Migration and the Case for Global Distributive Justice in Liberal Political Theory" (2007), http://lsr.nellco.org/upenn/wps/papers/159. Studies documenting the benign impact of immigration on labor markets include David Card, "Is the New Immigration Really So Bad?" *The Economic Journal* 115 (2005): F300–F323, which looks at national data and finds no evidence of immigration having an adverse impact on labor markets; Rachel Friedberg and Jennifer Hunt, "The Impact of Immigrants on Host Country Wages, Employment, and Growth," *Journal of Economic Perspectives* 9 (1995): 23–44, a metastudy concluding that "empirical estimates in a variety of settings and using a variety of approaches have shown that the effect of immigration on the labor market outcomes of natives is small. There is no evidence of economically significant reductions in native employment. Most empirical analysis of the United States and other countries finds that a 10 percent increase in the fraction of immigrants in the population reduces native wages by at most 1 percent" (42). Another study using a dynamic model finds that "the average wage of US-born workers experiences a significant increase (rather than a decrease) as a consequence of immigration." Gianmarco Ottaviano and Giovanni Peri, "Rethinking the Effects of Immigration on Wages," NBER Working Paper No. 12497, p. 4, http://creativeclass.com/rfcgdb/articles/Peri%20and%20Ottavanio,%20Rethinking%20Immigrations%20Effect.pdf. Another study of global immigration states that "even a small liberalization of international migration restrictions can still yield substantial gains. In particular, we estimate that a 10% increase in international migration corresponds to an efficiency gain of about US$774 billion (1998) dollars." Jonathan Moses and Bjørn Letnes, "The Economic Costs to International Labor Restrictions: Revisiting the Empirical Discussion," *World Development* 32 (2004): 1609.

111. Borjas's 1999 book *Heaven's Door* was reissued in 2001 in a paperback edition (Princeton, N.J.: Princeton University Press, 2001); Borjas has authored over dozens of books and articles on immigration economics that are widely quoted by immigration opponents.

112. The problem that many of his colleagues have with Borjas's findings is that his models have miserly assumptions that do not include income-generating functions of immigration, only costs, e.g., Chang, "The Economics of International Migration," 9–10; Ottaviano and Peri, "Rethinking the Effects of Immigration on Wages," 3.

113. Ana María Iregui, "Efficiency Gains from the Elimination of Global Restrictions on Labour Mobility: An Analysis Using a Multiregional CGE Model," Estudios Económicos, Banco de la República, Bogotá, Colombia (December 1999), http://www.banrep.org/docum/ftp/borra146.pdf. Irequi writes: According to our results, the elimination of global restrictions on labour mobility generates world-wide efficiency gains that could be of considerable magnitude, ranging from 15% to 67% of world GDP."

114. Bob Hamilton and John Whalley, "Efficiency and Distributional Implications of Global Restrictions on Labour Mobility," *Journal of Development Economics* 14 (1984): 61–75.

115. Gillian Hadfield, "Just Borders," in *Justice in Immigration*, 204–205.

116. Hadfield, "Just Borders," 201–211.

117. Hadfield, "Just Borders," 209.

118. Bruce Scott, "The Great Divide in the Global Village," *Foreign Affairs* (January/February, 2001).

119. "State Effects on Labor Exploitation: The INS and Undocumented Immigrants at the Mexico-U.S. Border," *Critique of Anthropology* 18 (1998): 158.

120. An excellent example of how nationality undercuts labor bargaining power is the decision of Agriprocessors, a kosher meat processing company, not to recognize a vote to unionize on the grounds that some of the voting workers were in the country illegally. A 1984 Supreme Court decision allows workers who lack documentation of their legal status to vote in union elections, but Agriprocessors has decided to appeal that decision on the grounds that federal laws on employing immigrants have changed. The union went on strike to protest this decision and in response Agriprocessors hired scabs, many of them reportedly also undocumented workers. Steven Greenhouse, "Meatpacker in Brooklyn Challenges a Union Vote," *New York Times* (September 1, 2008).

121. For a discussion of how ethnicity is predicated on the nation-state, see Stevens, *Reproducing the State*, 149–171.

122. For a discussion of how race is constituted by the state and its citizenship rules, see *Reproducing the State*, 172–208, which includes citations to other relevant works.

123. Avram Bornstein, "Borders and the Utility of Violence: State Effects on the 'Superexploitation' of West Bank Palestinians," *Critique of Anthropology* 22 (2002).

124. Joseph Nevins, *Operation Gatekeeper: The Rise of the 'Illegal Alien' and the Remaking of the U.S.-Mexican Border* (New York: Routledge, 2002), 65.

125. Jimmy Carter, *Peace Not Apartheid* (New York: Simon and Schuster, 2006).

126. Nevins, *Operation Gatekeeper*, 65.

127. Nevins, *Operation Gatekeeper*, 66.

128. Cox News Service, "Israel Plans to Fence Out Palestinians in West Bank: High Tech Barriers, Checkpoints, and Dog Patrols Are Attempt to Keep out Militant Violence," *The Gazette* (March 21, 1995).

129. Joseph Nevins and Mizue Aizeki, *Dying to Live: U.S. Immigration in an Age of Global Apartheid* (San Francisco: City Lights Books, 2008), 41–42.

130. Nevins, *Dying to Live*, 42.

131. *How Ah Kow v. Nunan*, 12 F. Cas. 252 (1879).

132. Edward J. M. Rhoads, *Manchus and Han: Ethnic Relations and Political Power in Late Qing and Early Republican China, 1861–1928* (Seattle: University of Washington Press, 2000), 60.

133. *How Ah Kow v. Nunan*, 256.

134. *How Ah Kow v. Nunan*, 255.

135. *Kwock Jan Fat v. White, as Commissioner of Immigration at the Port of San Francisco*, 253 U.S. 454, 64 (1920).

136. National Commission on Law Observance and Enforcement, *Report on the Enforcement of the Deportation Laws of the United States* (Washington, D.C.: Government Printing Office, 1931); Francisco Balderrama and Raymond Rodríguez, *Decade of Betrayal: Mexican Repatriation in the 1930s* (Albuquerque : University of New Mexico Press, 1995).

137. Since the 1990s, legal clinics and nonprofit civil rights law firms have been filing lawsuits against the Immigration and Naturalization Service and the Department of Homeland Security for violating the civil rights of U.S. citizens and legal residents. Between 1995 and 2002, the small San Francisco office of the Lawyers Committee for Civil Rights settled eight cases of civil rights violations by immigration agents for a total of $675,000. Memorandum from staff attorney at the Lawyers Committee for Civil Rights, received July 7, 2008.

138. Reynolds Holding, "Power of the INS Outweighs Proof," *San Francisco Chronicle* (June 4, 2000).

139. First in the 1994 Crime Bill and then in the 1996 Immigration Reform and Immigrant Responsibility Act (IRIRA), Congress attempted to bolster its alien criminal identification and deportation program. The goal was to induce the states to help deport "criminal aliens" by paying them per diems for those found in their prisons and jails. After being so identified, the states were supposed to parole nonviolent felons early, on condition of their deportation: "To the extent of available appropriations, funds otherwise made available under this section with respect to a State (or political subdivision, including a municipality) for incarceration of an undocumented criminal alien may, at the discretion of the recipient of the funds, be used for the costs of imprisonment of such alien in a State, local, or municipal prison or jail" (IRIRA, Sec. 328). In my research on a U.S. inmate in Georgia and correspondence and habeas writs filed by an attorney representing a U.S. citizen classified as an alien in Maryland, I learned how these monetary inducements may be leading to U.S. citizen inmates being incorrectly classified as aliens, leading to heightened security, longer sentences, and no due process for challenging this. My conversations with Georgia corrections officers, including an official on the parole board, indicates that prisoners the federal government expects will be paroled early on condition of deportation are being held for periods longer than inmates classified as U.S. citizens. Also, the Department of Homeland Security is recklessly disregarding the proof of citizenship being offered. In the case in Georgia, following the judge's order terminating deportation proceedings on grounds of U.S. citizenship, the DHS trial attorney failed to notify the inmate's attorney that the DHS was appealing the ruling and the parole order denying release was still in effect. The DHS issued a notice that it was withdrawing its appeal, which the client's attorney believes is an admission that it had

incorrectly been detaining this inmate for over 3 years. For details, see Stevens, "States Without Nations" posts tagged "David," http://stateswithoutnations.blogspot.com.

140. Stevens, "Thin ICE," *Nation* (June 23, 2008).

141. Personal communication with detainees and their attorneys and records submitted to immigration judges.

142. Other countries require the United States to obtain travel documents for persons the U.S. government alleges are nationals of their country. Otherwise the United States could simply ship its criminal population to foreign countries. This actually occurs in the case of Mexico, which the DHS singles out in its own nomenclature as a unique target destination by the abbreviation of OTM, Other Than Mexico, because Mexico has an agreement with the United States not to require these travel documents, facilitating the easy removal of U.S. residents and those apprehended entering the United States without authenticating their Mexican citizenship. Department of Homeland Security, Office of Inspector General, "Detention and Removal of Illegal Aliens, U.S. Immigration and Customs Enforcement," OIG--06-33 (2006), http://www.dhs.gov/xoig/assets/mgmtrpts/OIG_06-33_Apr06.pdf. U.S.-born criminals have strategically used this to avoid arrest in the United States, citizens from other countries in Central America lie and are dropped off in Tijuana because it is easier to attempt reentry from there, and U.S. citizens can be illegally removed to Mexico because no one in that government is checking their internal records to verify Mexican citizenship. *Rivera v. Ashcroft*, 394 F. 3d 1129, and interview with southern Arizona immigration attorney, September 3, 2008, describing U.S.-born citizen held in July to August 2008 by ICE for one month after ICE first deported her client to Mexico based on client's false statement to border-patrol agent that he was a Mexican citizen.

143. Caroline Danielson, *Citizen Acts: Citizenship and Political Agency in the Works of Jane Addams, Charlotte Perkins Gilman, and Emma Goldman*, dissertation, University of Michigan, 1996. This is a distinction that is only relevant for democracies. Dictatorships of various sorts do not have citizens but subjects who by definition must endure what their leaders decide.

144. George Will, "Good Citizenship Can Include Cash," *Times Union* (Albany) (July 29, 1999).

145. These examples reveal a double standard for citizenship and other admissions criteria but do not mean that the right standards for citizenship should be wealth or education tests.

146. T. H. Marshall, *Citizenship and Social Class* [1950] (London: Pluto Press, 1992), 15.

147. Yasmin Soysal, *Limits of Citizenship: Migrants and Postnational Membership in Europe* (Chicago: University of Chicago Press, 1994), 130-131; citing Anthony Giddens, *The Nation-State and Violence* (Berkeley: University of California Press, 1985), 198-221. Soysal accurately paraphrases Giddens, but Giddens does a disservice to the complexity of Marshall's analysis.

148. Giddens also makes this point by reference to the nineteenth-century German state. Oddly, Giddens inaccurately claims that his evidence on Bismarck refutes rather than reinforces the same approach Marshall assesses in early nineteenth-century England. Giddens, *Nation-State*, 205. It might be noted that Soysal's observations on citizenship were developed during a small window of time just after the collapse of communism and during the first Clinton administration. It is not clear that she would find the same ideological climate inducing such an approach in today's post-9/11 reterritorialized security states.

149. Mary Dietz, "Citizenship with a Feminist Face: The Problem of Maternal Thinking," *Political Theory* 13 (1984): 30.

150. "All income earned by a U.S. citizen, whether from sources within or without the United States, is taxable, whether or not the individual lives in the United States." The same is true for a "resident alien," defined as either as someone who is a legal resident ("green card") or who is "present in the United States for 31 or more days during the current calendar year and has been present in the United States . . . for 183 or more weighted toward the present year," or who "makes an election to be treated as a resident of the United States." Nonresident aliens are "subject to United States tax on income from United States sources or income that is effectively connected with the conduct of a trade or business within the United States," subject to exceptions from bilateral treatises. United States Joint Committee on Taxation (USJCT), "Present Law and Background Relating to Individual Taxpayer Identification Numbers (ITNS)" (March 5, 2004), 3, http://www.house.govjet/x<->16-04.pdf.

151. USJCT, "Present Law," 3.

152. When St. Augustine paraphrased Cicero in pointing out that without justice governments were no different from pirates, he was referring to imperial powers in the Mediterranean who rarely blushed at their own use of force to extract at sea whatever they needed from colonized seafaring subjects, in other words, "official" sailors whose effects were, but for the alleged justice of their leaders, in practice indistinguishable from pirates. *City of God*, book 19, chap. 21, c. 412.

153. See Frede Løkkegaard, *Islamic Taxation in the Classic Period* (Copenhagen: Brauner and Korch, 1950), esp. 92–108; Roy Douglas, *Taxation in Britain Since 1660* (New York: St. Martin's Press, 1999).

154. Joseph Vogt, *Ancient Slavery and the Idea of Man* (Cambridge, Mass.: Harvard University Press, 1975), 42.

155. Xenophon, *Persian War* (Harmondsworth: Penguin, 1972), 46.

156. Michael Kirsch, "The Tax Code as Nationality Law," *Harvard Journal on Legislation* 13 (2006), 375–377.

157. The residents of California are too familiar with this, as each annual budget crisis is accompanied by arbitrary, very steep, and of course regressive increases in penalties for traffic violations and administrative fines, such as lateness for court appearances, that do not have the pretense of being rooted in any policy preferences. The increase of speeding-ticket fines purely for revenue raising and not to deter accidents means that the state is arbitrarily casting about for ways to use its police force to extract money in a way that is unmoored from any principle of distributive justice and used for its ease of enforcement and collection. If California's assembly decided it could gain more money from using traffic guards to collect from children walking to school, it would be doing this instead.

158. Immanuel Kant, *Perpetual Peace*, http://www.constitution.org/kant/perpeace.htm; Locke, "Second Treatise of Government," especially §113, §115, §119, §122; Carens, "Aliens and Citizens," 261–262.

159. For a review of this literature, see Henri Tafjel, "Social Psychology of Intergroup Relations," *Annual Review of Psychology* 33 (1982): esp. 19–20.

160. Groups organized by ethnicity, i.e., groups based on past, current, or aspirational nations elsewhere, may in some countries garner enough support to start a civil war, but groups without these, e.g., soccer hooligans, have individuals with the same "human nature" as found in other groups and never organize mass slaughters. A rough tally of total deaths from soccer-hooligan violence suggests deaths in the dozens.

161. Jacob Rabbie and Murray Horwitz, "Arousal of Ingroup-Outgroup Bias by a Chance Win or Loss," *Journal of Personality and Social Psychology* 13 (1969): 272.

162. I was referred to this article by a colleague in political science who told me in- and out-group violence was simply human nature. If intergenerational states withered, states would still pursue military campaigns designed to destroy the enemy, he claimed. The study to which my colleague referred me in support of this claim is one indeed frequently cited to make this very point, e.g., Roy Baumeister and Mark Leary, "The Need to Belong: Desire for Interpersonal Attachments as a Fundamental Human Motivation," *Psychological Bulletin* 117 (1995): 513. The Rabbie and Horwitz study says that the authors found more coherence after a group was given a prize based on a coin toss than if the group was not given a prize, but they omit mention in the main summary that the cohesion is reversed when the tester awards the transistor radio to a group in which one member was presumed by the others to have swayed the result toward the group. In that case, individuals prefer members of the other group. Yet one article cites the Rabbie and Horwitz study after stating, "Research on group processes consistently show that considering oneself as a member of a particular group leads to discriminatory, competitive behavior toward other groups." Robert Kurzban and Mark Leary, "Evolutionary Origins of Stigmatization: The Functions of Social Exclusion," *Psychological Bulletin* 127 (2001): 195. Another study cites Rabbie and Horwitz for the claim, "People evaluate members of their own group more favorably than others." Don Moore, Terri Kurtzberg, Leigh Thompson, and Michael Morris, "Long and Short Routes to Success in Electronically Mediated Negotiations: Group Affiliation and Good Vibrations,"

Organizational Behavior and Human Decision Processes 77 (1999): 22–43, http://www.cbdr.cmu.edu/mpapers/emn.pdf. And another article states, "Experiments on 'minimal' groups, first conducted by Rabbie and Horwitz (1969) ... were a crucial hallmark in this domain of research. Results observed in these studies indicate that the mere categorization of individuals into arbitrary social categories can be sufficient to elicit in-group formation." Sabine Otten and Dirk Wentura, "About the Impact of Automaticity in the Minimal Group Paradigm: Evidence from the Effective Primary Tasks," *European Journal of Social Psychology* 29 (1999): 1049.

163. Rabbie and Horwitz, "Arousal of Ingroup-Outgroup Bias," 273.

164. Rabbie and Horwitz, "Arousal of Ingroup-Outgroup Bias," 274.

165. E. O. Wilson, *Sociobiology: The New Synthesis* (Cambridge, Mass.: Harvard University Press, 2000), 553; citing V. Reynolds, "Kinship and the Family in Monkeys, Apes, and Man," *Man* 3 (1968): 209–233; Lila Leibowitz, "Founding Families," *Journal of Theoretical Biology* 21 (1968): 153–169.

166. Garrett Hardin. "Population Skeletons in the Environmental Closet." *Bulletin of the Atomic Scientists* 28 (1972): 37–41; quoted in Wilson, *Sociobiology*, 565.

167. Wilson, *Sociobiology*, 565.

168. Konrad Lorenz, *On Aggression*, trans. Marjorie Latzke (London: Routledge, 1996), 245–246.

169. Lorenz, *Aggression*, 205.

170. Lorenz, *Aggression*, 207.

171. Joshua Goldstein, *Gender and War* (Princeton, N.J.: Princeton University Press, 2001), 408.

172. Roosevelt, quoted in Goldstein, *Gender and War*, 275–276.

173. Woodrow Wilson, "Report of Address to Universal Peace Union" (February 9, 1912), quoted in Thomas Knoch, *To End All Wars: Woodrow Wilson and the Quest for a New World Order* (Oxford: Oxford University Press, 1992), 19.

174. Woodrow Wilson, "A Message to Democratic Rallies," quoted in Knoch, *To End All Wars*, 19.

175. Woodrow Wilson, "A Fourth of July Address," quoted in Knoch, *To End All Wars*, 28.

176. Erasmus, "Complaint of Peace," in *In Praise of Folly and Other Writings* (New York: Norton, 1989), 90.

177. While this is a correct claim about systematic fighting, there is a widely studied species of chimpanzees that on rare occasions raid in small numbers other nearby chimpanzee communities. A group from one will attack a single chimpanzee from another. Another species genetically similar to humans displays relatively little aggression, the bonobo. Primatologists have had heated debates on the accuracy of these generalizations and their

significance, but none of these observe one community attacking more than one member of another community. For a summary of the debates in response to an article reevaluating the bonobo data, see Craig Stanford, "The Social Behavior of Chimpanzees and Bonobos: Empirical Evidence, Shifting Assumptions," *Current Anthropology* 4 (1998), 399–420. The last section includes comments by primatologists on this debate, making the point that studies indicate changes within the species over time and variations within each of them, both data indicating malleability and thus sensitivity to nongenetic stimuli.

178. A. C. Beier, *Masterless Men: The Vagrancy Problem in England, 1560–1640* (New York: Methuen, 1985); William Harrison, *The Description of England* (Ithaca, N.Y.: Cornell University Press, 1968).

179. David Brion Davis, *The Problem with Slavery in the Western World* (Ithaca, N.Y.: Cornell University Press, 1966), 40.

180. Torpey, *The Invention of the Passport*, 19.

181. Torpey, *The Invention of the Passport*, 21.

182. Torpey, *The Invention of the Passport*, 55.

183. Torpey, *The Invention of the Passport*, 114, 124.

184. Torpey, *The Invention of the Passport*, 25, 28.

185. Torpey, *The Invention of the Passport*, 31, 32, 41.

186. Torpey, *The Invention of the Passport*, 153.

187. Torpey, *The Invention of the Passport*, 153.

188. Torpey, *The Invention of the Passport*, 72.

189. Torpey, *The Invention of the Passport*, 72.

190. For more on English citizenship laws, see Stevens, *Reproducing the State*, 138–139.

191. Stevens, *Reproducing the State*, 67.

192. Stevens, *Reproducing the State*, 68.

193. Torpey, *The Invention of the Passport*.

194. Quoted in Larry Rohter, "Las Palomas Journal: Pillow Talk of U.S.-Mexico Towns: What Border?" *New York Times* (February 17, 1990).

195. Quoted in Rohter, "Las Palomas Journal."

196. Charlie LeDuff, "Jacumba Journal: Border Towns Are Close Enough to Touch but Worlds Apart," *New York Times* (February 24, 2003).

197. Joseph Nevins, *Operation Gatekeeper*, 1–2.

198. LeDuff, "Jacumba Journal," quoting Raleigh Leonard.

199. The city council of Hazelton, Pennsylvania, passed a law requiring fines of $1,000 per day for landlords who rent to anyone who does not pay the city for a background check. Altoona, Pennsylvania, then passed a similar measure. Pahrump, Nevada, passed a law stating that "illegal aliens are undocumented immigrants are not entitled to any benefits." Farmers Branch, Texas, also set penalties for renting to undocumented immigrants and directed police to report them to Homeland Security. Many other cities are considering similar measures. Perhaps the most draconian is in Escondido, California, where landlords were given ten days to evict undocumented immigrants. The data above are from Eunice Moscoso, "Thumbnails of Towns That Are Cracking Down on Illegal Immigration," Cox News Service (November 22, 2006).

200. For an excellent overview of this period and its relevance to contemporary policies, see Nevins, *Operation Gatekeeper*, 15–38.

201. Migration Dialogue, University of California at Davis, http://migration.ucdavis.edu/ rmn/rural_data/carucom/cal_counties/tulare/london.html; http://www.civilrights.org/pub lications/reports/ c2k_report/charts/chart11.pdf.

202. "As every man is equal before God and every sojourner in this life must be left undisturbed in his legitimate possessions, especially in his natural and political life, it is the wish of this assembly that individual liberty be guaranteed to all the French, and therefore that each must be free to move about or to come, within and outside the Kingdom, without permissions, passports, or other formalities that tend to hamper the liberty of its citizens." *Cahiers des États Généraux* (Paris: A. Guyot, 1834), 4:509, quoted in Torpey, *The Invention of the Passport*, 22. Although strictly speaking this law applies only to the French, it is impossible to abandon such "formalities" and also regulate the movement of foreigners.

203. *Le Moniteur*, 5:351–352, quoted in Torpey, *The Invention of the Passport*, 25, quoting Georges Lefebvre, *The French Revolution*, trans. Elizabeth Moss Evanson (New York: Columbia University Press, 1962), vol. 1.

204. Torpey, *The Invention of the Passport*, 88.

205. Bradley Hope, "Festive Atmosphere in Manhattan as Immigrant Marches Converge," *New York Sun* (May 2, 2006).

206. This sentence refers to the efforts of governments to discriminate against immigrant minority populations during the consolidation of postempire modern, territorial states and the organizing against them on the same national and ethnic basis, the catastrophic consequences of which were the Jewish genocide and the creation of the state of Israel.

207. For details, see Stevens, *Reproducing the State*, 77–79.

208. Torpey, *The Invention of the Passport*, 24.

209. *Phenomenology of Spirit* [1807], trans. A. V. Miller (Oxford: Oxford University Press, 1977), 288–289. Hegel goes on to say that the risk of life in war propels citizens into a strong feeling of self-consciousness. For men, this ensues because of their own immediate potential sacrifice. For women, this results from being sisters or wives to such full citizens.

210. Hegel, *Phenomenology of Spirit*, 111–138.

211. For more on the psychodynamics of this scene, see Stevens, *Reproducing the State*, 275–280.

1. Rawls, *The Law of Peoples* (Cambridge, Mass.: Harvard University Press, 1999), 83.

2. Martha Nussbaum, "Patriotism and Cosmopolitanism," in *For Love of Country*, ed. Joshua Cohen (Boston: Beacon Press, 1996); Thomas Pogge, "Priorities of Global Justice," in *Global Justice*, ed. Thomas Pogge (Oxford: Blackwell, 2001), 6–24; Thomas Pogge, "World Poverty and Human Rights," *Ethics and International Affairs* 19 (2005): 1–7, http://www.cceia.org/media/5109_eia19-1_poggeo1.pdf. Jeremy Waldron, "Minority Cultures and the Cosmopolitan Alternative," *University of Michigan Journal of Law Reform* 25 (1992): 751; Jeremy Waldron, "What Is Cosmopolitan?" *Journal of Political Philosophy* 8 (2000): 227–243. Seyla Benhabib's work on the "end of the unitary model of citizenship" echoes Yasmin Soysal's overreading of foreigners' ambiguous civil rights. Benhabib also celebrates a discourse of abstract human rights as a legal norm to challenge oppression, but does not explain how these might be implemented. See, e.g., "Twilight of Sovereignty of the Emergence of Cosmopolitan Norms? Rethinking Citizenship in Volatile Times," *Citizenship Studies* 11 (2007): 19–36.

3. Ayelet Shachar and Ran Hirschl, "Citizenship as Inherited Property," *Political Theory* 35 (2007): 279.

4. For an excellent analysis of the ambiguities of origin in the book of Ruth, see Bonnie Honig, "Ruth, the Model Émigré: Mourning and the Symbolic Politics of Immigration," *Political Theory* 25 (1997): 128; citing Eric Santer, *Stranded Objects: Mourning, Memory and Film in Postwar Germany* (Ithaca, N.Y.: Cornell University Press, 1990). There is of course a very large literature following the lead of historian Ernst Renan in debating how the nation and nationalism arose. I discuss these texts in *Reproducing the State* (Princeton, N.J.: Princeton University Press, 1999). Since then some postcolonial scholars have been questioning the relevance of the European nation for these inquiries, or whether much of anything from Europe is useful for scholarly and particularly global heuristics. See especially Dipesh Chakrabarty, *Provincializing Europe: Postcolonial Thought and Historical Difference*, 2nd ed. (Princeton, N.J.: Princeton University Press, 2007); and Ranjit Guha, *History at the Limit of World History* (New York: Columbia University Press, 2002). One might say that the first wave of postcolonial scholarship, especially work inspired by Edward Said, pointed out the inconsistencies in discourses that aspired to universality and equality but were particularist and racist. Current research is questioning why scholars from outside Europe would even bother with this literature, rather than mining their own luminaries. The ressentiment is palpable: no one has prevented Chakrabarty, a tenured anthropologist at the University of Chicago, from using an Indian archive for his historiography, so it seems strange to advocate for this cause rather than simply pursue it. Substantively, the historiographical research attentive to the hybridity of research and political movements seems a more fruitful line of inquiry than the call to "provincialize Europe," which of course only

places Europe center stage. From W. E. B. DuBois's and other antiracist scholars' strategic appropriation of tropes from European nationalism, to Edward Said's work on the use of the authentic "Oriental," to Martin Bernal's documentation of African intellectual culture's impact on that of ancient Greece, to more recent work revealing the elevation of Southeast Asian intellectual culture through the work of European philologists rooting Indo-European languages in Sanskrit, the evidence seems to suggest that our most influential ideas are hybrids of ambiguous origin and are often expressed this way by writers and received as such by readers. Thus the attempts to found inquiry on the archive of one country or region seems doomed. See David Lewis, *W. E. B. Du Bois: Biography of a Race, 1868–1919* (New York: John MacRae Books, 1994); Edward Said, *Orientalism* (New York: Vintage, 1978); Martin Bernal, *Black Athena: The Afroasiatic Roots of Classical Civilization* (London: Free Association Books, 1987).

5. Bernard Lazare, *Anti-Semitism: Its History and Causes* [1894] (London: Brilon Publishers, 1962), 125.

6. Lazare, *Anti-Semitism*, 87, note 190, quoting from Talmud Bablim Perdchim.

7. Freud, "Moses and Monotheism" [1938] in *The Complete Psychological Works of Sigmund Freud, Standard Edition*, ed. and trans. James Strachey (London: Hogarth Press, 1955), 23:3–137.

8. This analysis follows Hegel's discussion of knowledge in the *Phenomenology of Spirit* (1809). Hegel describes how consciousness is created by different categories of knowledge. These do not exist independently but move dynamically such that one moment's fact can be the question for another, and vice versa.

9. Hannah Arendt, *The Human Condition* (Chicago: University of Chicago, 1958).

10. See Wendy Sarvassy, "Social Citizenship from a Feminist Perspective," *Signs* 12 (1997): 54–73.

11. Sarvassy, "Social Citizenship."

12. In his *Social Contract* (1762).

13. G. W. F. Hegel, *Philosophy of Right*, trans. T. M. Knox, (Oxford: Oxford University Press, 1952), §258.

14. The mantra of no taxation without representation implies a reciprocal relation that at least in principle would allow for people to opt out of representation in exchange for paying no taxes. Indeed this is precisely the position of the libertarian Freeman's Movement, who claim that because they never consented to the United States government's sovereignty over them, they are not obliged to pay taxes, a claim that the courts not only dismiss but that prosecutors find literally incomprehensible: "It becomes extremely frustrating," an attorney dealing with these groups in Montana told a reporter, "because lawyers are not trained in law school to deal with unrecognizable pleadings." Quoted in Wynn Miller, "Montana 'Freemen' Clog Court System," *National Law Journal* (July 16, 1995). Although most taxpayers appreciate that they benefit from collective projects such as public education, roads, and utilities, the notion of representation following from taxation has no logical relation to one's obligation to follow the law. The provision of desired services, without self-rule per se, could also entail obligation, regardless of tax policies. The Boston Tea Party slogan was about colonial rule, the fear that money from the colonies was being distributed in England. This is a principle that requires that money collected in one society be spent on that society. But it does not by itself require that the government be accountable to a representative government.

15. Whether these changes actually occurred during the period to which Plutarch ascribes them is a matter of debate, and they may have been instituted a few hundred years later. However, that these reforms were put in place for the reasons Plutarch offers is not in dispute, and the relevant corporate groups existed through the early Roman empire. Emilio Gabra, "The *Collegia* of Numa: Problems of Method and Political Ideas," *The Journal of Roman Studies* 74 (1984): 81–86.

16. William Blackstone, *Commentaries on the Laws of England* (New York: W. E. Dean, 1841), 2:48–49.

17. For a discussion and references pertaining to Athenian citizenship, see Stevens, *Reproducing the State*, 113–117.

18. Howard Chang defends open borders on very different grounds, suggesting that absent legal sanction, people still self-segregate into ethnic enclaves, thereby alleviating Walzer's fear that cosmopolitan norms will eradicate ancestral communities. Chang, "Cultural Communities," 9. It is true that such patterns presently prevail but only because birthright citizenship makes these differences indelible and salient.

19. The third item is explored in chapter 3.

20. Tyche Hendricks, "Life Without a License," *San Francisco Chronicle* (February 10, 2002).

21. There is some confusion about immigration crimes: most of those whose presence is being challenged by anti-immigrant groups arrived in the country legally and then overstayed their visas. Their presence is not a criminal matter but an administrative violation.

22. The approach to driver's licenses presently suggests that defining residency is not that challenging. The California Department of Motor Vehicles Web site states: "Residency is established by voting in a California election, paying resident tuition, filing for a homeowner's property tax exemption, or any other privilege or benefit not ordinarily extended to nonresidents." California Department of Motor Vehicles. "How to Apply for a Driver's License If Over 18," http://www.dmv.ca.gov/dl/dl_info.htm#2500. These last criteria imply that there may be problems of fairly denoting the financial obligations and prerogatives of governance to newcomers, but states, without restricting movement, manage to reconcile the privileges

of membership with the obligations of regulation and taxation. Driver's license and registration fees are an especially interesting example of how states that do not allow free movement hurt themselves. Laws preventing undocumented immigrants from registering cars and obtaining driver's licenses both impede enforcement and cost state governments tens of millions of dollars. If one assumes, conservatively, that just one-quarter of the approximately twelve million undocumented U.S. immigrants own cars and that registration and license fees are about $75 annually, then states lose $225 million each year from the inability to collect these payments—over $1 billion in five years lost from just this one unpaid user fee.

23. Just over 190 million people worldwide are foreign-born, 2.9 percent of the total world population. United Nations, *International Migration 2006*, http://www.un.org/esa/popula tion/publications/ittmig2002/Migration2002.pdf; Bruce Scott, "The Great Divide in the Global Village," *Foreign Affairs* 80 (2001): 160.

24. "The President's Agenda for Tax Relief," http://www.whitehouse.gov/news/reports/ taxplan.html. The inference from low taxation to high economic performance is misguided. The reason the United States has a large portion of the world's capital is that approximately 80 percent of the world's cash reserves are in U.S. dollars, which leads to artificially low interest rates for U.S. citizens only, as banks with U.S. dollars largely refuse to lend to foreigners.

25. According to the most recent U.S. census data, the three states with the highest rates of emigration between 2001 and 2002 were Nebraska, North Dakota, and Mississippi, states with relatively low rates of taxation. http://eire.census.gov/popest/data/counties/tables/CO -EST2002/CO-EST2002-04-28.php; http://eire.census.gov/popest/data/counties/tables/CO-EST2002/CO-EST2002-04-12.php. For comparative data on tax rates, see http://dab.nfc .usda.gov/pubs/docs/taxformulas/statecitycounty.

26. U.S. Census, table DP-3, "Selected Economic Characteristics, New Hampshire, 2000," http://censtats.census.gov/data/NH/04033.pdf#page=3. U.S. Census, table DP-3, "Selected Economic Characteristics, Nevada, 2000," http://censtats.census.gov/data/NV/04032.pdf #page=3.

27. For the New York City income-tax table for 2004, see http://dab.nfc.usda.gov/pubs/ docs/taxformulas/formulas/statecitycounty/taxny-c/taxny-c.html.

28. U.S. Census, "American Factfinder, QT-P32, Income Distribution of Households and Families, 1999," http://www.factfinder.census.gov.

29. John Salt and James Clark, "International Migration in the UNECE Region: Patterns, Trends, Policies," *International Social Science Journal* 52 (2000): 314, 316.

30. Salt and Clark, "International Migration in the UNECE Region," 316.

31. *OECD News Release, Standardized Unemployment Rates* (July 9, 1999), cited in U.S. Census Bureau, *Statistical Abstract of the United States 1999*, table 1375.

32. French GDP per capita in 1997 was $22,210; in Greece, it was $12,540. U.S. Census Bureau, *Statistical Abstracts*, table 1362. Calculation based on Anna Triandafyllidou and Ruby Gropas, *European Immigration* (Hampshire: Ashgate, 2007), 133.

33. U.S. Department of Labor, *Foreign Labor Trends: Greece (2003)*, 10, http://www.ilr .cornell.edu/library/downloads/keyWorkplaceDocuments/ForeignLaborTrends/greece -2003.pdf.

34. Ayhan Kaya, research survey author, personal communication, December 3, 2004.

35. For the United States, see George Borjas and Bernt Bratsbert, "Who Leaves? The Outmigration of the Foreign-Born," *The Review of Economics and Statistics* 78 (1996): 165–176; for Europe, see Christian Dustmann, Samuel Bentolila, and Riccardo Faini, "Return Migration: The European Experience," *Economic Policy* 11 (1996): 213–250.

36. Will Kymlicka, *Multicultural Citizenship: A Liberal Theory of Minority Rights* (Oxford: Oxford University Press, 1995); Will Kymlicka, *Politics in the Vernacular: Nationalism, Minority Rights, and Multicultural Citizenship* (Oxford: Oxford University Press, 2001); Charles Taylor, *Multiculturalism and the Politics of Recognition: An Essay* (Princeton, N.J.: Princeton University Press, 1992).

37. Other scholars refer to all of these as "multinational" democracies, but this seems misleading, because only nations, not ethnicities, are able to regulate their membership. Among these countries, only Canada allows separate immigration authority to its provinces, and even this is contingent on the overarching rules of Canada. See http://www.cic.gc.ca/eng lish/sponsor/index.html.

38. James Tully, "Introduction," in *Multinational Democracies*, ed. Alan-G. Gagnon and James Tully (Cambridge: Cambridge University Press, 2001), 3.

39. Jean-Benoî Nadeau and Julie Barlow, "Words Fail Them," *New York Times* (December 27, 2006).

40. Article 2, League of Nations, quoted in Zelim Skurbaty, *As If Peoples Mattered: A Critical Appraisal of 'People' and 'Minorities' from the International Human Rights Perspective and Beyond* (Boston: Martinus Nijhoff, 2000), 314.

41. Presently there are more Kurds in Istanbul, the west of Turkey, than in any other part of the country.

42. Tully, "Introduction," 30.

43. Gregory Jusdanis, *The Necessary Nation* (Princeton, N.J.: Princeton University Press, 2001), 10.

44. Jusdanis, *The Necessary Nation*, 16.

45. Jusdanis, *The Necessary Nation*, 13.

46. Jusdanis, *The Necessary Nation*, 10 and, more generally, 3–16.

47. For evidence on the longstanding history of the nation-state, see Stevens, *Reproducing the State*, chaps. 1–3.

48. Jusdanis, *The Necessary Nation*, 15.

49. Tully, "Introduction," 25.

50. Tully, "Introduction," 25.

51. Authors may object to an organization with the monopoly on force but have very different reasons for the criticism and understandings of the alternatives. Max Stirner and Peter Kropotkin are two antistatists who, despite different views of social interdependence—Stirner denies its importance and Kropotkin embraces it—both protest government restrictions based on force.

52. Henry David Thoreau, "Civil Disobedience," http://www.thoreau.thefreelibrary.com/Civil-Disobedience.

53. Locke, "A Letter Concerning Toleration," http://www.constitution.org/jl/tolerati.htm.

54. Melissa Williams provides a defense of minority-group rights in the context of race and ethnic politics in the United States, arguing that a causal connection between historical oppression and current inequality, as opposed to redress for past inequality, justifies special rights. *Voice, Trust, and Memory: Marginalized Groups and the Failings of Liberal Representation* (Princeton, N.J.: Princeton University Press, 1998), esp. 172, 176, 192, 195. Her analysis would therefore exclude from special recognition those minorities that do not experience current economic hardships due to political discrimination, e.g., Francophones in Canada. Her argument reveals a weakness similar to that of the national minority–rights authors, as Williams too does not explain why structural changes are necessary to compensate for the systematic oppression of some groups and not others. Under her analysis, anarchists too should receive special benefits and state recognition, although her examples speak only to the hardships endured by intergenerational minorities in the United States. Williams might concede this possibility, but that raises the problem of a government in which numerous minorities may be recognized as such, all competing for special benefits. If everyone is part of a privileged minority, then the distributive consequences seem to wash out.

55. Rawls, *The Law of Peoples*, 11.

56. Rawls, *The Law of Peoples*, 39.

57. Rawls, *The Law of Peoples*, 39.

58. Carens, "Aliens and Citizens," 261–262.

59. Walzer, *Spheres of Justice*, 34.

60. NewsMax.com Wires, "Sierra Club Feuds Over Immigration" (February 18, 2004), http://www.newsmax.com/archives/articles/2004/2/18/101437.shtml.

61. SUSPS homepage (April 1, 2004), http://www.susps.org.

62. NewsMax.com Wires, "Sierra Club Feuds Over Immigration."

63. Maude Barlow and Tony Clarke, *Blue Gold: The Fight to Stop the Corporate Theft of the World's Water* (New York: New York Press, 2002); Vandana Shiva, *Water Wars: Privatization, Pollution, and Profit* (London: Pluto Press, 2002).

64. C. Michael Hall and Dieter Müller, *Tourism, Mobility, and Second Homes* (Buffalo, N.Y.: Channel View Publications, 2004).

65. Steven Camarota, "Immigrants in the United States, 2002," Center for Immigration Studies, analysis of the U.S. Current Population Survey, Census Bureau, http://www.cis.org/articles/2002/back1302.html.

66. Charles Beitz, *Political Theory and International Relations* (Princeton, N.J.: Princeton University Press, 1979); Brian Barry, *Democracy, Power, and Justice* (Oxford: Clarendon, 1989); Henry Shue, "Mediating Duties," *Ethics* 98 (1988): 687–704; Onora O'Neill, "Transnational Justice," in *Political Theory Today*, ed. David Held (Cambridge: Polity Press, 1991), 276–304; Hillel Steiner, "Libertarianism and the Transnational Migration of People," in *Free Movement*, ed. Brian Barry and Robert Goodin, 87–94.

67. Preamble, at www.wfm.org.

68. Kant, "Perpetual Peace" [1795], http://www.constitution.org/kant/perpeace.htm.

69. The United States Congress has clearly disproven the conventional wisdom on democracies not going to war against each other. In Korea, Vietnam, Palestine/Israel, the Bay of Pigs attack on the popularly supported government of Cuba, the assassination of the democratically elected president of Chile, the installation of the Shah of Iran, and the support of the Contras against the popularly elected Sandinista government, the United States has consistently shown that democratic regimes it finds distasteful may be attacked.

70. Kant, "Perpetual Peace."

71. Dale Fuchs, "Is the Beach Party Over for the 'Florida of Europe'? Spain's Coastal Building Boom Is Fueling the Economy, but at a Price," *International Herald Tribune* (July 22, 2006).

72. Land rights will be discussed in chapter 7.

73. Christian Dustmann, "Why Go Back? Return Motives of Migrant Workers" (2000), http://www.ucl.ac.uk/~uctpb21/pdf/Return1.pdf.

74. Charlotte Waddell, Harriet MacMillan, and Anna Pietrantonio, "How Important Is Permanency Planning for Children? Considerations for Pediatricians Involved in Child Protection," *Journal of Developmental & Behavioral Pediatrics* 25 (2004): 285–292; citing M. McClure, "An Integrative Ecology," in *Family Matters: Interfaces Between Child and Adult Mental Health*, ed. P. Reder, M. McClure, and A. Jolley (London: Routledge, 2000), 303–317.

75. Amy Goldstein, director, *The Hooping Life* (2007).

76. Mikhail Bakunin, *God and the State* (Mineola: Dover, 1970).

77. Barbara Cruikshank, *The Will to Empower: Democratic Citizens and Other Subjects* (Ithaca, N.Y.: Cornell University Press, 1999).

78. Established to fight proprietary copyright claims and their prohibitions against sharing knowledge, communities from Linux (an operating system) developers to the wikipedia.org content providers are organizing sophisticated and useful services without the use of coercion or individually assigned property rights. The result is some of the highest-quality technical and substantive knowledge available. A study comparing the accuracy of answers to scientific questions by Encyclopedia Britannica and Wikipedia found that they both made the same number of serious errors. The most stable Internet browser, Mozilla, is also open source. "Special Report: Internet Encyclopedias Go Head to Head," *Nature* 438 (2005): 900–901.

79. Robert Paul Wolff, *In Defense of Anarchism* (New York: Harper and Row, 1970), 79.

3. A THEORY OF WEALTH FOR MORTALS

1. Damon Darlin, "Your Money: With a Little Estate Planning, Your House Can Stay in the Family," *New York Times* (January 21, 2006), citing 2002 IRS statistics.

2. 2002 National Election Survey, cited in Marylin Birney, Michael Graetz, and Ian Shapiro, "Public Opinion and the Push to Repeal the Estate Tax," *National Tax Journal* 59 (2003): 444.

3. James Davis, Susanna Sandstrom, Anthony Shorrocks, and Edward Wolff, "The World Distribution of Household Wealth," WIDER Project Meeting on Personal Assets from a Global Perspective (December 5, 2006), table 10s, "Global Wealth Distribution in 2000," http://www.wider.unu.edu/research/2006-2007/2006-2007-1/wider-wdhw-launch-5-12 -2006/wider-wdhw-report-5-12-2006.pdf.

4. U.S. Statistical Abstract, table 803, "Farm Operators—Tenure and Characteristics: 1997 and 2002" (2007), http://www.census.gov/compendia/statab/agriculture/farms_and_ farmland.

5. U.S. Statistical Abstract, table 803.

6. John Locke, "Second Treatise," §38 in *Two Treatises of Government*, ed. Peter Laslett (Cambridge: Cambridge University Press, 1960).

7. Certainly others might object that wealth's utility is best assessed by how much pleasure it provides or how much pain it helps people avoid, separate from life expectancy. In response to the question asked during a robbery, "your money or your life," some even pick the latter.

8. CIA World Factbook, http://www.cia.gov/cia/publications/factbook/geos/sl.html.

9. United Nations Development Program, *Human Development Report* (New York: Oxford University Press, 2000).

10. Fran Baum, "Wealth and Health: The Need for More Strategic Public Health Research," *Journal of Epidemiological Community Health* 59 (2005): 542–545; Dalton Conley, *Being Black, Living in the Red* (Berkeley: University of California Press, 1999); G. William Domhoff, *The Higher Circles* (New York: Vintage, 1971); G. William Domhoff, *The Power Elite and the State: How Policy Is Made in America* (New York: Aldine de Gruyter, 1990); C. W. Mills,

The Power Elite [1959] (New York: Oxford University Press, 2000); Melvin Oliver and Thomas Shapiro, *Black Wealth/White Wealth* (New York: Routledge, 1995); Joan Ostrove, Pamela Feldman, and Nancy Adler, "Relations Among Socioeconomic Status Indicators and Health for African-Americans and Whites," *Journal of Health Psychology* 4 (1999): 451–463.

11. George Simmel, *The Philosophy of Money*, trans. Tom Bottomore and David Frisby (London: Routledge and Kegan Paul, 1978), 217.

12. Lisa Keister and Stephanie Moller, "Wealth Inequality in the United States," *Annual Review of Sociology* 26 (2000): 65; citing Eric Wolff, *Top Heavy: A Study of the Increasing Inequality of Wealth in America* (New York: Twentieth Century Fund); and R. B. Avery et al., "Survey of Consumer Finances, 1983: A Second Report" *Federal Reserve Bulletin* 72: 163–177.

13. Davis et al., "The World Distribution of Household Wealth."

14. Davis et al., "The World Distribution of Household Wealth," table 10s.

15. These estimates come from Davis et al., "World Distribution of Household Wealth," tables 5, 10a, and 11. The first numbers in these ranges represent estimates of purchasing power parity and the latter are based on exchange rate dollar values.

16. Arthur Kinickell, "An Examination of Changes in the Distribution of Wealth from 1989 to 1998: Evidence from the Survey of Consumer Finances," prepared for the Conference on Saving, Intergenerational Transfers, and the Distribution of Wealth, Jerome Levy Economics Institute, Bard College (June 7–9, 2000), table 5, "Proportion of Total Net Worth Held by Different Percentile Groups: 1989, 1992, 1995 and 1998 SCFs," http://www.federalreserve.gov/Pubs/OSS/oss2/papers/wdist98.pdf.

17. Kinickell, "Examination of Changes in the Distribution of Wealth," appendix, table 2, "Percentage Distribution of Families Over Constant-dollar Wealth Groups"; 1989, 1992, 1995, and 1998 Survey of Consumer Finances.

18. Early work on this topic are Yaari Menahem, "On the Consumer's Lifetime Allocation Process," *International Economic Review* 5 (3): 304–317; and Yaari Menahem, "Uncertain Lifetime, Life Insurance, and the Theory of the Consumer," *Review of Economic Studies* 32 (2): 137–150. For a more recent study and review of the literature, see Michael Hurd, "Bequests: By Accident or Design?" in *Death and Dollars*, ed. Alicia Munnell and Annika Sunden (Washington, D.C., Brookings Institute: 2003), 93–117.

19. Keister and Moller, "Wealth Inequality in the United States," 63.

20. Keister and Moller, "Wealth Inequality in the United States," 65; citing D. L. Lerman and J. J. Mikesell, "Rural and Urban Poverty: An Income/Net Worth Approach," *Policy Studies Review* 7 (1988): 779.

21. One of the key disputes on the rate of intergenerational transfers bears on whether college payments should be included. For purposes of public policy, this transfer is clearly a relevant contribution to an individual's potential prosperity and must be taken into account.

See Laurence Kotlikoff, "Intergenerational Transfers and Saving," *Journal of Economic Perspectives* 2 (1988): 41–58.

22. Karl Marx, *Capital*, trans. Samuel Moore and Edward Aveling (London: Lawrence and Wishart, 1974).

23. Paul Baran, *Monopoly Capital: An Essay on the American and Social Order* (New York: Monthly Review Press, 1966).

24. For reasons of theoretical integrity, Marx was deliberately blind to this possibility. He thought it important that his be a theory of an entirely new economic mode of accumulation. Unique to the proliferation of capitalism, he argued, was that the only important sources of inequality would come from the synchronic, cross-sectional relations to the means of production, not diachronic, longitudinal, hereditary wealth. Inequality in wealth based on family background and the laws of inheritance associated with families was a vestige of feudalism. For Marx's theory of exploitation to be truly revolutionary, it had to focus on a truly new source of inequality, one that he claimed occurred strictly in the disparities between the resources of the capitalist and the worker and not the different family resources they might have accumulated through inheritance practices. A second failure of the Marxist schema is that it underestimates the impact of nationalism and thus overestimates the likelihood of a truly global market for labor as well as capital, the symptoms of which are discussed in chapter 1.

25. Laurence Kotlikoff and Lawrence Summers, "The Role of Intergenerational Transfers in Aggregate Capital Accumulation," *Journal of Political Economy* 89 (1981): 706–732.

26. Edward Wolff, "Wealth Accumulation by Age Cohort in the U.S., 1962–92: The Role of Savings, Capital Gains, and Intergenerational Transfers," *Geneva Papers on Risk and Insurance, Issues and Practice* 24: 27–49. Wolff estimates inheritance, *inter vivos* transfers from parents, and savings each contribute one-third to an individual's lifetime wealth. For a review of the debate over the proportion of wealth attributable to lifetime savings versus intergenerational transfers, see Laurence Kotlikoff, "Intergenerational Transfers and Saving," 41–58. Kotlikoff is responding to his critics. One key difference is that Kotlikoff and Summers treat college tuition as a transfer of wealth, to which their major critic Franco Modigliani objects ("The Role of Intergenerational Transfers and Life Cycle Saving in the Accumulation of Wealth," *Journal of Economic Perspectives* 2 [1988]: 15–40).

27. C. Wright Mills, *The Power Elite* [1956] (Oxford: Oxford University Press, 2000), 107.

28. http://en.wikipedia.org/wiki/Bill_Gates.

29. William Gale and John Scholz, "Intergenerational Transfers and the Accumulation of Wealth," *Journal of Economic Perspectives* 4 (1994): 147.

30. For a review citing studies with a similar range, see Pierre Pestieua, "The Role of Gift and Estate Transfers in the United States and Europe," in *Death and Dollars*, 72.

31. Most bequests go to family members. According to a study of results from the Survey of Consumer Finances, conducted by the Federal Reserve, and data from the IRS, 60 percent of estates goes to relatives and 20 percent to charities, John Havens, "Notes on Wealth Transfer Estimates Originally Presented in 'Millionaires and Millenium,'" Center on Wealth and Philanthropy, Boston College (February 13, 2006), 2. The balance goes to estate fees and taxes.

32. Stephen McNamee and Robert Miller, "Inheritance and Stratification," in *Wealth in America*, 207.

33. Ralph Brashier, *Inheritance Law and the Evolving Family* (Philadelphia: Temple University Press, 2004), 30. Technically, Georgia is an exception in formally allowing complete free will to testators, but in practice judges divide estates so that spouses are supported for at least one year.

34. Lee Anne Fennell, "Death, Taxes, and Cognition," (January 2003), *North Carolina Law Review* 81: 578.

35. Even arch-social biologist Garrett Hardin attacks current inheritance practices as opposed to principles of natural selection and hence in tension with evolution: "If there are to be differences in individual inheritance, legal possession should be perfectly correlated with biological inheritance—that those who are biologically more fit to be the custodians of property and power should legally inherit more. But genetic recombination continually makes a mockery of the doctrine of 'like father, like son' implicit in our laws of legal inheritance. An idiot can inherit millions, and a trust fund can keep his estate intact." "The Tragedy of the Commons," *Science* 162 (1968): 1243-1248.

36. Articles explaining these tensions include Jane Baron, "Intention, Interpretation, and Stories," *Duke Law Journal* 42 (1992); Frances Foster, "The Family Paradigm of Inheritance Law," *North Carolina Law Review* 80 (2001); Susan Gary, "Adapting Intestacy Laws to Changing Families," *Law and Inequality* 18 (2000): 1-82; and Lawrence Waggoner, "Tribute to William F. Fratcher: Marital Property Rights in Transition," *Missouri Law Review* 59 (1994): 21-30.

37. Peter Hall and George Marcus, "Why Should Men Leave Great Fortunes to their Children? Class, Dynasty and Inheritance in America," in *Inheritance and Wealth in America*, ed. Robert Miller and Stephen McNamee (New York: Plenum, 1998), 139-171.

38. Brashier, *Inheritance Law and the Evolving Family*, 4.

39. Wojcieh Kopczuk and Joel Slemrod, "Wealth Accumulation and Transfers of the Rich," in *Death and Dollars*, 216-217.

40. Pestieau gives a higher figure of two-thirds leaving a will but provides no citation for this claim; also uncited is his claim that in France fewer than 10 percent have wills. "Role of Gift and Estate Transfers," 77. Perhaps his figure is based on the research from a study of 521 elderly, which also uses this figure: Marsha Goetting and Peter Martin, "Characteristics of

Older Adults with Written Wills," *Journal of Family and Economic Issues* 22 (2001): 243–264. The problem with this study is that it oversamples people who are conscientious and responsive. The sort of people who will reply to repeated, extensive, and invasive questions about their estate planning are self-selected and more likely to write wills than elderly who do not reply to requests for this data. Goetting and Martin write, "Because the study sample had significantly higher incomes, greater net worth, and more education than the sample with deleted cases, the results are biased toward older adults with the aforementioned characteristics. Caution should be exercised in generalizing the results for the older adult population in the United States" (248).

41. Alaska Statute 13.12.102 Share of Spouse.

42. Idaho Statute 15–2–102.

43. For instance, if someone dies without children or a spouse, and if that person has just two parents, and each of them have two parents, and if each parent has one sibling and they each have two children, this provision means that there are eighteen people eligible for that estate.

44. California Statute 240.6402.5, sect. 5.

45. Locke, "Second Treatise," §26–28.

46. Eileen Spring, *Law, Land, and Family: Aristocratic Inheritance in England, 1300–1800* (Chapel Hill: University of North Carolina, 1993), 31.

47. Mary Fellows, Rita Simon, and William Rau, "Public Attitudes About Property Distribution at Death and Intestate Succession Laws in the United States," *American Bar Foundation Research Journal* (1978): 321, 323.

48. U.S. law does recognize "implied consent" for a narrow range of practices and laws that are transparent and well established, such as a driver's license—awarded at the state's discretion—implying consent to sobriety tests. Implied consent does not apply to situations with the large degrees of variation in intent and behavior we see in inheritance practices.

49. J. L. Austin, *How to Do Things with Words* (Cambridge, Mass.: Harvard University Press, 1962).

50. It is true that couples may be aware of common-law rules, but more often the status is invoked during separations, when one party believes it advantageous to stress a marital relation. The state's interest in deciding on the question of what counts as the right family is separate from the tacit commitments the couple may have made to each other. Although prosecutions or lawsuits often occur for fraudulent contracts, outside of family law there are no other norms where the state claims its judgments should be substituted for the null judgment indicated by silence.

51. Fellow, Simon, and Rau, "Public Attitudes About Property Distribution at Death," 339, 346, 374. A separate study of those who were taking an estate-planning course in Montana found that 68 percent thought the state law would not "distribute property according to their wishes if they died without having a written will." Marsha Goetting, "Home Study Courses: An Education Option," *Journal of Extension* 24 (1981): 14–18; cited in Marsha Goetting and Peter Martin, "Characteristics of Older Adults with Written Wills," *Journal of Family and Economic Issues* 22 (2001): 244.

52. Fellow, Simon, and Rau, "Public Attitudes About Property Distribution at Death," 339, 346, 374.

53. In a follow-up study, researchers noted that intestacy laws were also inconsistent with the preferences of unmarried different- and same-sex committed couples who lacked written wills. All the same-sex couples and 75 percent of the different-sex couples would prefer their partners receive a portion of their wealth when they die, although "current laws award them nothing and aware their parents everything." Mary Fellows, Monica Johnson, Amy Chiericozzi, Ann Hale, Christopher Lee, Robin Preble, and Michael Voran, "Committed Partners and Inheritance: An Empirical Study," *Law and Inequality* 16 (1998): 37.

54. Fellow, Simon, and Rau, "Public Attitudes about Property Distribution at Death," 334–335.

55. The phenomenology of moral theory suggests timeless commitments to abstract principles, but its content is always political. The presence of political commitments is not a defect nor sign of bad character, although Nietzsche might say that the desire to call them moral reveals a weakness.

56. Robert Nozick, *Anarchy, the State, and Utopia* (New York: Basic Books, 1974), 8–9.

57. It may seem odd that a work drawing so heavily on psychoanalytic theory would find flaws with Nozick's hypothetical narrative on the state of nature. If Nozick used evidence from other countries, justified the language he was using for the ideas he explores, considered competing examples, and entertained alternative hypotheses, then I would not have these reservations.

58. Robert Nozick, *Anarchy, the State, and Utopia*, 100, 159.

59. Hillel Steiner, *An Essay on Rights* (Oxford: Blackwell, 1994). The critique of Nozick here follows closely on lines indicated by Steiner.

60. Blackstone, *Commentaries* 10–12 (St. George Tucker ed., 1803). Blackstone's sentiment on inheritance as a feature of positive and not natural law was echoed in the beliefs of American politicians before the Revolution; see Stanley Katz, "Republicanism and the Law of Inheritance in the American Revolutionary Era," *Michigan Law Review* 76 (1977): esp. 7–8.

61. Chester, *Inheritance, Wealth, and Society* (Bloomington: University of Indiana, 1982), 37.

62. From *Selected Essays* (1936), quoted in Austin Scott, *The Law of Trusts*, 4th ed. (New York: Little Brown, 1987), 1:1–2.

63. Without political societies, there are no rules to designate what counts as the family unit through which wealth might be distributed.

64. *The Complete Writings of Thomas Paine*, ed. P. Foner (1945), 251; quoted by Chester, *Inheritance, Wealth, and Society*, 35. The latter quotation is from A. Koch, *Jefferson and Madison: The Great Collaboration* (1964), 86; in Chester, *Inheritance, Wealth and Society*, 35.

65. Andrew Carnegie, *The Gospel of Wealth and Other Timely Essays* (Cambridge, Mass.: Harvard University Press, 1962), 22.

66. Carnegie, *The Gospel of Wealth*, 19-20.

67. "The Economics of Taxing the Rich," in *Does Atlas Shrug? The Economic Consequences of Taxing the Rich* (New York: Russell Sage, 2000), 13.

68. Alfred Marshall, *Principles of Economics* [1890] (London: MacMillan for the Royal Society, 1961), book 4, chap 7, para. 6; quoted in Barry Bracewell-Milnes, *The Wealth of Giving: Everyone in His Inheritance* (London: Institute of Economic Affairs, 1989), 45.

69. James Poterba, "The Estate Tax and After Tax Investment," in *Does Atlas Shrug?* 345; Michael Hurd and James Smith, "Anticipated and Actual Bequests," Working Paper no. 7380, National Bureau of Economic Research (1999): 9, http://nber.org/papers/w7380.pdf.

70. Hurd and Smith, "Anticipated and Actual Bequests," 9.

71. Fennell, "Death, Taxes, and Cognition," 582.

72. Michael Hurd, "Bequests: Accidental or by Design?" in *Death and Dollars*, 114.

73. Jagadeesh Gokhale and Laurence Kotlikoff, "The Baby Boomers' Mega-Inheritance—Myth or Reality?" Federal Reserve Bank of Cleveland (October 1, 2000), 2.

74. Christopher Carroll, "Why Do the Rich Save So Much?" in *Does Atlas Shrug?* 471.

75. Gokhale and Kotlikoff, "The Baby Boomers' Mega-Inheritance," 2; citing Jagadeesh Gokhale, Laurence Kotlikoff, and John Sabelhaus, "Understanding the Postwar Decline in National Saving: A Cohort Analysis," in *Brookings Papers on Economic Activity*, vol. 1 (Washington, D.C., Brookings Institution, 1996), note 3.

76. *U.S. Survey of Consumer Finances* (1998), http://www.federalreserve.gov/pubs.

77. Charles Horioka, "Are the Japanese Selfish, Altruistic, or Dynastic?" *Japanese Economic Review* 53 (March 2002): 26-54.

78. Carroll, "Why Do the Rich Save So Much?" 472; quoting Arthur Kennickell, M. Starr-McCleuer, and Annika Sunden, "Saving and Financial Planning: Some Findings from a Focus Group," unpublished paper, Board of Governors, Federal Reserve System (1995). For a contrary and minority view that is not based on observed data but economic modeling, see Mariacristina De Nardi, "Wealth Inequality and Intergenerational Links," *Review of Economic Studies* 71 (2004): 743-768.

79. Federal Reserve Board, *U.S. Survey of Consumer Finances* (1998) dataset, http://www.federalreserve.gov/pubs/oss/oss2/method.html. The question states, "Some people think it is important to leave an estate or inheritance to their surviving heirs, while others don't. Which is closer to your and your (spouse/partner)'s feelings? Would you say it is very important, important, somewhat important, or not important?" The open-ended question states: "Now I'd like to ask you a few questions about your savings. People have different reasons for saving, even though they may not be saving all the time. What are your most important reasons for saving?"

80. Arthur Kennickell and Annamaria Lusardi, "Wealth Accumulation and the Importance of Precautionary Savings," table A.1, "Motives to Save in the 1995 SCF," Dartmouth College (2003), http://www.federalreserve.gov/pubs/oss/oss2/papers/precautionary.nov05 .2.pdf.

81. Karen Dynan, Jonathan Skinner, and Stephen Zeldes, "The Importance of Bequests and Life-cycle Saving in Capital Accumulation: A New Answer," *The American Economic Review, Papers and Proceedings of the 114th Annual Meeting of the American Economic Association* (2002): 274–278.

82. For references, see Jonathan Gruber, comment on Hurd, "Bequests," in *Death and Dollars*, 128.

83. Gruber, comment on Hurd, "Bequests," in *Death and Dollars*, 128.

84. Wilmoore Kendall, *John Locke and the Doctrine of Majority Rule* (Urbana: University of Indiana, 1959); Richard Ashcraft, *Revolutionary Politics and John Locke's Two Treatises of Government* (Princeton, N.J.: Princeton University Press, 1986).

85. For further discussion of the relevant passages, see Jacqueline Stevens, "The Reasonableness of John Locke's Majority: Property Rights, Consent, and Resistance in the Second Treatise," *Political Theory* 24 (1996): 424–463.

86. Jeremy Waldron, "Locke's Account of Inheritance and Bequest," *Journal of the History of Philosophy* 19 (1981): 39–51.

87. Locke, "Second Treatise," §28.

88. Waldron, "Locke's Account of Inheritance," 39–40.

89. Waldron, "Locke's Account of Inheritance," 43.

90. C. B. MacPherson, *Possessive Individualism: Hobbes to Locke* (Oxford: Clarendon Press, 1962).

91. I differ in my interpretation on one point: Locke does not have the theory of natural rights that the possessive individualist thesis imputes to him. Hence I see the tension between Locke's accounts of inheritance and property rights differently from Waldron. Locke allows for a majority passing laws that might tax or otherwise fetter property in ways that an Andrew Carnegie might not appreciate, without any compunction over natural rights. This is because Locke has a two-tiered system of rights: one for their acquisition in the state of nature, absent a legitimate government occasioned by the consent of the majority, and another theory of property and other rights after this legitimate government has been established. See Stevens, "Reasonableness."

92. Locke, "First Treatise," §89.

93. Locke, "First Treatise," §87. Waldron reads these passages as being at odds with the reference Locke makes to the right that fathers have to "bequest" portions of their estates to those who are not their children (I.87) and concludes that the "right of bequest occupies at most a secondary position in Lockean theory of property and is always a matter of civil law, never of natural right," "Inheritance and Bequest," 51.

94. In the "First Treatise," Locke constantly chides Filmer for overlooking the Biblical injunction to 'honor thy father *and mother.*' For instance: "God says, '*Honour thy father and mother*'; but our author contents himself with half, leaves out *they mother* quite, as little serviceable to his purpose" (I. §6). And see I. §11, §55, §61, §62, §64, §65, §66, §67 and *passim*; II. §52, §53, §64, §65, §66, §69 and *passim*.

95. Locke, "Second Treatise," §86.

96. The psychoanalytic framework explaining this debt emerges from a literature on pregnancy envy. For more, see Eve Feder Kittay, "Womb Envy: An Explanatory Concept," in *Mothering—Essays in Feminist Theory*, ed. Joyce Trebilcot (Totowa, N.J.: Rowman and Allanheld, 1983); see also chaps. 5 and 6 below.

97. In addition to the above, see also Bruno Bettelheim, *Symbolic Wounds: Puberty Rites and the Envious Male* (New York: Collier Books, 1962).

98. This is where my interpretation of Locke diverges from that of Lorenne Clark's excellent essay "Who Owns the Apples in the Garden of Eden?" in *The Sexism of Social and Political Theory: Women and Reproduction from Plato to Nietzsche*, ed. Lorenne M. G. Clark and Lynda Lange (Toronto: University of Toronto Press, 1979), 16–40. Clark argues that Locke premises paternal control of inheritance to men's naturally superior strength: "Because women are less able, and are weaker than men, they either do not appropriate, or, even if they do, have no claim to ownership. They are naturally inferior because weaker than men and are, therefore, naturally subject to their domination" (32).

99. Locke, I §88. Although Locke here and in a few other places refers to the "parents' possessions," he clearly understands fathers as the source of and arbiter over the "property of the parents," e.g., "though the dying parents, by express words, declare nothing about [their property], nature appoints the descent of their property to their children, who thus come to have a title, and natural right of inheritance to their fathers goods, which the rest of mankind cannot pretend to" (I. §89). Here and elsewhere Locke treats the parents' property in the plural as synonymous with the "fathers goods."

100. The fantasies about birth's importance are just that. Kinship rules and other ruses to assert male authority do not reflect an innate supremacy in the ability to give birth *but a series of infant fantasies about the lack of this potential.*

101. Locke, "First Treatise," §54.

102. Locke, "First Treatise," §55.

103. Locke, "Second Treatise," §65.

104. Locke, "Second Treatise," §69, emphasis added.

105. Locke, "Second Treatise," §70, emphasis added.

106. Locke, "First Treatise," §90.

107. Spring, *Law, Land, and Family*, quoting J. Prowden, H. Baker, and S. F. C. Milson, *Sources in English History: Private Law to 1750* (London, 1986).

108. A more recent example is a "73-year-old Briton who fears that his family name will die with him" and therefore "took to the airwaves to appeal for anyone else with the same moniker to get in touch." Alan Cowell, "Britain: Dying Surname," *New York Times* (July 28, 2004).

109. Locke attributes to a "principle of nature" the "increase of mankind" and considers the "distinction of families, with the security of the marriage bed, as necessary thereunto." "First Treatise," §59.

110. Bettelheim, *Symbolic Wounds*.

111. G. W. F. Hegel, *Phenomenology of Spirit* [1807] (Oxford: Oxford University Press, 1977), 273; G. W. F. Hegel, *Philosophy of Right* (Oxford: Oxford University Press, 1953), §132.

112. Hegel, *Philosophy of Right*, §169. See also §178 and §180.

113. Hegel, *Philosophy of Right*, §180, addition 114.

114. Alas, his work also lacks the appropriate audience in the United States, where his ideas are rarely taught to undergraduates.

115. Hegel, *Philosophy of Right*, §173.

116. Hegel, *Philosophy of Right*, §306; Hegel, *Phenomenology of Spirit*, 274–275.

117. Hegel, *Philosophy of Right*, §167, remark.

118. Hegel, *Philosophy of Right*, §167.

119. This observation finds anecdotal confirmation by my students, who seem a bit chagrined to realize the extent to which the promise of an inheritance may subtly influence interactions with their parents, my inference from the nervous giggle elicited when asked, "Would you be so anxious about what your parents thought about your choices if you were certain that you would never receive a penny in inheritance?"

120. Hegel, *Philosophy of Right*, §180.

121. Hegel, *Philosophy of Right*, §178, §179.

122. Hegel, *Philosophy of Right*, §174.

123. Hegel, *Philosophy of Right*, §176.

4. ABOLISHING INHERITANCE

1. Jim Hopkins, "Wal-Mart Family Lobbies for Tax Cuts," *USA Today* (April 5, 2005).

2. Citizens for Tax Justice, IRS 990 form, line 17.

3. James Davis, Susanna Sandstrom, Anthony Shorrocks, and Edward Wolff, "The World Distribution of Household Wealth," WIDER Project Meeting on Personal Assets from a Global Perspective (December 5, 2006), table 10a, "Global Wealth Distribution in 2000," http://www.wider.unu.edu/research/2006-2007/2006-2007-1/wider-wdhw-launch-5-12 -2006/wider-wdhw-report-5-12-2006.pdf.

4. Matthew Lynn, "A Lesson for Britain: Capitalism Without Capital Doesn't Work," *The Business* (May 19, 2007); Carl Mortished, "Tax Mobility Trumps French Loyalty," *The Globe and Mail* (December 28, 2006).

5. Machiko Nissanke, "Revenue Potential of the Tobin Tax for Development Finance: A Critical Appraisal," paper presented at the WIDER Conference on Sharing Global Prosperity (September 6–7, 2003), Helsinki, p. 15, http://62.237.131.23/publications/dps/dps2003/ dp2003-081.pdf.

6. Nissanke, "Revenue Potential," 19.

7. Nissanke, "Revenue Potential," 21.

8. Nissanke, "Revenue Potential," 22.

9. Bruce Ackerman and Anne Alstott, *The Stakeholder Society* (New Haven, Conn.: Yale University, 1999), 4.

10. Ackerman and Alstott, *The Stakeholder Society*, 5.

11. They write that "too generous an embrace of immigrants at too early a stage would be counterproductive" and "the only feasible way to save the Treasury from the most cynical abuses is by imposing a residency requirement on birthright citizens." Ackerman and Alstott, *The Stakeholder Society*, 48–49.

12. CIA World Factbook Rank Order Pages, World Health Organization, "Health Spending as Percent of GNP," http://www.emro.who.int/emrinfo/#HealthExpenditure, https://www .cia.gov/library/publications/the-world-factbook/docs/rankorderguide.html. Tabular data available from author.

13. CIA World Factbook, Rank Order Pages, for life expectancy. Tabular data available from author.

14. The phrase "family paradigm" appears in the social science literature first in social psychology, when David Riess used it to describe variations among family norms in *The Family's Construction of Reality* (Cambridge, Mass.: Harvard University Press, 1981). It is used rather differently in work by critics of inheritance law to describe a legal framework that establishes the family as the most important constituent for inheritance law. Foster discusses this trend, including the first use of the phrase for this purpose by Ralph Brashier, in "Children and Inheritance in the Nontraditional Family," *Utah Law Review* 93 (1996). See Frances Foster, "The Family Paradigm of Inheritance Law," *North Carolina Law Review* 80 (2001): 271, notes 6 and 16.

15. Tanya Hernandez, "The Property of Death," *University of Pittsburgh Law Review* 60 (1999): 971; E. Gary Spitko, "The Expressive Function of Succession Law and the Merits of Nonmarital Inclusion," *Arizona Law Review* 41 (1999): 1063; Lawrence Waggoner, "Tribute to William F. Fratcher: Marital Property Rights in Transition," *Missouri Law Review* 59 (1994):21–30.

16. Lee Anne Fennell, "Death, Taxes, and Cognition," *North Carolina Law Review* 81 (2003): 641–642.

17. Larry Bartels, "Homer Gets a Tax Cut: Inequality and Public Policy in the American Mind," *Perspectives on Politics* 30 (2005): 16.

18. Chicago Council on Foreign Relations "Worldviews 2002: American Public Opinion and Foreign Policy," http://www.worldviews.org/detailreports/usreport/public_topline_report.pdf/.

19. Helen Milner, "Why Delegate the Allocation of Aid to Multilateral Organizations? Principal Agent Problems and Multilateralism" (August 25, 2003), p. 10, v. 3.0., http://faculty.wm .edu/mjtier/milner8–03.pdf; citing Alberto Alisina and David Dollar, "Who Gives Foreign Aid to Whom and Why?" *Journal of Economic Growth* 5: 33.

20. David Lumsdaine, *Moral Vision in ·International Politics* (Princeton, N.J.: Princeton University Press, 1993), 43; cited in Milner, "Why Delegate the Allocation of Aid," 22.

21. Milner, "Why Delegate the Allocation of Aid," 22; citing Ida McDonnell, Henri-Bernard Solignac Lecomte, and Liam Wegimont, eds., *Public Opinion and the Fight Against Poverty* (Paris: OECD), 20.

22. United Nations Office of the High Commissioner of Human Rights, *Fact Sheet No. 21, The Human Right to Adequate Housing*, http://193.194.138.190/html/menu6/2/fs21.htm# entitlements.

23. Kofi Anan, *We the Peoples: The Role of the United Nations in the Twenty-first Century* (2000), paras. 66 to 188, http://www.un.org/millennium/sg/report/full.htm.

24. Kevin Watkins, *Human Development Report: Beyond Scarcity: Power, Poverty, and the Global Water Crisis* (New York: United Nations and MacMillan, 2006), 31, http://hdr .undp.org/hdr2006/pdfs/report/HDR06-complete.pdf.

25. John Havens, "Notes on the Wealth Transfer Estimates Originally Presented in 'Millionaires and the Millennium,'" Center on Wealth and Philanthropy, Boston College (February 13, 2006), 2, http://www.bc.edu/research/swri/meta-elements/pdf/noteswte.pdf. This figure is based on data on charitable giving and the inference from IRS estate filings that noncharitable wealth is 86 percent of an estate. Direct data on estates are unavailable. It is likely that this estimate overestimates charitable giving and underestimates the total amount of wealth, so that on balance the figure should be close to the actual amount of wealth transferred at death.

26. Watkins, *Human Development Report*, 47.

27. Watkins, *Human Development Report*, 42.

28. Watkins, *Human Development Report*, 58, citing WHO research commissioned for its report.

29. Watkins, *Human Development Report*, 42.

30. Watkins, *Human Development Report*, 58.

31. *The Public Acts of the General Assembly of North Carolina*, chap. 22 (J. Iredell ed. F. X. Martin rev. 1804); cited in Stanley Katz, "Republicanism and the Law of Inheritance in the American Revolutionary Era," *Michigan Law Review* 76 (1977): 15.

32. Katz, "Republicanism and the Law of Inheritance," 23.

33. United Nations, "Compendium on Human Settlements Statistics, 2001," table 2, "Households by type of living quarters: country or area, urban/rural, cities, latest available year," http://unstats.un.org/unsd/demographic/sconcerns/housing/housing2.htm#DYB.

34. One can see the exact principle at work in determining tuition for elite colleges. The fees are quite high, but most of the students receive financial aid. Effectively, some people pay $45,000 per year, many people pay half that, and a few receive stipends. However, the funding techniques are such that the tuition costs for everyone are the same (e.g., $50,000) and most people receive subsidies.

35. Freud, "Mourning and Melancholia" (1917) in *The Complete Psychological Works of Sigmund Freud, Standard Edition*, ed. and trans. James Strachey (London: Hogarth Press, 1955), 14:239–258.

36. Eric Partridge, *Origins: A Short Etymological Dictionary of the English Language* (New York: MacMillan, 1958).

37. Robert Burton, *The Anatomy of Melancholy*, ed. Floyd Dell and Paul Jordan-Smith (London: George Routledge and Son, 1931), 16.

38. Burton, *The Anatomy of Melancholy*, 65–67.

39. Peter Goodrich, *Oedipus Lex: Psychoanalysis, History, Law* (Berkeley: University of California Press, 1995), 7.

40. Brian Smith, "Kharles Demore v. Hyung Joon Kim: Another Step Away from Full Due Process Protections," *Akron Law Review* 38 (2005): 207.

41. Between 2001 to 2005, the IRS collected $290 million through this program. Because the IRS has its own ability to directly monitor transactions, the amount gained from such reporting is a very small percentage of the overall IRS collections. Source: Treasury Inspector General For Tax Administration, "June 2006 Report," compiled at TaxWhistles.org, http://www.taxwhistleblowers.org/main/page.php?page_id=11.

42. It might seem that countries that collect more of the GPA funds than they receive would be less inclined to cooperate, but there are countless examples of federal and other representative governments where this is not the case. Income tax collected from Californians is certainly subsidizing the Medicare of Mississippians. EU taxes on Germans are supporting arts initiatives in Portugal. And in private firms, not all divisions are equally profitable, but for reasons of branding and other vertical advantages of integration corporations will retain these units and continue to subsidize them. The advantages for a state, especially if it has a large number of wealthy citizens, being part of an integrated global system with the benefits of a global citizenry guaranteed a safety net are large and fairly obvious. Leaving aside norms of justice, it is pragmatic to subsidize programs that have a good chance of decreasing global war and poverty and, in turn, their repercussions in one's own country.

43. Steven Greenhouse, "Meatpacker in Brooklyn Challenges a Union Vote," *New York Times* (September 1, 2008).

44. The federal government defended the constitutionality of the 1964 Civil Rights Act's intrusion into private businesses by invoking its responsibilities under the Interstate Commerce Clause, on the theory that an interdependent economy required a free labor market and free movement among the states—hence the provision for public accommodations not to discriminate based on race. *Heart of Atlanta Motel Inc. v. United States*, 379 U.S. 241 (1964).

45. To be clear, it seems that Rubashkin is doing whatever he can to make the most money possible. This means suing the union for allowing undocumented laborers to vote as well as hiring undocumented scabs to replace them. Greenhouse, "Meatpacker in Brooklyn Challenges a Union Vote."

5. THE LAW OF THE MOTHER

1. Chapters 5 and 6 draw on work that appeared in Jacqueline Stevens, "Methods of Adoption: Eliminating Genetic Privilege," in *Adoption Matters: Philosophical and Feminist Essays*, ed. Sally Haslanger and Charlotte Witt (Ithaca, N.Y.: Cornell University Press, 2005), 68–94; and Stevens, "Pregnancy Envy and Compensatory Masculinities," *Gender and Politics* 1 (2006): 265–296.

2. Citations are in the relevant sections below.

3. Of course, religious zealots will offer interpretations of why we wash dishes at odds with those of atheists, as well. But since no important question of public policy hangs on the right justification for dishwashing, such potential rationales are irrelevant. Marriage cannot be necessary because God demanded this ten thousand years ago *and* because of evolutionary pressures initiated by unknown causes billions of years ago in a random, godless universe. That these two discourses are incompatible is the point Nietzsche makes: evil has been as successful in surviving as good. Moralists have to choose. If they embrace social Darwinism, then they must concede that evil has been naturally selected for. Friedrich Nietzsche, *On the Genealogy of Morals* [1887] (New York: Vintage Books, 1967).

4. The chapter's premise is indebted to related work by Lisa Duggan, especially "Queering the State," *Social Text* 39 (1994): 1–14.

5. Maria Sanminatelli, "Pope Urges Couples to Resist Modern Pressures, Stick to Traditional Family Values," *AP* (October 8, 2006).

6. Lambda Legal Defense Organization, http://wwwlamdalegal.org/cgi-bin/iowa/nws/fact.html?record=1530; and Chris Jenkins, "Ban on Same-Sex-Unions Added to Virginia Constitution," *New York Times* (November 8, 2006).

7. Jerome Taylor, "Protection from Harsh Penalties or Legalised Prostitution?" *The Independent* (September 28, 2006).

8. FBI's Most Wanted List, http://www.fbi.gov/pressrel/2006/px/050/606.htm. The specific charge was assisting rape, in Jeff's capacity as a minister performing a marriage for a minor. Since the other criminals on the "Most Wanted" list are charged with personally committing multiple heinous crimes, and as none of the other suspects in the United States wanted for assisted rape appear on the FBI's Most Wanted list, it seems fair to infer that it was Jeff's support for polygamy that led to this special attention.

9. Catholic Answers, "Gay Marriage," at http://www.catholic.com/library/gay_marriage.asp.

10. Peter Sprigg, *Outrage: How Gay Activists and Liberal Judges are Trashing Democracy to Redefine Marriage* (New York: Regnery, 2004), 98.

11. Brad Knickerbocker, "Crackdown on Polygamy Group," *Christian Science Monitor* (May 9, 2006), http://www.csmonitor.com/2006/0509/p02s01-ussc.html.

12. Congressional Record, *Proceedings and Debates of the 104th Congress*, 2nd sess., vol. 142, no. 123 (September 10, 1996).

13. Heritage Foundation, "What Is Marriage?" http://www.heritage.org/Research/Family/MarriageDebate/WhatIsMarriage.cfm.

14. Human Rights Campaign Web site, "Top 10 Reasons for Marriage Equality," http://www.hrc.org.

15. Evan Wolfson, *Why Marriage Matters: America, Equality, and Gay People's Right to Marry* (New York: Simon and Schuster, 2004), 7–8.

16. Wolfson, *Why Marriage Matters*, 7.

17. Ruth Vanita, *Same-sex Marriage in India and the West* (New York: Palgrave-MacMillan, 2005), 237.

18. An excellent survey of these arguments with an extensive bibliography appears in Jyl Josephson, "Citizenship, Same-Sex Marriage, and Feminist Critiques of Marriage," *Perspectives on Politics* 3 (2005): 269–284.

19. Duggan, "Queering the State," 1–14.

20. Nancy Cott, *Public Vows: A History of Marriage and the Nation* (Cambridge, Mass.: Harvard University Press, 2000); Patricia Hill Collins, "African-American Women and Economic Justice: A Preliminary Analysis of Wealth, Family, and African-American Social Class," *University of Cincinnati Law Review* 65 (1997): 825.

21. Michael Warner, *The Trouble with Normal: Sex, Politics, and the Ethics of Queer Life* (New York, Free Press, 1999).

22. "Stalemate: Rethinking the Politics of Marriage," *Feminist Theory* 3 (2002): 52–53.

23. Foucault voices caution on the prospect of liberation: "I've always been a little distrustful of the general theme of liberation, to the extent, that, if one does not treat it with a certain number of safeguards and within certain limits, there is a danger that it will refer back to the idea that there does exist a nature or human foundation which as a result of a certain number of historical, social, or economic processes, found itself concealed, alienated or imprisoned in and by some repressive mechanism. In that hypothesis it would suffice to unloosen these repressive locks so that man can be reconciled with himself." "The Ethic of Care for the Self as a Practice of Freedom: An Interview with Michel Foucault on January 20, 1984," conducted by Raul Fornet-Betancourt, Helmut Becker, and Alfredo Gomez-Mueller, *Philosophy and Social Criticism* 12 (Summer 1987): 113; quoted in Terry Alajdem, "The Philosopher's Prism: Foucault, Feminism, and Critique," *Political Theory* 19 (1991): 279. The reason Foucault distrusts liberation is that he believes there is no true human nature, only the one created through politics. Alajdem refers to Foucault's resistance "even to modestly transcendent categories of humanism" and explains this as based on Foucault's belief that the "political question is not error, illusion, alienated consciousness or ideology; it is truth itself," quoting Foucault from *Power/Knowledge: Selected Interviews and Other Writings, 1972–1977*, ed. Colin Gordon (New York: Pantheon, 1980), 133. One cannot criticize any particular political regime based on a supposedly prepolitical concept of liberation.

24. Foucault invents a specific aesthetic of Greco-Roman self-restraint that he avows occurred separately from marriage laws. If this could happen in antiquity, then marriage law should be seen as separate from a society's moral and political codes. *The Use of Pleasure* [1984], trans. Robert Hurley (Vintage Books, New York: 1985), 69.

25. According to the mission statement, which I have joined many others in endorsing: "Marriage is not the only worthy form of family or relationship, and it should not be legally and economically privileged above all others. A majority of people—whatever their sexual and gender identities—do not live in traditional nuclear families. They stand to gain from alternative forms of household recognition beyond one-size-fits-all marriage." "Beyond Marriage," http://www.beyondmarriage.org.

26. *Sociobiology: The New Synthesis* (Cambridge, Mass.: Harvard University Press, 2000), 553; citing V. Reynolds, "Kinship and the Family in Monkeys, Apes, and Man," *Man* 3, no. 2 (1968): 209–233; and Lila Leibowitz, "Founding Families," *Journal of Theoretical Biology* 21, no. 2 (1968): 153–169.

27. There is actually a great deal of evidence to the contrary. For a survey, see Bruce Bagemihl, *Biological Exuberance: Animal Homosexuality and Natural Diversity* (New York: St. Martin's Press, 1998).

28. These are the same six from chapter 1, selected by their placement at fixed intervals in an alphabetical list of countries: Afghanistan, Democratic Republic of Congo, Honduras, Monaco, Senegal, and Zimbabwe.

29. Ella Landau-Tasseron, "Adoption, Acknowledgement of Paternity, and False Genealogical Claims in Arabian and Islamic Societies," *Bulletin of School of Oriental and African Studies* 66 (2003): 176.

30. Stevens, *Reproducing the State*, 209–235.

31. Jelili A. Omotola, "Primogeniture and Illegitimacy in African Customary Law: The Battle for Survival of Culture," *Indiana International and Comparative Law Review* 15 (2004): 136.

32. Gary Barker, "Men's Participation as Fathers in Latin American and Caribbean Region: A Critical Literature Review with Policy Considerations," document prepared for the World Bank (2003), http://promundo.org.br.

33. I define a "family" as a custodial group facilitated by the state for the purpose of providing care across generations. These families will require mutual financial and other support among caregiving members of the group. While it is currently colloquial to regard only two-generation households with genetic or legal ties as "family," this is only a subset of the more general definition offered above.

34. I am using the pronoun "he" because kinship rules for the father come out of a sexed difference in the relation to birth that prompts compensatory behaviors from that sex which cannot give birth, whom we call males. This is discussed below.

35. Absent such a community, people may of course procreate and care for children, but they would lack guidelines for living in kinship groups. There is no record of any such community, but instead kinship rules appear ubiquitous.

36. Reciprocally, men's obligations to support children would be similarly ad hoc.

37. A political society usually exists by parents recruiting, so to speak, their progeny, ensuring the parental group's continuity. The importance of this particular parent-child unit to political societies is clear in legislation that allows citizens to sponsor their parents and children but not other family members.

38. Modern states are very clear in their use of legal and not genetic ancestry for determining ethnicity and race. One quick illustration of the centrality of family to ethnicity is how people respond to questions about their ethnicity by referencing the ethnicity of their parents and their parents. The same holds for race.

39. Alberto Alesina, Edward Glaeser, and Bruce Sacerdote, "Why Doesn't the United States Have a European-style Welfare State?" *Brookings Papers on Economic Activity* (2003): 187– 277. Available online at http://muse.jhu.edu/journals/brookings_papers_on_economic _activity/v2001/2001.2durlauf.pdf.

40. Stevens, "Pregnancy Envy and Compensatory Masculinities."

41. There are numerous psychoanalysts' whose observations support this statement, especially Sigmund Freud in his earlier work "Three Essays on Sexuality" (1905), in *The Standard Edition of the Complete Psychological Works of Sigmund Freud*, trans. James Strachey (London: Hogarth Press, 1955), 7:124–245; Otto Rank, *The Trauma of Birth* (New York: Robert Brunner, 1952); Karen Horney, *Feminine Psychology* (New York: W. W. Norton: 1967); Ida Macalpine and Richard Hunter, "The Schreber Case: A Contribution to Schizophrenia, Hypochondria, and Psychosomatic Symptom Formation," *Psychoanalytic Quarterly* 22 (1953): 328–371; Bruno Bettelheim, *Symbolic Wounds: Puberty Rites and the Envious Male* (New York: Collier, 1961); and Eva Feder Kittay, "Womb Envy: An Explanatory Concept," in *Mothering: Essays in Feminist Theory*, ed. Joyce Trebilcot (Totowa, N.J.: Rowman and Allanheld), 94–128. For a full analysis of the relevant passages in their work, see Stevens, "Pregnancy Envy."

42. See Stevens, "Pregnancy Envy," 280, for further discussion of the literature on this, especially work by Philip Slater.

43. Stevens, "Pregnancy Envy," 265.

44. I use Baum's text because the narrative is familiar enough for its themes to be used to explain dynamics in contexts whose scripts are more challenging to decipher, i.e., the daily plots and roles occasioned by the law of the father in which we are daily immersed. The use of this widely known text here is therefore one of analogy, a method of investigation used at least since Plato for making the familiar seem unfamiliar so as to assist in its logical comprehension.

45. George Gilder, *Sexual Suicide* [1973] (New York: Bantam, 1975), 17.

46. Gilder, *Sexual Suicide*, 98.

47. Gilder, *Sexual Suicide*, 98.

48. Further underscoring the "wizard's" fraud is that the acronym for his entire given name spelled OZPINHEAD. To avoid his nominal status as a pinhead, Oscar used only his first two names, Oscar Zoraster. L. Frank Baum, *The Wizard of Oz and Who He Was* (East Lansing: Michigan State University Press, 1957), 198, note 18.

49. Baum, *The Wizard of Oz*, 154.

50. Gilder, *Sexual Suicide*, 18.

51. Gilder, *Sexual Suicide*, 204.

52. I am alluding to the extensive literature pointing out national and racial identities' contingent and nonbiological, nonessential origins. For specific references, see Stevens, *Reproducing the State*, esp. chaps. 2–5.

53. Dorothy Roberts proposes that black families are less committed than are white families to a genetic definition of family. See "The Genetic Tie," *University of Chicago Law Review* 62 (1995): 209–273.

54. For a detailed discussion and critique of recent efforts to establish this continuity, see Nadia abu El-Haj, "A Tool to Recover Past Histories: Genealogy and Identity after the Genome," http://www.sss.ias.edu/publications/papers/paper19.pdf. For a discussion of Freud's hypotheses about genes for group memory, see Jacqueline Stevens, "Freud and International Relations," *Law, Culture, and the Humanities* 2 (2006): 201–217.

55. The use of the scientific idiom below and elsewhere should seem off-putting to Foucauldians, who believe the power/knowledge from scientific approaches themselves confine us to artifacts of rules and practices thought objective but that are really low-key false gods. In short, Foucault gave science a bad name, one to which it has lived up by its own empty procedures for a long time. For more on methods, see the appendix, below.

56. For an excellent example first authored by a leading ideologue in this field, see Owen Jones and Timothy Goldfield, "Law and Behavioral Biology," *Columbia Law Review* 105: 405–502.

57. United States Census Bureau, "America's Families and Living Arrangements," tables A2 and FG2, "Current Population Survey Reports, March 2000," http://www.census.gov/population/www/socdemo/hh-fam.html.

58. United States Census Bureau, "America's Families and Living Arrangements," tables A2 and FG2, "Current Population Survey Reports, March 2000," http://www.census.gov/population/www/socdemo/hh-fam.html.

59. See Stevens, *Reproducing the State*, chap. 6. Daly and Wilson attempt to explain this by pointing out that the vast majority of this violence is men attacking their partners, a behavior they claim does not jeopardize their own genetic survival. However, these are very frequently attacks on the mothers of their children. Hence, since Daly and Wilson also believe that being raised by a genetic mother enhances the fitness of one's progeny, they make an empirical mistake by not noticing that killing one's children's mother would indeed adversely impact one's genes.

60. Even Wilson's own personal experiences do not fit his narrative. After his parents divorced when he was seven, he was raised by his father and stepmother. Edward O. Wilson, *Naturalist* (Washington, D.C.: Island Press, 2006), 52.

61. Martin Daly and Margo Wilson, *Homicide* (New York: Aldine de Gruyter, 1988).

62. "The Risk of Abusive Violence Among Children with Nongenetic Caregivers," *Family Relations* 40 (1991): 82.

63. B. Ewigman, C. Kivlatan, and G. Land, "The Missouri Child Fatality Study: Underreporting of Maltreatment Fatalities Among Children Younger Than Five Years of Age," *Pediatrics* 91 (1993): 330–337; A. Wilcynski, *Child Homicide* (London: Oxford University Press, 1997); A. S. Botash, S. Blatt, and V. Meguid, "Child Abuse and Sudden Infant Death Syndrome," *Current Opinions in Pediatrics* 10 (1998): 217–223; cited in Susan Friedman, Sarah

Horwitz, and Philip Resnick, "Child Murders by Mothers: A Critical Analysis of the Current State of Knowledge and a Research Agenda," *American Journal of Psychiatry* 162 (2005): 1578.

64. H. Temrin, S. Buchmayer, and M. Enquist, "Stepparents and Infanticide: New Data Contradict Evolutionary Predictions," *Proceedings. Biological Sciences* 267 (2000): 944; see also Richard Gelles, "Child Abuse and Violence in Single Parent Families: Parent-absent and Economic Deprivation," *American Journal of Orthopsychiatry* 59: 492–501.

65. T. Vanamo, A. Kauppo, K. Karkola, et al. "Intrafamilial Child Homicide in Finland 1970–1994: Incidence, Causes of Death, and Demographic Characteristics," *Forensic Science International* 117 (2001): 202.

66. S. Rohwer, J. C. Herron, and M. Daly, "Stepparental Behavior as Mating Effort in Birds and Other Animals," *Evolution & Human Behavior* 20 (1999): 367–390.

67. Matt Keating, "What they Said About . . . Heshu Yones," *Guardian* (October 2, 2003), http://www.guardian.co.uk/editor/story/0,12900,1053731,00.html.

68. http://childtrendsdatabank.org. Between 1970 and 2000, the official reported rate of infant homicide per 100,000 had gone from 4.3 to 8.6, a figure the researchers said underestimated the actual rate of parents killing their infants (largely mothers before the age of one and fathers or stepfathers after the age of one). Among developed countries, the United States has the highest rate of child homicide: 8 per 100,000. Friedman, Horwitz, and Resnick, "Child Murders by Mothers," 1578; citing D. Finkelhor, "The Homicide Rates of Children and Youth: A Developmental Perspective," in *Out of the Darkness: Contemporary Perspectives on Family Violence*, ed. G. K. Kanto and J. L. Jasinski (Thousand Oaks, Calif.: Sage Publications, 1997), 17–34.

69. Marcia Herman-Giddens et al., "Underascertainment of Child Abuse Mortality in the United States," *JAMA* 281: 466.

70. Levinson, cited in Krug et al., eds., *World Report on Violence and Health*, 100.

71. Krug et al., eds., *World Report on Violence and Health*, 102.

72. Krug et al., eds., *World Report on Violence and Health*, 102.

73. Krug et al., eds., *World Report on Violence and Health*, 102.

74. Krug et al., eds., *World Report on Violence and Health*, 162.

75. L. R. Eskow, "The Ultimate Weapon?: Demythologizing Spousal Rape and Reconceptualizing its Prosecution," *Stanford Law Review* 48 (1995): 677–709.

76. Krug et al., eds., *World Report on Violence and Health*, 163.

77. Nuran Hortaçsu and Sibel Kalaycioğluŏ, "Intrafamily Aggression in Turkey: Frequency, Instigation, and Acceptance," *Journal of Social Psychology* 143 (2003): 166.

78. The main proponents of using evolutionary theory in legal analyses have been John Beckstrom, Richard Epstein, Owen Jones, and Richard Posner. For a discussion of their work, see Jacqueline Stevens, "Legal Aesthetics of the Family and Nation: agoraXchange

and Notes Toward Reimaging the Future," *New York Law Review* 49 (2004/2005): 317–352, esp. 325–331.

79. The report also describes research on two Indian states in which another controlled study found that "women who had been beaten were significantly more likely than non-abused women to have experienced an infant death or pregnancy loss (abortion, miscarriage or stillbirth)." Krug et al., eds., *World Report on Violence and Health*, 103.

80. In a cross-sectional survey of children in Egypt, 37 percent reported being beaten or tied up by their parents and 26 percent reported physical injuries such as fractures, loss of consciousness, or permanent disability as a result of being beaten or tied up. A study in the Republic of Korea found that two-thirds of parents reported whipping their children and 45 percent confirmed that they had hit, kicked, or beaten them. A survey of households in Romania found that 4.6 percent of children reported suffering severe and frequent physical abuse, including being hit with an object, being burned, or being deprived of food. Nearly half of Romanian parents admitted to beating their children "regularly" and 16 percent to beating their children with objects. In Ethiopia, 21 percent of urban schoolchildren and 64 percent of rural schoolchildren reported bruises or swellings on their bodies resulting from parental punishment. And a study in China indicated an annual rate of "severe violence against children, as reported by parents, of 461 per 1000." Krug et al., eds., *World Report on Violence and Health*, 63.

81. Hortaçsu and Kalaycioğluö, "Intrafamily Aggression in Turkey," 164; citing M. Arı et. al, "Aile İçi İlişkilerde Siddet [Violence in Interfamily Relationships]," in *Aile Kuraltayı Degisim Sürecinde Aile*, ed. R. Karadayı et al. (Ankara: Aile Kurumu: 1994), 300–312.

82. They define a patriarchal household as one in which the "husband is named as the head of the family, has the first say concerning the family's place of residence, and has primary responsibility for taking care of his wife and children." Hortaçsu and Kalaycioğluö, "Intrafamily Aggression in Turkey," 164; citing M. Arı et al., "Violence in Interfamily Relationships," 300–312.

83. Hortaçsu and Kalaycioğluö, "Intrafamily Aggression in Turkey," 166, 167.

84. Hortaçsu and Kalaycioğluö, "Intrafamily Aggression in Turkey," table 3.1, reporting the results of WorldSAFE study.

85. Callie Rennison, "Intimate Partner Violence, 1993–2001," U.S. Bureau of Justice Statistics, Crime Data Brief, February 2003, NCJ 197838. For a comparative study of partner violence, see Krug et al., eds., *World Report on Violence and Health*, 89–121.

86. Bill Leadbetter, "The Illegitimacy of Constantine and the Birth of the Tetrarchy," in *Constantine: History, Historiography, Legend*, ed. Samuel Lieu and Dominic Montserrat (London: Routledge, 1998).

87. Warren Treadgold, *A History of the Byzantine State and Society* (Stanford, Calif.: Stanford University Press), 44.

88. Treadgold, *A History of the Byzantine State and Society*, 44.

89. George Palermo, "Murderous Parents," *International Journal of Offender Therapy and Comparative Criminology* 46 (2002): 126.

90. Constantine affiliated himself and his regime with Christianity in the course of being brought into an internecine exegetical debate. The question at hand was whether Jesus was entirely divine or partly human. Constantine joined those staking out the former position, thus cementing this as what became the official doctrine of the Catholic Church.

91. Abimelech, the son of Gideon, killed his seventy brothers so that he alone would be king, significantly diminishing the survival of his genes (Judges 9:5); Ahaz, a son of David, sacrificed his son to fire (2 Kings 16:1–4), which we learn was a common custom in the region (2 Chronicles 28:3). King Leovigild killed his son Hermangild in 585. In the late eighth century, Irene of the Eastern Roman Empire killed her son, the emperor, and declared herself monarch. Treadgold, *A History of the Byzantine State and Society*, 422. Algernon Sidney, a political writer and philosopher who was eventually executed by the Stuarts, writes: "Artaxerxes killed his son Darius: Herod murder'd the best of his wives, and all his sons except the worst. Tiberius destroy'd Agrippa Posthumus, and Germanicus with his wife and two sons. How highly soever Constantine the Great be commended, he was polluted with the blood of his father-in-law, wife, and son. Philip the second of Spain did in the like manner deliver himself from his fears of Don Carlos; and 'tis not doubted that Philip the fourth, for the same reasons, dispatched his brother Don Carlos, and his son Balthasar. The like cases were so common in England, that all the Plantagenets, and the noble families allied to them being extinguish'd, our ancestors were sent to seek a king in one of the meanest in Wales." *Discourses Concerning Government* [1698], section 2:24, http://www.constitution.org/as/dcg_224.htm.

92. Richard Dawkins, *The Selfish Gene* (Oxford: Oxford University Press, 1989), 88–108.

93. Leadbetter, "The Illegitimacy of Constantine," 80.

94. Donna Haraway, *Primate Visions: Gender, Race, and Nature in the World of Modern Science* (New York: Routledge, 1989).

95. Rights justified despite sex, it seems, and only because of genes, is not captured by general references to a "biological" or "natural" parent. It is not biological narratives but specifically genetic ones prompting women to want their own eggs, inseminated by their husbands' sperm, to be carried by others. What could be more "biological" than carrying a fetus in one's womb for nine months and then giving birth? Yet these are considered "surrogate" and also not "real" mothers. "Biological" and "natural" ties are assumed to produce a parenting status parasitic on acts thought "genetic," and hence this last term is the one that will be used and scrutinized.

96. For an overview on the father's rights movement's major legal challenges, see "My Two Dads: Disaggregating Biological and Social Paternity," *Arizona State Law Journal* 38 (2006).

For an article advocating changing laws to enhance fathers' so-called rights, see Robbin Pott Gonzalez, "The Rights of Putative Fathers to Their Infant Children in Contested Adoptions: Strengthening State Laws That Currently Deny Adequate Protection," *Michigan Journal of Gender & Law* 13 (2006).

97. I refer to narratives affirming children's ties to "genetic parents"—not the more idiomatic "birth parents," "natural parents," or "biological parents"—because these latter categories are overinclusive. "Genetic parents" is preferable to the other labels because men never give birth, but they are often parents and often claim that parental status, informally as well as legally, based only on a genetic tie.

98. See M. R. Anderlik and M. A. Rothstein, "DNA-based Identity Testing and the Future of the Family: A Research Agenda," *American Journal of Law and Medicine* 28 (2002): 215–232. A study of paternity testing in Canada from 1992 to 1998 "finds no significant increase in either the number of cases brought to court or the percentage of cases in which genetic testing was ordered. However, the authors' analysis suggests that courts are placing a growing value on the importance of genetic evidence and that they justify its use by reference to the importance of complete medical information for the future health of the child, to the state's interest in ensuring that a child receives financial support, and to the certainty which genetic evidence affords." Timothy Caulfield, "Canadian Family Law and the Genetic Revolution: A Survey of Cases Involving Paternity Testing," *Queen's Law Journal* 26 (2000): 67.

99. This is clearly an inconsistency. It seems to follow from the government's failure to provide sufficient support for children's welfare, leading legislators to search for alternative revenue streams, including men whose sperm resulted in progeny.

100. Melanie McCulley argues that if women have the right to abortion, then genetic fathers should have the right to terminate their interests in unborn children, based on the notion of obligations imposed by not doing so. However, McCulley does not believe that women should have the right to abortions: "the author's purpose in writing this article is to demonstrate the inequities in the abortion decision and to propose legislation promoting male equality in the procreative decision. This article should not be construed to promote or advocate the women's right to abortion," "The Male Abortion: The Putative Father's Right to Terminate His Interests in and Obligations to the Unborn Child," *Missouri Law Review* 64 (1999): 517. See also Dalton Conley, "A Man's Right to Choose," *New York Times* (December 1, 2005).

101. Geraldine Sealey, "Duped Dads: Men Fight Centuries-Old Paternity Laws," *ABC News* (October 2, 2002), http://www.canadiancrc.com/articles/ABC_Duped_Dads_02OCT02.htm.

102. Two good works on the subject are Richard Lewontin, Steven Rose, and Leon Kamin, *Not in Our Genes* (New York: Pantheon, 1984); and Sahotra Sarkar, *Genetics and Reductionism* (Cambridge: Cambridge University Press, 1998).

103. Jeffrey Ming and Maximilian Muenke, "Multiple Hits During Early Embryonic Development: Digenic Diseases and Holoprosencephaly," *American Journal of Human Genetics* 71 (2002): 1017–1032.

104. For research debunking twin studies, see Troy Duster, *Backdoor to Eugenics* (New York: Routledge, 1990); Leon Kamin, *The Science and Politics of IQ* (Potomac, Md.: L. Erlbaum, 1974); Leon Kamin and H. J. Eysenck, *The Intelligence Controversy* (New York: Wiley, 1981); Stephen Jay Gould, *The Mismeasure of Man* (New York: Norton, 1996).

105. For the last several decades, cognitive linguistics has been the home of heated debates on this question, not entirely separable from the genetic themes discussed here. (Some of those staking out the extreme view of our minds as "hardwired" for certain concepts are now turning to genetic research.) For much of this period, the experiments were unpersuasive for either approach, and scholars were divided between the linguistic relativists and the brain determinists. However, new experimental techniques and studies appear to have confirmed at least a weak version of the claim that one's native language shapes cognitive abilities. For instance, an Amazonian tribe whose language lacked numbers was unable to be taught how to perform other mathematical functions, including counting, even after the words and concepts for this were explained. Daniel Everett, "Cultural Constraints on Grammar and Cognition in Pirahã," *Current Anthropology* 46 (2005): 621–646. See also Asifa Majid et al., "Can Language Restructure Cognition? The Case for Space," *Trends in Cognitive Sciences* 8 (2004): 108–114. For a survey of these themes, see also the essays in *Language in Mind: Advances in the Study of Thought*, ed. Dedre Gentner and Susan Goldin-Meadow (Cambridge, Mass.: The MIT Press, 2003).

106. The discussion here focuses on paternal rights but the reciprocal point holds as well. Citizenship for mortals means that children have their financial support guaranteed by a fund derived from estate wealth, therefore removing the equation of paternal obligations with paternal rights from the table of arguments for custody rights.

107. John Locke, "Second Treatise," §28, in *Two Treatises on Government*, ed. Peter Laslett (Cambridge: Cambridge University Press, 1960).

108. John Locke, "First Treatise," §53, §54, in *Two Treatises on Government*, ed. Peter Laslett (Cambridge: Cambridge University Press, 1960).

109. For a discussion of ethically (in)defensible entitlements following from genetic ties, see Hillel Steiner, *An Essay on Rights* (Cambridge: Blackwell, 1994), 274–277.

110. *John Moore v. Regents of the University of California* 793 P.2d 479, citing *Diamond v. Chakrabarty* 447 U.S. 303 (1980); emphasis in original.

111. In *Moore v. Regents of California*, the California Court ruled that Moore's caregivers should have informed him of their intention to his cells in their research and allow him the right to refuse this, on the grounds that the research might interfere with his care and thus Moore should be apprised so he might evaluate any potential conflicts of interest. Presumably, all men having intercourse are aware that unless they take certain precautions this will result in the creation of another organism separate from the biological matter they discharge pursuant to sex. Unless they are being raped, their ejaculations imply consent to the consequences of this activity.

6. ABOLISHING MARRIAGE

1. See Martha Fineman's excellent analyses in *The Illusion of Equality* (Chicago: Chicago University Press, 1991); and especially *The Neutered Mother, the Sexual Family, and Other Twentieth-century Tragedies* (New York: Routledge, 1995). See also Cheshire Calhoun, *Feminism, the Family, and the Politics of the Closet: Lesbian and Gay Displacement* (New York: Oxford University Press, 2000); Gill Jagger and Caroline Wright, *Changing Family Values* (New York: Routledge, 2000); Ruthann Robson, "Making Mothers: Lesbian Legal Theory and the Judicial Construction of Lesbian Mothers," *Women's Rights Law Reporter* 22 (2000): 15; Kath Weston, *Families We Choose: Lesbians, Gays, Kinship* (New York: Columbia University Press, 1991); Ellen Lewin, *Lesbian Mothers: Accounts of Gender in American Culture* (Ithaca, N.Y.: Cornell University Press, 1993).

2. Shulamith Firestone, *The Dialectic of Sex: The Case for Feminist Revolution* (New York: Bantam, 1970), 188.

3. Firestone, *The Dialectic of Sex*, 193.

4. Catharine MacKinnon, *Towards a Feminist Theory of the State* (Cambridge, Mass.: Harvard University Press, 1989).

5. Jessica Benjamin, *Bonds of Love* (New York: Pantheon, 1988); Nancy Chodorow, *Reproduction of Mothering* (Berkeley: University of California, 1978); Dorothy Dinnerstein, *The Mermaid and the Minotaur: Sexual Arrangements and Human Malaise* (New York: Harper and Row, 1976).

6. Fineman, *The Neutered Mother*, 146–147, 155, 172–173 note 36, 228, 230–231, 234–235.

7. Fineman, *The Neutered Mother*, 5.

8. Anna Marie Smith, *Welfare and Sexual Regulation* (Cambridge: Cambridge University Press, 2007). Sympathetic critics have followed up by modifying Fineman's proposals. Drucilla Cornell largely endorses Fineman's approach but questions the connotations and denotations of Fineman's concept of motherhood, *The Heart of Freedom* (Princeton, N.J.: Princeton University Press, 1998), 116. Also contrary to Fineman, Cornell believes that the state *should* use marriage to recognize sexual relations, including polygamous ones, but without stipulating the subject positions or who may occupy them (124–125).

9. This claim is supported in Stevens, *Reproducing the State*, chap. 5. This current chapter draws on those findings for proposing child-care laws alternative to marriage.

10. Cornell makes just this point, turning around the Lockean position outlined above by using the fact of such masculine compensations as evidence that there is nothing so special about pregnancy. Cornell, *At the Heart of Freedom*, 130.

11. Locke, "First Treatise," §55 and *passim*.

12. Carla Abhou Zahr, "Global Burden of Maternal Death and Disability," *British Medical Bulletin* 67 (2003): 6, table 2.

13. Zahr, "Maternal Death and Disability," 6, table 2. In the United States, between 1991 and 1999 about 4,200 women died from complications during pregnancy, and the rate of deaths in 1999 was actually higher than in 1982. Jerry Chang, et al., "Pregnancy-related Mortality Surveillance: United States, 1991–1999," U.S. Division of Reproductive Health National Center for Chronic Disease Prevention and Health Promotion (2003), http://www.cdc.gov/mmwR/preview/mmwrhtml/ss5202a1.htm.

14. Donald Regan, "Rewriting *Roe v. Wade*," *Michigan Law Review* 7 (1979): 1569–1646.

15. U.S. Federal Code 42, section 273 (b), http://www.optn.org/downloadables/42_USC_273_274_274a-g.pdf. The Interstate Commerce Clause is the congressional hook for passing this legislation and has been broadly construed to prevent organ donations for financial gain. The penalty is $50,000 or up to five years in prison. States and other countries have similar laws.

16. Catharine MacKinnon, "Prostitution and Civil Rights," *Michigan Journal of Gender and Law* (1993): 13–57.

17. Behaviors with far fewer health-threatening consequences, from car ownership to being a beautician, are restricted through cumbersome regulations, yet millions of women every day expose themselves to the risks of pregnancy without filling out a single form. Countries that regulate the conditions of pregnancy are thought authoritarian and intrusive because the burdens and risks of pregnancy are distinguishable from other individual decisions fundamentally affecting the lives of others.

18. Donating eggs for use in another uterus is actually far more cumbersome and dangerous than donating sperm, but still does not match the overall risks and labor of pregnancy.

19. If, for reasons of superstition regarding their sperm and DNA, men do not want "their" children to be conceived without assurances of custody, they can either wear condoms or decide to have sex only with those women whom they trust to comply with these desires, a situation similar to that confronting women who are anxious about conception. If genetics companies may "own" someone else's DNA because the company's research created something of use, then surely mothers too come to possess the consequences of the sperm, especially as the use of it in the creation of a child is always an implied possibility and therefore a matter of presumptive consent when men ejaculate in women's vaginas.

20. If the state provides basic provisions for raising children such as health care and child care, then there is little argument for pursuing child support payments from "fleeing inseminators," who, under current regimes, do not pay in any case. For an excellent discussion of the law and theory of paternal obligations for children of poor women, see Smith, *Welfare Reform.*

21. In 2008, seventeen states had laws or constitutional amendments prohibiting the recognition of same-sex married couples, even when these couples were legally formed elsewhere; many of these also have denied recognition to domestic-partner relations as well. For current data, see the National Council of State Legislatures Web site, http://www.ncsl.org/ programs/cyf/samesex.htm#DOMA, and also the Human Rights Campaign national map of Statewide Marriage Prohibitions, at http://www.hrc.org/documents/marriage_prohibitions .pdf.

22. David Chambers writes, "A final criticism of the laws bearing on married persons is more fundamental: even if legal marriage would offer benefits to a broad range of same-sex couples, some might claim that all these advantages are illegitimate—illegitimate for both same-sex and opposite-sex couples—because they favor persons in two-person units over single persons and over persons living in groups of three or more, and because they favor persons linked to one other person in a sexual-romantic relationship over persons linked to another by friendship or other allegiances." "What If: The Legal Consequences of Marriage and the Legal Needs of Lesbian and Gay Male Couples," *Michigan Law Review* 95 (1996): 447–491.

23. Matthew Bramlett and William Mosher, "First Marriage Dissolution, Divorce, and Remarriage, United States," Center for Disease Control, Division of Vital Statistics, National Center for Health Statistics (May 31, 2001), http://www.cdc.gov/nchs/data/ad/ad323.pdf.

24. Laws do not have to fit every situation but must simply bear a rational relation to the objective. Some children will fit these criteria for self-sufficiency at earlier ages and some later. If legislatures make a poor judgment as to the right age where enough people can care for themselves, they are free to change it. It is precisely the fact that assessments on these dimensions may be subjective that an age is necessary to avoid parents' and children's uncertainty on the extent of their legal responsibilities and obligations. Current law allows self-sufficient minors to emancipate themselves and also for the state to care for those above the age of majority who cannot care for themselves, though in the latter case this care is often inadequate and would be improved through a GPA to distribute estate wealth.

25. James Peterson and Nicholas Zill, "Marital Disruption, Parent-Child Relationships, and Behavior Problems in Children," *Journal of Marriage and Family* 48 (1981): 295–307.

26. Parents who do not serve three meals daily to their three-year-olds can be imprisoned for child neglect; parents who do serve three meals daily to their thirty-year-olds can be interviewed as freakish oddballs on "Oprah."

27. The above status seems to formalize not only discrimination against genetic fathers— it does, for reasons explained above—but it may appear also to disadvantage the parent in a

lesbian relation who does not give birth. However, this is not the case for two reasons. First, the arrangement above precludes any state recognition of sexual arrangements altogether, so same-sex couples would have no different relation to the state than different-sex couples. Second, while the status of "mother" is held by only the person giving birth, the effect of this in the context of laws denying the status of "father" is to put all nonmaternal parents on equal footing. Instead of the non–birth parent in a lesbian couple being inferior to the mother, the emphasis here is on providing juridical parity for parents, making the female non-birth parent in a lesbian relation legally identical to the male partner in a different-sex relation where the mother maintains custody with the man who may be the one whose sperm inseminated the maternal egg. That maternity and its prerogatives assigned here are not sex specific can be seen in the case of the transgendered female to male who gave birth in 2008, and who, by the rules here, would be considered a mother. Russell Goldman and Katie Thompson, "'Pregnant Man' Gives Birth to Girl," *ABC News* (July 3, 2008), http://abcnews .go.com/Health/story?id=5302756&page=1.

7. ABOLISHING PRIVATE LAND RIGHTS

1. The quotation from Jefferson in the epigraph appears in Mahoney, "The Illusion of Perpetuity and the Preservation of Privately Owned Lands," *Natural Resources Journal* (Spring 2004): note 3.

2. A keyword search on September 28, 2008, for "Robinson Crusoe" in economics journals indexed by JSTOR listed 929 publications.

3. Daniel Defoe, *Robinson Crusoe* [1719], chap. 20, http://etext.virginia.edu/etcbin/toccer -new2?id=DefCru1.sgm&images=images/modeng&data=/texts/english/modeng/parsed& tag=public&part=20&division=div1.

4. Defoe, *Robinson Crusoe*, chap. 20.

5. Defoe, *Robinson Crusoe*, chap. 20.

6. Stephen Hodgson, Cormac Cullinan, and Karen Campbell, "Land Ownership and Foreigners: A Comparative Analysis of Regulatory Approaches to the Acquisition and Use of Land by Foreigners," *FAO Legal Papers Online* (1999): 1, http://www.fao.org/Legal/default .htm.

7. Robert Ellickson, "Property in Land," *Yale Law Journal* 102 (April 1993): 1322.

8. Hodgston, Cullinan, and Campbell, "Land Ownership and Foreigners," 2.

9. Edward Coke, *The First Part of the Institutes of the Laws of England*, 16th ed. (London: L. Hansard and Sons, 1809); and see the background discussions to current land-rights disputes in Eduardo Penalver, "Is Land Special? The Unjustified Preference for Landownership in Regulatory Takings Law," *Ecology Law Quarterly* 31 (2004): 247–249.

10. Kendall Burr, "The Evolution of the International Law of Alienability: The 1997 Land Law of Mozambique as a Case Study," *Columbia Journal of Transnational Law* 43 (2005); Natasha Robinson, "The World Summit on Sustainable Development and Women's Access to Land: Why Nigeria Should Adopt the Eritrean Land Proclamation," *William and Mary Journal of Women and the Law* 10 (Spring 2004): 593, 604–605; Karol Boudreaux, "The Human Face of Resource Conflict: Property and Power in Nigeria," *San Diego International Law Journal* 7 (2005).

11. *Kelo v. New London* 545 U.S. 469 (2005). The relevant portion of the Fifth Amendment states: "nor shall private property be taken for public use, without just compensation."

12. There are several cases that are very close to the facts and law in the Kelo case cited in the majority decision, especially an early case, *Berman v. Parker* 348 U.S. 26 (1954), where an area of Washington, D.C., was condemned as blighted and set to be destroyed, including a building in perfectly good condition owned by someone who had not agreed to sell his land and argued that commercial redevelopment was not a "public benefit" but a private one. The decision in *Kelo* follows the same logic as *Berman*, explaining that a "public benefit" is defined by whatever the legislative body indicates it is. Exercising eminent domain to establish a revitalized commercial area is very similar to doing the same for an industrial park. If Kelo's team were to have prevailed, they would have established a very different precedent. See also Bernard Bell, "Legislatively Revising *Kelo v. City of New London*: Eminent Domain, Federalism, and Congressional Powers," *Journal of Legislation* 32 (2005): 165.

13. Elisabeth Sperow, "Perspective on *Kelo v. City of New London*: The Kelo Legacy: Political Accountability, Not Legislation, Is the Cure," *McGeorge Law Review* 38 (2007): 417; citing Castle Coalition, "2006 Election Wrap Up: Voters Overwhelmingly Passed Eminent Domain Reform" (November 8, 2006); and John Hill, "Mixed Verdict Nationwide on Eminent Domain Proposals," *Sacramento Bee* (November 9, 2006).

14. Susan Haigh, "Conn. Changes Eminent Domain Laws Two Years After Court Ruling," *Associated Press* (June 3, 2007).

15. In addition to the principle of stare decisis, there is the less noble principle of corporate politics: with the current institutions for land management, large corporations and those preferring strong government have a common interest in preserving the right of the government to make land-use decisions.

16. Richard Epstein, *Takings: Regulations, Private Property, and Eminent Domain* (Cambridge, Mass.: Harvard University Press, 1985).

17. Epstein, *Takings: Regulations, Private Property, and Eminent Domain*.

18. Eduardo Penalver, "Is Land Special?" offers an incisive and thorough critique of the Supreme Court's regulatory takings rulings and the underlying doctrine.

19. *Lucas v. S.C. Coastal Commission*, 505 U.S. 1003 (1992).

20. The six-to-three decision included three separate dissents by Souter, Blackmun, and Stevens, and a separate concurring opinion by Kennedy.

21. *Lucas v. S.C. Coastal Commission*, at 1017.

22. This depiction also entails a scenario whereby taxpayers are forced to subsidize Lucas's investment preferences. By asserting the land's only value is in its potential for development, the court concedes that the land is primarily an investment for Lucas, especially because it accepted its appraised market value and not the initial value of the land when he bought it.

23. "It is correct that many of our prior opinions have suggested that 'harmful or noxious uses' of property may be proscribed by government regulation without the requirement of compensation. For a number of reasons, however, we think the South Carolina Supreme Court was too quick to conclude that that principle decides the present case." *Lucas v. S.C. Coastal Commission*.

24. James Burling, "The Latest Take on Background Principles and the States' Law of Property After Lucas and Palazzolo," *University of Hawaii Law Review* 24 (2002): 497.

25. Burling, "The Latest Take on Background Principles," 507.

26. John Hart, "The Land Use Law in the Early Republic and the Original Meaning of the Takings Clause," *Northwestern University Law Review* 94 (2000): 1150.

27. Hart, "The Land Use Law in the Early Republic," 1102.

28. Hart, "The Land Use Law in the Early Republic," 1101, 1106, 1107, and note 262.

29. Gary Libecap, "Bureaucratic Issues and Environmental Concerns: A Review of the History of Federal Land Ownership," *Harvard Journal of Law and Public Policy* 15 (1992): 3.

30. Libecap, "Bureaucratic Issues and Environmental Concerns," 3.

31. Marx and Engels could never really integrate land prices into their analysis of capitalism, because unlike every other commodity its value had no relation to labor. Even the value of gold could be reduced to the high expense of the labor and machinery requisite to its extraction, or the value of agricultural products to the labor to cultivate or gather them, but land value was in this respect *sui generis*, and Marx and Engels did their best to slough it off as a residual remnant of capitalism. See *Capital* [1867], vol. 3 (New York: International Publishers, 1970); and Engels, "On the Housing Question" (1872), 2nd. ed., rev. 1887 (Moscow: Foreign Languages Publisher, 1955), 31.

32. Libecap, "Bureaucratic Issues and Environmental Concerns," 3.

33. William Casey, "Letter to the Editor," *Pittsburgh Tribune Review* (November 2005).

34. George Will, in the *Washington Post* (March 25, 1993).

35. For a few of many examples of an association of Locke with private property rights and with the founding of the United States, see also William Safire, "Poletown Wrecker's Ball," *New York Times* (April 30, 1981); and "What Is Government For?" *New York Times* (March 2,

1981); Becerril Coca and Becerril Legal Department, "The Promotion and Defense of Intellectual Property in Mexico as Motor of Development," Business and Management Practices, Mondaq Business Briefing (October 23, 2002).

36. Epstein, *Takings: Regulations, Private Property, and Eminent Domain*, 10.

37. Epstein, *Takings: Regulations, Private Property, and Eminent Domain*, 12.

38. Epstein, *Takings: Regulations, Private Property, and Eminent Domain*, 12.

39. Jacqueline Stevens, "The Reasonableness of John Locke's Majority: Property Rights, Consent, and Resistance in the Second Treatise," *Political Theory* 24 (1996): 424–463.

40. David Herszenhorn, "Residents of New London Go to Court, Saying Project Puts Profit Before Homes," *New York Times* (December 21, 2000).

41. Herszenhorn, "Residents of New London Go to Court."

42. Hodgson, Cullinan, and Campbell, "Land Ownership and Foreigners," 6.

43. *UK 2005: Official Yearbook of the United Kingdom of Britain and Northern Ireland*, 281–282, http://www.statistics.gov.uk/onlineproducts.

44. http://www.gao.gov/financial/fy2005/05stew.pdf.

45. Libecap, "Bureaucratic Issues and Environmental Concerns," 11.

46. During the war, refugees were created when warlords confiscated land. The government is establishing a commission to establish clear records, but it is not very successful. http://www.hq.usace.army.mil/cepa/pubs/jan03/jan03.htm. Liz Wiley, "Land and the Constitution," AREU Policy Brief, 2003, p. 12, http://www.areu.org.af/publications/land%20and%20the%20constitution_eng.pdf.

47. Customary leaders must authorize land use as a freehold and farmers must pay taxes and develop the land to continue their freehold. Up to ninety-nine-year leases are given to large farms. In practice, there are major fights among customary leaders about which group controls the land. African Development Fund, "Democratic Republic of Congo: Agricultural and Rural Sector Rehabilitation Support Project in Bas-Congo and Bandundu Provinces (PARSAR) Appraisal Report" (2004), 6, http://www.afdb.org/pls/portal/docs/page/adb_admin_pg/documents/operationsinformation/adf_bd_wp_2004_35_e.pdf.

48. Frances Heyward Currin, "Transformation of Paradise: Geographical Perspectives on Tourism Development on a Small Caribbean Island (Utila, Honduras)," masters thesis submitted to the Graduate Faculty of the Louisiana State University and Agricultural and Mechanical College (2003), 16, http://etd.lsu.edu/docs/available/etd-1114102-141915/unrestricted/Currin_thesis.pdf.

49. Christian Sylt, "The Powerhouse Principality," *CNBC European Business* (2005), http://europeanbusiness.eu.com/features/2005/dec/monaco.html.

50. Jacques Faye, "Land and Decentralisation in Senegal," IIED Drylands Issue Paper 149 (2008), http://www.iied.org/pubs/pdfs/12550IIED.pdf.

51. Karol Boudreaux, "The Human Face of Resource Conflict: Property and Power in Nigeria," note 87; citing U.N. Integrated Regional Information Networks (June 8, 2004), http://irinnews.org/report.asp?ReportID =41476.

52. "The Land Proclamation restricts Eritrean citizens from selling or inheriting land, and it prohibits the government from granting ownership rights in land." Natasha Robinson, "The World Summit on Sustainable Development and Women's Access to Land," 593, 604–605; citing Jason Wilson, "Eritrean Land Reform: The Forgotten Masses," *North Carolina Journal of International and Comparative Regulations* 24 (1999); citing Eritrean Proceeding No. 58/1994, in Jonathan M. Linsay, *Creating a Legal Framework for Land Registration in Eritrea: Consolidated Final Report of the International Legal Consultant*, U.N. Food and Agriculture Organization, Main Report, at 9, U.N. Doc TCP/ERI/4554 (1997).

53. Burr, "The Evolution of the International Law of Alienability," 973.

54. Burr, "The Evolution of the International Law of Alienability," 973.

55. Burr, "The Evolution of the International Law of Alienability," 973.

56. Burr, "The Evolution of the International Law of Alienability," 973.

57. Burr, "The Evolution of the International Law of Alienability," 972.

58. Burr, "The Evolution of the International Law of Alienability," 972.

59. Robinson, "The World Summit on Sustainable Development and Women's Access to Land," 592–593.

60. Burr, "The Evolution of the International Law of Alienability," 961.

61. Burr, "The Evolution of the International Law of Alienability," 972; citing Tanzania Land Act, 1999, 3(1)(a).

62. Burr, "The Evolution of the International Law of Alienability," 972; citing Uganda Const. art. 237(1), "Land in Uganda belongs to the citizens of Uganda and shall vest in them in accordance with the land tenure systems provided for in this Constitution."

63. Burr, "The Evolution of the International Law of Alienability," 971.

64. The United Nations also is on record as concerned about the earth's degradation. http://www.un.org/esa/sustdev/documents/agenda21/english/agenda21toc.htm.

65. Burr, "The Evolution of the International Law of Alienability," 976–977.

66. Indeed, Burr points out that the American Convention on Human Rights requires only the "use and enjoyment" of property and the First Protocol to the European Convention on Human Rights requires states to respect a right to the "enjoyment" of property. Burr, "The Evolution of the International Law of Alienability," 978; quoting the American Convention on Human Rights, opened for signature November 22, 1969, art. 21(1), OASTS 36, 9 ILM 673 (1920) (entered into force 1978) ("Everyone has the right to the use and enjoyment of his property,"); and the First Protocol for the Protection of Human Rights and Fundamental Freedoms, March 20, 1952, art. 1, ETS. no. 009 ("Every natural or legal person is entitled to the peaceful enjoyment of his possessions"). Neither the right to enjoy or use

property guarantees rights to exclude others or to be able to alienate land titles but only gives people the right to use and enjoy whatever the government at any point considers property.

67. Burr, "Evolution of Law of Alienability," 975; citing Restatement (Third) of the Foreign Relations Law of the United States (1987).

68. Hart, "Colonial Land Use Law in the Early Republic," 1124.

69. Hart, "Colonial Land Use Law in the Early Republic," 1263; citing the Act of June 13, 1716, 2 The Statutes At Large of South Carolina 641, 641–642 (Thomas Cooper, ed., Columbia, S.C., A.S. Johnston 1837).

70. Hart, "Colonial Land Use Law in the Early Republic," note 72, citing the Act of June 13, 1716.

71. Hodgston, Cullinan, and Campbell, "Land Ownership and Foreigners," 2. The "Trading with the Enemy Act" defines an enemy as "(a) Any individual, partnership, or other body of individuals, of any nationality, resident within the territory (including that occupied by the military and naval forces) of any nation with which the United States is at war." http://www.access.gpo.gov/uscode/title50a/50a_2_1_.html. In addition, the act says that "the President, if he shall find the safety of the United States or the successful prosecution of the war shall so require, may, by proclamation, include within the term 'enemy'" any other resident or citizen of any other country.

72. Hodgson, Cullinan, and Campbell, "Land Ownership and Foreigners," 2.

73. Hodgson, Cullinan, and Campbell, "Land Ownership and Foreigners," 8; citing Article 47(1) of the Lithuanian legal code.

74. Hodgson, Cullinan, and Campbell, "Land Ownership and Foreigners," 9, 16.

75. One example of this is the Philippines. In Thailand, Bulgaria, and other places, foreign heirs must dispose of such estates within a year of receiving them. Hodgson, Cullinan, and Campbell, "Land Ownership and Foreigners," 10.

76. Hodgson, Cullinan, and Campbell, "Land Ownership and Foreigners," 12.

77. Hodgson, Cullinan, and Campbell, "Land Ownership and Foreigners," 12.

78. Boudreaux, "The Human Face of Resource Conflict," 81.

79. Boudreaux, "The Human Face of Resource Conflict," 82.

80. Indigeneity is a misleading concept because all populations save those in southern Africa are immigrant communities at some point.

81. See especially Paul Collier and Anke Hoeffler, "Greed and Grievance in Civil War," *Oxford Economic Papers* 56 (2004): 563–595.

82. Boudreaux, "The Human Face of Resource Conflict," 61.

83. Boudreaux, "The Human Face of Resource Conflict," 93, also provides fascinating counterexamples, of "strangers" becoming adopted as part of the kin group as a means of obtaining property rights.

84. For an exploration of this myth and other myths of national belonging, see Stevens, *Reproducing the State*, chaps. 1–3.

85. For a further discussion of the institutional inducements to ethnic and tribal conflicts in Africa, see Richard Joseph, "Africa: States in Crisis," *Journal of Democracy* 14 (2003): 159–170.

86. Defoe, *Robinson Crusoe*, chap. 20.

87. Burr, "The Evolution of the International Law of Alienability," 962.

88. This argument is influenced by Martin Bernal, only emphasizing the Roman and Greek manifestation of African institutions, ideas, and people on so-called Europe. *Black Athena: The Afroasiatic Roots of Classical Civilization* (London: Free Association Books, 1987).

89. Burr, "The Evolution of the International Law of Alienability," note 15, quoting Keba M'Baye, "The African Conception of Law," in *International Encyclopedia of Comparative Law* ed. K. Zweigert and Ulrich Drobnig (1974), 2:149.

90. John Locke, *Two Treatises on Government*, I §41.

91. John Medearis, "Labor, Democracy, Utility, and Mill's Critique of Private Property," *American Journal of Political Science* 49 (2005): 143; quoting John Stuart Mill, *Principles of Political Economy, with Some of Their Applications to Social Philosophy*, ed. J. M. Robson (Toronto: University of Toronto Press, 1965), 230.

92. John Smith, *The Complete Works of Captain Smith*, ed. Philip Barbour (Williamsburg: University of North Carolina, 1986), 247; quoted in Ellickson, "Property in Land," 1337.

93. Mancur Olsen, *The Logic of Collective Action; Public Goods and the Theory of Groups* (Cambridge, Mass.: Harvard University Press, 1965).

94. "The sorry environmental records of federal land agencies and Communist regimes are a sharp reminder that governments are often particularly inept managers of large tracts." Ellickson, "Property in Land," 1326.

95. Hardin, "The Tragedy of the Commons," *Science* 162 (1968): 1243–1248.

96. Susan Hanna, Carl Folke, and Karl-Göan Mäler, "Property Rights and Environmental Resources," in *Property Rights and the Environment: Social and Ecological Issues*, ed. Susan Hanna and Mohan Munasinghe (Washington, D.C.: World Bank, 1995), 15–32.

97. Libecap, "Bureaucratic Issues and Environmental Concerns," 10.

98. Elizabeth Douglas and Richard Simon, "Scandal at Federal Oil Royalty Collection Agency," *Los Angeles Times* (September 11, 2008), http://www.latimes.com/news/printedi tion/front/la-fi-oilsex11-2008sep11,0,4053044.story.

99. Hardin, "The Tragedy of the Commons," 1245.

100. Hardin, "The Tragedy of the Commons," 1245.

101. Hardin, "The Tragedy of the Commons," 1248.

102. Hardin also writes with some sadness that each generation is in the habit of forgetting the lessons of previous generations. It is indeed a sign of the times that Hardin's lessons on the dangers of overpopulation and the commons, which have not proven the problem he thought they would be, would be the ones for which he is remembered, while his more astute observations about the harms of property rights have been ignored.

103. Bernard Fernow, *Economics of Forestry: A Reference Book for Students of Political Economy and Professional and Lay Students of Forestry* (1902); quoted in Libecap, "Bureaucratic Issues and Environmental Concerns," 6–7.

104. Burr, "The Evolution of the International Law of Alienability," 994; citing Julian Quan "Land Tenure, Economic Growth, and Poverty in Sub-Saharan Africa," in *Evolving Land Rights, Policy, and Tenure in Africa*, ed. Camilla Toulmin and Julian Quan (London, 2000), 31–32.

105. Burr, "The Evolution of the International Law of Alienability," note 174.

106. Burr, "The Evolution of the International Law of Alienability," 995; citing Quan, "Land Tenure," 46.

107. Robinson, "Why Nigeria Should Adopt the Eritrean Land Proclamation," 609.

108. Martin Mowforth and Ian Munt, *Tourism and Sustainability: New Tourism in the Third World* (New York: Routledge, 1998); William Ascher, *Why Governments Waste Natural Resources: Policy Failures in Developing Countries* (Baltimore, Md.: The Johns Hopkins University Press, 1998).

109. "Mozambique has enjoyed a peaceful democracy for over a decade, and duly elected representatives have opted to preserve the vesting of ultimate title in the State." Burr, "The Evolution of the International Law of Alienability," 995, note 53.

110. See Rodney Carlisle and Joan Zenzen, *Supplying the Nuclear Arsenal: American Production-Reactors, 1942–1992* (Baltimore, Md.: The Johns Hopkins University Press, 1996); National Research Council, *Ground Water and Soil Cleanup: Improving Management of Persistent Contaminants* (National Academy Press: Washington, D.C., 1999); Lisa Stiffler, "Radioactive Contamination at Hanford is on the Move," *Seattle Post-Intelligencer* (June 15, 2005), http://seattlepi.nwsource.com/local/228573_hanford15.html.

111. Judy Pasternak, "Oases in Navajo Desert Contained a 'Witch's Brew,'" *Los Angeles Times* (November 20, 2006), http://www.latimes.com/news/nationworld/nation/la-na-navajo20nov20,0,6106722.story?page=1.

112. Pasternak, "Oases in Navajo Desert Contained a 'Witch's Brew.'"

113. Silke Pfeiffer, "Vote Buying," 76–77; Fred Schaffer, "Vote Buying in East Asia," in *Transparency International, Global Corruption Report, 2004* (London: Pluto Press and Transparency International, 2004), 83, http://www.transparency.org/publications/gcr/download_gcr/download_gcr_2004.

114. Chenglin Liu, "Informal Rules, Transaction Costs, and the Failure of the 'Takings' Law in China," *Hastings International and Comparative Law Review* 29 (2005): 8.

115. Simon Coldham, "Legal Responses to State Corruption in Commonwealth Africa," *Journal of African Law* 39 (1995): 115–126.

116. Coldham, "Legal Responses to State Corruption in Commonwealth Africa," 124.

117. Richard Joseph, "Africa: States in Crisis," *Journal of Democracy* 14 (2003): 159–170.

118. Hannah Arendt, *On Violence* (New York: Harcourt, Brace and World, 1970), 78.

119. Ellickson, "Property in Land," 1368.

120. Ellickson, "Property in Land," 1368.

121. It is unclear how this process benefits the unborn as well, since most bequests go to living relatives. To the point, the world will be inhabited by someone who is not yet born and regardless of whether that person is genetically related or simply a member of a common species, the legal regimes that dispose of land rights are not reflecting preexisting preferences but instructing citizens on the sorts of people for whom they should care. As shown in chapter 3, the regime of inheritance rights gives lessons that have had tragic consequences, resulting in enormous systemic inequalities and extreme poverty.

122. A critique of conservation trusts, on grounds that their "perpetuity" clauses constrain public land-use decisions in the future, applies as well to the dead hand of land trusts issued to private individuals. Julia Mahoney, "The Illusion of Perpetuity and the Preservation of Privately Owned Lands," *Natural Resources Journal* 44 (2004): 573–599 and notes.

123. Ellickson, "Property in Land," 1400, note 11.

124. Arendt, *The Human Condition*, 262.

125. United States Constitution, Article I, Section 2.

126. James Krier, "The Tragedy of the Commons, Part Two," *Harvard Journal of Law and Public Policy* 15 (1992): 325–348; one text popularizing the concept Krier attacks is Terry Anderson and Donald Leal, *Free Market Environmentalism*, published first by the libertarian Pacific Research Institute in 1991 and then issued in a revised edition by Palgrave in 2001. I mention this first point because the deep pockets of the libertarian cause are one reason its ideas have been so resonant despite their inability to tie their cause to U.S. law and history.

127. Krier, "The Tragedy of the Commons, Part Two," section B. See also Peter Menell, "Institutional Fantasylands: From Scientific Management to Free Market Environmentalism," *Harvard Journal of Law and Public Policy* 15 (1992): 489–511.

128. Wendy Brown, "American Nightmare Neoliberalism, Neoconservatism, and Dedemocratization," *Political Theory* 34 (2006): 704–706.

129. Ron Suskind, *The One Percent Doctrine: Deep Inside America's Pursuit of Its Enemies Since 9/11* (New York: Simon and Schuster, 2006). Even before the Federal Reserve gave away money to failed banks, Naomi Klein pointed out that neoliberalism was only tried outside the United States, because governments formed by majority rule need to print money on occasion. Naomi Klein, *The Shock Doctrine: The Rise of Disaster Capitalism* (New York: Simon and Schuster, 2007).

130. Jonathan Simon, *Governing Through Crime: How the War on Crime Transformed American Democracy and Created a Culture of Fear* (Oxford: Oxford University Press, 2007), 76–77.

131. Simon, *Governing Through Crime*, 76.

132. It is certainly true that some industries have benefitted enormously from the effects of this, but instrumental explanations cannot account for the rhetoric's success. Some industries also reap major benefits from environmentalism and the businesses it sustains as well.

133. Hannah Arendt, "Public Rights and Private Interests," in *Small Comforts for Hard Times: Humanists on Public Policy*, ed. Michael Mooney and Florian Stuber (New York: Columbia University Press, 1977), 104.

134. Grand juries generally are based on names drawn from pools using drivers licenses and voter registration lists, both of which rely on residence for eligibility.

135. A 30,000-inhabitant district with thirty members on the land jury, for instance, would have ten old members exit and ten new members join each year. This size does not guarantee that it will be representational of all the characteristics of the community. For a discussion of the politics of lotteries, see Philip Green, *The Pursuit of Inequality* (New York: Pantheon, 1981); and Barbara Goodwin, *Justice by Lottery* (Chicago: University of Chicago Press, 1992); and see also the chapter on the Athenian use of the lot in Emily Hauptmann, *Putting Choice Before Democracy: A Critique of Rational Choice Theory* (Albany, N.Y.: SUNY, 1996).

136. Peter McLaverty, "The Public Sphere and Local Democracy," *Democratization* 5 (1998): 224–239.

137. Arendt, "Public Rights and Private Interests."

8. RELIGION AND THE NATION-STATE

1. In Jacqueline Stevens, *Reproducing the State* (Princeton, N.J.: Princeton University Press, 1999), chap. 7.

2. On the continuity of early Christian habits, including celibacy, through the sixth century, see Peter Brown, *The Body and Society: Men, Women, and Sexual Renunciation in Early Christianity* (New York: Columbia University Press, 1988).

3. Genesis 17:2–9.

4. Josephus, *The Jewish War* (Middlesex: Penguin, 1981).

5. Koran, The Bee, 1–4.

6. Carolos Conde, "Clans Complicate Philippine Conflict," *New York Times* (October 28, 2007).

7. S. J. Connolly, *Religion, Law, and Power: The Making of Protestant Ireland, 1660–1760* (Oxford: Clarendon Press, 1992), 13.

8. Connolly, *Religion, Law, and Power*, 103.

9. Forrest Wood, *The Arrogance of Faith: Christianity and Race in America from the Colonial Era to the Twentieth Century* (New York: Knopf, 1990).

10. Merriam-Webster online dictionary, http://www.merriam-webster.com.

11. Cults resemble religious groups except that they do not have a long history and may have few followers.

12. http://en.wikipedia.org/wiki/Heaven's_Gate_(cult).

13. Hobbes still would be troubled by their appearance, realizing that actions diminishing the importance of the body and life on earth weaken the state's threats of bodily pain and death instrumental to the sovereign's ability to coerce obedience.

14. Facts on File World News Digest, "U.S. Congressman, Four Others Killed in Guyana Ambush; Hundreds Commit Suicide at American Religious Commune" (November 24, 1978).

15. Philip Dine, "At Hearing, Danforth Absolves Government in Waco Fire," *St. Louis Post-Dispatch* (July 27, 2000).

16. Karl Marx, "A Contribution to the Critique of Hegel's Philosophy of Right: Introduction," in *Early Writings*, trans. Rodney Livingston (Middlesex: Penguin, 1992), 244, 243–258.

17. Weber actually makes an even less defensible claim, that the sixteenth century's Christian sects were echoing earlier religious motifs: "Baxter's principal work is dominated by the continually repeated, often almost passionate preaching of hard, continuous bodily or mental labour. It is due to a combination of two different motives. Labour is, on the one hand, an approved ascetic technique, as it always has been in the Western Church, in sharp contrast not only to the Orient but to almost all monastic rules the world over." *The Protestant Ethic and the Spirit of Capitalism*, chap. 5, http://www.ne.jp/asahi/moriyuki/abukuma/weber/world/ethic/pro_eth_frame.html. The early Christians would not recognize this claim on their behalf. To the extent it applies to the Catholic Church, it would be due to its political functions, not its spiritual ones. All self-sufficient communities need to encourage members to work, but there is nothing in the New Testament that mentions salvation through labor.

18. Marx, "Contribution to a Critique," 244.

19. Islam's doctrinal requirement of sovereignty, as well as the notion that children born to Muslim parents are Muslim, advocates a return to the political and national character of Abraham's Israelites and away from the Christian interpretation of monotheism.

20. Jane Bennett, *The Enchantment of Modern Life* (Princeton, N.J.: Princeton University Press, 2001), 12.

21. Bennett, *The Enchantment of Modern Life*, 111.

22. Marx, "Contribution to a Critique," 245, emphasis in original.

23. Rory McCarthy, "Hamas Hints at Talks as Chaos Reigns in Divided Palestine," *Guardian* (June 16, 2007), http://www.guardian.co.uk/world/2007/jun/16/israel.

24. Mona El-Naggar, "Egypt Arrests Opposition Leaders After a Protest," *New York Times* (December 15, 2006).

25. Lydia Polgreen, "Dozens Are Killed in Raids of Darfur Camp," *New York Times* (August 25, 2008).

26. VOA English Service, "Recent Slaying Highlights Dangers Faced by Journalists in Somalia" (October 22, 2007).

27. Associated Press, "Inquiry Says Ethiopian Troops Killed 193 in Ballot Protests in '05," *New York Times* (October 19, 2006).

28. Many parliamentary constitutions contain explicit language allowing a president to declare a state of emergency or state of exception and absorb all government functions into the presidency. This was the case for Germany and Palestine, although the latter clearly violated its constitutional rules for taking over these powers. The U.S. Constitution does not allow for such a declaration and hence the unilateral powers seized by President Bush without the consent of the Congress were simply the maneuvers of a private man abusing his office and lack the paradoxical qualities of legitimacy and legality Schmitt explores in the period leading to Hitler's appointment as chancellor.

29. Even more particularly, the substantive policy of land reform shifted conservatives into Hitler's camp. Chancellor Heinrich Brüning wanted to expropriate selected large estates to more equitably fund the war repayments demanded by the Versailles Treaty: "Hopelessly indebted properties were to be used for resettling some of the unemployed on the land." Brüning's attempt to spread the war's debt burden more evenly led the landed friends of President Hindenberg to pressure him to fire Brüning, which opened the door to Hitler's appointment. Joachim Fest, *Hitler*, trans. Richard Winston and Clara Winston (New York: Harcourt Brace Jovanovich, 1973), 333. Of course, absent a regime of private land rights, such a situation would not have arisen.

30. It is also the case that Islamist leaders in countries such as Iran and Somalia are using the perceived and actual threats of foreign powers to legitimate their extralegal powers.

31. For a rich and helpful exploration of the politics of recognition that Hegel's work engenders, see Patchen Markell, *Bound by Recognition* (Princeton, N.J.: Princeton University Press, 2002).

32. Schmitt mentions Hegel by name, and his general ideas appear throughout the text. Carl Schmitt, *The Concept of the Political* (Chicago: University of Chicago Press, 2007), 62–63.

33. Schmitt, *The Concept of the Political*, esp. 33, 35.

34. Schmitt, *The Concept of the Political*, 49.

1. An exception, because it highlights methods in practice and not as an abstraction, are the essays in Dvora Yanow and Peregrine Schwartz-Shea, eds., *Interpretation and Method: Empirical Research and the Interpretive Turn* (Armonk, N.Y.: M. E. Sharpe, 2006).

2. Paul Feyerabend's ressentiment in relation to his teacher Karl Popper is a symptom of how the antimethods camp is about friends and enemies, not ideas and knowledge. Feyerabend writes: "Popper's philosophy, which some people would like to lay on us as the one and only humanitarian rationalism in existence today, is but a pale reflection of Mill.... We can understand its peculiarities when we consider ... the unrelenting puritanism of its author (and of most of his followers), and when we remember the influence of Harriet Taylor on Mill's life and philosophy. There is no Harriet Taylor in Popper's life." *Against Method: Outline of an Anarchistic Theory of Knowledge* (New York: Verso, 1993), 34. Feyerabend's beliefs are largely complementary to those of Popper; Feyerabend's suggestion to the contrary has demarcated unnecessary enemy lines and impeded the development of knowledge in the social sciences. The inappropriate outburst directed against Popper's wife—to whom Popper dedicated his *The Logic of Scientific Discovery* (London: Hutchison, 1959)—raises questions about the family dramas fantasized by Feyerabend, the son in Popper's intellectual household.

3. Sheldon Wolin, "Political Theory as a Vocation," *American Political Science Review* 63 (1969): 1063.

4. Emily Hauptmann, "A Local History of 'the Political,'" *Political Theory* 32 (2004): 34–60.

5. For a longer discussion of the relevance of Popper's epistemology to science studies debates, see Jacqueline Stevens, "Symbolic Matter: DNA and Other Linguistic Stuff," *Social Text*, 20 (2002): 106–140.

6. Karl Popper, *The Open Society and Its Enemies* (New York: Routledge, 2003), 3–4; and Karl Popper, *Conjectures and Refutations: The Growth of Scientific Knowledge* (New York: Routledge, 2002), 34–35.

7. Karl Popper, "Prediction and Prophecy in the Social Sciences," in *Conjectures and Refutations*, 336.

8. Popper, "Prediction and Prophecy in the Social Sciences," 336.

9. Feyerabend, *Against Method*, 23, 150, 154.

10. Friedrich Hayek, *The Road to Serfdom* (Chicago: University of Chicago Press, 1944).

11. Wolin, "Political Theory as a Vocation," 1064.

12. Karl Popper, *The Logic of Scientific Discovery*, 53.

13. Karl Popper, "Prediction and Prophecy in the Social Sciences," 338.

14. Karl Popper, "Prediction and Prophecy in the Social Sciences," 339.

15. James Fearon and David Laitin, "Ethnicity, Insurgency, and Civil War," *American Political Science Review* 97 (2003): 75–90.

16. Karl Popper, *The Logic of Scientific Discovery*, 251.

17. See, e.g., Steven Jay Gould, *Full House: The Spread of Excellence from Plato to Darwin* (New York: Random House, 1997).

18. Karl Popper, "Science: Conjectures and Refutations," in *Conjectures and Refutations*, 57.

19. Claude Levi-Strauss, *The Elementary Structures of Kinship*, trans. James Bell (Boston: Beacon Press, 1969).

20. See chapter 1, which explains apparent exceptions to this.

21. Popper, *The Logic of Scientific Discovery*, 33.

22. Popper, *The Logic of Scientific Discovery*, 33.

23. Popper, "Science: Conjectures and Refutations," 49.

24. Feyerabend, *Against Method*, 18–19, emphasis in original.

25. Popper, *The Logic of Scientific Discovery*, preface to first English edition (1959), 16.

26. Popper, *The Logic of Scientific Discovery*, 31.

27. Thomas Kuhn, *The Structure of Scientific Revolutions* (Chicago: University of Chicago Press, 1970).

28. Popper, "Three Views Concerning Human Knowledge," in *Conjectures and Refutations*, 102.

29. Galileo Galilei, *Dialogue Concerning the Two Chief World Systems* (Berkeley: University of California Press, 1958) 256; quoted in Feyerabend, *Against Method*, 56.

30. Feyerabend, *Against Method*, e.g., 118.

31. Naomi Klein, *The Shock Doctrine: The Rise of Disaster Capitalism* (New York: Simon and Schuster, 2007), 79.

32. Klein, *The Shock Doctrine*, 53.

33. Klein, *The Shock Doctrine*, 89.

34. Klein, *The Shock Doctrine*, 51.

35. Klein, *The Shock Doctrine*, 183.

36. One subtle and important point Klein makes is that the one place these policies could not be implemented was the United States itself, which had a somewhat functional democracy that would never tolerate these policies. An excellent example of this is the Federal Reserve's and Congress's interventions in the 2008 housing-loan crises. The IMF in the 1980s would never have allowed any of the policies implemented by the Bush and Obama administrations.

37. Klein, *The Shock Doctrine*, 39.

38. Popper, "Prediction and Prophecy in the Social Sciences," 344.

39. Popper, "Prediction and Prophecy in the Social Sciences," 344.

40. The introduction and chapter 1 discuss Schmitt's understanding of the fundamentally antiutilitarian and therefore antieconomic motives of political violence.

41. See Steven Goldstein, "Nationalism and Internationalism: Sino-Soviet Relations," in *Chinese Foreign Policy: Theory and Practice*, ed. Thomas Robinson and David Shambaugh (Oxford: Clarendon Press, 1994), pp. 224–265; see Tianbiao Zhu, "Nationalism and Chinese Foreign Policy," *The China Review* 1, no. 1 (Fall 2001): 1–27.

42. Michael Rogin's essays on demonology in *Ronald Reagan, the Movie, and Other Episodes in Political Demonology* (Berkeley: University of California Press, 1987) advance this claim, locating the parallels between the nation-building strategies of Jacksonian demonology (of the Native Americans) and the demonology of the foreign ideas of communism. It was Russia's foreignness that metonymically contaminated Marxism.

43. Rogin, "Ronald Reagan, the Movie," in *Ronald Reagan, the Movie*, 27.

44. Rogin, "Ronald Reagan, the Movie," 30.

45. Rogin, "Political Repression in the United States," in *Ronald Reagan, the Movie*, 79–80.

46. Rogin, "Kiss Me Deadly: Communism, Motherhood, and Cold War Movies," in *Ronald Reagan, the Movie*, 237.

47. Fred Weir, "United Russia Wins, Putin sees 'Moral Mandate' in Vote," *Christian Science Monitor* (December 4, 2007).

48. Oleg Schedrov, "Putin's Foreign Policy Is a Hit at Home, Polls Say," *Reuters*.

49. Shlomo Avineri, "It Seemed to Be Working," *Haaretz* (October 8, 2008), http://ww .haaretz.com/hasen/pages/1027061.html.

50. Alessandra Ferrara, *The Force of the Example: Explorations in the Paradigm of Judgment* (New York: Columbia University Press, 2008).

51. Immanuel Kant, *Critique of Judgment*, trans. James Meredith (Oxford: Oxford University Press, 1952), 18.

52. Ferrara, *The Force of the Example*, 48; quoting Arendt, *Lectures on Kant's Political Philosophy* (Chicago: University of Chicago Press, 1982).

53. Ferrara, *The Force of the Example*, 53.

54. This is explained in detail in Stevens, *Reproducing the State* (Princeton, N.J.: Princeton University Press, 1999), esp. chaps. 1 and 2.

55. Jürgen Habermas, *Between Facts and Norms: Contributions to a Discourse Theory of Law and Democracy* (Cambridge, Mass.: The MIT Press, 1996), p. 23.

56. Habermas, *Between Facts and Norms*, 26.

57. Habermas, *Between Facts and Norms*, 28.

58. Habermas, *Between Facts and Norms*, 33.

59. Habermas' work anticipated a host of writers who, in the aftermath of the USSR's collapse and the rise of so-called globalization, foresaw what Habermas calls a "postnational society" that was steadily advancing. Residents of Kosovo, or the Minutemen, or the participants in the world-trade talks that collapsed in 2008, leading to an increasing trend of closed markets and nationally driven tax and tariff policies, might have a different view. For an especially glaring example of Habermas' poor predictions, see "Popular Sovereignty as Procedure" (1988) and "Citizenship and National Identity" (1990) in *Between Facts and Norms*, 463–489 and 491–514.

60. Habermas, *Between Facts and Norms*, 514–515.

61. For more on the interplay between Nietzsche's ideas and the legal imaginary, see Adam Gearey, *Law and Aesthetics* (Portland, Me.: Hart Publishing, 2001).

Bibliography

Ackerman, Bruce, and Anne Alstott. *The Stakeholder Society*. New Haven, Conn.: Yale University Press, 1999.

Adams, Richard, and John Page. "Do International Migration and Remittances Reduce Poverty in Developing Countries?" *World Development* 33 (2005): 1645–1669.

Addison, Tony. "Reconstruction from War in Africa: Communities, Entrepreneurs, and States." CSAE Conference 2001: Development Policy in Africa. Centre for the Study of African Economies. Oxford: University of Oxford, 2001. Available online at http://www.csae.ox.ac.uk/conferences/2001-DPiA/pdfs/Addison.pdf.

African Development Fund. "Democratic Republic of Congo: Agricultural and Rural Sector Rehabilitation Support Project in Bas-Congo and Bandundu Provinces (PARSAR) Appraisal Report." 2004. Available online at http://www.afdb.org/pls/portal/docs/page/adb_admin_pg/documents/operationsinformation/adf_bd_wp_2004_35_e.pdf.

Agamben, Giorgio. *Homo Sacer: Sovereign Power and Bare Life*. Stanford, Calif.: Stanford University Press, 1995.

Alajdem, Terry. "The Philosopher's Prism: Foucault, Feminism and Critique." *Political Theory* 19 (1991): 277–291.

Alesina, Alberto, and David Dollar. "Who Gives Foreign Aid to Whom and Why?" *Journal of Economic Growth* 5: 33–63.

Alesina, Alberto, Edward Glaeser, and Bruce Sacerdote. "Why Doesn't the United States Have a European-style Welfare State?" *Brookings Papers on Economic Activity* (2003): 187– 277. Available online at http://muse.jhu.edu/journals/brookings_papers_on_economic_activity/v2001/2001.2durlauf.pdf.

Allen, Amy. *The Politics of Our Selves: Power, Autonomy, and Gender in Contemporary Critical Theory*. New York: Columbia University Press, 2008.

Anan, Kofi. *We the Peoples: The Role of the United Nations in the Twenty-first Century*. United Nations, 2000. Available online at http://www.un.org/millennium/sg/report/full.htm.

Anderlik, M. R., and M. A. Rothstein. "DNA-based Identity Testing and the Future of the Family: A Research Agenda." *American Journal of Law and Medicine* 28 (2002): 215–232.

Anderson, Terry, and Donald Leal. *Free Market Environmentalism*. New York: Palgrave, 2001.

Angell, Norman. "The Great Illusion." *New York Times Magazine* (June 15, 1913).

Arendt, Hannah. *Between Past and Future: Eight Exercises in Political Thought*. New York: Viking Press, 1968.

——. "Christianity and Revolution." *The Nation* (September 1945).

——. *Eichmann in Jerusalem: A Report on the Banality of Evil*. New York: Penguin, 1965.

——. *The Human Condition*. Chicago: University of Chicago Press, 1958.

——. *The Jew as Pariah: Jewish Identity and Politics in the Modern Age*. New York: Random House, 1978.

——. *Lectures on Kant's Political Philosophy*. Chicago: University of Chicago Press, 1982.

——. *On Violence*. New York: Harcourt, Brace and World, 1970.

——. "Public Rights and Private Interests." In *Small Comforts for Hard Times: Humanists on Public Policy*, ed. Michael Mooney and Florian Stuber, 103–108. New York: Columbia University Press, 1977.

Ari, M., et al. "Aile İçi İliskilerde Siddet [Violence in Interfamily Relationships]." In *Aile Kuraltayı Degisim Sürecinde Aile*, ed. R. Karadayı et al., 300–312. Ankara: Aile Kurumu: 1994.

Arnold, Kathleen. *Homelessness, Citizenship, and Identity: The Uncanniness of Late Modernity*. Albany, N.Y.: SUNY Press, 2004.

Ascher, William. *Why Governments Waste Natural Resources: Policy Failures in Developing Countries*. Baltimore, Md.: The Johns Hopkins University Press, 1998.

Ashcraft, Richard. *Revolutionary Politics and John Locke's Two Treatises of Government*. Princeton, N.J.: Princeton University Press, 1986.

Associated Press. "Inquiry Says Ethiopian Troops Killed 193 in Ballot Protests in '05." *New York Times* (October 19, 2006).

Austin, J. L. *How to Do Things with Words*. Cambridge, Mass.: Harvard University Press, 1962.

Avery, R. B., et al. "Survey of Consumer Finances, 1983: A Second Report." *Federal Reserve Bulletin* 72 (March): 163–177.

Avineri, Shlomo. "It Seemed to Be Working." *Haaretz* (October 8, 2008). Available online at http://ww.haaretz.com/hasen/pages/1027061.html.

Bagemihl, Bruce. *Biological Exuberance: Animal Homosexuality and Natural Diversity*. New York: St. Martin's Press, 1998.

Bakunin, Mikhail. *God and the State*. Mineola, N.Y.: Dover, 1970.

Balderrama, Francisco, and Raymond Rodríguez. *Decade of Betrayal: Mexican Repatriation in the 1930s*. Albuquerque: University of New Mexico Press, 1995.

Bales, Kevin. *Disposable People: New Slavery in the Global Economy*. Berkeley: University of California, 1999.

Baran, Paul. *Monopoly Capital: An Essay on the American and Social Order*. New York: Monthly Review Press, 1966.

Barker, Gary. "Men's Participation as Fathers in the Latin American and Caribbean Region: A Critical Literature Review with Policy Considerations." Prepared for the World Bank (2003). Available online at http://www.promundo.org.br.

Barlow, Maude, and Tony Clarke. *Blue Gold: The Fight to Stop the Corporate Theft of the World's Water*. New York: New York Press, 2002.

Baron, Jane. "Intention, Interpretation, and Stories." *Duke Law Journal* 42 (1992): 630–678.

Barry, Brian. *Democracy, Power, and Justice*. Oxford: Clarendon, 1989.

Bartels, Larry. "Homer Gets a Tax Cut: Inequality and Public Policy in the American Mind." *Perspectives on Politics* 30 (2005): 15–31.

Baum, Fran. "Wealth and Health: The Need for More Strategic Public Health Research." *Journal of Epidemiological Community Health* 59 (2005): 542–545.

Baum, L. Frank. *The Wizard of Oz and Who He Was*. East Lansing: Michigan State University Press, 1957.

Baumeister, Roy, and Mark Leary. "The Need to Belong: Desire for Interpersonal Attachments as a Fundamental Human Motivation." *Psychological Bulletin* 117: 497–529.

Becerril, Coca, and Becerril Legal Department. "The Promotion and Defense of Intellectual Property in Mexico as Motor of Development." Business and Management Practices, Mondaq Business Briefing (October 23, 2002).

Behdad, Ali. *A Forgetful Nation: On Immigration and Cultural Identity in America*. Durham, N.C.: Duke University Press, 2005.

Beier, A. C. *Masterless Men: The Vagrancy Problem in England, 1560–1640*. New York: Methuen, 1985.

Beitz, Charles. *Political Theory and International Relations*. Princeton, N.J.: Princeton University Press, 1979.

Bell, Bernard. "Legislatively Revising *Kelo v. City Of New London*: Eminent Domain, Federalism, and Congressional Powers." *Journal of Legislation* 32 (2005): 165–219.

Bell, Daniel. *The End of Ideology: The Exhaustion of Ideas in the Fifties*. New York: Free Press, 1960.

Bellamy, Carol. *The State of the World's Children*. New York: Oxford University Press, 1996.

Benhabib, Seyla. "Twilight of Sovereignty or the Emergence of Cosmopolitan Norms? Rethinking Citizenship in Volatile Times." *Citizenship Studies* 11 (2007): 19–36.

Benjamin, Jessica. *Bonds of Love*. New York: Pantheon, 1988.

Bennett, Jane. *The Enchantment of Modern Life*. Princeton, N.J.: Princeton University Press, 2001.

Berlin, Isaiah. *Crooked Timber of Humanity*. New York: Random House, 1990.

Bernal, Martin. *Black Athena: The Afroasiatic Roots of Classical Civilization*. London: Free Association Books, 1987.

Bettelheim, Bruno. *Symbolic Wounds: Puberty Rites and the Envious Male*. New York: Collier Books, 1962.

Birney, Marylin, Michael Graetz, and Ian Shapiro. "Public Opinion and the Push to Repeal the Estate Tax." *National Tax Journal* 59 (2003): 439–461.

Bisharat, George. "Land, Law, and Legitimacy in Israel and the Occupied Territories." *American University Law Review* 43 (1994): 467–561.

Blackstone, William. *Commentaries on the Laws of England*. W. E. Dean: New York, 1841.

Borjas, George. *Heaven's Door*. Princeton, N.J.: Princeton University Press, 2001.

Borjas, George, and Bernt Bratsbert. "Who Leaves? The Outmigration of the Foreign-born." *The Review of Economics and Statistics* 78 (1996): 165–176.

Bornstein, Avram. "Borders and the Utility of Violence: State Effects on the 'Superexploitation' of West Bank Palestinians." *Critique of Anthropology* 22 (2002): 201–220.

Botash, A. S., S. Blatt, and V. Meguid. "Child Abuse and Sudden Infant Death Syndrome." *Current Opinions in Pediatrics* 10 (1998): 217–223.

Boudreaux, Karol. "The Human Face of Resource Conflict: Property and Power in Nigeria." *San Diego International Law Journal* 7 (2005): 61–87.

Bozniak, Linda. *Citizen and Alien: Dilemmas of Contemporary Membership*. Princeton, N.J.: Princeton University Press, 2007.

Bracewell-Milnes, Barry. *The Wealth of Giving: Everyone in His Inheritance*. London: Institute of Economic Affairs, 1989.

Brashier, Ralph. "Children and Inheritance in the Nontraditional Family." *Utah Law Review* (1996): 93–94.

———. *Inheritance Law and the Evolving Family*. Philadelphia: Temple University Press, 2004.

Brecht, Bertolt. *Mother Courage and Her Children*. Trans. David Hare. New York: Arcade, 1996.

Brook, Heather. "Stalemate: Rethinking the Politics of Marriage." *Feminist Theory* 3 (2002): 52–53.

Brooks, Karen. "Illegal Immigration's Give-and-Take: Study—Their Taxes Lift State but Services Drain Counties." *Dallas Morning News* (December 8, 2006).

Brooks, Rosa. "An SAT for Citizenship: Natural-born Citizens Should Take the New Naturalization Test for Immigrants—and Be Deported If They Fail." *Los Angeles Times* (December 8, 2006).

Brown, Norman Oliver. *Life Against Death: The Psychoanalytical Meaning of History*. London: Routledge, Kegan and Paul, 1959.

Brown, Peter. *The Body and Society: Men, Women, and Sexual Renunciation in Early Christianity*. New York: Columbia University Press, 1988.

Brown, Wendy. "American Nightmare Neoliberalism, Neoconservatism, and Dedemocratization." *Political Theory* 34 (2006): 690–714.

Burling, James. "The Latest Take on Background Principles and the States' Law of Property After Lucas and Palazzolo." *University of Hawaii Law Review* 24 (2002): 497.

Burr, Kendall. "The Evolution of the International Law of Alienability: The 1997 Land Law of Mozambique as a Case Study." *Columbia Journal of Transnational Law* 43 (2005): 962.

Burton, Robert. *The Anatomy of Melancholy*. London: George Routledge and Son, 1931.

Butler, Judith. "Imitation and Gender Insubordination." In *Inside/Out: Lesbian and Gay Theories*, ed. Diana Fuss, 13–31. New York: Routledge, 1991.

Calhoun, Cheshire. *Feminism, the Family, and the Politics of the Closet: Lesbian and Gay Displacement*. New York: Oxford University Press, 2000.

California Department of Motor Vehicles. "How to Apply for a Driver's License If Over 18." 2004. Available online at http://www.dmv.ca.gov/dl/dl_info.htm#2500.

Camarota, Steven. "Immigrants in the United States, 2002." Center for Immigration Studies, analysis of the U.S. Current Population Survey, Census Bureau. Available online at http://www.cis.org/articles/2002/back1302.html.

Card, David. "The Impact of the Mariel Boatlift on the Miami Labor Market." *Industrial and Labor Relations Review* 43 (1990): 245–257.

———. "Is the New Immigration Really So Bad?" *The Economic Journal* 115 (2005): F300–F323.

Carens, Joseph. "Aliens and Citizens: The Case for Open Borders." *Review of Politics* 49 (1987): 251–273.

Carlisle, Rodney, and Joan Zenzen. *Supplying the Nuclear Arsenal: American Production Reactors, 1942–1992*. Baltimore, Md.: The Johns Hopkins University Press, 1996.

Carnegie, Andrew. *The Gospel of Wealth and Other Timely Essays*. Cambridge, Mass.: Harvard University Press, 1962.

Carrier, Paul. "Group Drops Antigay Effort." *Morning Sentinel* (June 20, 2008). Available online at http://morningsentinel.mainetoday.com/news/local/5170407.html.

Carroll, Christopher. "Why Do the Rich Save So Much?" In *Does Atlas Shrug? The Economic Consequences of Taxing the Rich*, ed. Joel Slemrod. Cambridge, Mass.: Harvard University Press, 2000.

Carter, Jimmy. *Peace Not Apartheid*. New York: Simon and Schuster, 2006.

Castle Coalition. "2006 Election Wrap Up: Voters Overwhelmingly Passed Eminent Domain Reform." (November 8, 2006). Available online at http://www.castlecoalition.org.

Chakrabarty, Dipesh. *Provincializing Europe: Postcolonial Thought and Historical Difference*. 2nd ed. Princeton, N.J.: Princeton University Press, 2007.

Chambers, David. "What If: The Legal Consequences of Marriage and the Legal Needs of Lesbian and Gay Male Couples." *Michigan Law Review* 95 (1996): 447–491.

Chang, H. F. "Cultural Communities in a Global Labor Market: Immigration Restrictions as Residential Segregation." American Law & Economics Association, 16th Annual Meeting, Working Paper 28. May 2006. Available online at http://law.bepress.com/alea/16th/bazaar/art28.

——. "The Economics of International Labor Migration and the Case for Global Distributive Justice in Liberal Political Theory." University of Pennsylvania Law School. Scholarship at Penn Law. Paper 159. December 24, 2007. Available online at http://lsr.nellco.org/upenn/wps/papers/159.

——. "Immigration Policy, Liberal Principles, and the Republican Tradition." *Georgetown Law Journal* 85 (1997): 2105–2119.

Chang, Jerry, et al. "Pregnancy-related Mortality Surveillance: United States, 1991–1999." U.S. Division of Reproductive Health National Center for Chronic Disease Prevention and Health Promotion, 2003. Available online at http://www.cdc.gov/mmwR/preview/mmwrhtml/ss5202a1.htm.

Chester, Ronald. *Inheritance, Wealth, and Society*. Bloomington: University of Indiana Press, 1982.

Chicago Council on Foreign Relations. "Worldviews 2002: American Public Opinion and Foreign Policy." Available online at http://www.worldviews.org/detailreports/usreport/public_topline_report.pdf.

Chodorow, Nancy. *Reproduction of Mothering*. Berkeley: University of California, 1978.

Clark, Lorenne. "Who Owns the Apples in the Garden of Eden?" In *The Sexism of Social and Political Theory: Women and Reproduction from Plato to Nietzsche*, ed. M. G. Clark and Lynda Lange, 16–40. Toronto: University of Toronto Press, 1979.

Cocks, Joan. *Passion and Paradox: Intellectuals Confront the National Question*. Princeton, N.J.: Princeton University Press, 2002.

Coghlan, Benjamin, et al. "Mortality in the Democratic Republic of Congo: A Nationwide Survey." *Lancet* 367 (2006): 44–51.

Coke, Edward. *The First Part of the Institutes of the Laws of England*. 16th ed. London: L. Hansard and Sons, 1809.

Coldham, Simon. "Legal Responses to State Corruption in Commonwealth Africa." *Journal of African Law* 39 (1995): 115–126.

Coleman, Jules, and Sarah Harding. "Citizenship, Justice, and Political Borders." In *Justice in Immigration*, ed. Warren Schwartz, 18–62. Cambridge: Cambridge University Press, 1995.

Coleman, Mathew. "Immigration Geopolitics Beyond the Mexico-U.S. Border." *Antipode* 39 (2007): 54–76.

Collier, Paul, and Anke Hoeffler. "Greed and Grievance in Civil War." *Oxford Economic Papers* 56 (2004): 563–595.

Collins, Patricia Hill. "African American Women and Economic Justice: A Preliminary Analysis of Wealth, Family, and African American Social Class." *University of Cincinnati Law Review* 65 (1997).

Conde, Carlos. "Clans Complicate Philippine Conflict." *New York Times* (October 28, 2007).

Conley, Dalton. *Being Black, Living in the Red.* Berkeley: University of California Press, 1999.

——. "A Man's Right to Choose." *New York Times* (December 1, 2005).

Connolly, S. J. *Religion, Law and Power: The Making of Protestant Ireland, 1660–1760.* Oxford: Clarendon Press, 1992.

Connolly, William. "Discipline, Politics, and Ambiguity." *Political Theory* 11 (1983): 325–341.

Cooper, Marc. "Twelve Die on the U.S. Border: A New Season of Death Begins." *Nation Online* (May 25, 2006). Available online at http://www.thenation.com/doc/20050606/cooperweb.

Cornell, Drucilla. *The Heart of Freedom: Feminism and Sex Equality.* Princeton, N.J.: Princeton University Press, 1998.

Cott, Nancy. *Public Vows: A History of Marriage and the Nation.* Cambridge, Mass.: Harvard University Press, 2000.

Coutin, Susan. *Nations of Emigrants: Shifting Boundaries of Citizenship in El Salvador and the United States.* Ithaca, N.Y.: Cornell University Press, 2007.

Cowell, Alan. "Britain: Dying Surname." *New York Times* (July 28, 2004).

Cramer, Christopher. "*Homo Economicus* Goes to War: Methodological Individualism, Rational Choice, and Political Economy." *World Development* 30 (2002): 1845–1864.

Cruikshank, Barbara. *The Will to Empower: Democratic Citizens and Other Subjects.* Ithaca, N.Y.: Cornell University Press, 1999.

Curran, John. "Vermont Gay Marriage Debate Tamer This Time." *USA Today.* Available online at http://www.usatoday.com/news/nation/2008-01-13-3932657192_x.htm.

Currin, Frances Heyward. "Transformation of Paradise: Geographical Perspectives on Tourism Development on a Small Caribbean Island (Utila, Honduras)." Masters thesis submitted to the Graduate Faculty of the Louisiana State University and Agricultural and Mechanical College. 2003. Available online at http://etd.lsu.edu/docs/available/etd-1114102-141915/unrestricted/Currin_thesis.pdf.

Daly, Martin, and Margo Wilson. *Homicide.* New York: Aldine de Gruyter, 1988.

Danielson, Caroline. *Citizen Acts: Citizenship and Political Agency in the Works of Jane Addams, Charlotte Perkins Gilman, and Emma Goldman.* Dissertation. Ann Arbor: University of Michigan, 1996.

Darlin, Damon. "Your Money: With a Little Estate Planning, Your House Can Stay in the Family." *New York Times* (January 21, 2006).

Davis, David Brion. *The Problem with Slavery in the Western World.* Ithaca, N.Y.: Cornell University Press, 1966.

Davis, James, et al. "The World Distribution of Household Wealth." WIDER Project Meeting on Personal Assets from a Global Perspective (2006): Table 10a. Available online at http://www.wider.unu.edu/research/2006-2007/2006-2007-1/wider-wdhw-launch-5-12-2006/wider-wdhw-report-5-12-2006.pdf.

Dawkins, Richard. *The Selfish Gene.* Oxford: Oxford University Press, 1989.

Dafoe, Daniel. *Robinson Crusoe*. Available online at http://etext.virginia.edu/etcbin/toccer
-new2?id=DefCru1.sgm&images=images/modeng&data=/texts/english/modeng/
parsed&tag=public&part=20&division=div1.

De Nardi, Mariacristina. "Wealth Inequality and Intergenerational Links." *Review of Economic Studies* 71 (2004): 743–768.

DePalma, Anthony. "Farmers Caught in Conflict Over Illegal Migrant Workers." *New York Times* (October 3, 2000).

Detwiler, Edward. "The Anglo-Saxon Myth in the United States." *American Sociological Review* 3 (1938): 183–189.

Dietz, Mary. "Citizenship with a Feminist Face: The Problem of Maternal Thinking." *Political Theory* 13 (1984): 19–35.

Dine, Philip. "At Hearing, Danforth Absolves Government in Waco Fire." *St. Louis Post-Dispatch* (July 27, 2000).

Dinnerstein, Dorothy. *The Mermaid and the Minotaur: Sexual Arrangements and Human Malaise*. New York: Harper and Row, 1976.

Domhoff, G. William. *The Higher Circles*. New York: Vintage, 1971.

——. *The Power Elite and the State: How Policy Is Made in America*. New York: Aldine de Gruyter, 1990.

Douglas, Elizabeth, and Richard Simon. "Scandal at Federal Oil Royalty Collection Agency." *Los Angeles Times* (September 11, 2008).

Douglas, Roy. *Taxation in Britain Since 1660*. New York: St. Martin's Press, 1999.

Duggan, Lisa. "Queering the State." *Social Text* 39 (1994): 1–14.

Durant, Will. *Our Oriental Heritage*. New York: Simon and Schuster, 1951.

Duster, Troy. *Backdoor to Eugenics*. New York: Routledge, 1990.

Dustmann, Christian. "Why Go Back? Return Motives of Migrant Workers." London: University College, 2000. Available online at http://www.ucl.ac.uk/~uctpb21/pdf/Return1.pdf.

Dustmann, Christian, Samuel Bentolila, and Riccardo Faini. "Return Migration: The European Experience." *Economic Policy* 11 (1996): 213–250.

Dworkin, Ronald. *Taking Rights Seriously*. Cambridge, Mass.: Harvard University Press, 1978.

Dynan, Karen, Jonathan Skinner, and Stephen Zeldes. "The Importance of Bequests and Lifecycle Saving in Capital Accumulation: A New Answer." *American Economic Review* (2002): 274–278.

El-Haj, Nadia abu. "A Tool to Recover Past Histories: Genealogy and Identity after the Genome." 2004. Available online at http://www.sss.ias.edu/publications/papers/paper19.pdf.

Ellickson, Robert. "Property in Land." *Yale Law Journal* 102 (1993): 1394–1397.

El-Naggar, Mona. "Egypt Arrests Opposition Leaders After a Protest." *New York Times* (December 15, 2006).

Elster, Jon. "Motivations and Beliefs in Suicide Missions." In *Making Sense of Suicide Missions*, ed. Diego Gambetta. Oxford: Oxford University Press, 2005.

Engels, Freidrich. *On the Housing Question*. Moscow: Foreign Languages Publisher, 1955.

Epstein, Richard. *Takings: Regulations, Private Property, and Eminent Domain*. Cambridge, Mass.: Harvard University Press, 1985.

Erasmus. "Complaint of Peace." In *In Praise of Folly and Other Writings*. New York: Norton, 1989.

Eskow, L. R. "The Ultimate Weapon?: Demythologizing Spousal Rape and Reconceptualizing Its Prosecution." *Stanford Law Review* 48 (1995): 677–709.

Everett, Daniel. "Cultural Constraints on Grammar and Cognition in Pirahã." *Current Anthropology* 46 (2005): 621–646.

Ewigman, B., C. Kivlatan, and G. Land. "The Missouri Child Fatality Study: Underreporting of Maltreatment Fatalities Among Children Younger Than Five Years of Age." *Pediatrics* 91 (1993): 330–337.

Ezzati, Majid, et al. "Selected Major Risk Factors and Global and Regional Burden of Disease." *Lancet* 360 (2002): 1347–1360.

Facts on File World News Digest. "U.S. Congressman, Four Others Killed in Guyana Ambush; Hundreds Commit Suicide at American Religious Commune." (November 24, 1978).

Faye, Jacques. "Land and Decentralisation in Senegal." IIED Drylands Issue Paper 149 (2008). Available online at http://www.iied.org/pubs/pdfs/12550IIED.pdf.

Fearon, James. "Ethnic and Cultural Diversity by Country." *Journal of Economic Growth* 8 (2003): 195–222.

Fearon, James, and David Laitin. "Ethnicity, Insurgency, and Civil War." *American Political Science Review* 97 (2003): 75–90.

Fellows, Mary, Monica Johnson, Amy Chiericozzi, Ann Hale, Christopher Lee, Robin Preble, and Michael Voran. "Committed Partners and Inheritance: An Empirical Study," *Law and Inequality* 16 (1998): 1–94.

Fellows, Mary, Rita Simon, and William Rau. "Public Attitudes About Property Distribution at Death and Intestate Succession Laws in the United States." *American Bar Foundation Research Journal* (1978): 319–391.

Fennell, Lee Anne. "Death, Taxes, and Cognition." *North Carolina Law Review* 81 (2003): 567–642.

Ferrara, Alessandra. *The Force of the Example: Explorations in the Paradigm of Judgment.* New York: Columbia University Press, 2008.

Fest, Joachim. *Hitler.* Trans. Richard Winston and Clara Winston. New York: Harcourt Brace Jovanovich, 1973.

Feyerabend, Paul K. *Against Method: Outline of an Anarchistic Theory of Knowledge.* New York: Verso, 1993.

Fineman, Martha. *The Illusion of Equality.* Chicago: Chicago University Press, 1991.

——. *The Neutered Mother, the Sexual Family, and Other Twentieth-century Tragedies.* New York: Routledge, 1995.

Finkelhor, D. "The Homicide Rates of Children and Youth: A Developmental Perspective." In *Out of the Darkness: Contemporary Perspectives on Family Violence,* ed. G. K. Kanto and J. L. Jasinski, 17–34. Thousand Oaks, Calif.: Sage Publications, 1997.

Firestone, Shulamith. *The Dialectic of Sex: The Case for Feminist Revolution.* New York: Bantam, 1970.

Fornet-Betancourt, Raul, Helmut Becker, and Alfredo Gomez-Mueller. "The Ethic of Care for the Self as a Practice of Freedom: An Interview with Michel Foucault on January 20, 1984." *Philosophy and Social Criticism* 12 (1987): 112–131.

Foster, Frances. "The Family Paradigm of Inheritance Law." *North Carolina Law Review* 80 (2001): 199–273.

Foucault, Michel. *Power/Knowledge: Selected Interviews and Other Writings, 1972–1977.* Ed. Colin Gordon. New York: Pantheon, 1980.

——. *The Use of Pleasure.* Trans. Robert Hurley. New York: Vintage Books, 1985.

Freud, Sigmund. "Civilization and its Discontents." In *Civilization, Society and Religion*, ed. James Strachey, 274–275. London: Penguin, 1991.

——. *Future of an Illusion*. London: Penguin, 1991.

——. *Moses and Monotheism*. New York: Vintage, 1955.

——. "Mourning and Melancholia." In *The Standard Edition of the Complete Psychological Works of Sigmund Freud*, trans. James Strachey, 14:239–258. London: Hogarth Press, 1955.

——. "Thoughts for the Times on War and Death." In *The Standard Edition of the Complete Psychological Works of Sigmund Freud*, trans. James Strachey, 14:275–300. London: Hogarth Press, 1955.

——. "Three Essays on Sexuality." In *The Standard Edition of the Complete Psychological Works of Sigmund Freud*, trans. James Strachey, 7:124–245. London: Hogarth Press, 1955.

——. *Totem and Taboo: Resemblances Between the Psychic Lives of Savages and Neurotics*. New York: Routledge, 1919.

——. "Why War?" In *The Standard Edition of the Complete Psychological Works of Sigmund Freud*, trans. James Strachey, 22:197–221. London: Hogarth Press, 1955.

Friedberg, Rachel, and Jennifer Hunt. "The Impact of Immigrants on Host Country Wages, Employment, and Growth." *Journal of Economic Perspectives* 9 (1995): 23–44.

Friedman, Susan, Sarah Horwitz, and Philip Resnick. "Child Murders by Mothers: A Critical Analysis of the Current State of Knowledge and a Research Agenda." *American Journal of Psychiatry* 162 (2005): 1578–1587.

Fuchs, Dale. "Is the Beach Party Over for the 'Florida of Europe'? Spain's Coastal Building Boom Is Fueling the Economy, but at a Price." *International Herald Tribune* (July 22, 2006).

Fukuyama, Francis. *The End of History and the Last Man*. New York: Free Press, 1992.

Gabra, Emilio. "The Collegia of Numa: Problems of Method and Political Ideas." *The Journal of Roman Studies* 74 (1984): 81–86.

Gale, William, and John Scholz. "Intergenerational Transfers and the Accumulation of Wealth." *Journal of Economic Perspectives* 4 (1994): 145–160.

Galilei, Galileo. *Dialogue Concerning the Two Chief World Systems*. Berkeley: University of California Press, 1958.

Gaouette, Nicole. "Worker Rules Called Likely to Hurt the Economy." *Los Angeles Times* (August 11, 2007).

Gary, Susan. "Adapting Intestacy Laws to Changing Families." *Law and Inequality* 18 (2000): 1–82.

Gearey, Adam. *Law and Aesthetics*. Portland, Me.: Hart Publishing, 2001.

Gelles, Richard. "Child Abuse and Violence in Single-parent Families: Parent-absent and Economic Deprivation." *American Journal of Orthopsychiatry* 59: 492–501.

——. "The Risk of Abusive Violence Among Children with Nongenetic Caregivers." *Family Relations* 40 (1991): 78–83.

Gentner, Dedre, and Susan Goldin-Meadow, eds. *Language in Mind: Advances in the Study of Thought*. Cambridge, Mass.: The MIT Press, 2003.

Ghobarah, Hazem, Adam Paul Huth, and Bruce Russett. "Civil Wars Kill and Maim People— Long After the Shooting Stops." *American Political Science Review* 97 (2003): 189–202.

Giddens, Anthony. *The Nation-State and Violence*. Berkeley: University of California Press, 1985.

Gilder, George. *Sexual Suicide*. New York: Bantam, 1975.

Giles, Jim. "Special Report: Internet Encyclopedias Go Head to Head." *Nature* 438 (2005): 900–901.

Gilligan, Carol. *In a Different Voice*. Cambridge, Mass.: Harvard University Press, 1978.

Gleditsch, Petter. "Monitoring Trends in Global Combat: A New Dataset of Battle Deaths." *European Journal of Population* (2005): 145–166.

Goetting, Marsha. "Home Study Courses: An Education Option," *Journal of Extension* 24: 14–18.

Goetting, Marsha, and Peter Martin. "Characteristics of Older Adults with Written Wills." *Journal of Family and Economic Issues* 22 (2001): 243–264.

Goggin, Malcolm. "The Courts, Interest Groups, and Public Opinion About Abortion." *Public Behavior* 15 (1993): 381–405.

Gokhale, Jagadeesh, and Laurence Kotlikoff. "The Baby Boomers' Mega-Inheritance—Myth or Reality?" Federal Reserve Bank of Cleveland, October 1, 2000.

Gokhale, Jagadeesh, Laurence Kotlikoff, and John Sabelhaus. "Understanding the Postwar Decline in National Saving: A Cohort Analysis." In *Brookings Papers on Economic Activity*, vol. 1. Washington, D.C.: Brookings Institution, 1996.

Goldman, Russell, and Katie Thompson. "'Pregnant Man' Gives Birth to Girl." *ABC News* (July 3, 2008), http://abcnews.go.com/Health/story?id=5302756&page=1.

Goldstein, Amy. *The Hooping Life* [film]. 2007.

Goldstein, Joshua. *Gender and War*. Princeton, N.J.: Princeton University Press, 2001.

Gonzalez, Robbin Pott. "The Rights of Putative Fathers to Their Infant Children in Contested Adoptions: Strengthening State Laws That Currently Deny Adequate Protection." *Michigan Journal of Gender & Law* 13, no. 39 (2006).

Goodhand, J., and D. Hulme. "From Wars to Complex Political Emergencies: Understanding Conflict and Peace-building in the New World Disorder." *Third World Quarterly* 20 (1999): 13–26.

Goodrich, Peter. *Oedipus Lex: Psychoanalysis, History, Law*. Berkeley: University of California Press, 1995.

Goodwin, Barbara. *Justice by Lottery*. Chicago: University of Chicago Press, 1992.

Gould, Stephen Jay. *Full House: The Spread of Excellence from Plato to Darwin*. New York: Random House, 1997.

——. *The Mismeasure of Man*. New York: Norton, 1996.

Green, Philip. *The Pursuit of Inequality*. New York: Pantheon, 1981.

Greenhouse, Steven. "Congress Looks to Grant Legal Status to Immigrants." *New York Times* (October 13, 2003).

——. "Foreign Workers at Highest Level in Decades." *New York Times* (September 4, 2000).

——. "Meatpacker in Brooklyn Challenges a Union Vote." *New York Times* (September 1, 2008).

Grossman, H. I. "A General Equilibrium Model of Insurrections." *American Economic Review* 81 (1991): 912–921.

Gruber, Jonathan. "Bequests." In *Death and Dollars*, ed. Alicia Munnell and Annika Sunden. Washington, D.C.: The Brookings Institution, 2003.

Guha, Ranjit. *History at the Limit of World History*. New York: Columbia University Press, 2002.

Habermas, Jürgen. *Between Facts and Norms: Contributions to a Discourse Theory*. Cambridge, Mass.: The MIT Press, 1996.

Hadfield, Gillian. "Just Borders: Normative Economics and Immigration Law." In *Justice in Immigration*, ed. W. Schwartz, 204–205. Cambridge: Cambridge University Press, 1995.

Haigh, Susan. "Conn. Changes Eminent Domain Laws Two Years After Court Ruling." *Associated Press* (June 3, 2007).

Hall, C. Michael. *Tourism, Mobility, and Second Homes*. Buffalo, N.Y.: Channel View Publications, 2004.

Hall, Peter, and George Marcus. "Why Should Men Leave Great Fortunes to Their Children? Class, Dynasty, and Inheritance in America." In *Inheritance and Wealth in America*, ed. Robert Brashier and Stephen McNamee, 139–171. New York: Plenum, 1998.

Hamilton, Bob, and John Whalley. "Efficiency and Distributional Implications of Global Restrictions on Labour Mobility." *Journal of Development Economics* 14 (1984): 61–75.

Hanna, Susan, Carl Folke, and Karl-Göan Mäler. "Property Rights and Environmental Resources." In *Property Rights and the Environment: Social and Ecological Issues*, ed. S. Hanna and M. Munasinghe, 15–32. Washington, D.C.: World Bank, 1995.

Haraway, Donna. *Primate Visions: Gender, Race, and Nature in the World of Modern Science*. New York: Routledge, 1989.

Hardin, Garrett. "Population Skeletons in the Environmental Closet." *Bulletin of the Atomic Scientists* 28 (1972): 37–41.

——. "The Tragedy of the Commons." *Science* 162 (1968): 1243–1248.

Hardt, Michael, and Antonio Negri. *Empire*. Cambridge, Mass.: Harvard University Press, 2000.

Harris, W. V. "The Theoretical Possibility of Extensive Infanticide in the Greco-Roman World." *Classical Quarterly* 32 (1982): 114–116.

Harrison, William. *The Description of England*. Ithaca, N.Y.: Cornell University Press, 1968.

Hart, John F. "Colonial Land Use Law and Its Significance for Modern Takings Doctrine." *Harvard Law Review* 109 (1996): 1252–1300.

——. "Land Use Law in the Early Republic and the Original Meaning of the Takings Clause." *Northwestern University Law Review* 94 (2000): 1099–1156.

Harvey Oliver. "Entering the Promised Land." *The Sun Online* (September 19, 2006). Available online at http://www.thesun.co.uk/article/0,,2-2006430362,00.html.

Hauptmann, Emily. "A Local History of 'The Political.'" *Political Theory* 32 (2004): 34–60.

——. *Putting Choice Before Democracy: A Critique of Rational Choice Theory*. Albany, N.Y.: SUNY, 1996.

Havens, John. "Notes on the Wealth Transfer Estimates Originally Presented in 'Millionaires and the Millennium.'" Boston College Center on Wealth, 2006. Available online at http://www.bc.edu/research/cwp/meta-elements/pdf/noteswte.pdf.

Hegel, G. W. F. *Phenomenology of Spirit*. Trans. A. V. Miller. Oxford: Oxford University Press, 1977.

——. *Philosophy of Right*. Trans. T. M. Knos. Oxford: Clarendon Press, 1952.

Heiber, Helmut. *Hitler's Lagebesprechungen*. In *Hitler*, by Joachim Fest, trans. Richard Winston and Clara Winston. New York: Harcourt Brace Jovanovich, 1974.

Held, David. *Democracy and the Global Order*. Stanford, Calif.: Stanford University Press, 1996.

——, ed. *Political Theory Today*. Cambridge: Polity Press, 1991.

Hendricks, Tyche. "Life Without a License." *San Francisco Chronicle* (February 10, 2002).

Herder, Johann Gottfried. *Philosophical Writings*. Trans. Michael N. Forster. New York: Cambridge University Press, 2002.

Herman-Giddens, Marcia, et al. "Underascertainment of Child Abuse Mortality in the United States." *JAMA* 281: 463–467.

Hernandez, Tanya. "The Property of Death." *University of Pittsburgh Law Review* 60 (1999): 971–1028.

Herszenhorn, David. "Residents of New London Go to Court, Saying Project Puts Profit Before Homes." *New York Times* (December 21, 2000).

Hertz, Robert. *Death and the Right Hand*. London: Black, 1965.

Herzl, Theodore. *The Jewish State*. New York: Dover, 1988.

Heyman, Josiah. "State Effects on Labor Exploitation: The INS and Undocumented Immigrants at the Mexico-U.S. Border." *Critique of Anthropology* 18 (1998): 157–180.

Hilberg, Raul. *The Destruction of European Jewry*, 3rd ed. New Haven, Conn.: Yale University, 2003.

Hill, John. "Mixed Verdict Nationwide on Eminent Domain Proposals." *Sacramento Bee* (November 9, 2006).

Hitchens, Christopher. *God Is Not Great: How Religion Poisons Everything*. New York: Twelve, 2007.

Hobbes, Thomas. *Leviathan*. London: Penguin, 1985.

Hodgson, Stephen, Cormac Cullinan, and Karen Campbell. "Land Ownership and Foreigners: A Comparative Analysis of Regulatory Approaches to the Acquisition and Use of Land by Foreigners." FAO Legal Papers Online (1999). Available online at http://www.fao.org/Legal/default.htm.

Holding, Reynolds. "Power of the INS Outweighs Proof." *San Francisco Chronicle* (June 4, 2000).

Honig, Bonnie. *Democracy and the Foreigner*. Princeton, N.J.: Princeton University Press, 2001.

——. "Ruth, the Model Émigré: Mourning and the Symbolic Politics of Immigration." *Political Theory* 25 (1997): 112–136.

Hope, Bradley. "Festive Atmosphere in Manhattan as Immigrant Marches Converge." *New York Sun* (May 2, 2006).

Hopkins, Jim. "Wal-Mart Family Lobbies for Tax Cuts." *USA Today* (April 5, 2005).

Horioka, Charles. "Are the Japanese Selfish, Altruistic, or Dynastic?" *Japanese Economic Review* 53 (2002): 26–54.

Horney, Karen. *Feminine Psychology*. New York: W. W. Norton, 1967.

Hortaçsu, Nuran, and Sibel Kalaycioğluö. "Intrafamily Aggression in Turkey: Frequency, Instigation, and Acceptance." *Journal of Social Psychology* 143 (2003): 163–184.

Hunt, Peter. *Slaves, Warfare, and Ideology in the Greek Historians*. Cambridge, Mass.: Harvard University Press, 1998.

Hurd, Michael. "Bequests: By Accident or Design?" In *Death and Dollars*, ed. Alicia Munnell and Annika Sunden, 93–117. Washington, D.C., Brookings Institute, 2003.

Hurd, Michael, and James Smith. "Anticipated and Actual Bequests." Working Paper no. 7380. National Bureau of Economic Research. 1999. Available online at http://nber.org/papers/w7380.pdf.

Iregui, Ana María. "Efficiency Gains from the Elimination of Global Restrictions on Labour Mobility: An Analysis Using a Multiregional CGE Model." Estudios Económicos, Banco de la República, Bogotá, Colombia. December 1999. Available online at http://www.banrep.org/docum/ftp/borra146.pdf.

Jacobs, Melanie. "My Two Dads: Disaggregating Biological and Social Paternity." *Arizona State Law Journal* 38 (2006): 809–856.

Jagger, Gill, and Caroline Wright. *Changing Family Values*. New York: Routledge, 2000.

Jenkins, Chris. "Ban on Same-Sex-Unions Added to Virginia Constitution." *New York Times* (November 8, 2006).

Jones, Owen, and Timothy Goldfield. "Law and Behavioral Biology." *Columbia Law Review* 406 (2005): 405–502.

Joppke, Christian. "How Immigration Is Changing Citizenship: A Comparative View." *Ethnic and Racial Studies* 22 (1999): 629–655.

Joseph, Richard. "Africa: States in Crisis." *Journal of Democracy* 14 (2003): 159–170.

Josephson, Jyl. "Citizenship, Same-sex Marriage, and Feminist Critiques of Marriage." *Perspectives on Politics* 3 (2005): 269–284.

Josephus. *The Jewish War*. Middlesex: Penguin, 1981.

Jusdanis, Gregory. *The Necessary Nation*. Princeton, N.J.: Princeton University Press, 2001.

Kamber, Michael. "Shame of Imported Labor in Kurdish North of Iraq." *New York Times* (December 29, 2007).

Kamin, Leon. *The Science and Politics of IQ*. Potomac: L. Erlbaum, 1974.

Kamin, Leon, and H. J. Eysenck. *The Intelligence Controversy*. New York: Wiley, 1981.

Kant, Immanuel. *Critique of Judgment*. Trans. James Meredith. Oxford: Oxford University Press, 1952.

——. *Perpetual Peace*. 1795. Available online at http://www.constitution.org/kant/perpeace.htm.

Katz, Stanley. "Republicanism and the Law of Inheritance in the American Revolutionary Era." *Michigan Law Review* 76 (1977): 1–29.

Kearl, Michael, and Anoel Rinaldi. "The Political Uses of the Dead as Symbols in Contemporary Civil Religions." *Social Forces* 61 (1983): 693–708.

Keating, Matt. "What They Said About . . . Heshu Yones." *Guardian* (October 2, 2003). Available online at http://www.guardian.co.uk/editor/story/0,12900,1053731,00.html.

Keister, Lisa, and Stephanie Moller. "Wealth Inequality in the United States." *Annual Review of Sociology* 26 (2000): 63–81.

Kendall, Wilmoore. *John Locke and the Doctrine of Majority Rule*. Urbana: University of Indiana Press, 1959.

Kennickell, Arthur. "An Examination of Changes in the Distribution of Wealth from 1989 to 1998: Evidence from the Survey of Consumer Finances." Conference on Saving, Intergenerational Transfers, and the Distribution of Wealth (2001). Available online at http://www.federalreserve.gov/Pubs/OSS/oss2/papers/wdist98.pdf.

Kennickell, Arthur, and Annamaria Lusardi. "Wealth Accumulation and the Importance of Precautionary Savings." Motives to Save in the 1995 SCF. Hanover: Dartmouth College, 2003. Available online at http://www.federalreserve.gov/pubs/oss/oss2/papers/precautionary.nov05.2.pdf.

Kimche, Jon, and David Kimche. *The Secret Roads: The "Illegal" Migration of a People, 1938–1948*. London, 1954.

King, L. W., trans. "Hammurabi's Code." In *Ancient History Sourcebook: Code of Hammurabi, c. 1780*. Available online at http://www.fordham.edu/halsall/ancient/hamcod.html.

Kirsch, Michael. "The Tax Code as Nationality Law." *Harvard Journal on Legislation* 13 (2006): 375–377.

Kittay, Eva Feder. "Womb Envy: An Explanatory Concept." In *Mothering: Essays in Feminist Theory*, ed. Joyce Trebilcot, 94–128. Totowa, N.J.: Rowman and Allanheld, 1984.

Klein, Naomi. *The Shock Doctrine: The Rise of Disaster Capitalism*. New York: Simon and Schuster, 2007.

Knickerbocker, Brad. "Crackdown on Polygamy Group." *Christian Science Monitor* (May 9, 2006). Available online at http://www.csmonitor.com/2006/0509/p02s01-ussc.html.

Knock, Thomas. *To End All Wars: Woodrow Wilson and the Quest for a New World Order*. Oxford: Oxford University Press, 1992.

Koch, Adrienne. *Jefferson and Madison: The Great Collaboration*. New York: Knopf, 1964.

Kolsky, Thomas. *Jews Against Zionism: The American Council for Judaism, 1942–1948*. Philadelphia: Temple University Press, 1992.

Kopczuk, Wojcieh, and Joel Slemrod. "Wealth Accumulation and Transfers of the Rich." In *Death and Dollars*, ed. Alicia Munnell and Annika Sunden, 216–217. Washington, D.C.: Brookings Institute, 2003.

Kotlikoff, Laurence. "Intergenerational Transfers and Saving." *Journal of Economic Perspectives* (1988): 41–58.

Kotlikoff, Laurence, and Lawrence Summers. "The Role of Intergenerational Transfers in Aggregate Capital Accumulation." *Journal of Political Economy* 89 (1981): 706–732.

Krier, James. "The Tragedy of the Commons, Part Two." *Harvard Journal of Law and Public Policy* 15 (1992): 325–348.

Krug, E. G., et al., eds. *World Report on Violence and Health*. Geneva: World Health Organization, 2002.

Kuhn, Thomas. *The Structure of Scientific Revolutions*. Chicago: University of Chicago Press, 1970.

Kurzban, Robert, and Mark Leary. "Evolutionary Origins of Stigmatization: The Functions of Social Exclusion." *Psychological Bulletin* 127 (2001): 187–208.

Kymlicka, Will. *Multicultural Citizenship: A Liberal Theory of Minority Rights*. Oxford: Oxford University Press, 1995.

——. *Politics in the Vernacular: Nationalism, Minority Rights, and Multicultural Citizenship*. Oxford: Oxford University Press, 2001.

Lacina, Bethany, and Nils Petter Gleditsch. "Monitoring Trends in Global Combat." *European Journal of Population* 21 (2005): 145–166.

Landau-Tasseron, Ella. "Adoption, Acknowledgement of Paternity, and False Genealogical Claims in Arabian and Islamic Societies." *Bulletin of School of Oriental and African Studies* 66 (2003): 169–192.

Laurie, Nathan. "The Frightful Inadequacy of Most of the Statistics: A Critique of Collier and Hoeffler on Causes of Civil War." Crisis States Research Centre, University of Capetown, No. 5 (2005). Available online at http://www.crisisstates.com/Publications/dp/dp11.htm.

Lazare, Bernard. *Anti-Semitism: Its History and Causes*. London: Brilon Publishers, 1962.

Leadbetter, Bill. "The Illegitimacy of Constantine and the Birth of the Tetrarchy." In *Constantine: History, Historiography, Legend*, ed. Samuel Lieu and Dominic Montserrat. London: Routledge, 1998.

Leaning, Jennifer, Susan Briggs, and Lincoln Chen. "Introduction." In *Humanitarian Crises: The Medical and Public Health Response*, ed. Jennifer Leaning, Susan Briggs, and Lincoln Chen. Cambridge, Mass.: Harvard University Press, 1999.

LeDuff, Charlie. "Jacumba Journal: Border Towns Are Close Enough to Touch but Worlds Apart." *New York Times* (February 24, 2003).

Lefebvre, Georges. *The French Revolution: From Its Origins to 1793.* Trans. Elizabeth Moss Evanson. New York: Columbia University Press, 1962.

Leibowitz, Lila. "Founding Families." *Journal of Theoretical Biology* 21 (1968): 153–169.

Lerman, D. L., and J. J. Mikesell. "Rural and Urban Poverty: An Income/Net Worth Approach." *Policy Studies Review* 7 (1988): 779.

Lester, Will. "Acceptance of Gay Marriage Has Grown Since 2003 Decision." *The Berkshire Eagle* (July 13, 2005).

Levinson, D. "Family Violence in Cross-Cultural Perspective." In *Handbook of Family Violence*, ed. V. B. Van Hasselt et al. New York: Springer, 1987.

Levi-Strauss, Claude. *The Elementary Structures of Kinship.* Trans. James Bell. Boston: Beacon Press, 1969.

Levy, Barry, and Victor Sidel. *War and Public Health.* Oxford: Oxford University Press, 2000.

Lewin, Ellen. *Lesbian Mothers: Accounts of Gender in American Culture.* Ithaca, N.Y.: Cornell University Press, 1993.

Lewis, David. *W. E. B. Du Bois: Biography of a Race, 1868–1919.* New York: John MacRae Books, 1994.

Lewontin, Richard, Steven Rose, and Leon Kamin. *Not in Our Genes.* New York: Pantheon, 1984.

Libecap, Gary. "Bureaucratic Issues and Environmental Concerns: A Review of the History of Federal Land Ownership." *Harvard Journal of Law and Public Policy* 15 (1992).

Linsay, Jonathan M. *Creating a Legal Framework for Land Registration in Eritrea: Consolidated Final Report of the International Legal Consultant.* U.N. Food and Agriculture Organization, 1997. Doc. TCP/ERI/4554.

Liu, Chenglin. "Informal Rules, Transaction Costs, and the Failure of the 'Takings' Law in China." *Hastings International and Comparative Law Review* 29 (2005): 1–27.

Locke, John. *A Letter Concerning Toleration.* Available online at http://www.constitution.org/jl/tolerati.htm.

——. *Two Treatises on Government.* Ed. Peter Laslett. Cambridge: Cambridge University Press, 1960.

Løkkegaard, Frede. *Islamic Taxation in the Classic Period.* Copenhagen: Brauner and Korch, 1950.

Loraux, Nicole. *Children of Athena.* Princeton, N.J.: Princeton University Press, 1993.

Lorenz, Konrad. *On Aggression.* Trans. Marjorie Latzke. London: Routledge, 1996.

Lumsdaine, David. *Moral Vision in International Politics.* Princeton, N.J.: Princeton University Press, 1993.

Macalpine, Ida, and Richard Hunter. "The Schreber Case: A Contribution to Schizophrenia, Hypochondria, and Psychosomatic Symptom Formation." *Psychoanalytic Quarterly* 22 (1953): 328–371.

MacFarquhar, Neil. "After the War: Refugees; Iraqis in Iran: Unwanted in Both Countries." *New York Times* (June 12, 2003).

MacKinnon, Catharine. *Feminism Unmodified.* Cambridge, Mass.: Harvard University Press, 1987.

——. "Prostitution and Civil Rights." *Michigan Journal of Gender and Law* (1993): 13–57.

——. *Toward a Feminist Theory of the State.* Cambridge, Mass.: Harvard University Press, 1989.

MacPherson, C. B. *Possessive Individualism: Hobbes to Locke.* Oxford: Clarendon Press, 1962.

Maher, Joanne, ed. *Europa World.* Available online at http://www.europaworld.com.

Mahoney, Julia. "The Illusion of Perpetuity and the Preservation of Privately Owned Lands." *Natural Resources Journal* (2004): 573–600.

Majid, Asifa, et al. "Can Language Restructure Cognition? The Case for Space." *Trends in Cognitive Sciences* 8 (2004): 108–114.

Margalit, Avishai, and Joseph Raz. "National Self-Determination." *Journal of Philosophy* 87 (1990): 439–461.

Markell, Patchen. *Bound by Recognition.* Princeton, N.J.: Princeton University Press, 2003.

Markels, Alex. "Showdown for a Tool in Rights Suits." *New York Times* (June 15, 2003).

Marshall, Alfred. *Principles of Economics.* London: MacMillan for the Royal Society, 1961.

Marshall, Monty, comp. "Major Episodes of Political Violence, 1946–2006." Available online at http://members.aol.com/CSPmgm/warlist.htm.

Marshall, T. H. *Citizenship and Social Class.* London: Pluto Press, 1992.

Marx, Karl. *Capital.* London: Lawrence and Wishart, 1974.

——. "A Contribution to the Critique of Hegel's Philosophy of Right. Introduction." In *Early Writings,* trans. Rodney Livingston, 243–258. Middlesex: Penguin, 1992.

——. *Critique of Hegel's Philosophy of Right.* Cambridge: Cambridge University Press, 1977.

——. "On the Jewish Question." In *The Marx-Engels Reader,* trans. Robert Tucker. New York: W. W. Norton, 1978.

Massey, Douglas, and Nolan Malone. "Pathways to Legal Immigration." *Population Research and Policy Review* 21 (2002): 473–504.

M'Baye, Keba. "The African Conception of Law." In *International Encyclopedia of Comparative Law,* ed. K. Zweigert and Ulrich Drobnig. The Hague: Martinus Nijhoff Publishers, 1974.

McCarthy, Rory. "Hamas Hints at Talks as Chaos Reigns in Divided Palestine." *Guardian* (June 16, 2007).

McClure, M. "An Integrative Ecology." In *Family Matters: Interfaces Between Child and Adult Mental Health,* ed. P. Reder, M. McClure, and A. Jolley, 303–317. London: Routledge, 2000.

McCulley, Melanie. "The Male Abortion: The Putative Father's Right to Terminate His Interests in and Obligations to the Unborn Child." *Missouri Law Review* 64 (1999): 517.

McDonnell, Ida, Henri-Bernard Solignac Lecomte, and Liam Wegimont, eds. *Public Opinion and the Fight Against Poverty.* Paris: OECD, 2003.

McInnes, Colin, and Kelley Lees. "Health, Security, and Foreign Policy." *Review of International Studies* 32 (2006): 5–23.

McLaverty, Peter. "The Public Sphere and Local Democracy." *Democratization* 5 (1998): 224–239.

McNamee, Stephen, and Robert Brashier. "Inheritance and Stratification." In *Inheritance and Wealth in America,* ed. Robert Brashier and Stephen McNamee. New York: Plenum, 1998.

Medearis, John. "Labor, Democracy, Utility, and Mill's Critique of Private Property." *American Journal of Political Science* 49 (2005): 135–149.

Mehta, Uday. *Liberalism and Empire: A Study in Nineteenth-century Political Thought.* Chicago: University of Chicago, 1999.

Mendlovitz, Saul, and Burns H. Weston, eds. *Preferred Futures for the United Nations*. New York: Transnational Publishers, 1995.

Menell, Peter. "Institutional Fantasylands: From Scientific Management to Free Market Environmentalism." *Harvard Journal of Law and Public Policy* 15 (1992): 589–610.

Mercy, James, et al. "Preventing Violence." *Health Affairs* 12 (1993): 7–29.

Mill, John Stuart. *Considerations of Representative Government*. Toronto: University of Toronto Press, 1977.

Miller, Wynn. "Montana 'Freemen' Clog Court System." *National Law Journal* (July 16, 1995).

Mills, C. Wright. *The Power Elite*. Oxford: Oxford University Press, 2000.

Milner, Helen. "Why Delegate the Allocation of Aid to Multilateral Organizations? Principal Agent Problems and Multilateralism." 2003. Available online at http://faculty.wm.edu/mjtier/milner8-03.pdf.

Ming, Jeffrey, and Maximilian Muenke. "Multiple Hits During Early Embryonic Development: Digenic Diseases and Holoprosencephaly." *American Journal of Human Genetics* 71 (2002): 1017–1032.

Modigliani, Franco. "The Role of Intergenerational Transfers and Life Cycle Saving in the Accumulation of Wealth." *Journal of Economic Perspectives* 2 (Spring 1988): 15–40.

Moore, Don, et al. "Long and Short Routes to Success in Electronically Mediated Negotiations: Group Affiliation and Good Vibrations." *Organizational Behavior and Human Decision Processes* 77 (1999): 22–43.

Mortished, Carl. "Tax Mobility Trumps French Loyalty." *The Globe and Mail* (Canada) (December 28, 2006).

Moscoso, Eunice. "Thumbnails of Towns That Are Cracking Down on Illegal Immigration." *Cox News Service* (November 22, 2006).

Moses, Jonathan, and Bjørn Letnes. "The Economic Costs to International Labor Restrictions: Revisiting the Empirical Discussion." *World Development* 32 (2004): 1609–1626.

Mowforth, Martin, and Ian Munt. *Tourism and Sustainability: New Tourism in the Third World*. New York: Routledge, 1998.

Murray, C. J. L., et al. "Armed Conflict as a Public Health Problem." *British Medical Journal* 324 (2002): 346–349.

Nadeau, Jean-Benoî, and Julie Barlow. "Words Fail Them." *New York Times* (December 27, 2006).

Nassanke, Machiko. "Revenue Potential of the Tobin Tax for Development Finance: A Critical Appraisal." School of Oriental and African Studies, University of London (August 2003).

National Commission on Law Observance and Enforcement. *Report on the Enforcement of the Deportation Laws of the United States*. Washington, D.C.: Government Printing Office, 1931.

National Research Council. *Ground Water and Soil Cleanup: Improving Management of Persistent Contaminants*. National Academy Press: Washington, D.C., 1999.

Nevins, Joseph. "Israel Plans to Fence Out Palestinians in West Bank: High Tech Barriers." *The Gazette* (March 21, 1995).

——. *Operation Gatekeeper: The Rise of the "Illegal Alien" and the Remaking of the U.S.-Mexican Border*. New York: Routledge, 2002.

Nevins, Joseph, and Mizue Aizeki. *Dying to Live: U.S. Immigration in an Age of Global Apartheid*. San Francisco: City Lights Books, 2008.

Ngai, Mai. *Illegal Aliens and the Making of Modern America*. Princeton, N.J.: Princeton University Press, 2004.

Nietzsche, Friedrich. *On the Genealogy of Morals*. New York: Oxford University Press, 1998.

Nozick, Robert. *Anarchy, the State, and Utopia*. New York: Basic Books, 1974.

Nussbaum, Martha. *Liberty of Conscience: In Defense of America's Tradition of Religious Equality*. New York: Basic Books, 2008.

——. "Patriotism and Cosmopolitanism." In *For Love of Country*, ed. Joshua Cohen. 3–20. Boston: Beacon Press, 1996.

Okin, Susan. *Justice, Gender, and the Family*. New York: Basic Books, 1989.

Oliver, Melvin, and Thomas Shapiro. *Black Wealth/White Wealth*. New York: Routledge, 1995.

Olson, Mancur. *The Logic of Collective Action: Public Goods and the Theory of Groups*. Cambridge, Mass.: Harvard University Press, 1965.

Omotola, Jelili A. "Primogeniture and Illegitimacy in African Customary Law: The Battle for Survival of Culture." *Indiana International and Comparative Law Review* 15 (2004): 136.

O'Neill, Onora. "Transnational Justice." In *Free Movement: Ethical Issues in the Transnational Migration of People and of Money*, ed. Brian Barry and Robert E. Goodin, 87–94. London: Harvester Wheatsheaf, 2002.

Ostrove, Joan, Pamela Feldman, and Nancy Adler. "Relations Among Socioeconomic Status Indicators and Health for African-Americans and Whites." *Journal of Health Psychology* 4 (1999): 451–463.

Ottaviano, Gianmarco, and Giovanni Peri. "Rethinking the Effects of Immigration on Wages." NBER Working Paper No. 12497 (2006). Available online at http://creativeclass .com/rfcgdb/articles/Peri%20and%20Ottavanio,%20Rethinking%20Immigrations %20Effect.pdf.

Otten, Sabine, and Dirk Wentura. "About the Impact of Automaticity in the Minimal Group Paradigm: Evidence from the Effective Primary Tasks." *European Journal of Social Psychology* 29 (1999): 1049–1071.

Paine, Thomas. *The Complete Writings of Thomas Paine*. New York: Citadel Press, 1945.

Palermo, George. "Murderous Parents." *International Journal of Offender Therapy and Comparative Criminology* 46 (2002): 123–143.

Partridge, Eric. *Origins: A Short Etymological Dictionary of the English Language*. New York: MacMillan, 1959.

Passel, Jeffrey. "Size and Characteristics of the Unauthorized Migrant Population in the U.S." *PEW Foundation* (March 7, 2006). Available online at http://pewhispanic.org/ reports/report.php?ReportID=61.

Pasternak, Judy. "Oases in Navajo Desert Contained a 'Witch's Brew.'" *Los Angeles Times* (November 20 2006). Available online at http://www.latimes.com/news/nationworld/ nation/la-na-navajo20nov20,0,6106722.story?page=1.

Pateman, Carole. *Sexual Contract*. Stanford, Calif.: Stanford University Press, 1988.

Patterson, Cynthia. "'Not Worth Rearing': The Causes of Infant Exposure in Ancient Greece." *Transactions of the American Philological Association* 115 (1985): 103–123.

Penalver, Eduardo. "Is Land Special? The Unjustified Preference for Landownership in Regulatory Takings Law." *Ecology Law Quarterly* 31 (2004): 247–249.

Pestieua, Pierre. "The Role of Gift and Estate Transfers in the United States and Europe." In *Death and Dollars*, ed. Alicia Munnell and Annika Sunden. Washington, D.C.: The Brookings Institution, 2003.

Peterson, James, and Nicholas Zill. "Marital Disruption, Parent-Child Relationships, and Behavior Problems in Children." *Journal of Marriage and Family* 48 (1981): 295-307.

Pfeiffer, Silke. "Vote Buying and Its Implication for Democracy: Evidence from Latin America." In *Global Corruption Report*, 76-77. Sterling, Va.: Transparency International, 2004.

Plato. "Apology." In *Collected Works of Plato*, trans. Paul Shorey. New York: Bollingen, 1961.

——. *Republic*. In *Collected Works of Plato*, trans. Paul Shorey. New York: Bollingen, 1961.

Plutarch. "Lycurgus." Available online at http://classics.mit.edu/Plutarch/lycurgus.html.

Pogge, Thomas. "Priorities of Global Justice." In *Global Justice*, ed. Thomas Pogge, 6-24. Oxford: Blackwell, 2001.

——. "Recognized and Violated by International Law: The Human Rights of the Global Poor." *Leiden Journal of International Law* 18 (2005): 717-745.

——. "World Poverty and Human Rights." *Ethics and International Affairs* 19 (2005): 1-7.

Polgreen, Lydia. "Dozens Are Killed in Raids of Darfur Camp." *New York Times* (August 25, 2008).

Pomeroy, Sarah. *Goddesses, Whores, Wives, and Slaves: Women in Classical Antiquity*. New York: Schocken Books, 1975.

Popper, Karl. *Conjectures and Refutations: The Growth of Scientific Knowledge*. New York: Routledge, 2002.

——. *The Logic of Scientific Discovery*. London: Hutchison, 1959.

——. *The Open Society and Its Enemies*. New York: Routledge, 2003.

Posner, Daniel N. "Measuring Ethnic Fractionalization in Africa." *American Journal of Political Science* 48 (2004): 849-863.

Poterba, James. "The Estate Tax and After Tax Investment." In *Does Atlas Shrug?* ed. Joel Slemrod. Cambridge, Mass.: Harvard University Press, 2000.

Quan, Julian. "Land Tenure, Economic Growth, and Poverty in Sub-Saharan Africa." In *Evolving Land Rights, Policy, and Tenure in Africa*, ed. Camilla Toulmin and Julian Quan, 31-32. London, 2000.

Quirk, Joel. "Trafficked Into Slavery." *Journal of Human Rights* 6 (2007): 181-207.

Rabbie, Jacob, and Murray Horwitz. "Arousal of Ingroup-Outgroup Bias by a Chance Win or Loss." *Journal of Personality and Social Psychology* 13 (1969): 269-277.

Rank, Otto. *The Trauma of Birth*. New York: Robert Brunner, 1952.

Rawls, John. *The Law of Peoples*. Cambridge, Mass.: Harvard University Press, 1999.

——. *A Theory of Justice*. Cambridge, Mass.: Harvard University Press, 1972.

Ray, James Lee. "The Abolition of Slavery and the End of International War." *International Organization* 43 (1989): 405-439.

Regan, Donald. "Rewriting Roe v. Wade." *Michigan Law Review* 7 (1979): 1569-1646.

Rennison, Callie. "Intimate Partner Violence, 1993-2001." U.S. Bureau of Justice Statistics: February 2003, NCJ 197838.

Reynal-Querol, Marta. "Ethnicity, Political Systems, and Civil Wars." *Journal of Conflict Resolution* 46 (2001): 29-54.

Reynolds, Susan. *Kingdoms and Communities in Western Europe, 900-1300*. Oxford: Oxford University Press, 1997.

Reynolds, V. "Kinship and the Family in Monkeys, Apes, and Man." *Man* 3 (1968): 209–233.

Rezendes, Michael. "A Policy Lost at Sea: Worldwide Requests for Asylum Swamp the Immigration System." *Boston Globe* (July 10, 1994).

Rhoads, Edward. *Manchus and Han: Ethnic Relations and Political Power in Late Qing and Early Republican China, 1861–1928.* Seattle: University of Washington Press, 2000.

Riess, David. *The Family's Construction of Reality.* Cambridge, Mass.: Harvard University Press, 1981.

Roberts, Dorothy. "The Genetic Tie." *University of Chicago Law Review* 62 (1995): 209–273.

Roberts, Les. *Mortality in Eastern DRC: Results from Five Mortality Surveys.* New York/Bukavu: International Rescue Committee, 2000.

Roberts, Les, et al. "Mortality Before and After the 2003 Invasion of Iraq." *Lancet* (2004). Available online at http://image.thelancet.com/extras/04art10342web.pdf.

Robinson, Natasha. "The World Summit on Sustainable Development and Women's Access to Land: Why Nigeria Should Adopt the Eritrean Land Proclamation." *William and Mary Journal of Women and the Law* 10 (2004): 593–605.

Robson, Ruthann. "Making Mothers: Lesbian Legal Theory and the Judicial Construction of Lesbian Mothers." *Women's Rights Law Reporter* 22 (2000): 15–35.

Rogin, Michael. *Ronald Reagan, the Movie, and Other Episodes in Political Demonology.* Berkeley: University of California Press, 1987.

Rohter, Larry. "Las Palomas Journal: Pillow Talk of U.S.-Mexico Towns: What Border?" *New York Times* (February 17, 1990).

Rohwer, S., J. C. Herron, and M. Daly. "Stepparental Behavior as Mating Effort in Birds and Other Animals." *Evolution & Human Behavior* 20 (1999): 367–390.

Rosenthal, Elisabeth. "China and U.N. Meet on North Korea Immigrants." *New York Times* (June 28, 2001).

Ruggiero, Vincenzo. "Trafficking in Human Beings: Slaves in Contemporary Europe." *International Journal of the Sociology of Law* 25 (1997): 231–241.

Rummel, R. J. *Death by Government: Genocide and Mass Murder since 1900.* New Brunswick, N.J.: Transaction, 1994.

——. "Democracy, Power, Genocide, and Mass Murder." *Journal of Conflict Resolution* 39 (1995): 3–26.

Russett, Bruce, and Joel Slemrod. "Diminished Expectations of Nuclear War and Increased Personal Savings: Evidence from Individual Survey Data." *American Economic Review* 83 (1993): 1022–1033.

Safire, William. "Poletown Wrecker's Ball." *New York Times* (April 30, 1981).

——. "What Is Government For?" *New York Times* (March 2, 1981).

Said, Edward. *Orientalism.* New York: Vintage, 1978.

Salt, John. "Trafficking and Human Smuggling: A European Perspective." *International Migration* 38 (2000): 31–56.

Salt, John, and James Clark. "International Migration in the UNECE Region: Patterns, Trends, Policies." *International Social Science Journal* 52 (2000): 313–328.

Sanminatelli, Maria. "Pope Urges Couples to Resist Modern Pressures, Stick to Traditional Family Values." *AP* (October 8, 2006).

Santer, Eric. *Stranded Objects: Mourning, Memory, and Film in Postwar Germany.* Ithaca, N.Y.: Cornell University Press, 1990.

Sarkar, Sahotra. *Genetics and Reductionism.* Cambridge: Cambridge University Press, 1998.

Sarvassy, Wendy. "Social Citizenship from a Feminist Perspective." *Signs* 12 (1997): 54–73.

Schaffer, Fred. "Vote Buying in East Asia." In *Transparency International: Global Corruption Report*. London: Pluto Press and Transparency International, 2004.

Schmitt, Carl. *The Concept of the Political*. Chicago: University of Chicago Press, 2007.

Schuck, Peter, and Rogers Smith. *Citizenship Without Consent: Illegal Aliens in the American Polity*. New Haven, Conn.: Yale University Press, 1985.

Schultz, Bart. "Mill and Sidgwick, Imperialism and Racism." *Utilitas* 19: 104–130.

Scott, Austin. *The Law of Trusts*, 4th ed. New York: Little Brown, 1987.

Scott, Bruce. "The Great Divide in the Global Village." *Foreign Affairs* (January/February 2001).

Sealey, Geraldine. "Duped Dads: Men Fight Centuries-old Paternity Laws." *ABC News* (October 2, 2002). Available online at http://www.canadiancrc.com/articles/ABC_Duped_Dads_02OCT02.htm.

Seery, John Evan. *Political Theory for Mortals: Shades of Justice, Images of Death*. Ithaca, N.Y.: Cornell University Press, 1996.

Sengupta, Somini. "No Relief from War in African Refugee Camps." *New York Times* (May 19, 2003).

Shachar, Ayelet, and Ran Hirschl. "Citizenship as Inherited Property." *Political Theory* 35 (2007): 253–287.

Shiva, Vandana. *Water Wars: Privatization, Pollution, and Profit*. London: Pluto Press, 2002.

Shue, Henry. "Mediating Duties." *Ethics* 98 (1988): 687–704.

Sidgwick, Henry. *Elements of Politics*. London: Macmillan, 1897.

Sidney, Algernon. *Discourses Concerning Government*. Chicago: University of Chicago Press, 1987. Available online at http://www.constitution.org/as/dcg_224.htm.

Simmel, George. *The Philosophy of Money*. Trans. Tom Bottomore and David Frisby. London: Routledge, 1978.

Simon, Jonathan. *Governing Through Crime: How the War on Crime Transformed American Democracy and Created a Culture of Fear*. Oxford: Oxford University Press, 2007.

Sivard, R. I. *World Military and Social Expenditures*. Washington, D.C.: World Priorities, 1993.

Skön, Elisabeth, et al. "Military Expenditure." In *SIPRI Yearbook, 2005*. Oxford: Oxford University Press, 2005.

Skurbaty, Zelim. *As If Peoples Mattered: A Critical Appraisal of "People" and "Minorities" from the International Human Rights Perspective and Beyond*. Boston: Martinus Nijhoff, 2000.

Slemrod, Joel. "The Economics of Taxing the Rich." In *Does Atlas Shrug? The Economic Consequences of Taxing the Rich*, ed. Joel Slemrod. Cambridge, Mass.: Harvard University Press, 2000.

Smith, Anna Marie. *Welfare Reform and Sexual Regulation*. Cambridge: Cambridge University Press, 2007.

Smith, Brian. "*Charles Demore v. Hyung Joon Kim*: Another Step Away from Full Due Process Protections." *Akron Law Review* 38 (2005).

Smith, John. *The Complete Works of Captain Smith*. Ed. Philip Barbour. Williamsburg: University of North Carolina, 1986.

Soysal, Yasmin. *Limits of Citizenship: Migrants and Postnational Membership in Europe*. Chicago: University of Chicago Press, 1994.

Sperow, Elisabeth. "Perspective on *Kelo v. City Of New London*: The Kelo Legacy: Political Accountability, Not Legislation, Is the Cure." *McGeorge Law Review* 38 (2007).

Spitko, E. Gary. "The Expressive Function of Succession Law and the Merits of Nonmarital Inclusion." *Arizona Law Review* 41 (1999).

Sprigg, Peter. *Outrage: How Gay Activists and Liberal Judges Are Trashing Democracy to Redefine Marriage*. New York: Regnery, 2004.

Spring, Eileen. *Law, Land, and Family: Aristocratic Inheritance in England, 1300–1800*. Chapel Hill: University of North Carolina, 1993.

Stalker, Peter. *The No Nonsense Guide to International Migration*. New York: Verso, 2001.

Stanford, Craig. "The Social Behavior of Chimpanzees and Bonobos: Empirical Evidence, Shifting Assumptions." *Current Anthropology* 4 (1998): 399–420.

Steiner, Hillel. *An Essay on Rights*. Cambridge: Blackwell Publisher, 1994.

——. "Libertarianism and the Transnational Migration of People." In *Free Movement: Ethical Issues in the Transnational Migration of People and of Money*, ed. Brian Barry and Robert E. Goodin. London: Harvester Wheatsheaf, 2002.

Stern, Richard. "The Power of Faith." *International Herald Tribune*, letter to the editor (July 10, 2004).

Stevens, Jacqueline. "Legal Aesthetics of the Family and Nation: agoraXchange and Notes Toward Re-imaging the Future." *New York Law Review* 49 (2004/2005): 317–352.

——. "Methods of Adoption: Eliminating Genetic Privilege." In *Adoption Matters: Philosophical and Feminist Essays*, ed. Sally Haslanger and Charlotte Witt, 68–94. Ithaca, N.Y.: Cornell University Press, 2005.

——. "Pregnancy Envy and Compensatory Masculinities." *Gender and Politics* 1 (2006): 265–296.

——. "The Reasonableness of John Locke's Majority: Property Rights, Consent, and Resistance in the Second Treatise." *Political Theory* 24 (1996): 424–463.

——. *Reproducing the State*. Princeton, N.J.: Princeton University Press, 1999.

——. "Sigmund Freud and International Relations." *Journal of Law, Culture, and the Humanities* 2 (2006): 201–217.

——. "Symbolic Matter: DNA and Other Linguistic Stuff." *Social Text* 20 (2002): 106–140.

——. "Thin ICE." *The Nation* (June 23, 2008).

Stewart, Andrew. "Imag(in)ing the Other: Amazons and Ethnicity in Fifth-century Athens." *Poetics Today* 16 (1995): 571–597.

Stiffler, Lisa. "Radioactive Contamination at Hanford Is on the Move." *Seattle Post-Intelligencer* (June 15, 2005). Available online at http://seattlepi.nwsource.com/local/228573_hanford15.html.

Suskind, Ron. *The One Percent Doctrine: Deep Inside America's Pursuit of Its Enemies Since 9/11*. New York: Simon and Schuster, 2006.

Sylt, Christian. "The Powerhouse Principality." *CNBC European Business* (2005). Available online at http://europeanbusiness.eu.com/features/2005/dec/monaco.html.

Tafjel, Henri. "Social Psychology of Intergroup Relations." *Annual Review of Psychology* 33 (1982): 1–39.

Tamir, Yael. "Pro Patria Mori!: Death and the State." In *The Morality of Nationalism*, ed. Robert McKim and Jeff McMahan. Oxford: Oxford University Press, 1997.

Tavernise, Sabrina, and Robert Worth. "As Iraqis Flee, Few are Gaining Sanctuary in U.S." *New York Times* (January 2, 2007).

Taylor, Charles. *Multiculturalism and the Politics of Recognition: An Essay*. Princeton, N.J.: Princeton University Press, 1992.

Taylor, Jerome. "Protection from Harsh Penalties or Legalised Prostitution?" *The Independent* (September 28, 2006).

Temrin, H., S. Buchmayer, and M. Enquist. "Step-parents and Infanticide: New Data Contradict Evolutionary Predictions." *Proceedings, Biological Sciences* 267 (2000): 944.

Thoreau, Henry David. "Civil Disobedience." Available online at http://www.thoreau.the freelibrary.com/Civil-Disobedience.

Toledano, Ehud. *The Ottoman Slave Trade and Its Suppression, 1840-1890*. Princeton, N.J.: Princeton University Press, 1982.

Torpey, John. *The Invention of the Passport: Surveillance, Citizenship, and the State*. Cambridge: Cambridge University Press, 2000.

Treadgold, Warren. *A History of the Byzantine State and Society*. Stanford, Calif.: Stanford University Press.

Triandafyllidou, Anna, and Ruby Gropas. *European Immigration*. Hampshire: Ashgate, 2007.

Tully, James. "Introduction." In *Multinational Democracies*, ed. Allan Gagnon and James Tully. Cambridge: Cambridge University Press, 2001.

Tumlin, Karen. "Suspect First: How Terrorism Policy Is Reshaping Immigration Policy." *California Law Review* 92 (2004): 1173-1239.

UK 2005: Official Yearbook of the United Kingdom of Britain and Northern Ireland. Available online at http://www.statistics.gov.uk/onlineproducts.

Unamuno, Miguel de. *Tragic Sense of Life*. Available online at http://www.gutenberg.org/files/14636/14636.txt.

United Nations. "Compendium on Human Settlements Statistics, 2001." Available online at http://unstats.un.org/unsd/demographic/sconcerns/housing/housing2.htm#DYB.

——. *International Migration*. 2002. Available online at http://www.un.org/esa/population/publications/ittmig2002/Migration2002.pdf.

——. *International Migration*. 2006. Chart E.06xiii.6. Available online at http://www.un.org/esa/population/publications/2006Migration_Chart/2006IttMig_chart.htm.

——. *Millennium Development Goals Report 2005*. Available online at http://www.un.org/docs/summit2005/MDGBook.pdf.

——. *Population Database*. Available online at http://esa.un.org/unpp/p2k0data.asp.

United Nations Children's Fund (UNICEF). "Trafficking in Human Beings, Especially Women and Children, in Africa." Florence, 2005. Available online at http://www.unicef.org/irc.

United Nations Development Program. *Human Development Report, 1998*. New York: Oxford University Press, 1998.

——. *Human Development Report, 2000*. New York: Oxford University Press, 2000.

——. *Human Development Report, 2002*. New York: Oxford University Press, 2002.

United Nations Office of the High Commissioner of Human Rights. *Fact Sheet No. 21, The Human Right to Adequate Housing*. Available online at http://193.194.138.190/html/menu6/2/fs21.htm#entitlements.

United Nations Population Division. *World Population Prospects, 2002*. Available online at http://www.esa.un.org/unpp.

United States Census Bureau. "America's Families and Living Arrangements." Current Population Survey Reports (March 2000): table A2, FG2. Available online at http://www.census.gov/population/www/socdemo/hh-fam.html.

———. *American Factfinder: Income Distribution of Households and Families*. 1999. Available online at http://www.factfinder.census.gov.

———. *Current Population Survey*. Available online at http://www.cis.org/articles/2002/back1302.html.

United States Congressional Budget Office. *Immigration Policy in the United States*. 2006. Available online at http://www.cbo.gov/ftpdocs/70xx/doc7051/02-28-Immigration.pdf.

United States Department of Defense. *National Defense Budget Estimate for 2007*. Available online at http://defenselink.mil/comptroller/defbudget/fy2007.

United States Department of Homeland Security, Office of Inspector General. "Detention and Removal of Illegal Aliens, U.S. Immigration and Customs Enforcement, OIG-06-33." Washington, D.C. 2006. Available online at http://www.dhs.gov/xoig/assets/mgmtrpts/OIG_06-33_Apr06.pdf.

United States Department of Labor. "Foreign Labor Trends: Greece (2003)." Available online at http://www.ilr.cornell.edu/library/downloads/keyWorkplaceDocuments/Foreign-LaborTrends/greece-2003.pdf.

United States Federal Reserve Board. "1998 Survey of Consumer Finances Dataset." Available online at http://www.federalreserve.gov/pubs/oss/oss2/method.html.

United States Government Accountability Office. "United States Government Stewardship Information (Unaudited) for the Years Ended September 30, 2005, and September 30, 2004." Available online at http://www.gao.gov/financial/fy2005/05stew.pdf.

United States Joint Committee on Taxation. "Present Law and Background Relating to Individual Taxpayer Identification Numbers (ITNS)." 2004. Available online at http://www.house.gov/jct/x-16-04.pdf.

United States Statistical Abstract. "Farm Operators—Tenure and Characteristics: 1997 and 2002." Available online at http://www.census.gov/compendia/statab/agriculture/farms_and_farmland.

United States Treasury Inspector General for Tax Administration. "June 2006 Report." Available online at http://www.taxwhistleblowers.org/main/page.php?page_id=11.

Vanamo, Tuija, et al. "Intrafamilial Child Homicide in Finland 1970–1994: Incidence, Causes of Death, and Demographic Characteristics." *Forensic Science International* 117 (2001): 199–204.

Vanita, Ruth. *Same-sex Marriage in India and the West*. New York: Palgrave-MacMillan, 2005.

VOA English Service. "Recent Slaying Highlights Dangers Faced by Journalists in Somalia." (October 22, 2007).

Vogt, Joseph. *Ancient Slavery and the Idea of Man*. Cambridge, Mass.: Harvard University Press, 1975.

Waddell, Charlotte, Harriet MacMillan, and Anna Pietrantonio. "How Important Is Permanency Planning for Children? Considerations for Pediatricians Involved in Child Protection." *Journal of Developmental & Behavioral Pediatrics* 25 (2004): 285–292.

Waggoner, Lawrence. "Tribute to William F. Fratcher: Marital Property Rights in Transition." *Missouri Law Review* 59 (1994): 21–30.

Waldron, Jeremy. "Locke's Account of Inheritance and Bequest." *Journal of the History of Philosophy* 19 (1981): 39–51.

———. "Minority Cultures and the Cosmopolitan Alternative." *University of Michigan Journal of Law Reform* 25 (1992): 751–793.

———. "What Is Cosmopolitan?" *Journal of Political Philosophy* 8 (2000): 227–243.

———. "When Justice Replaces Affection: The Need for Rights." *Harvard Journal of Law and Public Policy* 11 (1988): 625–647.

Wall Street Journal Editorial Board. "In Praise of Huddled Masses." *Wall Street Journal* (July 3, 1984).

Walzer, Michael. *Spheres of Justice.* Cambridge, Mass.: Harvard University Press, 1983.

Warner, Michael. *The Trouble with Normal: Sex, Politics, and the Ethics of Queer Life.* New York, Free Press, 1999.

Watkins, Kevin. *Human Development Report: Beyond Scarcity: Power, Poverty, and the Global Water Crisis.* New York: United Nations, 2006. Available online at http://hdr .undp.org/hdr2006/pdfs/report/HDR06-complete.pdf.

Weber, Max. *The Protestant Ethic and the Spirit of Capitalism.* New York: Courier Dover Publications, 2003.

Weir, Fred. "United Russia Wins, Putin sees 'Moral Mandate' in Vote." *Christian Science Monitor* (December 4, 2007).

Westerman, William. *Slave Systems of Greek and Roman Antiquity.* Philadelphia: American Philosophical Society, 1955.

Weston, Kath. *Families We Choose: Lesbians, Gays, Kinship.* New York: Columbia University Press, 1991.

Widgren, J. "Multilateral Cooperation to Combat Trafficking in Migrants and the Role of International Organizations." 11th IOM Seminar on Migration. October 1994.

Wiley, Liz. "Land and the Constitution." AREU Policy Brief, 2003. Available online at http:// www.areu.org.af/publications/land%20and%20the%20constitution_eng.pdf.

Will, George. "Good Citizenship Can Include Cash." *Times Union* (Albany) (July 29, 1999).

Williams, Melissa. *Voice, Trust, and Memory: Marginalized Groups and the Failings of Liberal Representation.* Princeton, N.J.: Princeton University Press, 1998.

Wilson, Edward O. *Naturalist.* Washington, D.C.: Island Press, 2006.

———. *Sociobiology: The New Synthesis.* Cambridge, Mass.: Harvard University Press, 2000.

Wilson, Jason. "Eritrean Land Reform: The Forgotten Masses." *North Carolina Journal of International and Comparative Regulations* 24 (1999).

Wolf, Amy. *Deliver Us from Evil* [film]. 2006.

Wolff, Edward. *Top Heavy: A Study of the Increasing Inequality of Wealth in America.* New York: Twentieth Century Fund, 2002.

———. "Wealth Accumulation by Age Cohort in the U.S., 1962–1992: The Role of Savings, Capital Gains, and Intergenerational Transfers." *Geneva Papers on Risk and Insurance, Issues and Practice* 24 (1999): 27–49.

Wolff, Robert Paul. *In Defense of Anarchism.* New York: Harper and Row, 1970.

Wolfson, Evan. *Why Marriage Matters: America, Equality and Gay People's Right to Marry.* New York: Simon and Schuster, 2004.

Wolin, Sheldon S. "Political Theory as a Vocation." *American Political Science Review* 63 (1969).

Wood, Forrest. *The Arrogance of Faith: Christianity and Race in America from the Colonial Era to the Twentieth Century.* New York: Knopf, 1990.

World Bank Data and Research. Available online at http://devdata.worldbank.org/hnpstats/ cd.asp.

Xenophon. *Persian Wars.* Harmondsworth: Penguin, 1972.

Yaari, Menahem. "On the Consumer's Lifetime Allocation Process." *International Economic Review* 5 (1964): 304–317.

———. "Uncertain Lifetime, Life Insurance, and the Theory of the Consumer." *Review of Economic Studies* 32 (1965): 137–150.

Yanow, Dvora, and Peregrine Schwartz-Shea, eds.. *Interpretation and Method: Empirical Research and the Interpretive Turn.* Armonk, N.Y.: M. E. Sharpe, 2006.

Yenni, Kwok. "On Hire to the Cruelest Bidder." *South China Morning Post* (June 7, 2000).

Young-Bruehl, Elisabeth. *Hannah Arendt: For Love of the World.* New Haven, Conn.: Yale University Press, 1982.

Zahr, Carla Abhou. "Global Burden of Maternal Death and Disability." *British Medical Bulletin* 67 (2003): 6.

Zhu, Tianbiao. "Nationalism and Chinese Foreign Policy." *The China Review* 1 (Fall 2001): 1–27.

Zolberg, A. R. "International Migration Policies in a Changing World System." In *Human Migration: Patterns and Policies*, ed. W. H. McNeill and R. S. Adams, 241–286. Bloomington: Indiana University Press, 1978.

Index

domestic violence. *See under* partner abuse

Dominican Republic, 15, 21, 149

Dreyfus, Alfred, 76-77

early death. *See under* death

economics, 17, 41, 50, 80, 82, 83-84, 103, 105, 108, 185-186, 192, 198, 201-202, 205, 209; and citizenship, 28-31; classical, 29; inequality, 37, 106-107; and migration, 12, 28, 48, 49, 55, 67, 84, 92, 95, 99; neoclassical, 14, 193-194, 202-203, 207; neoliberal, 211; and religion, 220-221, 227; sanctions, 45, 201; and slavery 16-19; and war, 44-45. *See also* capitalism; Chicago School; inheritance; labor markets; political-economic theory; wealth

education, 12, 21, 43, 47, 48, 82, 93, 106, 124, 130, 138, 139, 140, 141, 142, 150, 153, 178, 211, 278n.14

Eichmann, Adolf, xi-xii, 224, 247n.1

Ellickson, Robert, 202, 207-208

Elster, Jon, 10

emigrant, emigrate, 19, 37, 38, 44-45, 49, 65, 66-67, 84, 99, 247n.4, 258n.4, 279n.25

empire, xiv, 16, 22, 31, 35, 77, 91, 169-170, 200-201, 215, 217, 249n.8, 278n.15, 304n.91

environment, 90, 93-95, 98, 99, 138, 151, 172, 191, 202, 205, 208, 210, 211, 257n.120, 316n94, 319n.132

Epstein, Richard, 189, 193

equality, 31, 51-56, 156, 175, 249n.10, 260n.22, 261n.28, 276n.4, 305n.100. *See also* United States, Fourteenth Amendment

Erasmus, 64

Eritrea, 195, 204, 314n.52

estate laws, 110-111. *See also* inheritance

Ethiopia, 42, 46, 195, 223, 264n.77, 303n.80

ethnicity, 3-4, 17, 19, 32, 33, 75, 76-77, 80, 98, 100-102, 149, 160, 163, 197-199, 201, 223, 260n.20, 264n.73, 264n.74; 268n.121; 272n.160; 275n.206, 278n.18; 280n.37; 281n.54; 299n.38; and apartheid, 38, 50-55; and religion, 215, 217-219; right of minorities, 85-92; violence, 9, 11, 14, 42, 61, 71

ethnocentrism, 17, 60-71

European Union, 28, 30, 82, 84, 295n.42

evolutionary, theory, xiii, 6, 60-65, 157-158, 164-171, 193, 252n.47, 286n.35, 302n.78

exclusion, benefits of, 38-55

existential, 71, 213, 224

family. *See under* children; inheritance; marriage

Fearon, James, 4, 230

feminist, 31, 78, 156, 157, 161, 162, 179, 260n.22; interventions, 175-177

Fennel, Lee Ann, 138-139

Ferrara, Alessandro, 238-239

feudal, 17, 32, 143, 285n.24; alongside capitalism, 107-109

Feyerabend, Paul, 225, 230-233, 239, 322n.2

Fiji, 197

filicide. *See under* child abuse

Filmer, Robert, 200, 291n.94

Fineman, Martha, 153, 176-177, 183, 307n.8

Finland, 165

Firestone, Shulamith, 175-176, 177

Foucault, Michel, 4, 43, 157, 250n.16, 258n.130, 298n.23, 301n.55

France, 66, 67, 69, 80, 81, 84, 141, 218, 234, 255n.97, 286n.40

persecution, xv, 45, 91

Persia, 17, 22, 29, 58

Philippines, 46, 217, 315n.75

Plato, 4, 6, 10, 17, 22, 74, 146, 234, 248n.2, 249n.4, 300n.44

Plutarch, 4–5, 80

Pogge, Thomas, 74

Poland, 86, 237

political-economic theory, 75, 108, 134, 189. See also capitalism; Chicago School

polygamy, 154, 155, 160, 297n.8, 307n.8

Pompilius, Numa, 80

Poor Laws (England), 57, 67

Popper, Karl, 14, 225; applied to *States Without Nations*, 238–242; on behavioral social science, 229–232; falsification of Popper's epistemology for anticommunists, 233–238; politics of 226–228

Portugal, 84

poverty, 9–10, 14, 82, 96, 105, 107, 127, 135, 137, 138, 154, 204, 234, 252n.45, 296n.42, 318n.121. See also Poor Laws

pregnancy, 132, 160–161, 172, 176–177, 249n.6, 249n.7, 308n.10; risks of, 166, 178–179, 303n.79, 308n.13, 308n.17, 308n.18; *sui generis*, 177–183

property rights, and inheritance, 124–127. See also inheritance; land rights; wealth

Protestants, 121, 218, 220–221, 320n.17

psychoanalytic theory, 12, 31, 161, 169, 176, 240, 288n.57, 291n.96, 300n.41

psychohistory, 237

psycholegal, 77

psychological, 3, 6, 10, 11, 15, 17, 26, 37, 39, 71, 99, 110, 124, 128, 132, 147, 166, 224, 260n.22, 266n.101, 293n.14

public benefit, 188–189. See also *Kelo v. New London*

public health. *See under* health

Putin, Vladimir (Russian prime minister), 237

race, 3, 5, 9, 10, 33, 34, 35, 38, 42, 61, 75, 77, 82, 100, 133, 147, 156, 160, 163, 195, 215, 268n.122, 281n.54, 299n.38; as mankind, 129, 131, 200; and racial apartheid, 50–55

racism, 31, 33, 75, 261n.28, 262n.40

rape, 9, 20, 46, 167, 297n.8, 306n.111

rational-choice theory, 10, 29, 32, 207, 230, 241

Rawls, John, 26, 31–35, 59, 68–70, 74, 87, 92–93

Raz, Joseph, 32–34

real estate, 98–100, 104. See also estate laws; inheritance

refugees, xii, xv, 20–21, 42, 45, 46–47, 55, 75, 89, 265n.91, 313n.46

religion, 3, 5, 7–11, 22, 23, 26, 40, 41–43, 51, 53, 65, 71, 79, 90, 101, 133, 147, 169, 170, 201, 249n.10, 252n.41, 253n.49; and disenchantment, 220–222; and the nation-state, 13–14; and rules for friends and enemies, 222–224; systemic violence, 215–220. See also Catholic Church; Christianity; Islam; Jews; Judaism; Muslims; Protestants; violence, religious

reproduction, 4, 161, 171, 176, 177, 179. See also pregnancy

residency, 29, 36, 66, 80, 81, 82, 88, 148, 278n.22, 293n.11

revolution, 42, 265n.88; American, 110, 193, 196, 288n.60; French, 66, 69; Marxism, 235